SAVERIO TENUTA

LEGENDS OF THE PIERCED VEIL

THE SCARLET BLADES

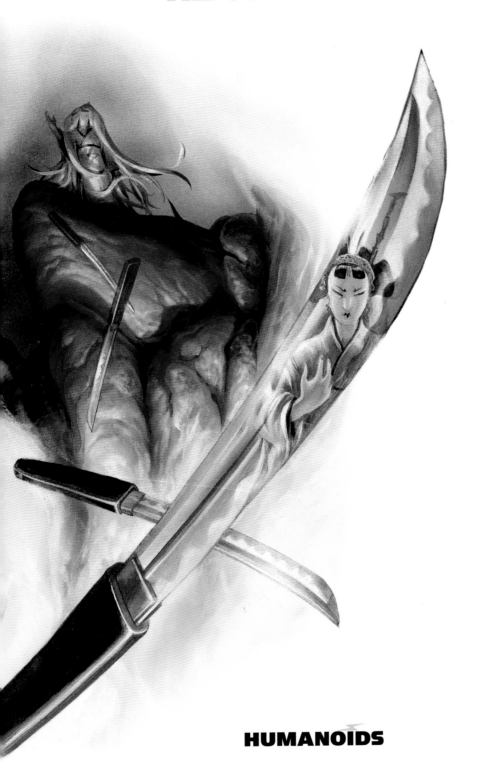

HUMANOIDS

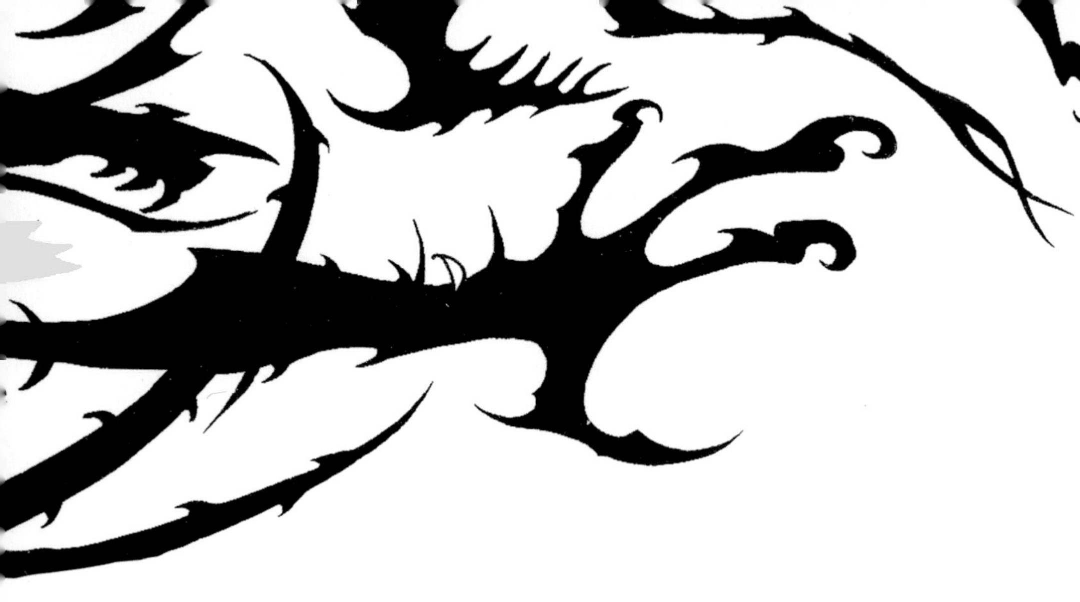

SAVERIO TENUTA
Writer & Artist

SAMANTHA DEMERS
for **WORLD LANGUAGE COMMUNICATIONS**
Translator

ALEX DONOGHUE
English-Language Edition Editor

CAMILLE THÉLOT-VERNOUX
Original Edition Editor

SANDY TANAKA
Designer

JERRY FRISSEN
Senior Art Director

FABRICE GIGER
Publisher

Rights & Licensing - licensing@humanoids.com
Press and Social Media - pr@humanoids.com

LEGENDS OF THE PIERCED VEIL: THE SCARLET BLADES. First Printing. This book is a publication of Humanoids, Inc. 8033 Sunset Blvd. #628, Los Angeles, CA 90046.

Library of Congress Control Number: 2021935527

Originally published in French by Les Humanoïdes Associés (Paris, France).

Raido Caym
AMNESIC RONIN

Meiki
YOUNG BUNRAKU PUPPETEER

Jera Isegawa
OLD WOMAN

Ogi
FRIEND TO MEIKI

Toteku Fujiwara
DECEASED SHOGUN

Ryin Fujiwara
DAUGHTER TO TOTEKU FUJIWARA
AND CURRENT SHOGUN

Yozeru Masa
TRANSCRIBER TO TOTEKU FUJIWARA

Nobu Fudo
PREMIER GENERAL TO THE SHOGUN

Kenzo Kawakami
CAPTAIN OF THE GUARDS

Izuna
LARGE VENOMOUS WOLVES
FROM THE ICE FOREST

Wunjo
BLACK WOLF, LEADER OF
THE IZUNA PACK

Shugendo
TRADITIONAL JAPANESE
ESOTERIC MAGIC

Yama-Ikki
REBEL ALLIANCE AND
SHUGENDO PRACTITIONERS

CHAPTER ONE:
The City that Speaks to the Sky

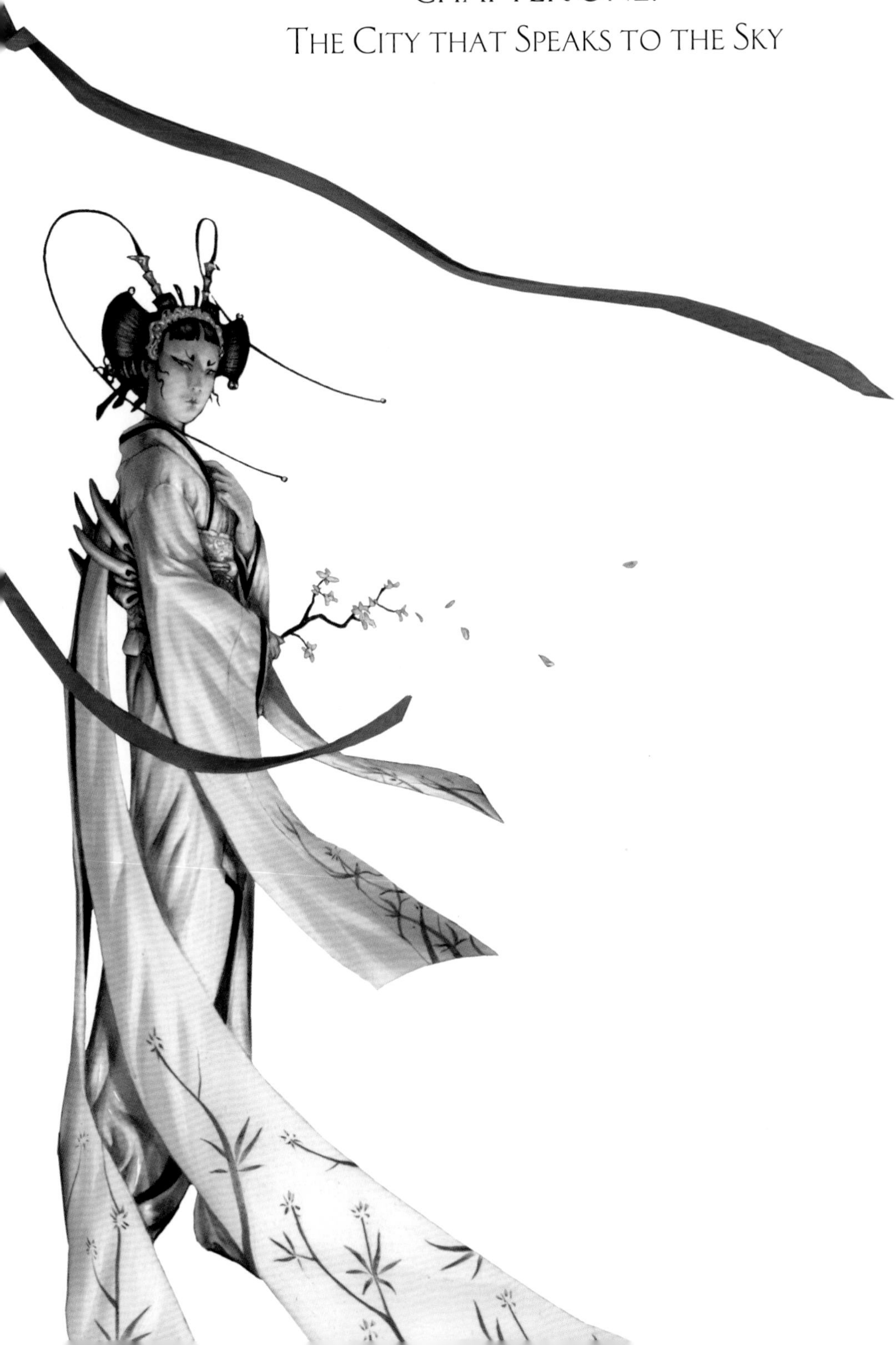

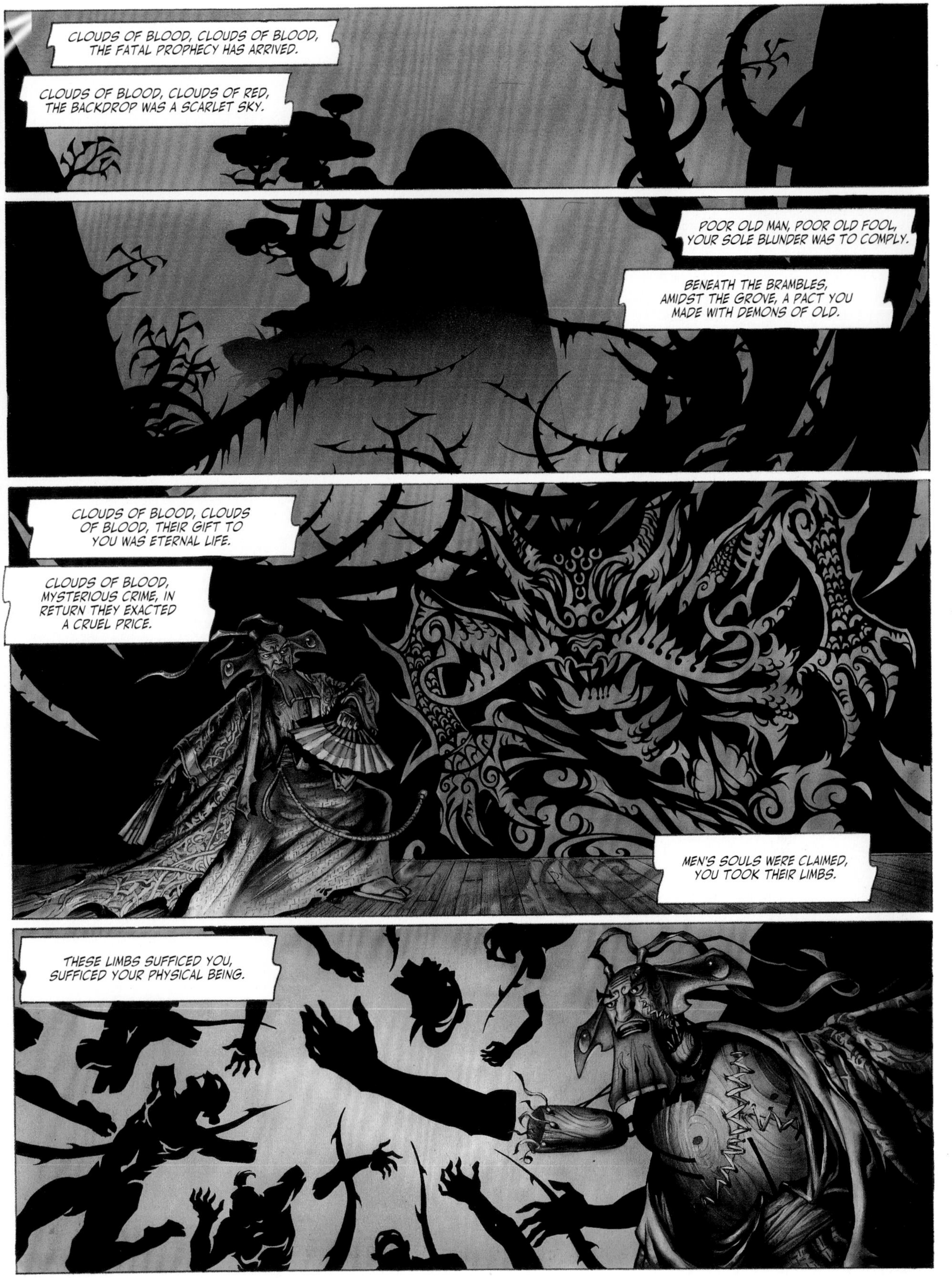
CLOUDS OF BLOOD, CLOUDS OF BLOOD, THE FATAL PROPHECY HAS ARRIVED.
CLOUDS OF BLOOD, CLOUDS OF RED, THE BACKDROP WAS A SCARLET SKY.
POOR OLD MAN, POOR OLD FOOL, YOUR SOLE BLUNDER WAS TO COMPLY.
BENEATH THE BRAMBLES, AMIDST THE GROVE, A PACT YOU MADE WITH DEMONS OF OLD.
CLOUDS OF BLOOD, CLOUDS OF BLOOD, THEIR GIFT TO YOU WAS ETERNAL LIFE.
CLOUDS OF BLOOD, MYSTERIOUS CRIME, IN RETURN THEY EXACTED A CRUEL PRICE.
MEN'S SOULS WERE CLAIMED, YOU TOOK THEIR LIMBS.
THESE LIMBS SUFFICED YOU, SUFFICED YOUR PHYSICAL BEING.

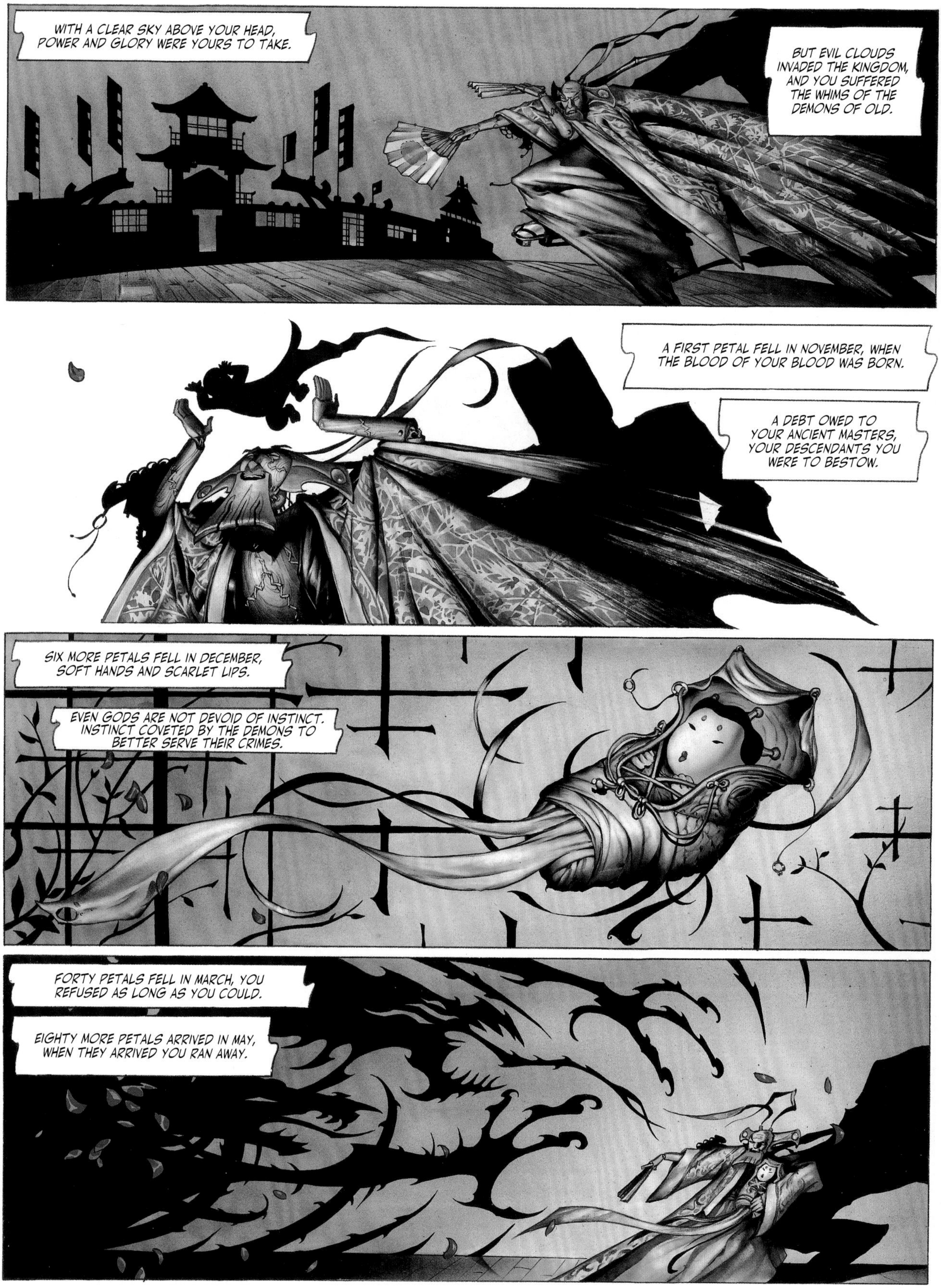
WITH A CLEAR SKY ABOVE YOUR HEAD, POWER AND GLORY WERE YOURS TO TAKE.
BUT EVIL CLOUDS INVADED THE KINGDOM, AND YOU SUFFERED THE WHIMS OF THE DEMONS OF OLD.
A FIRST PETAL FELL IN NOVEMBER, WHEN THE BLOOD OF YOUR BLOOD WAS BORN.
A DEBT OWED TO YOUR ANCIENT MASTERS, YOUR DESCENDANTS YOU WERE TO BESTOW.
SIX MORE PETALS FELL IN DECEMBER, SOFT HANDS AND SCARLET LIPS.
EVEN GODS ARE NOT DEVOID OF INSTINCT. INSTINCT COVETED BY THE DEMONS TO BETTER SERVE THEIR CRIMES.
FORTY PETALS FELL IN MARCH, YOU REFUSED AS LONG AS YOU COULD.
EIGHTY MORE PETALS ARRIVED IN MAY, WHEN THEY ARRIVED YOU RAN AWAY.

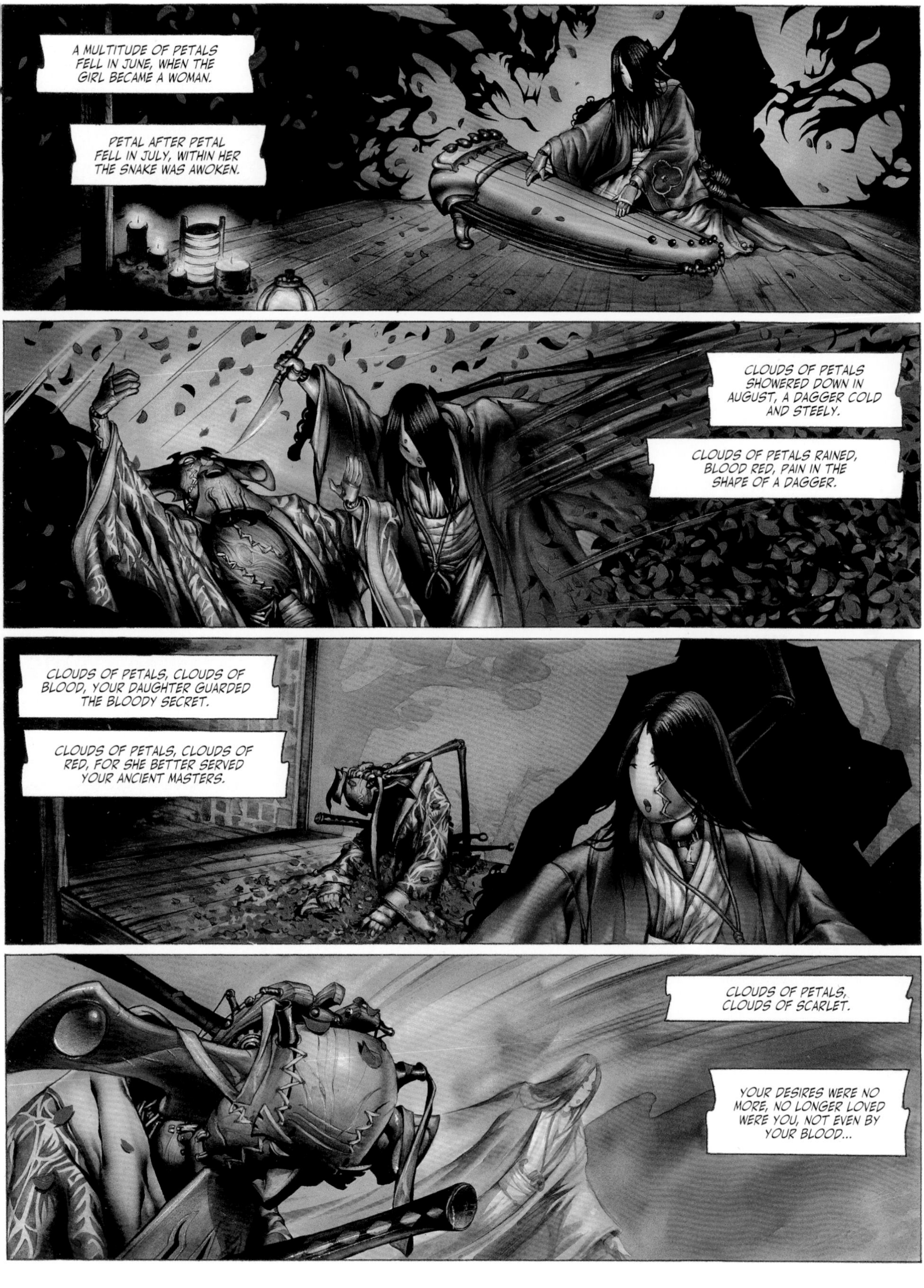
A MULTITUDE OF PETALS FELL IN JUNE, WHEN THE GIRL BECAME A WOMAN.
PETAL AFTER PETAL FELL IN JULY, WITHIN HER THE SNAKE WAS AWOKEN.
CLOUDS OF PETALS SHOWERED DOWN IN AUGUST, A DAGGER COLD AND STEELY.
CLOUDS OF PETALS RAINED, BLOOD RED, PAIN IN THE SHAPE OF A DAGGER.
CLOUDS OF PETALS, CLOUDS OF BLOOD, YOUR DAUGHTER GUARDED THE BLOODY SECRET.
CLOUDS OF PETALS, CLOUDS OF RED, FOR SHE BETTER SERVED YOUR ANCIENT MASTERS.
CLOUDS OF PETALS, CLOUDS OF SCARLET.
YOUR DESIRES WERE NO MORE, NO LONGER LOVED WERE YOU, NOT EVEN BY YOUR BLOOD...

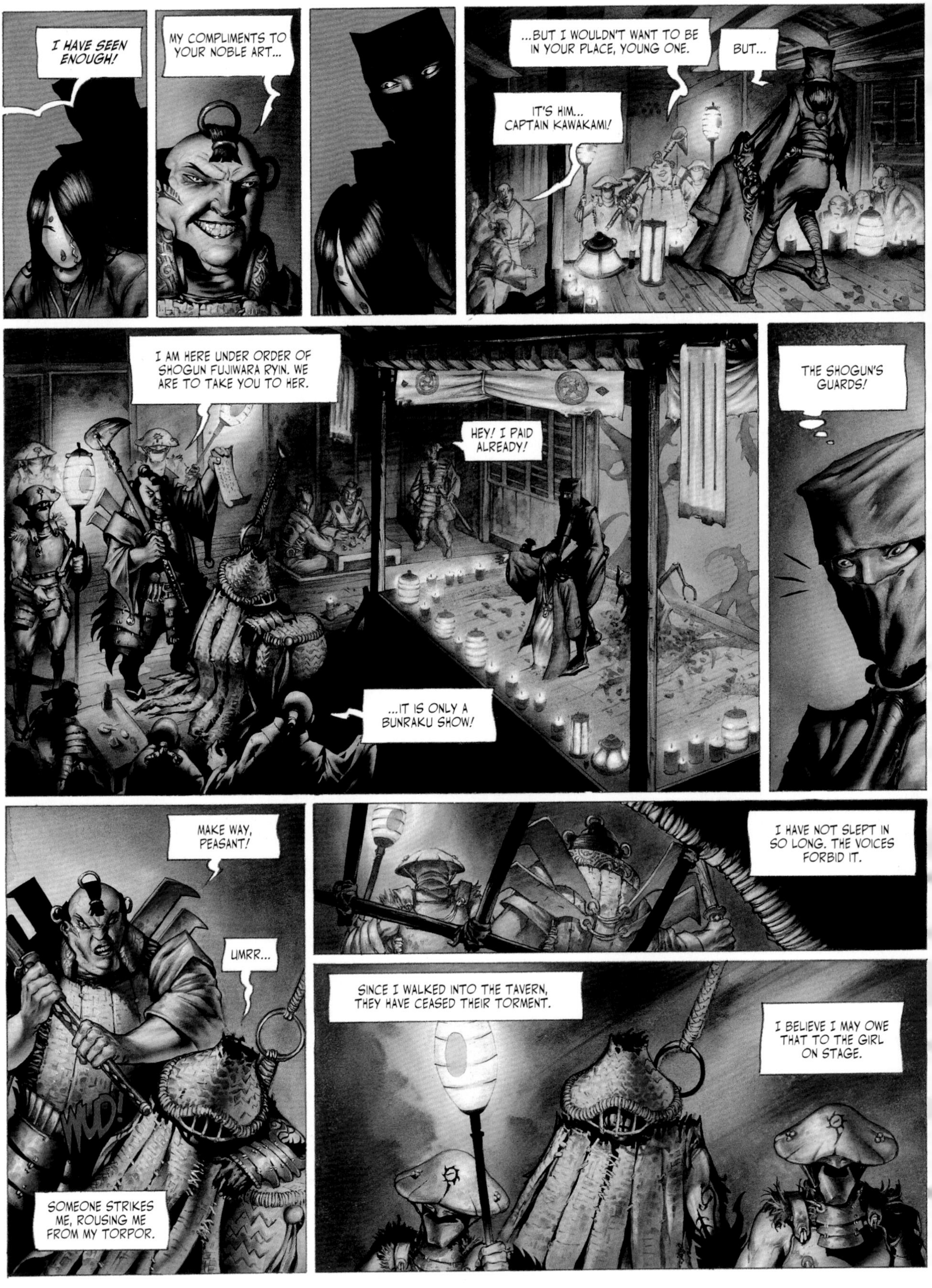
I HAVE SEEN ENOUGH!
MY COMPLIMENTS TO YOUR NOBLE ART...
...BUT I WOULDN'T WANT TO BE IN YOUR PLACE, YOUNG ONE.
BUT...
IT'S HIM... CAPTAIN KAWAKAMI!
I AM HERE UNDER ORDER OF SHOGUN FUJIWARA RYIN. WE ARE TO TAKE YOU TO HER.
HEY! I PAID ALREADY!
...IT IS ONLY A BUNRAKU SHOW!
THE SHOGUN'S GUARDS!
MAKE WAY, PEASANT!
UMRR...
WUD!
SOMEONE STRIKES ME, ROUSING ME FROM MY TORPOR.
I HAVE NOT SLEPT IN SO LONG. THE VOICES FORBID IT.
SINCE I WALKED INTO THE TAVERN, THEY HAVE CEASED THEIR TORMENT.
I BELIEVE I MAY OWE THAT TO THE GIRL ON STAGE.

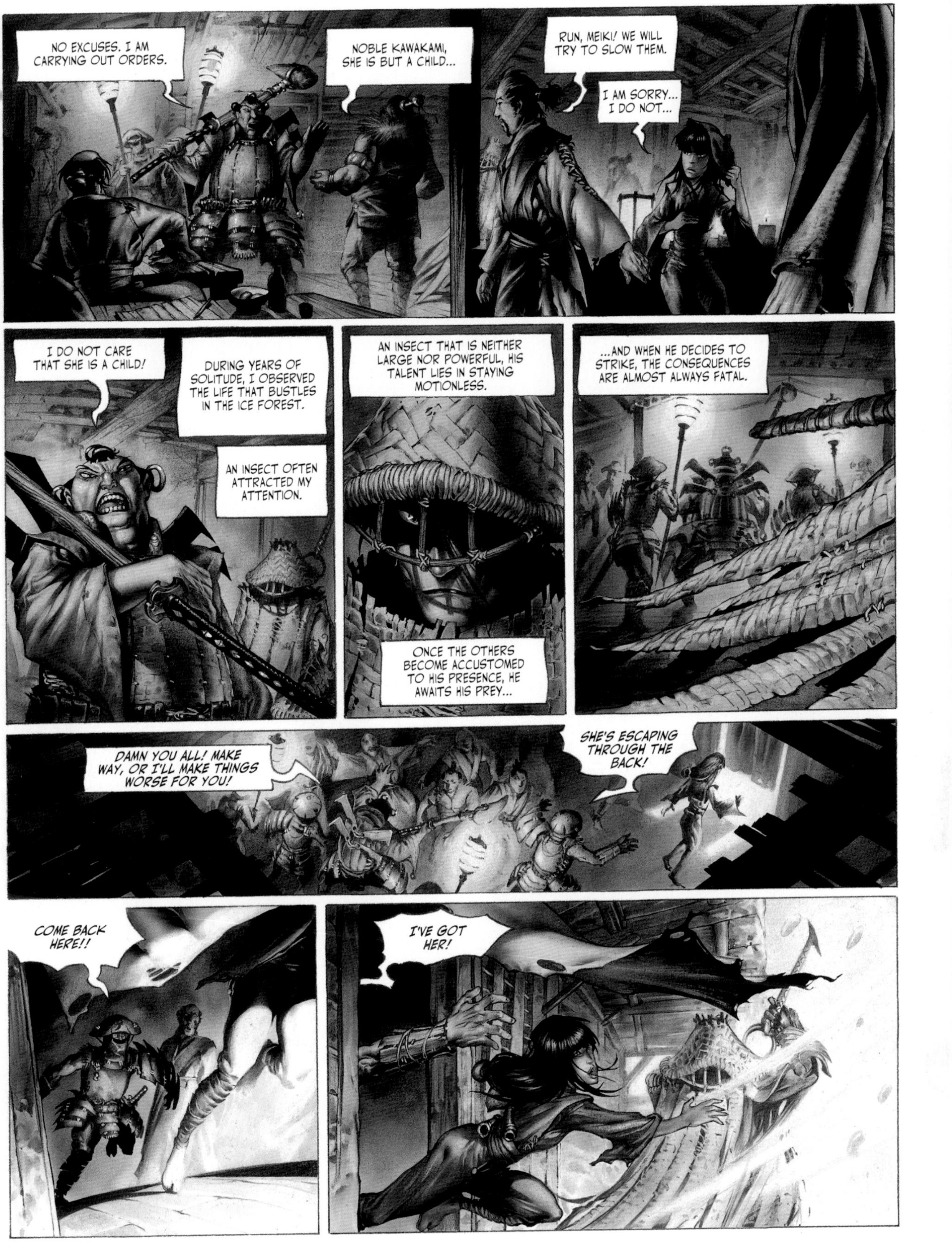

NO EXCUSES. I AM CARRYING OUT ORDERS.
NOBLE KAWAKAMI, SHE IS BUT A CHILD...
RUN, MEIKI! WE WILL TRY TO SLOW THEM.
I AM SORRY... I DO NOT...
I DO NOT CARE THAT SHE IS A CHILD!
DURING YEARS OF SOLITUDE, I OBSERVED THE LIFE THAT BUSTLES IN THE ICE FOREST.
AN INSECT OFTEN ATTRACTED MY ATTENTION.
AN INSECT THAT IS NEITHER LARGE NOR POWERFUL, HIS TALENT LIES IN STAYING MOTIONLESS.
ONCE THE OTHERS BECOME ACCUSTOMED TO HIS PRESENCE, HE AWAITS HIS PREY...
...AND WHEN HE DECIDES TO STRIKE, THE CONSEQUENCES ARE ALMOST ALWAYS FATAL.
DAMN YOU ALL! MAKE WAY, OR I'LL MAKE THINGS WORSE FOR YOU!
SHE'S ESCAPING THROUGH THE BACK!
COME BACK HERE!!
I'VE GOT HER!

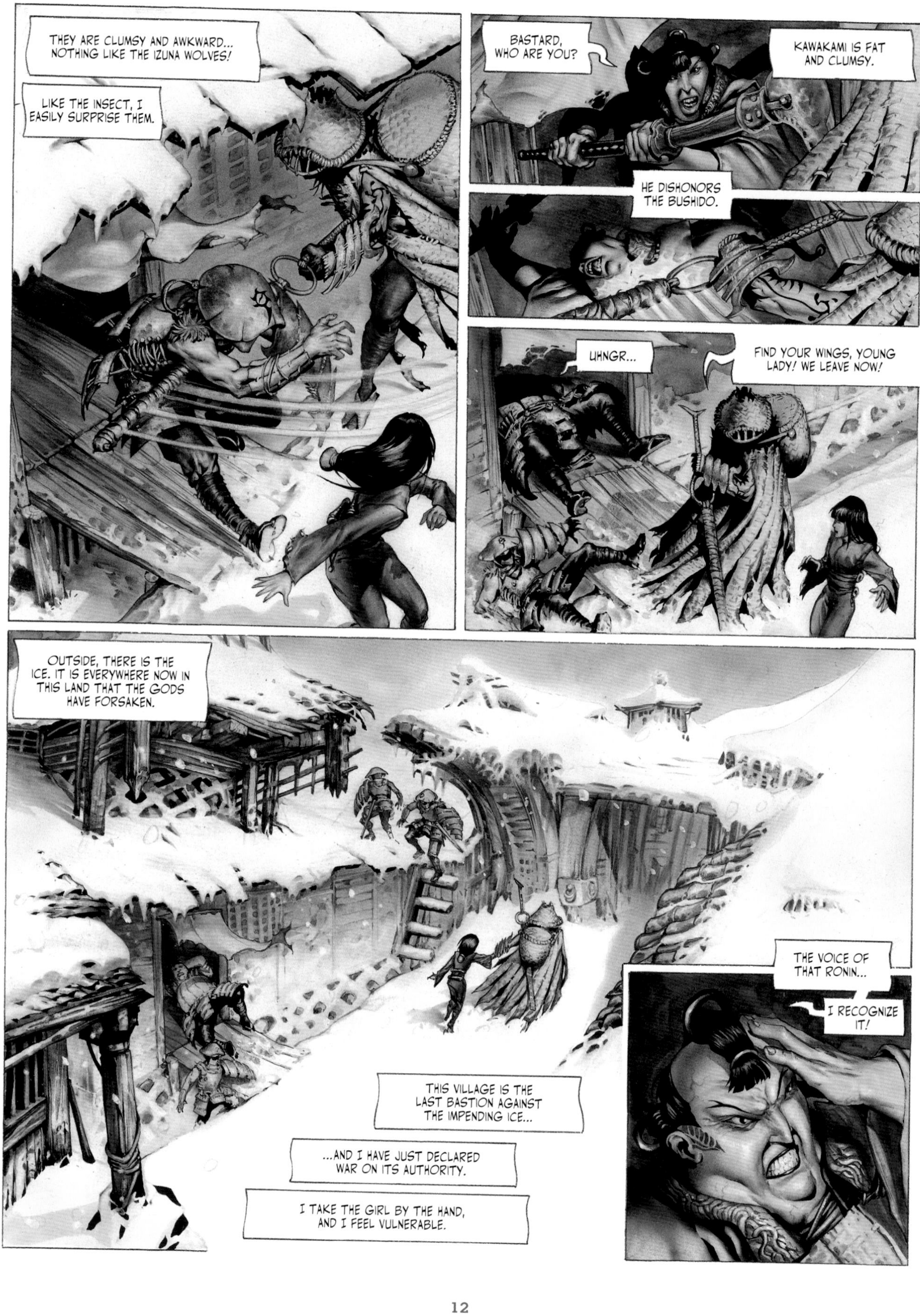
THEY ARE CLUMSY AND AWKWARD... NOTHING LIKE THE IZUNA WOLVES!
LIKE THE INSECT, I EASILY SURPRISE THEM.
BASTARD, WHO ARE YOU?
KAWAKAMI IS FAT AND CLUMSY.
HE DISHONORS THE BUSHIDO.
UHNGR...
FIND YOUR WINGS, YOUNG LADY! WE LEAVE NOW!
OUTSIDE, THERE IS THE ICE. IT IS EVERYWHERE NOW IN THIS LAND THAT THE GODS HAVE FORSAKEN.
THIS VILLAGE IS THE LAST BASTION AGAINST THE IMPENDING ICE...
...AND I HAVE JUST DECLARED WAR ON ITS AUTHORITY.
I TAKE THE GIRL BY THE HAND, AND I FEEL VULNERABLE.
THE VOICE OF THAT RONIN...
I RECOGNIZE IT!

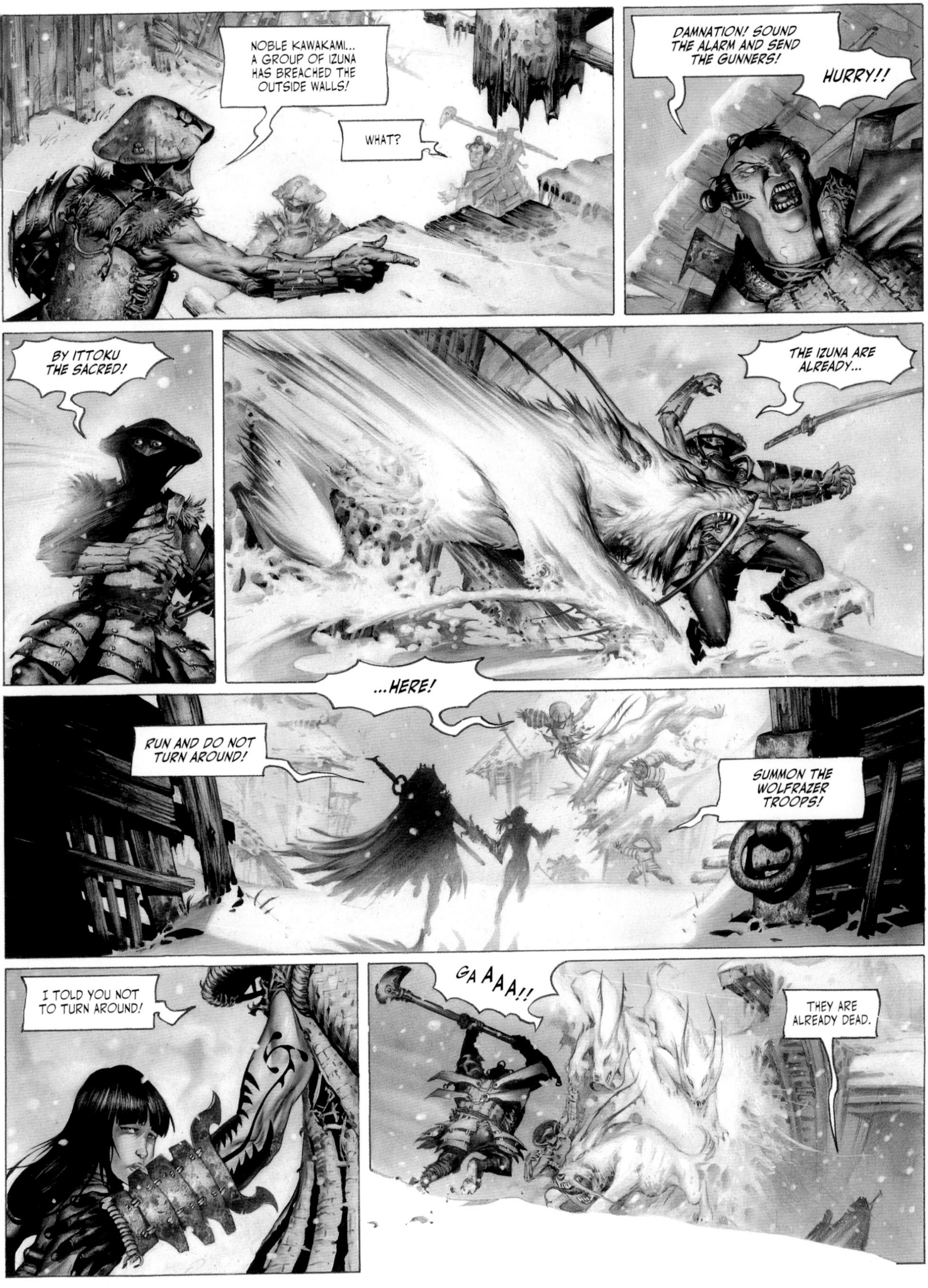

NOBLE KAWAKAMI... A GROUP OF IZUNA HAS BREACHED THE OUTSIDE WALLS!
WHAT?
DAMNATION! SOUND THE ALARM AND SEND THE GUNNERS!
HURRY!!
BY ITTOKU THE SACRED!
THE IZUNA ARE ALREADY...
...HERE!
RUN AND DO NOT TURN AROUND!
SUMMON THE WOLFRAZER TROOPS!
I TOLD YOU NOT TO TURN AROUND!
GA AAAA!!
THEY ARE ALREADY DEAD.

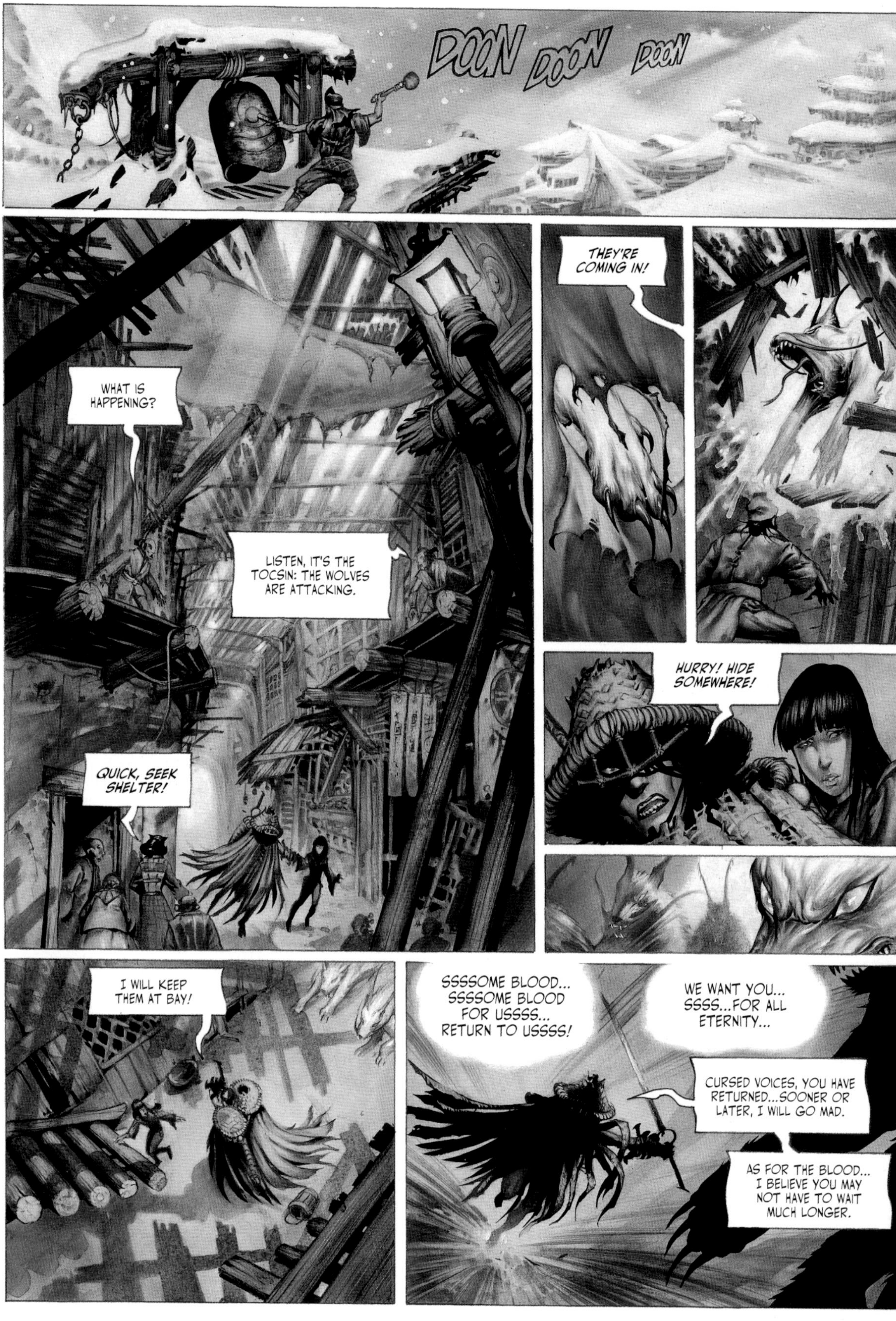
DOON DOON DOON
WHAT IS HAPPENING?
LISTEN, IT'S THE TOCSIN: THE WOLVES ARE ATTACKING.
QUICK, SEEK SHELTER!
THEY'RE COMING IN!
HURRY! HIDE SOMEWHERE!
I WILL KEEP THEM AT BAY!
SSSSOME BLOOD... SSSSOME BLOOD FOR USSSS... RETURN TO USSSSS!
WE WANT YOU... SSSS...FOR ALL ETERNITY...
CURSED VOICES, YOU HAVE RETURNED...SOONER OR LATER, I WILL GO MAD.
AS FOR THE BLOOD... I BELIEVE YOU MAY NOT HAVE TO WAIT MUCH LONGER.

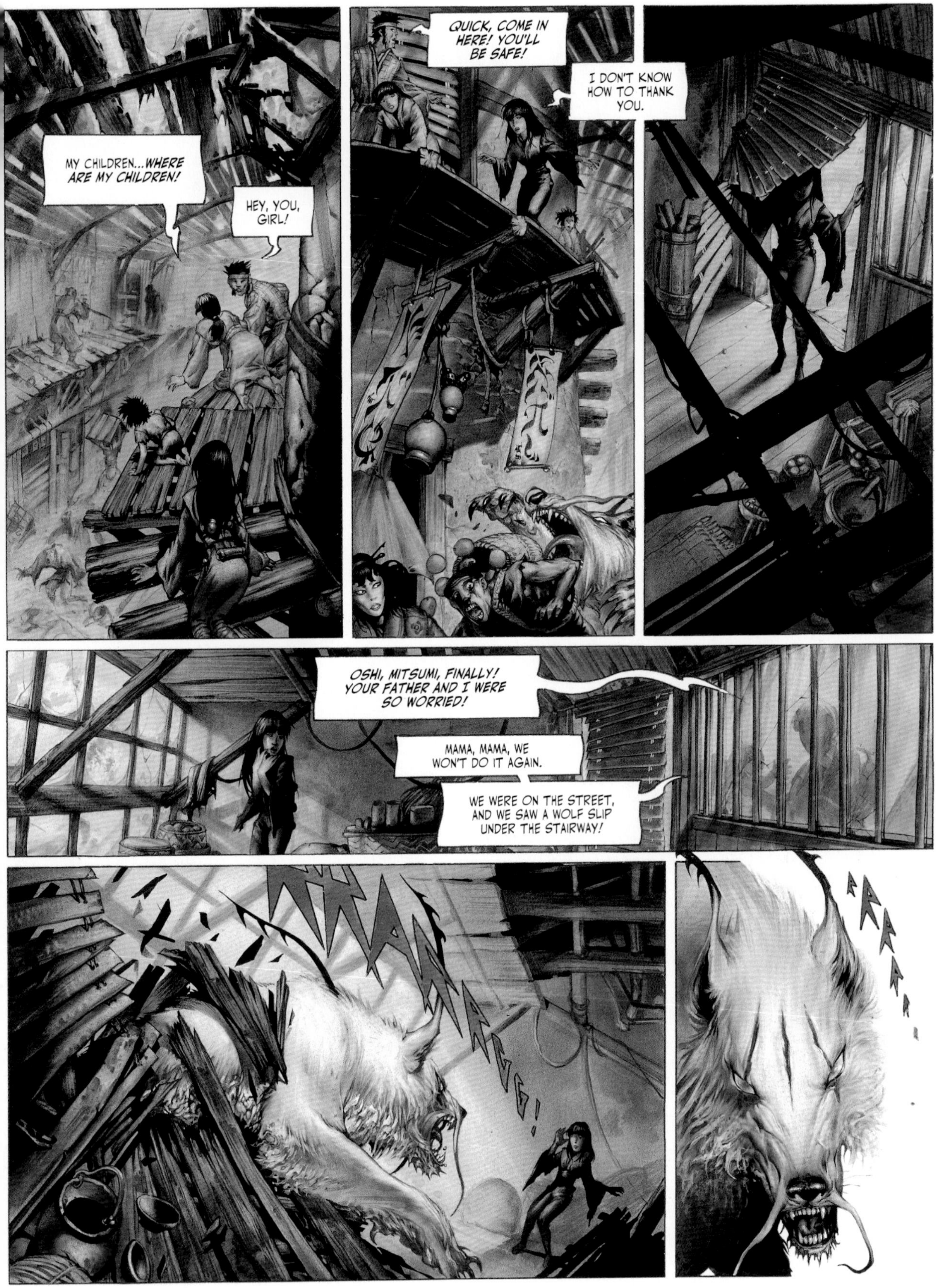
MY CHILDREN...WHERE ARE MY CHILDREN!
HEY, YOU, GIRL!
QUICK, COME IN HERE! YOU'LL BE SAFE!
I DON'T KNOW HOW TO THANK YOU.
OSHI, MITSUMI, FINALLY! YOUR FATHER AND I WERE SO WORRIED!
MAMA, MAMA, WE WON'T DO IT AGAIN.
WE WERE ON THE STREET, AND WE SAW A WOLF SLIP UNDER THE STAIRWAY!
RRRR

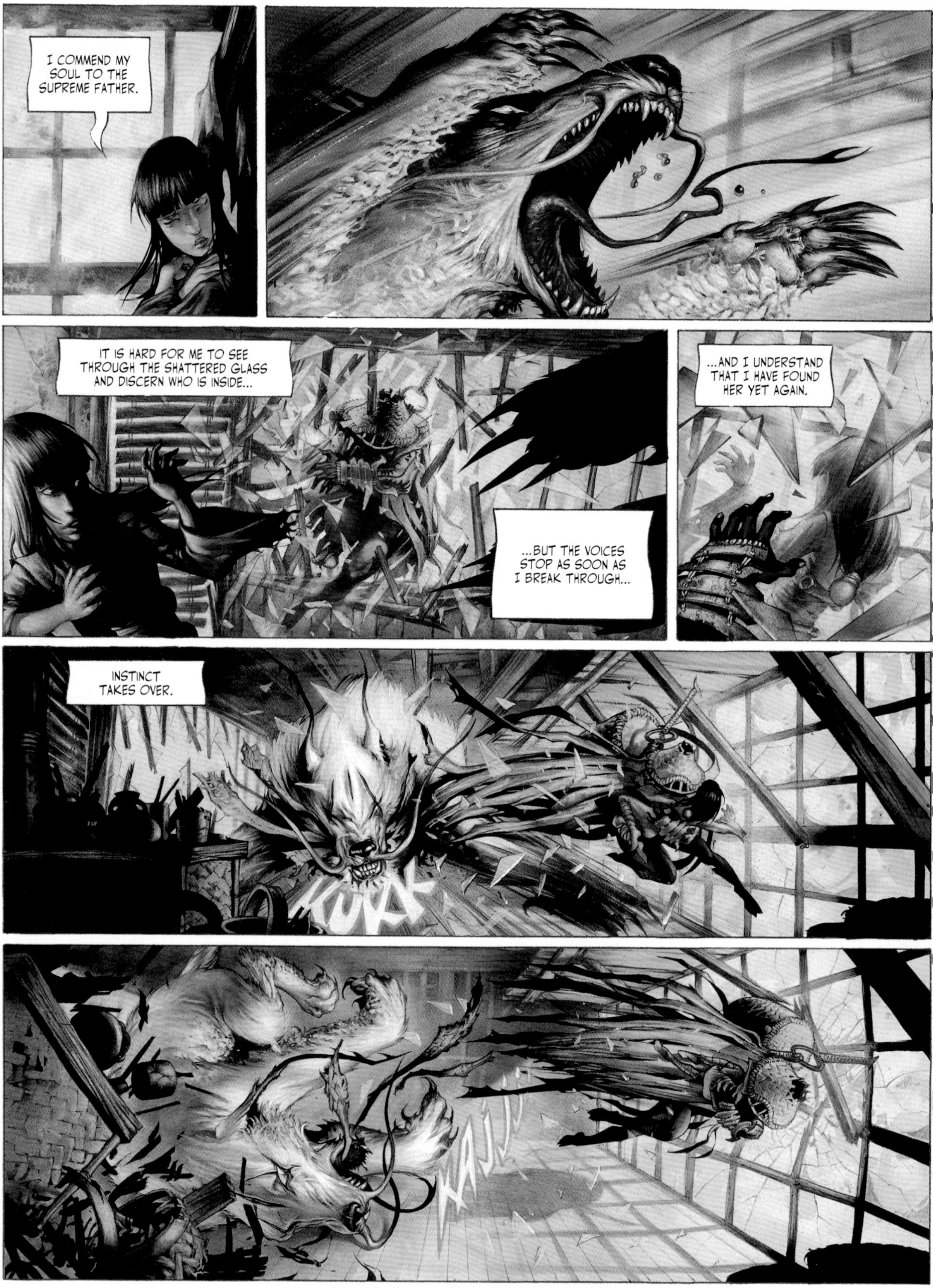
I COMMEND MY SOUL TO THE SUPREME FATHER.
IT IS HARD FOR ME TO SEE THROUGH THE SHATTERED GLASS AND DISCERN WHO IS INSIDE...
...BUT THE VOICES STOP AS SOON AS I BREAK THROUGH...
...AND I UNDERSTAND THAT I HAVE FOUND HER YET AGAIN.
INSTINCT TAKES OVER.

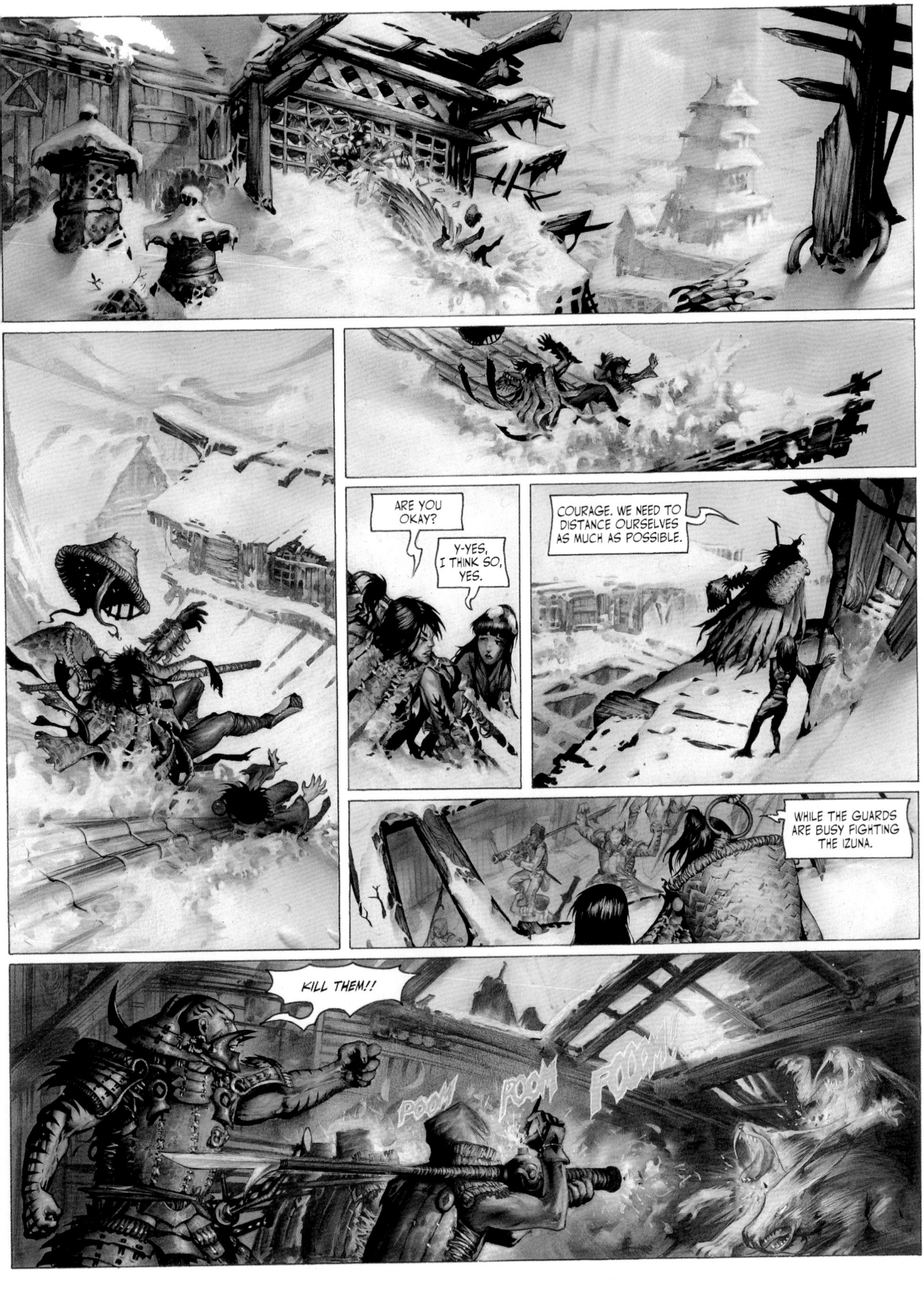
ARE YOU OKAY?
Y-YES, I THINK SO, YES.
COURAGE. WE NEED TO DISTANCE OURSELVES AS MUCH AS POSSIBLE.
WHILE THE GUARDS ARE BUSY FIGHTING THE IZUNA.
KILL THEM!!
POOM
POOM
FOOOM!!

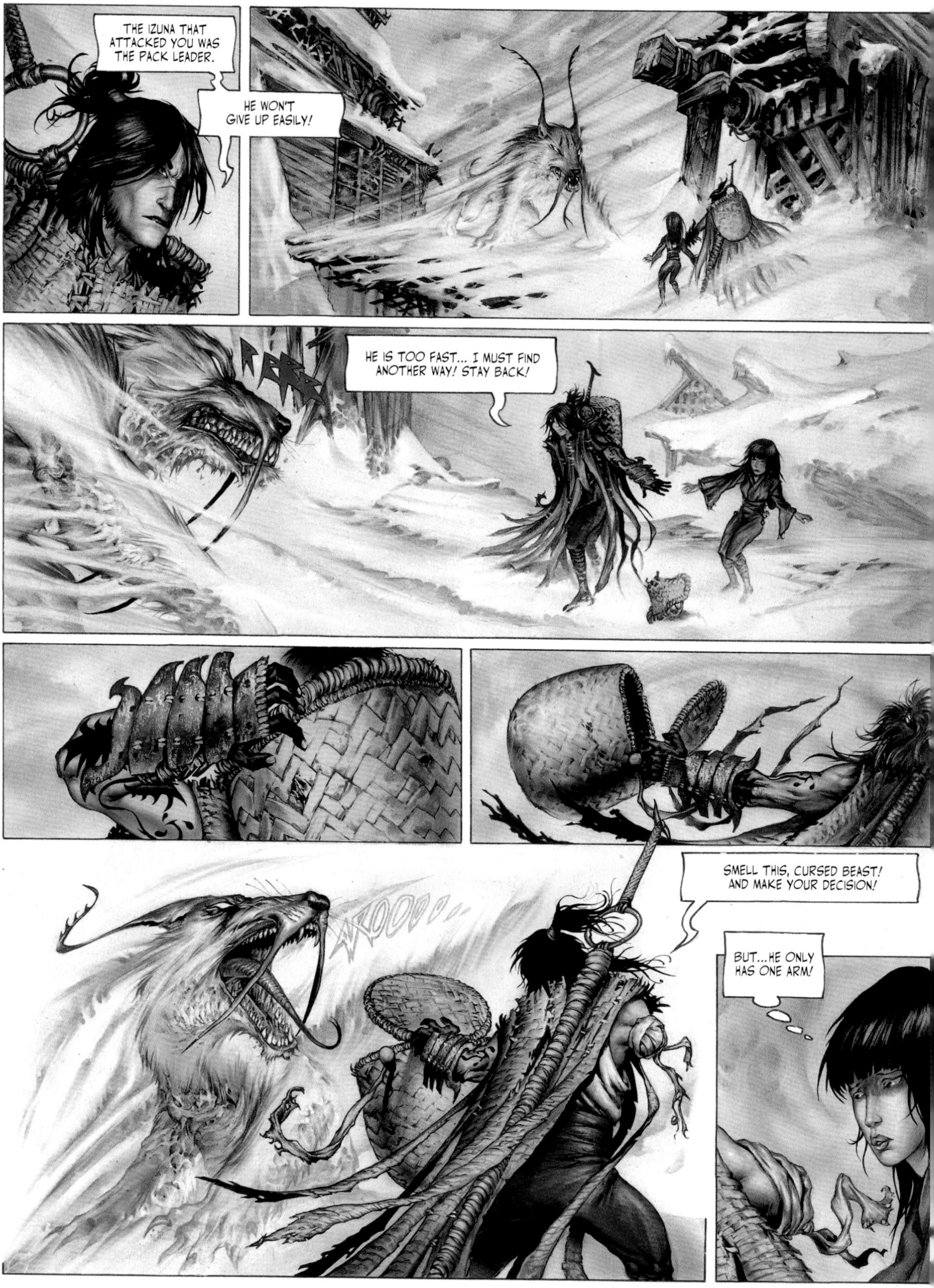
THE IZUNA THAT ATTACKED YOU WAS THE PACK LEADER.
HE WON'T GIVE UP EASILY!
RERR
HE IS TOO FAST... I MUST FIND ANOTHER WAY! STAY BACK!
SMELL THIS, CURSED BEAST! AND MAKE YOUR DECISION!
AROOO...
BUT...HE ONLY HAS ONE ARM!

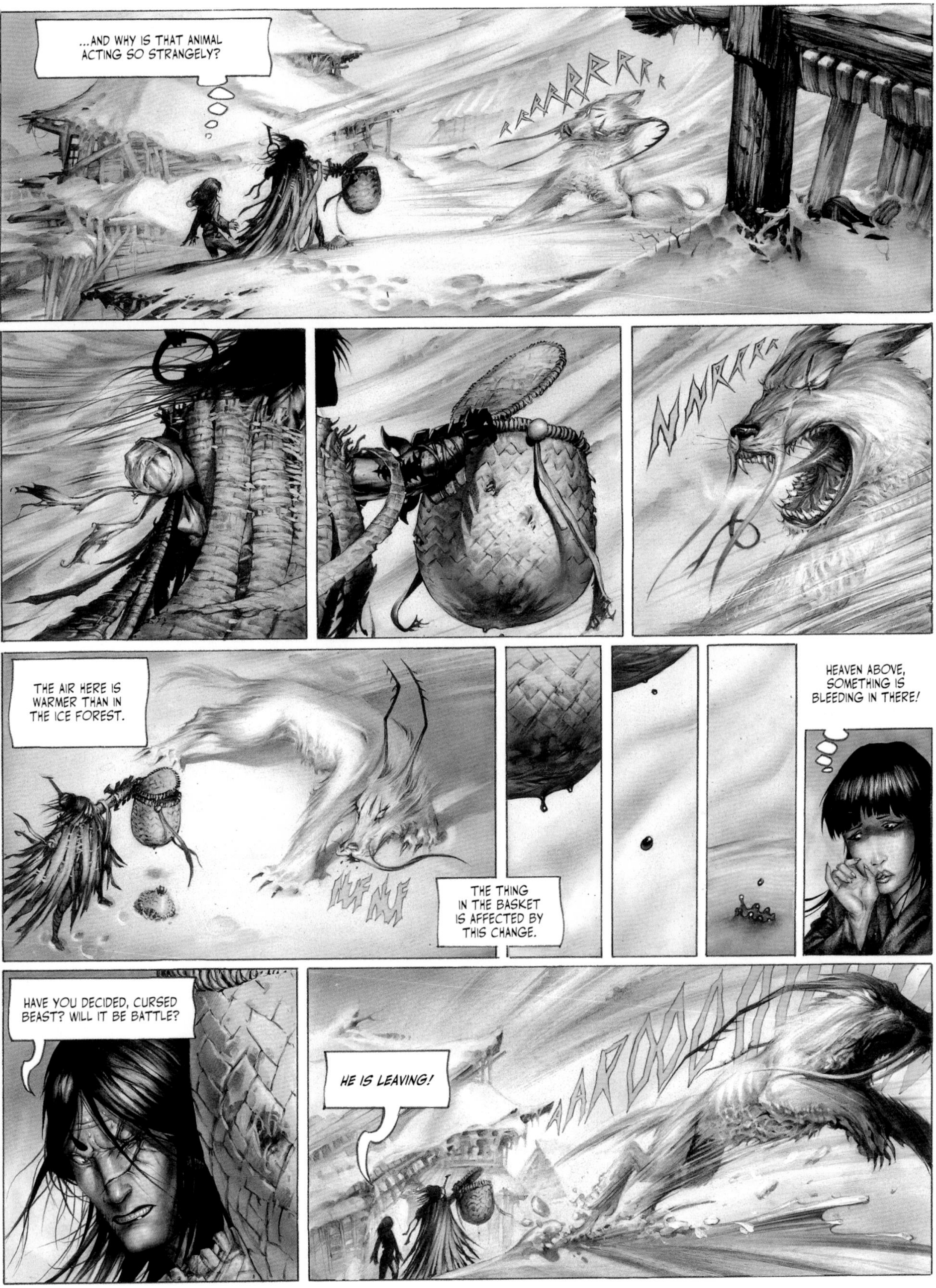

...AND WHY IS THAT ANIMAL ACTING SO STRANGELY?
RRRRRRRRR
NNRRRRR
THE AIR HERE IS WARMER THAN IN THE ICE FOREST.
NUF NUF
THE THING IN THE BASKET IS AFFECTED BY THIS CHANGE.
HEAVEN ABOVE, SOMETHING IS BLEEDING IN THERE!
HAVE YOU DECIDED, CURSED BEAST? WILL IT BE BATTLE?
HE IS LEAVING!

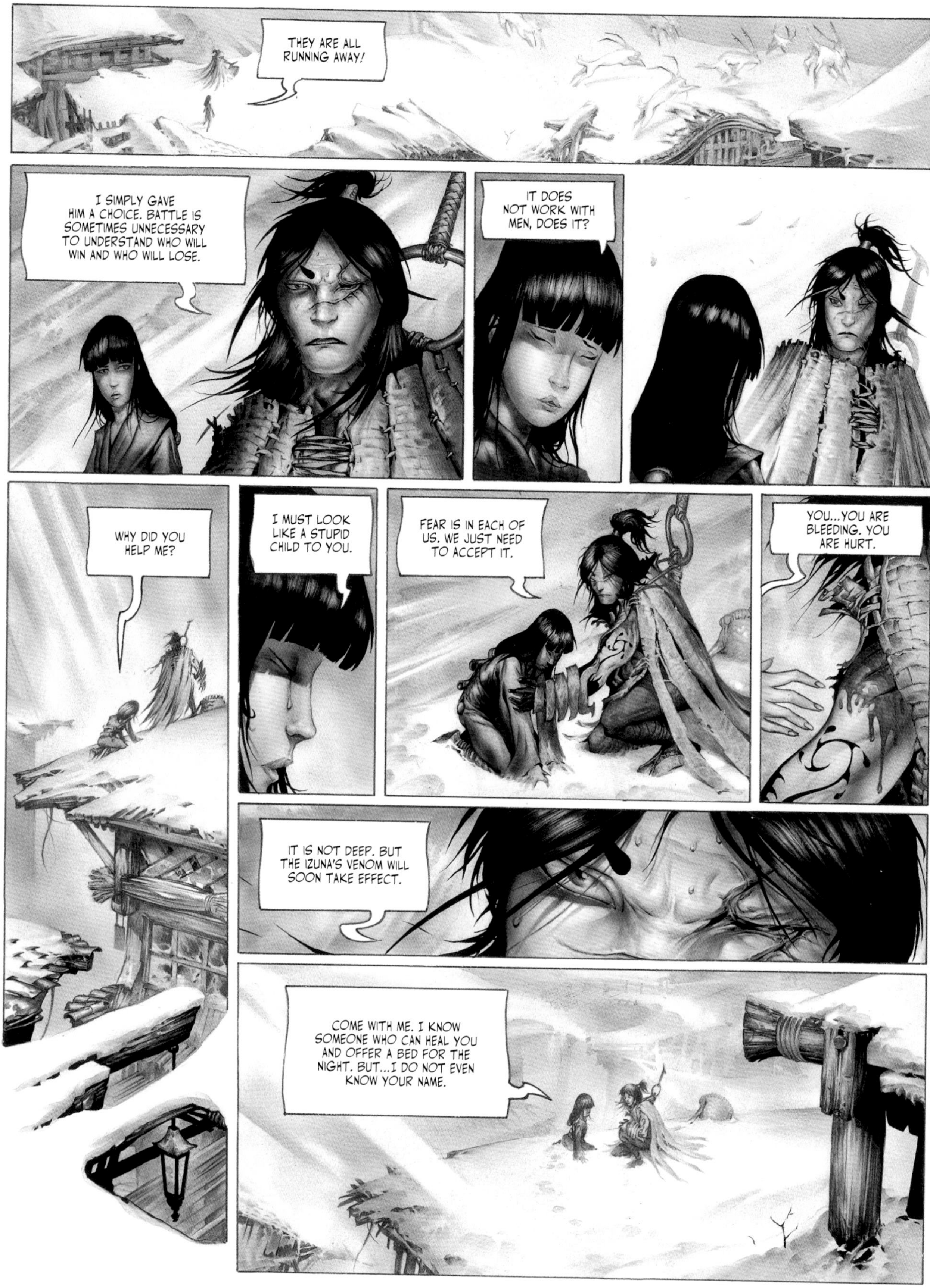
THEY ARE ALL RUNNING AWAY!
I SIMPLY GAVE HIM A CHOICE. BATTLE IS SOMETIMES UNNECESSARY TO UNDERSTAND WHO WILL WIN AND WHO WILL LOSE.
IT DOES NOT WORK WITH MEN, DOES IT?
WHY DID YOU HELP ME?
I MUST LOOK LIKE A STUPID CHILD TO YOU.
FEAR IS IN EACH OF US. WE JUST NEED TO ACCEPT IT.
YOU...YOU ARE BLEEDING. YOU ARE HURT.
IT IS NOT DEEP. BUT THE IZUNA'S VENOM WILL SOON TAKE EFFECT.
COME WITH ME. I KNOW SOMEONE WHO CAN HEAL YOU AND OFFER A BED FOR THE NIGHT. BUT...I DO NOT EVEN KNOW YOUR NAME.

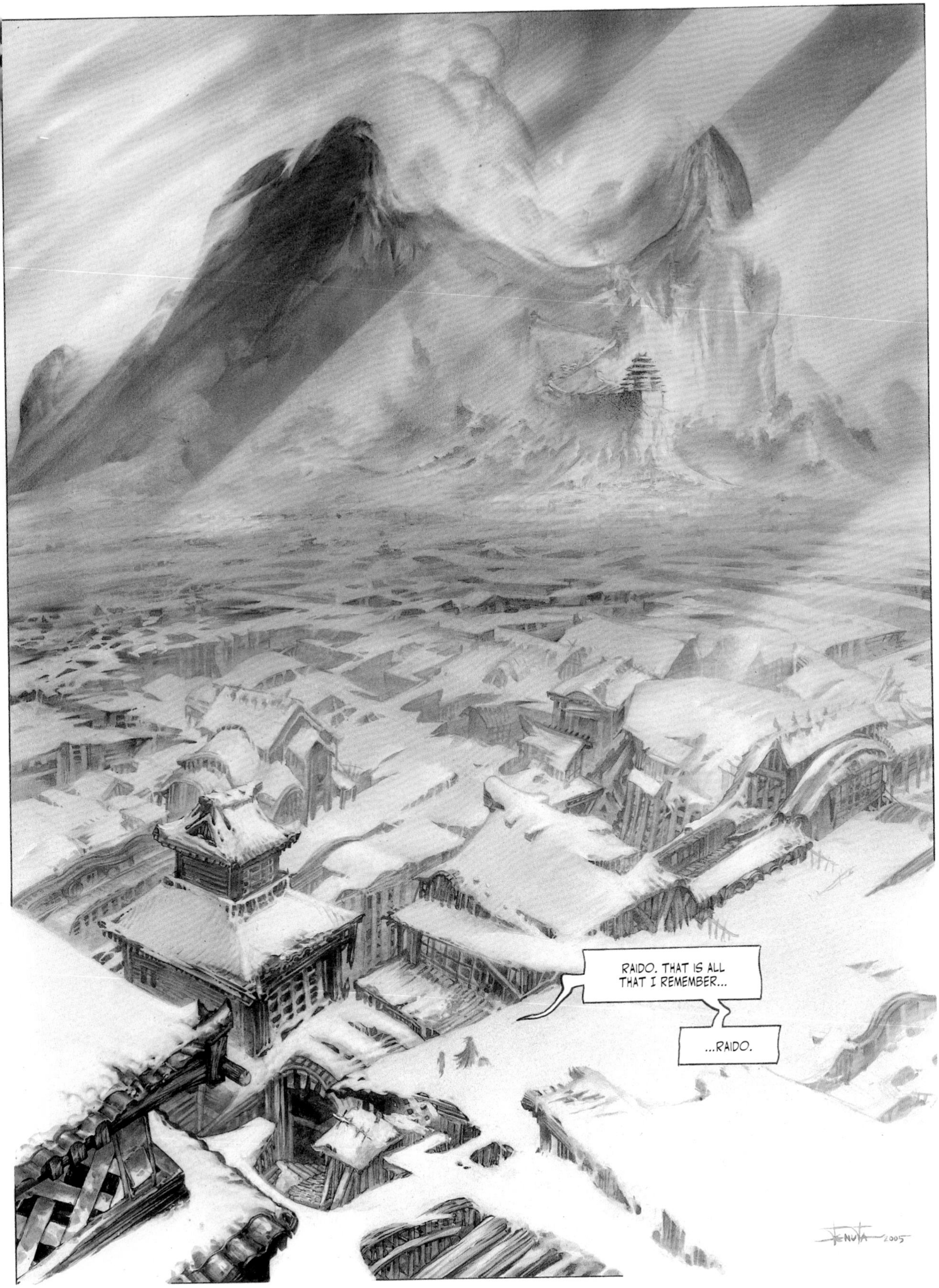
RAIDO. THAT IS ALL THAT I REMEMBER...
...RAIDO.

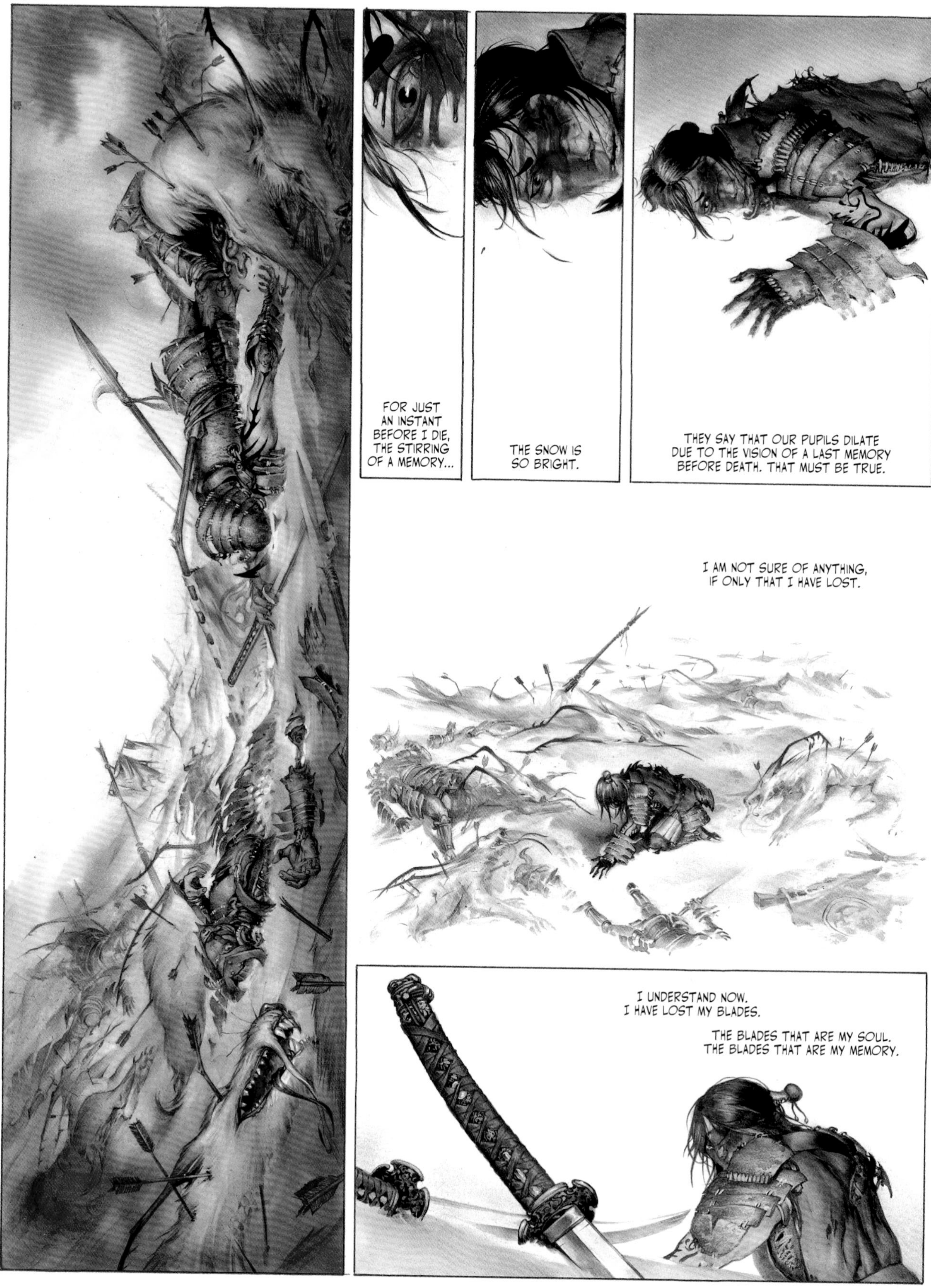
FOR JUST AN INSTANT BEFORE I DIE, THE STIRRING OF A MEMORY...
THE SNOW IS SO BRIGHT.
THEY SAY THAT OUR PUPILS DILATE DUE TO THE VISION OF A LAST MEMORY BEFORE DEATH. THAT MUST BE TRUE.
I AM NOT SURE OF ANYTHING, IF ONLY THAT I HAVE LOST.
I UNDERSTAND NOW. I HAVE LOST MY BLADES.
THE BLADES THAT ARE MY SOUL. THE BLADES THAT ARE MY MEMORY.

MY THOUGHTS ARE BUT DROPLETS OF DEW AMIDST THE RAIN. MY BLADES WASH AWAY WITH IT ALL.

I RAISE MY HEAD, AND I SMILE PAINFULLY. HE IS THERE BEFORE ME.

I TRY TO GRAB A BLADE, BUT MY ARM DOES NOT SEEM TO RESPOND. I REALIZE THAT I HAVE LOST IT COMPLETELY.

THE MAN BEFORE ME HAS NOT EVEN NOTICED MY ATTEMPT.

I WATCH AS HE SEIZES MY MEMORIES AND GRASPS THEM IN HIS FISTS... HE LAUGHS.

FOR JUST AN INSTANT BEFORE I DIE, THE STIRRING OF A MEMORY...

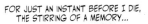

...THEN THE VOICES ASSAIL ME FOR THE VERY FIRST TIME.

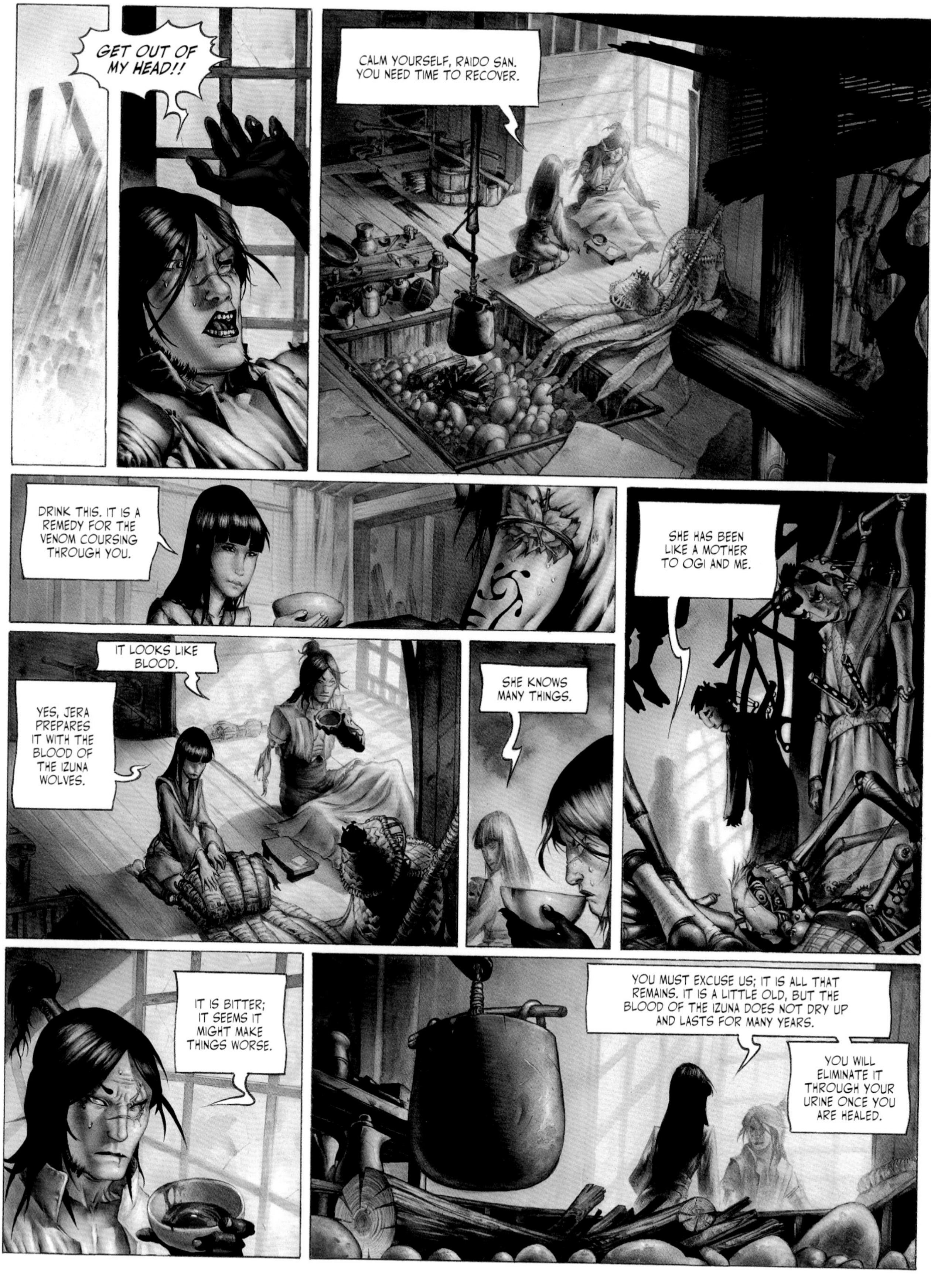
GET OUT OF MY HEAD!!
CALM YOURSELF, RAIDO SAN. YOU NEED TIME TO RECOVER.
DRINK THIS. IT IS A REMEDY FOR THE VENOM COURSING THROUGH YOU.
SHE HAS BEEN LIKE A MOTHER TO OGI AND ME.
IT LOOKS LIKE BLOOD.
YES, JERA PREPARES IT WITH THE BLOOD OF THE IZUNA WOLVES.
SHE KNOWS MANY THINGS.
IT IS BITTER; IT SEEMS IT MIGHT MAKE THINGS WORSE.
YOU MUST EXCUSE US; IT IS ALL THAT REMAINS. IT IS A LITTLE OLD, BUT THE BLOOD OF THE IZUNA DOES NOT DRY UP AND LASTS FOR MANY YEARS.
YOU WILL ELIMINATE IT THROUGH YOUR URINE ONCE YOU ARE HEALED.

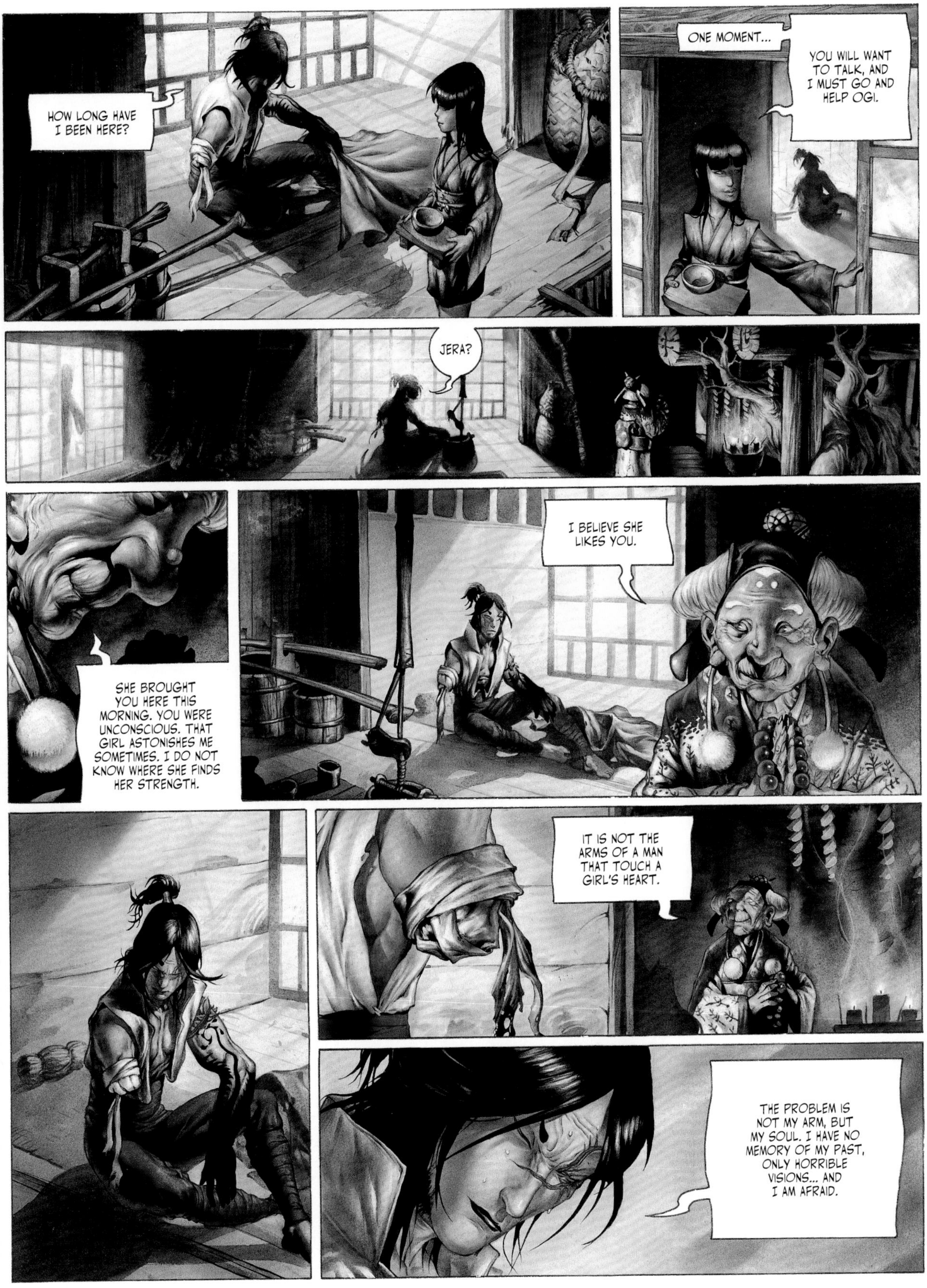
HOW LONG HAVE I BEEN HERE?
ONE MOMENT...
YOU WILL WANT TO TALK, AND I MUST GO AND HELP OGI.
JERA?
I BELIEVE SHE LIKES YOU.
SHE BROUGHT YOU HERE THIS MORNING. YOU WERE UNCONSCIOUS. THAT GIRL ASTONISHES ME SOMETIMES. I DO NOT KNOW WHERE SHE FINDS HER STRENGTH.
IT IS NOT THE ARMS OF A MAN THAT TOUCH A GIRL'S HEART.
THE PROBLEM IS NOT MY ARM, BUT MY SOUL. I HAVE NO MEMORY OF MY PAST, ONLY HORRIBLE VISIONS... AND I AM AFRAID.

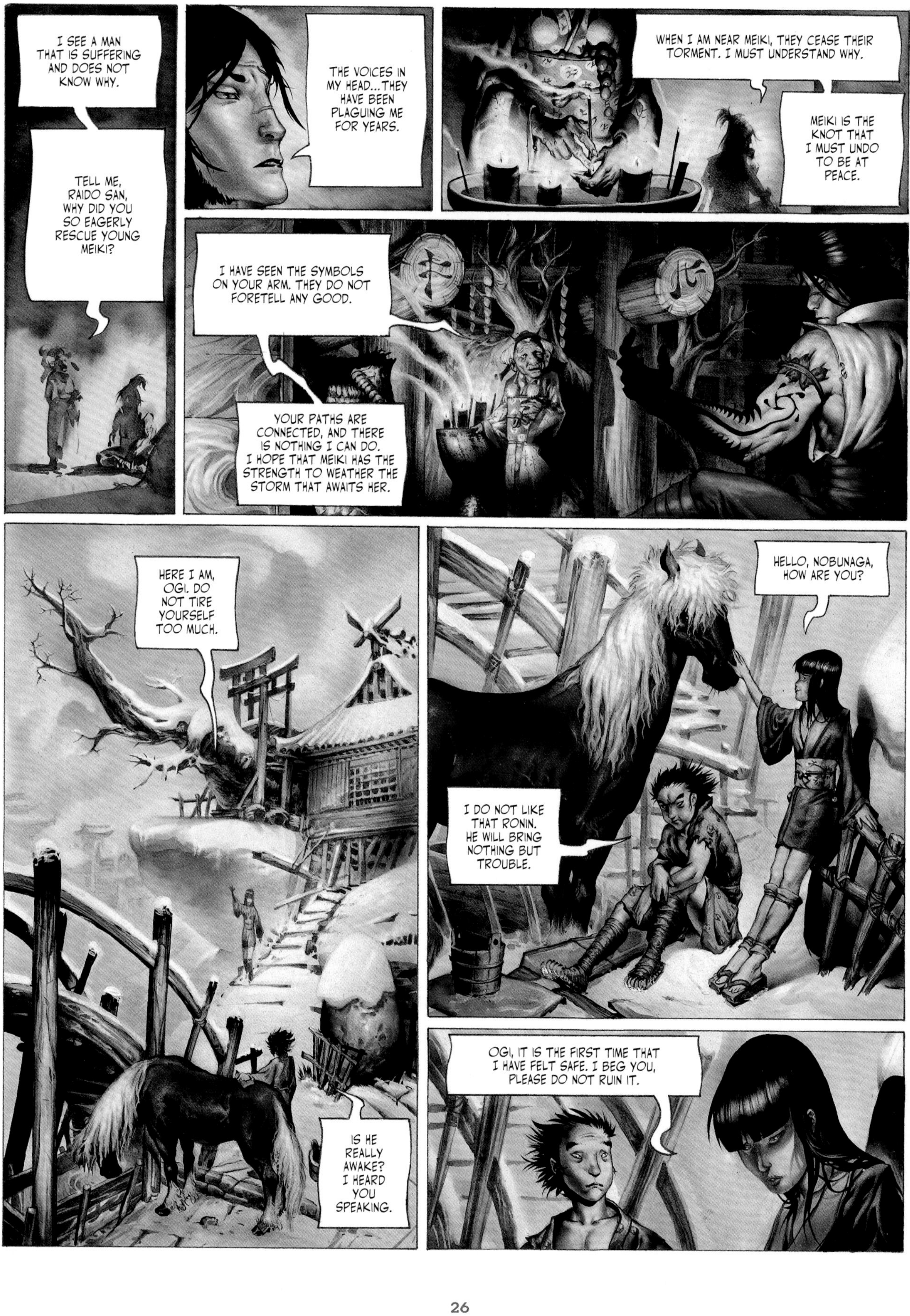
I SEE A MAN THAT IS SUFFERING AND DOES NOT KNOW WHY.
TELL ME, RAIDO SAN, WHY DID YOU SO EAGERLY RESCUE YOUNG MEIKI?
THE VOICES IN MY HEAD...THEY HAVE BEEN PLAGUING ME FOR YEARS.
WHEN I AM NEAR MEIKI, THEY CEASE THEIR TORMENT. I MUST UNDERSTAND WHY.
MEIKI IS THE KNOT THAT I MUST UNDO TO BE AT PEACE.
I HAVE SEEN THE SYMBOLS ON YOUR ARM. THEY DO NOT FORETELL ANY GOOD.
YOUR PATHS ARE CONNECTED, AND THERE IS NOTHING I CAN DO. I HOPE THAT MEIKI HAS THE STRENGTH TO WEATHER THE STORM THAT AWAITS HER.
HERE I AM, OGI. DO NOT TIRE YOURSELF TOO MUCH.
IS HE REALLY AWAKE? I HEARD YOU SPEAKING.
HELLO, NOBUNAGA, HOW ARE YOU?
I DO NOT LIKE THAT RONIN. HE WILL BRING NOTHING BUT TROUBLE.
OGI, IT IS THE FIRST TIME THAT I HAVE FELT SAFE. I BEG YOU, PLEASE DO NOT RUIN IT.

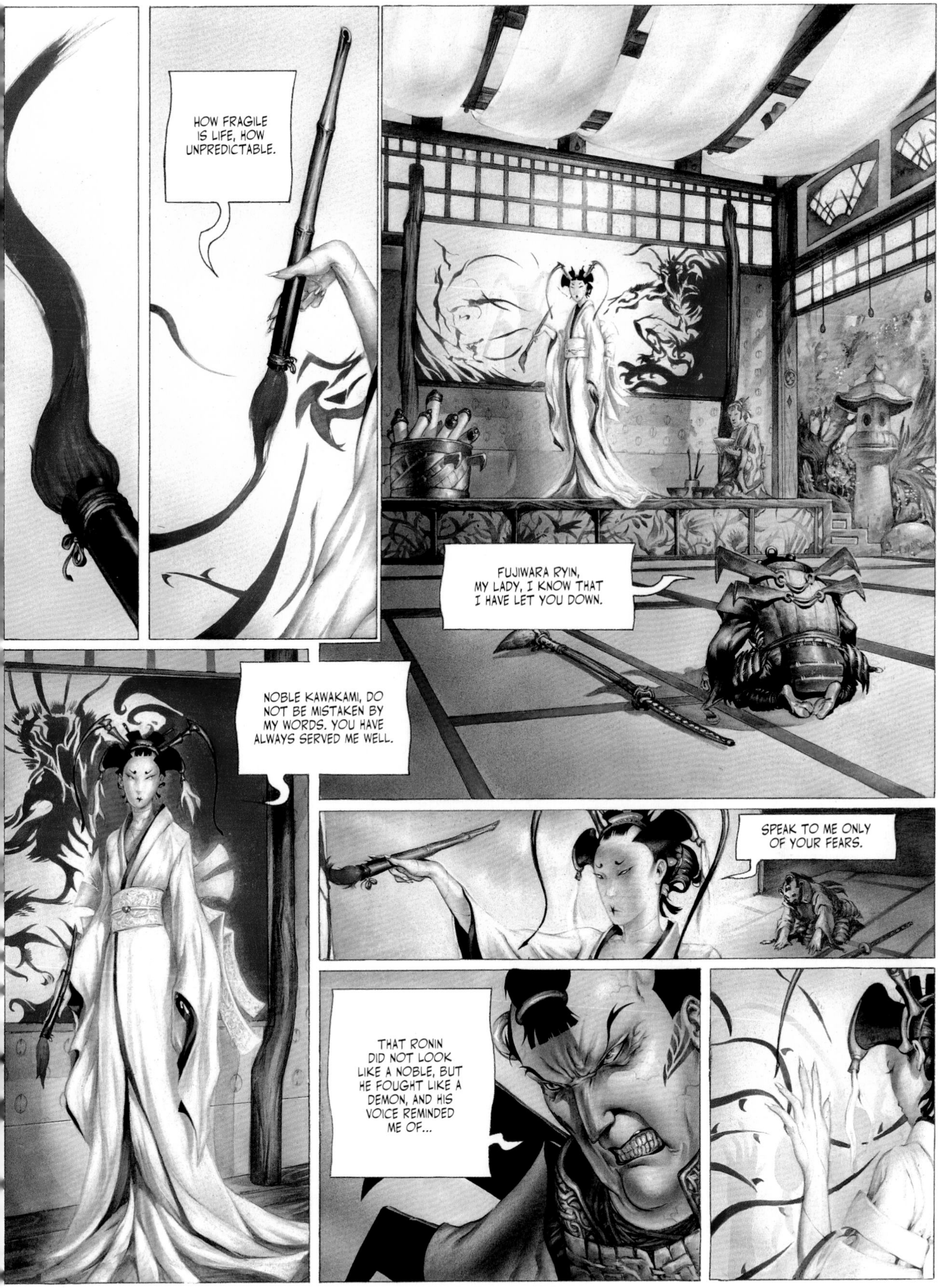
HOW FRAGILE IS LIFE, HOW UNPREDICTABLE.
FUJIWARA RYIN, MY LADY, I KNOW THAT I HAVE LET YOU DOWN.
NOBLE KAWAKAMI, DO NOT BE MISTAKEN BY MY WORDS. YOU HAVE ALWAYS SERVED ME WELL.
SPEAK TO ME ONLY OF YOUR FEARS.
THAT RONIN DID NOT LOOK LIKE A NOBLE, BUT HE FOUGHT LIKE A DEMON, AND HIS VOICE REMINDED ME OF...

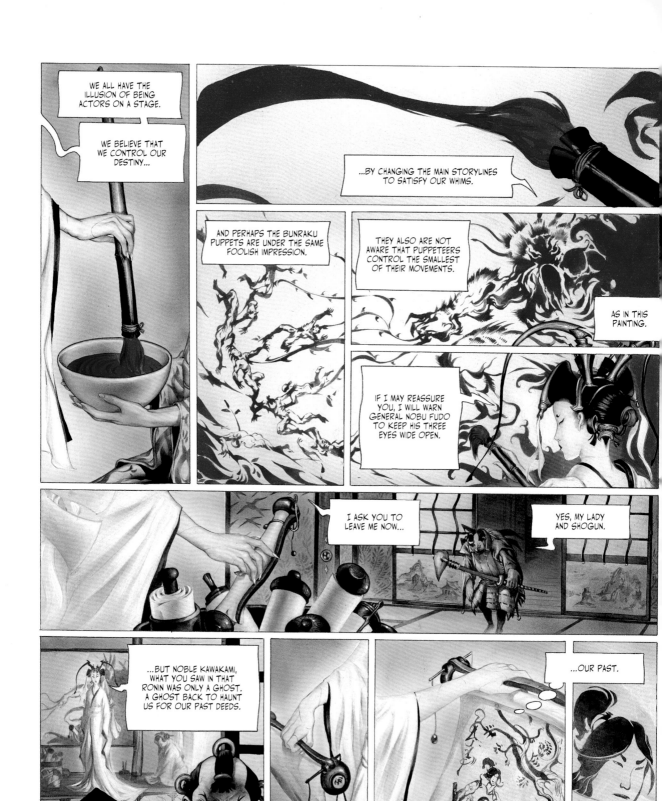

WE ALL HAVE THE ILLUSION OF BEING ACTORS ON A STAGE.

WE BELIEVE THAT WE CONTROL OUR DESTINY...

...BY CHANGING THE MAIN STORYLINES TO SATISFY OUR WHIMS.

AND PERHAPS THE BUNRAKU PUPPETS ARE UNDER THE SAME FOOLISH IMPRESSION.

THEY ALSO ARE NOT AWARE THAT PUPPETEERS CONTROL THE SMALLEST OF THEIR MOVEMENTS.

AS IN THIS PAINTING.

IF I MAY REASSURE YOU, I WILL WARN GENERAL NOBU FUDO TO KEEP HIS THREE EYES WIDE OPEN.

I ASK YOU TO LEAVE ME NOW...

YES, MY LADY AND SHOGUN.

...BUT NOBLE KAWAKAMI, WHAT YOU SAW IN THAT RONIN WAS ONLY A GHOST. A GHOST BACK TO HAUNT US FOR OUR PAST DEEDS.

...OUR PAST.

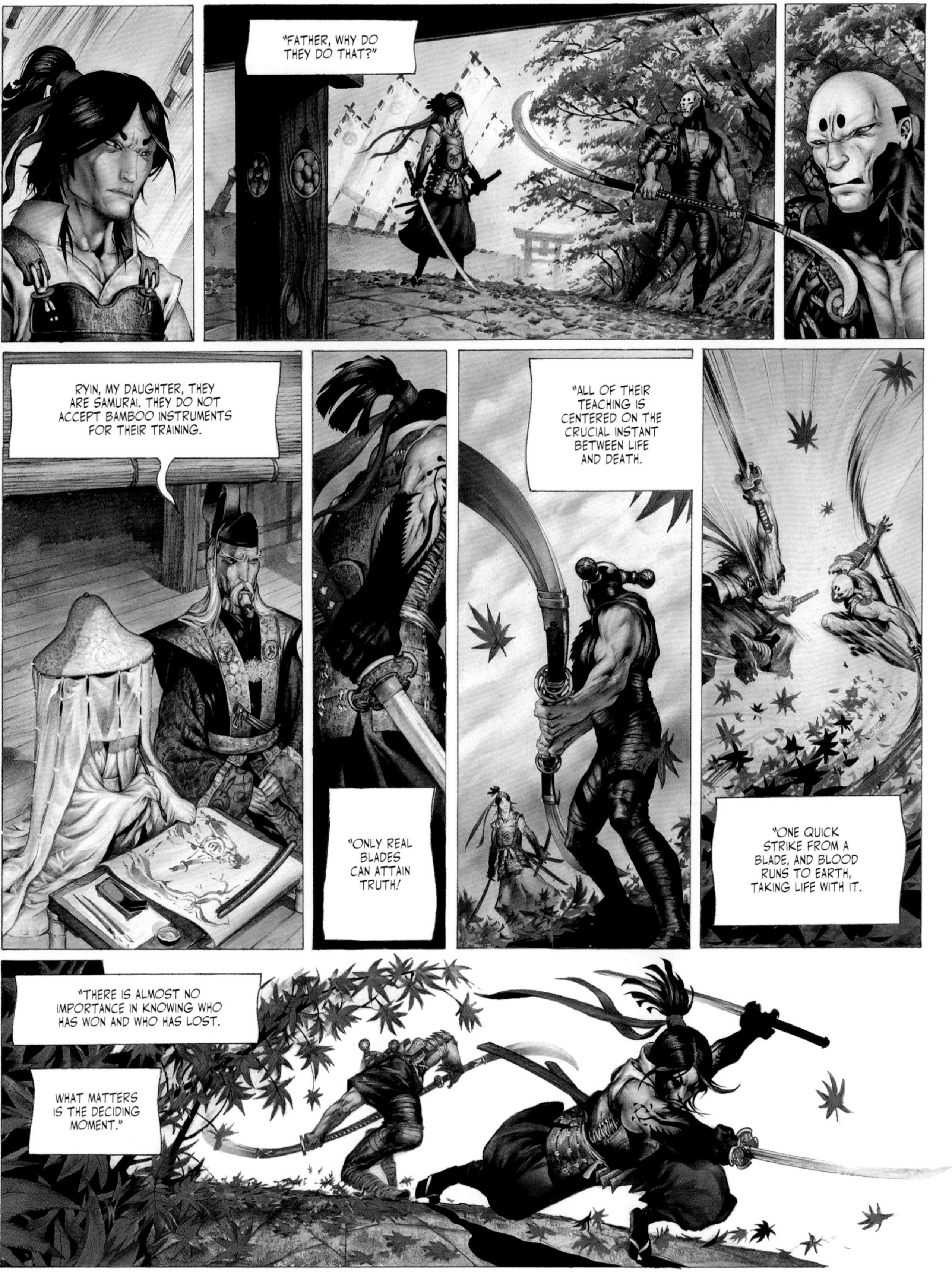
"FATHER, WHY DO THEY DO THAT?"
RYIN, MY DAUGHTER, THEY ARE SAMURAI. THEY DO NOT ACCEPT BAMBOO INSTRUMENTS FOR THEIR TRAINING.
"ONLY REAL BLADES CAN ATTAIN TRUTH!
"ALL OF THEIR TEACHING IS CENTERED ON THE CRUCIAL INSTANT BETWEEN LIFE AND DEATH.
"ONE QUICK STRIKE FROM A BLADE, AND BLOOD RUNS TO EARTH, TAKING LIFE WITH IT.
"THERE IS ALMOST NO IMPORTANCE IN KNOWING WHO HAS WON AND WHO HAS LOST.
WHAT MATTERS IS THE DECIDING MOMENT."

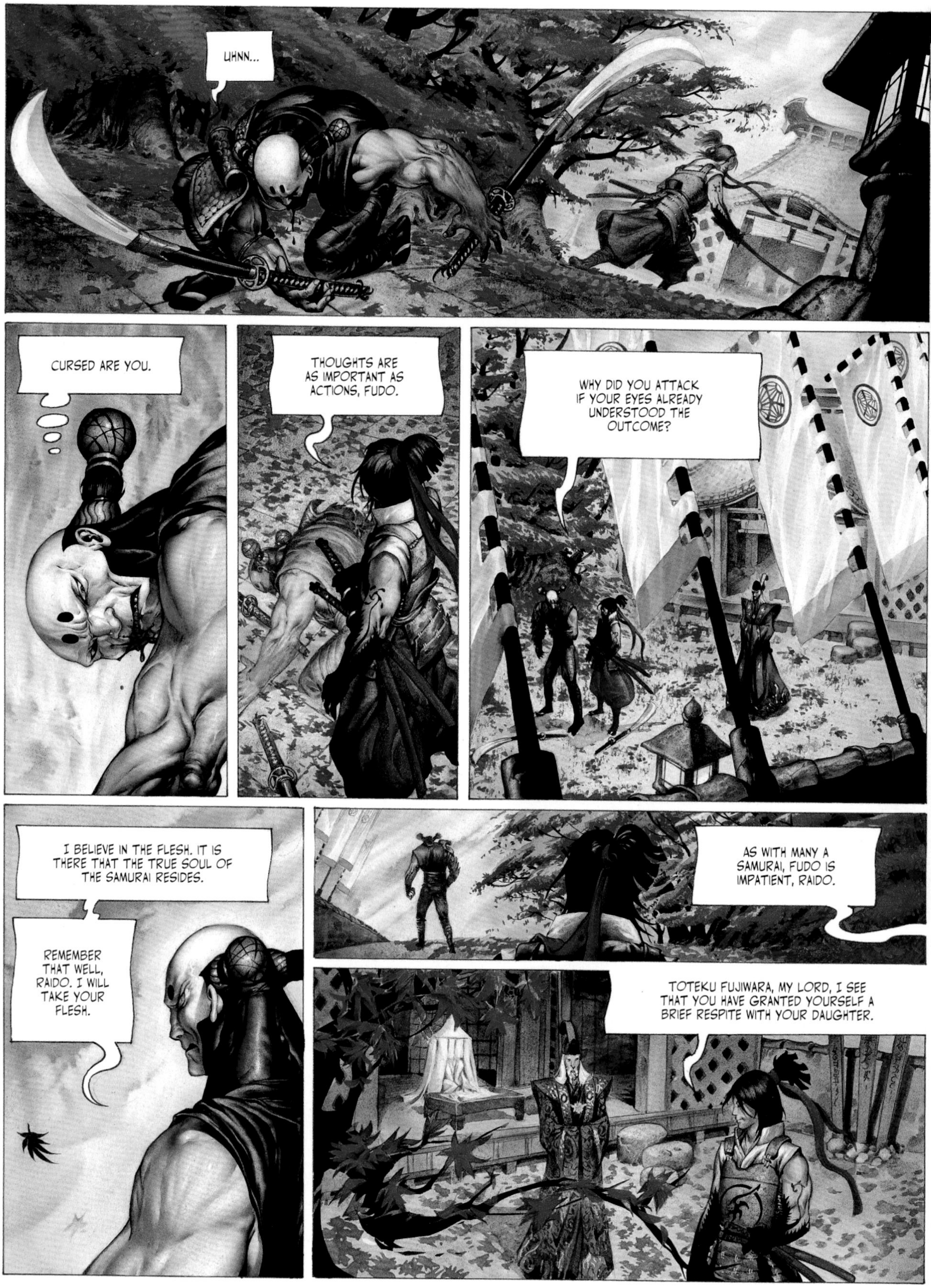
UHNN...
CURSED ARE YOU.
THOUGHTS ARE AS IMPORTANT AS ACTIONS, FUDO.
WHY DID YOU ATTACK IF YOUR EYES ALREADY UNDERSTOOD THE OUTCOME?
I BELIEVE IN THE FLESH. IT IS THERE THAT THE TRUE SOUL OF THE SAMURAI RESIDES.
REMEMBER THAT WELL, RAIDO. I WILL TAKE YOUR FLESH.
AS WITH MANY A SAMURAI, FUDO IS IMPATIENT, RAIDO.
TOTEKU FUJIWARA, MY LORD, I SEE THAT YOU HAVE GRANTED YOURSELF A BRIEF RESPITE WITH YOUR DAUGHTER.

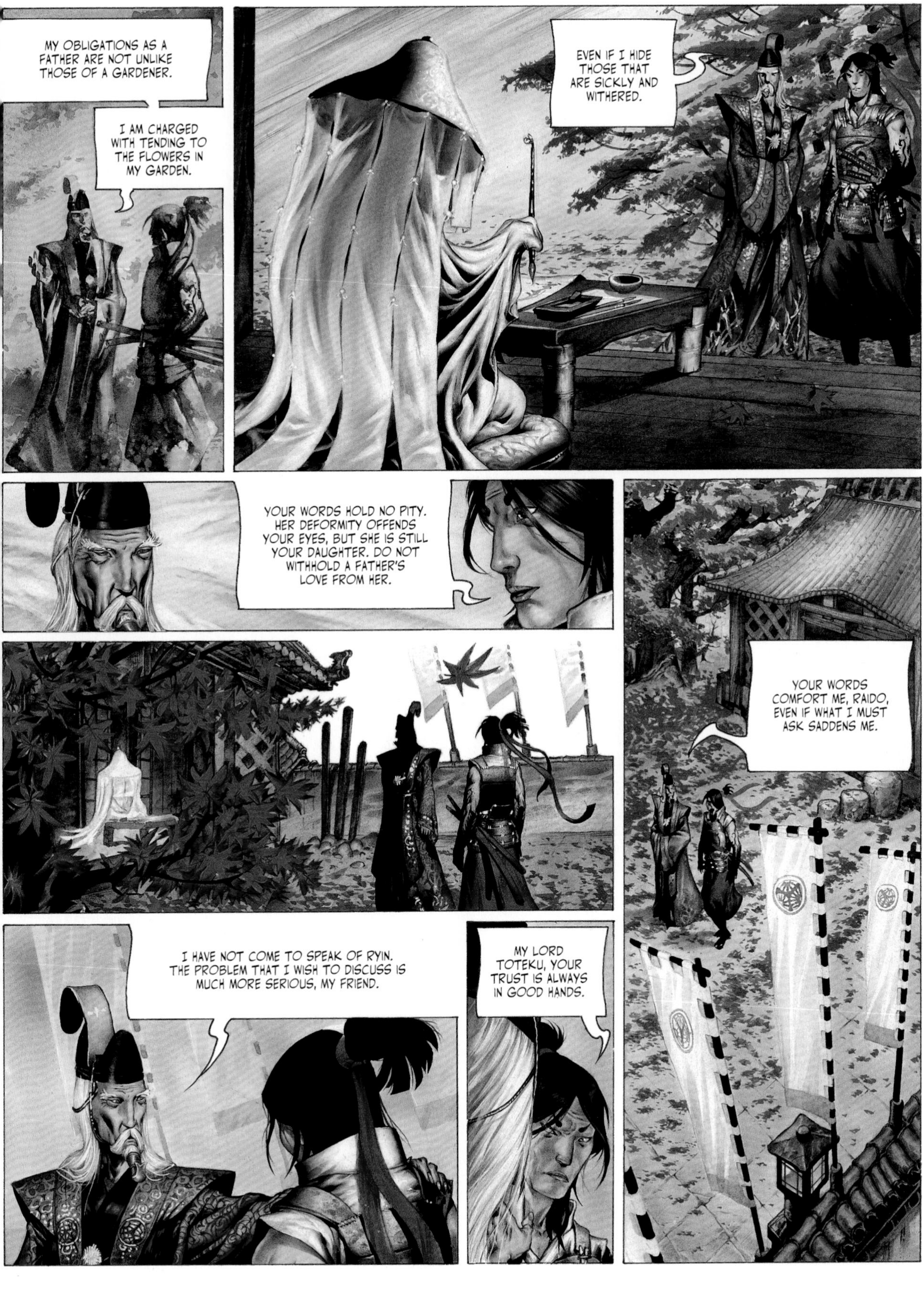

MY OBLIGATIONS AS A FATHER ARE NOT UNLIKE THOSE OF A GARDENER.
I AM CHARGED WITH TENDING TO THE FLOWERS IN MY GARDEN.
EVEN IF I HIDE THOSE THAT ARE SICKLY AND WITHERED.
YOUR WORDS HOLD NO PITY. HER DEFORMITY OFFENDS YOUR EYES, BUT SHE IS STILL YOUR DAUGHTER. DO NOT WITHHOLD A FATHER'S LOVE FROM HER.
YOUR WORDS COMFORT ME, RAIDO, EVEN IF WHAT I MUST ASK SADDENS ME.
I HAVE NOT COME TO SPEAK OF RYIN. THE PROBLEM THAT I WISH TO DISCUSS IS MUCH MORE SERIOUS, MY FRIEND.
MY LORD TOTEKU, YOUR TRUST IS ALWAYS IN GOOD HANDS.

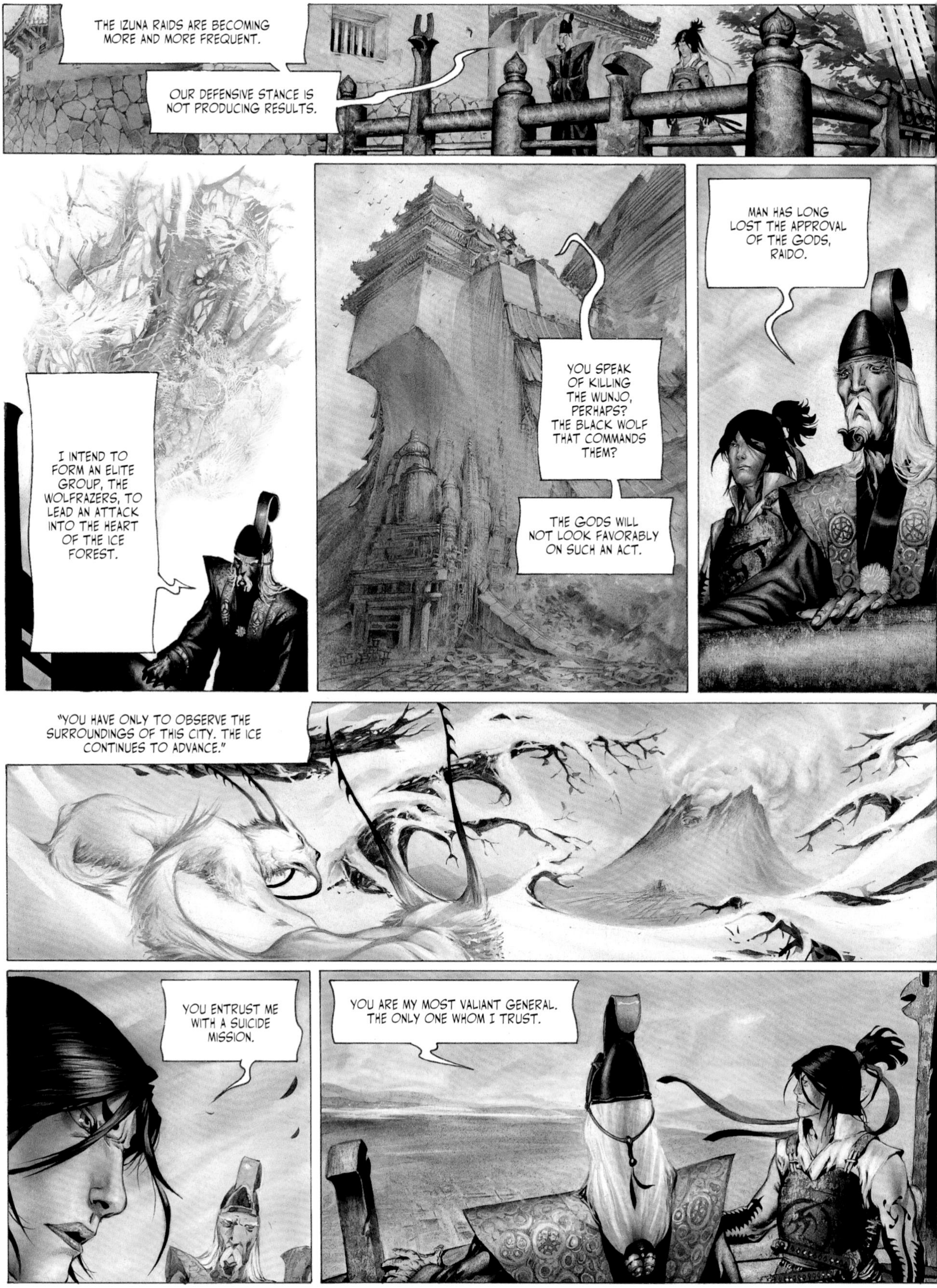
THE IZUNA RAIDS ARE BECOMING MORE AND MORE FREQUENT.
OUR DEFENSIVE STANCE IS NOT PRODUCING RESULTS.
I INTEND TO FORM AN ELITE GROUP, THE WOLFRAZERS, TO LEAD AN ATTACK INTO THE HEART OF THE ICE FOREST.
YOU SPEAK OF KILLING THE WUNJO, PERHAPS? THE BLACK WOLF THAT COMMANDS THEM?
THE GODS WILL NOT LOOK FAVORABLY ON SUCH AN ACT.
MAN HAS LONG LOST THE APPROVAL OF THE GODS, RAIDO.
"YOU HAVE ONLY TO OBSERVE THE SURROUNDINGS OF THIS CITY. THE ICE CONTINUES TO ADVANCE."
YOU ENTRUST ME WITH A SUICIDE MISSION.
YOU ARE MY MOST VALIANT GENERAL. THE ONLY ONE WHOM I TRUST.

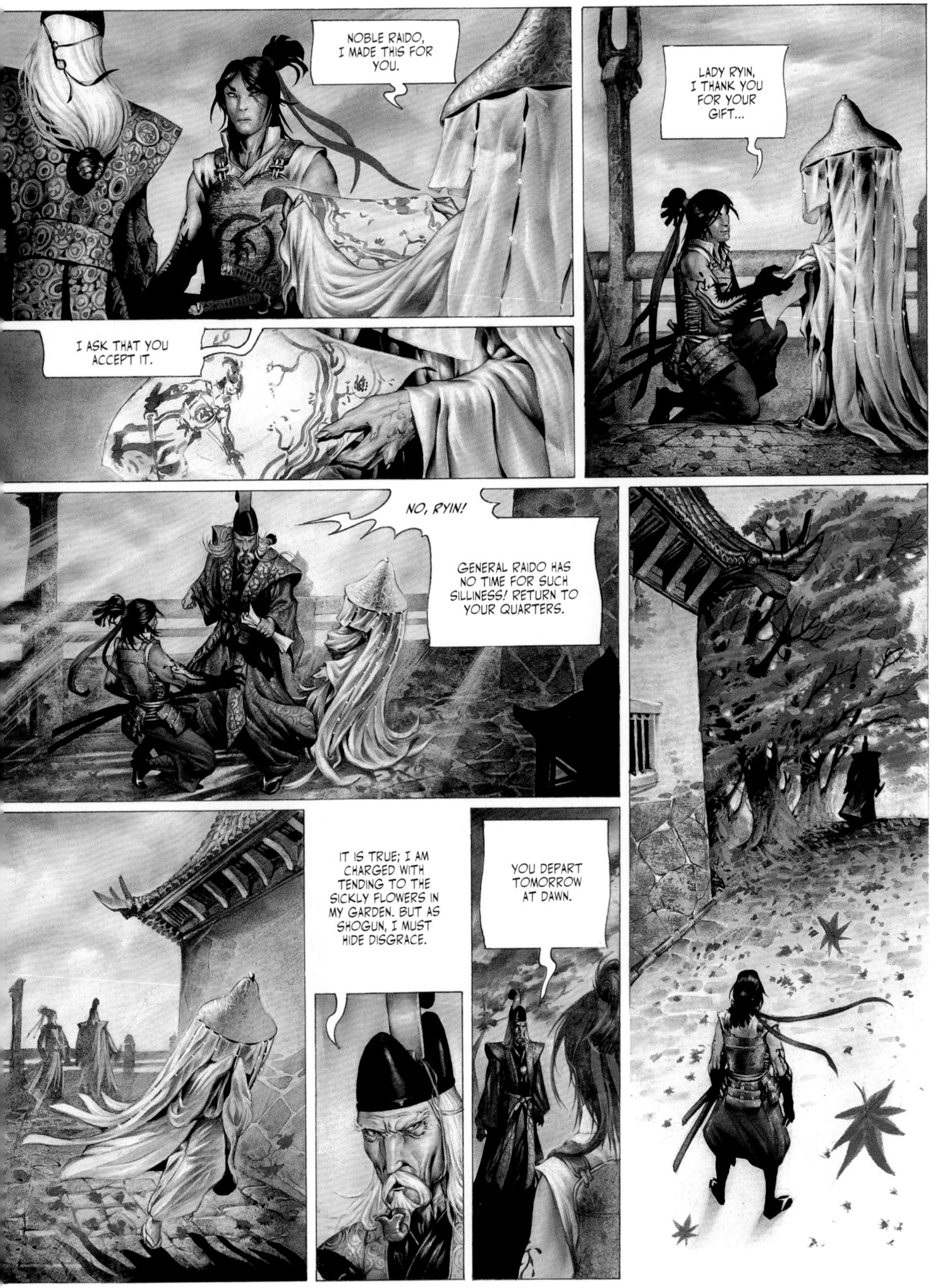
NOBLE RAIDO, I MADE THIS FOR YOU.
LADY RYIN, I THANK YOU FOR YOUR GIFT...
I ASK THAT YOU ACCEPT IT.
NO, RYIN!
GENERAL RAIDO HAS NO TIME FOR SUCH SILLINESS! RETURN TO YOUR QUARTERS.
IT IS TRUE; I AM CHARGED WITH TENDING TO THE SICKLY FLOWERS IN MY GARDEN. BUT AS SHOGUN, I MUST HIDE DISGRACE.
YOU DEPART TOMORROW AT DAWN.

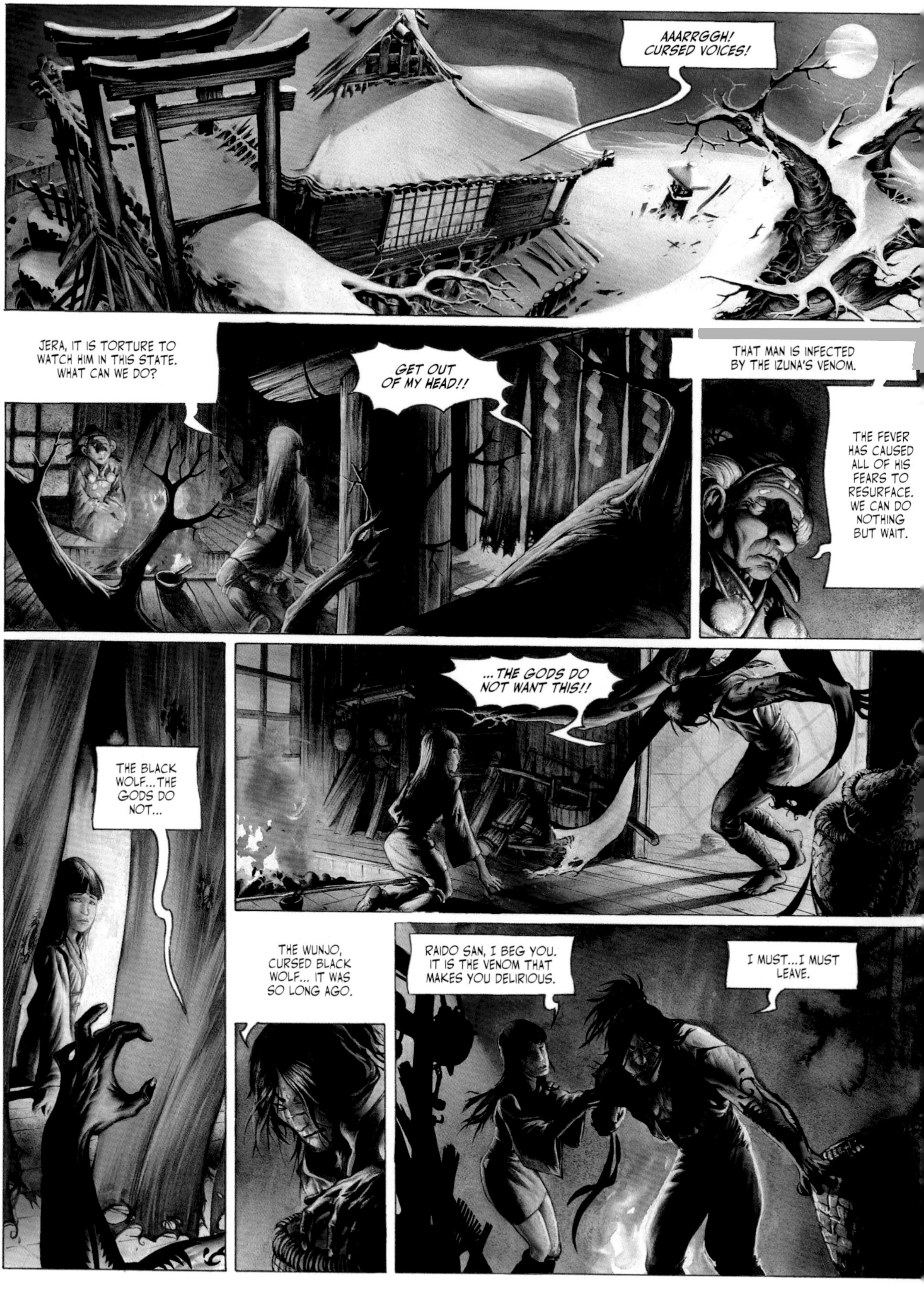
AAARRGGH! CURSED VOICES!
JERA, IT IS TORTURE TO WATCH HIM IN THIS STATE. WHAT CAN WE DO?
GET OUT OF MY HEAD!!
THAT MAN IS INFECTED BY THE IZUNA'S VENOM.
THE FEVER HAS CAUSED ALL OF HIS FEARS TO RESURFACE. WE CAN DO NOTHING BUT WAIT.
THE BLACK WOLF... THE GODS DO NOT...
...THE GODS DO NOT WANT THIS!!
THE WUNJO, CURSED BLACK WOLF... IT WAS SO LONG AGO.
RAIDO SAN, I BEG YOU. IT IS THE VENOM THAT MAKES YOU DELIRIOUS.
I MUST...I MUST LEAVE.

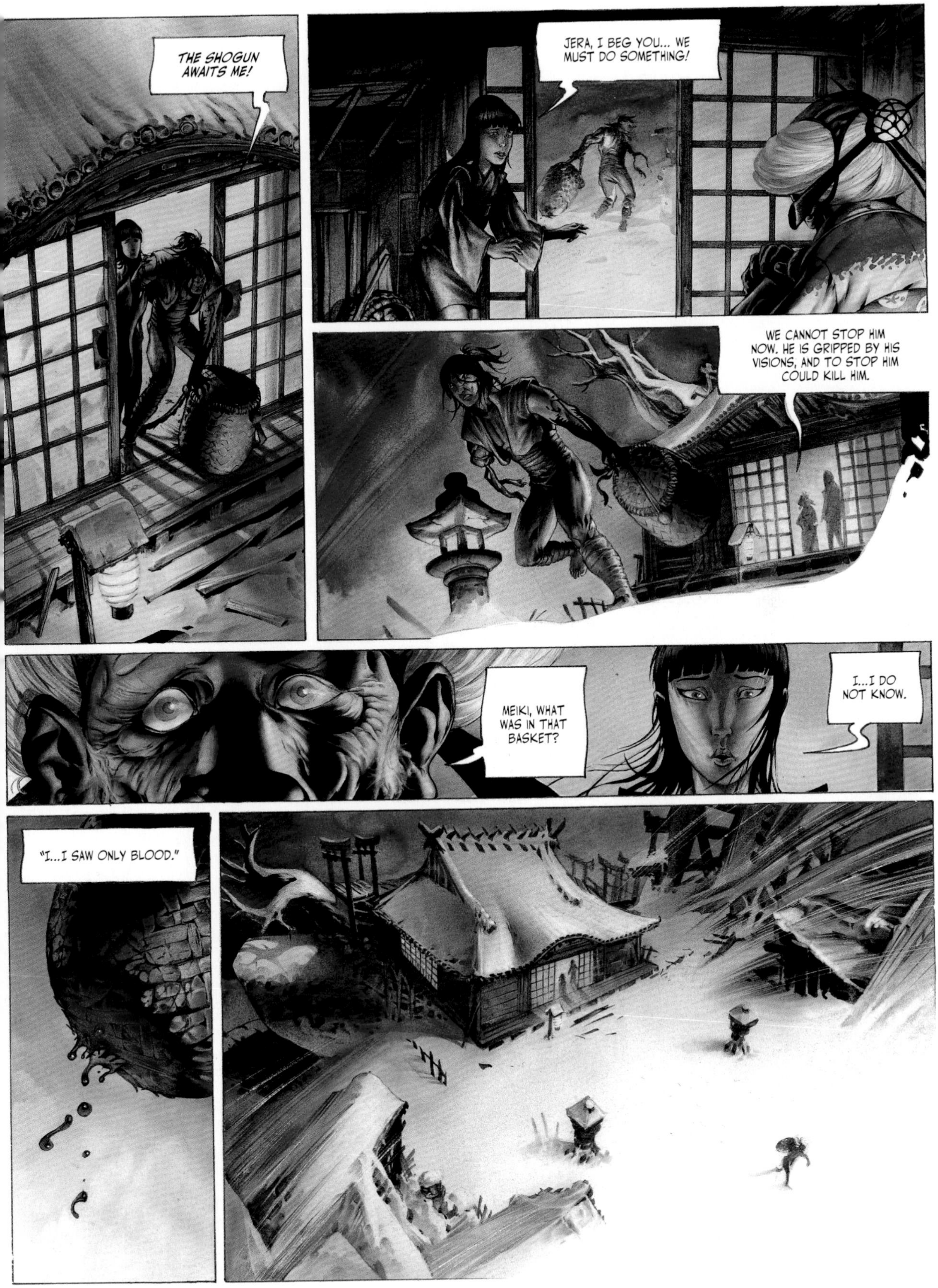
THE SHOGUN AWAITS ME!
JERA, I BEG YOU... WE MUST DO SOMETHING!
WE CANNOT STOP HIM NOW. HE IS GRIPPED BY HIS VISIONS, AND TO STOP HIM COULD KILL HIM.
MEIKI, WHAT WAS IN THAT BASKET?
I...I DO NOT KNOW.
"I...I SAW ONLY BLOOD."

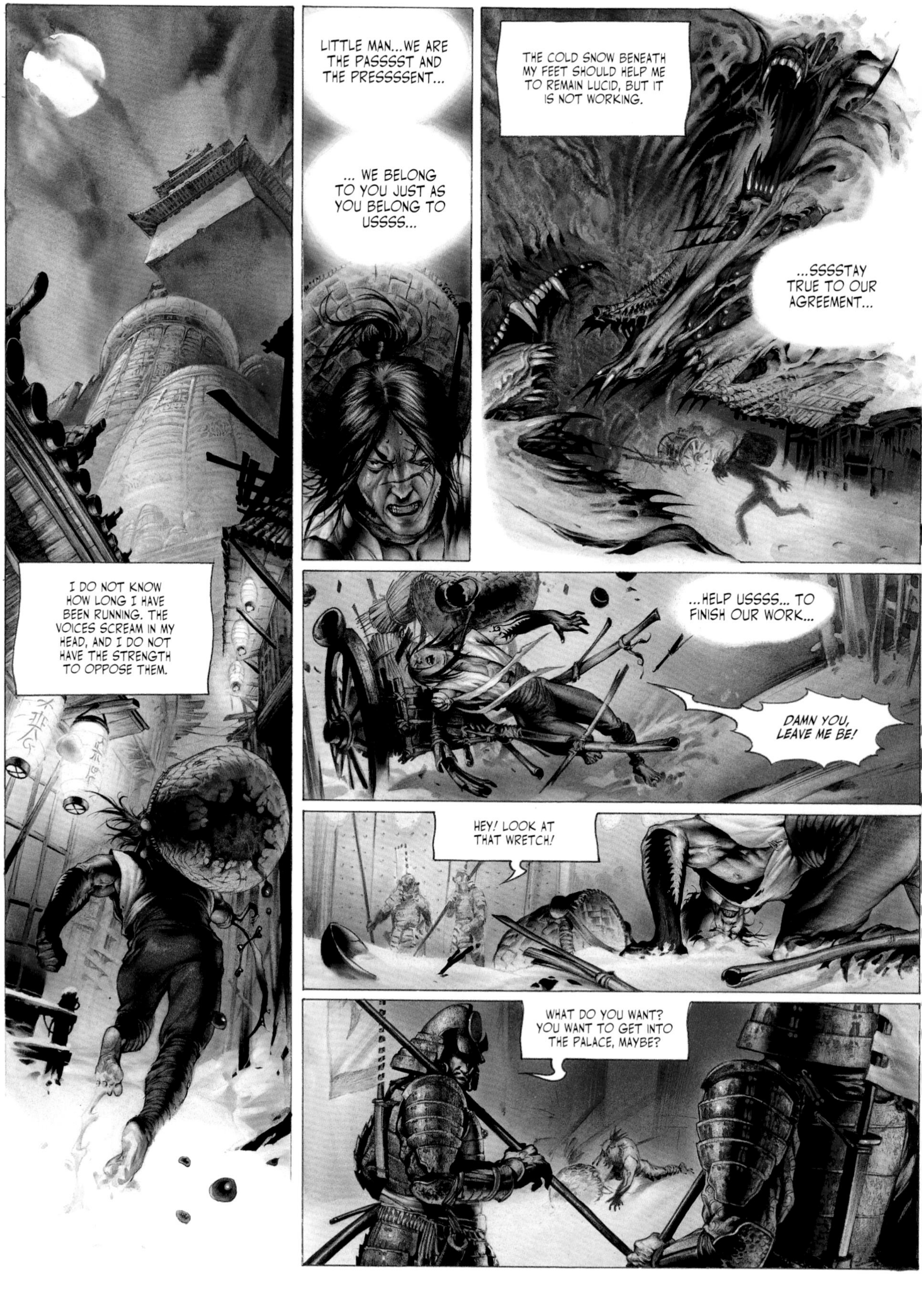
LITTLE MAN...WE ARE THE PASSSST AND THE PRESSSENT...
... WE BELONG TO YOU JUST AS YOU BELONG TO USSSS...
THE COLD SNOW BENEATH MY FEET SHOULD HELP ME TO REMAIN LUCID, BUT IT IS NOT WORKING.
...SSSSTAY TRUE TO OUR AGREEMENT...
I DO NOT KNOW HOW LONG I HAVE BEEN RUNNING. THE VOICES SCREAM IN MY HEAD, AND I DO NOT HAVE THE STRENGTH TO OPPOSE THEM.
...HELP USSSS... TO FINISH OUR WORK...
DAMN YOU, LEAVE ME BE!
HEY! LOOK AT THAT WRETCH!
WHAT DO YOU WANT? YOU WANT TO GET INTO THE PALACE, MAYBE?

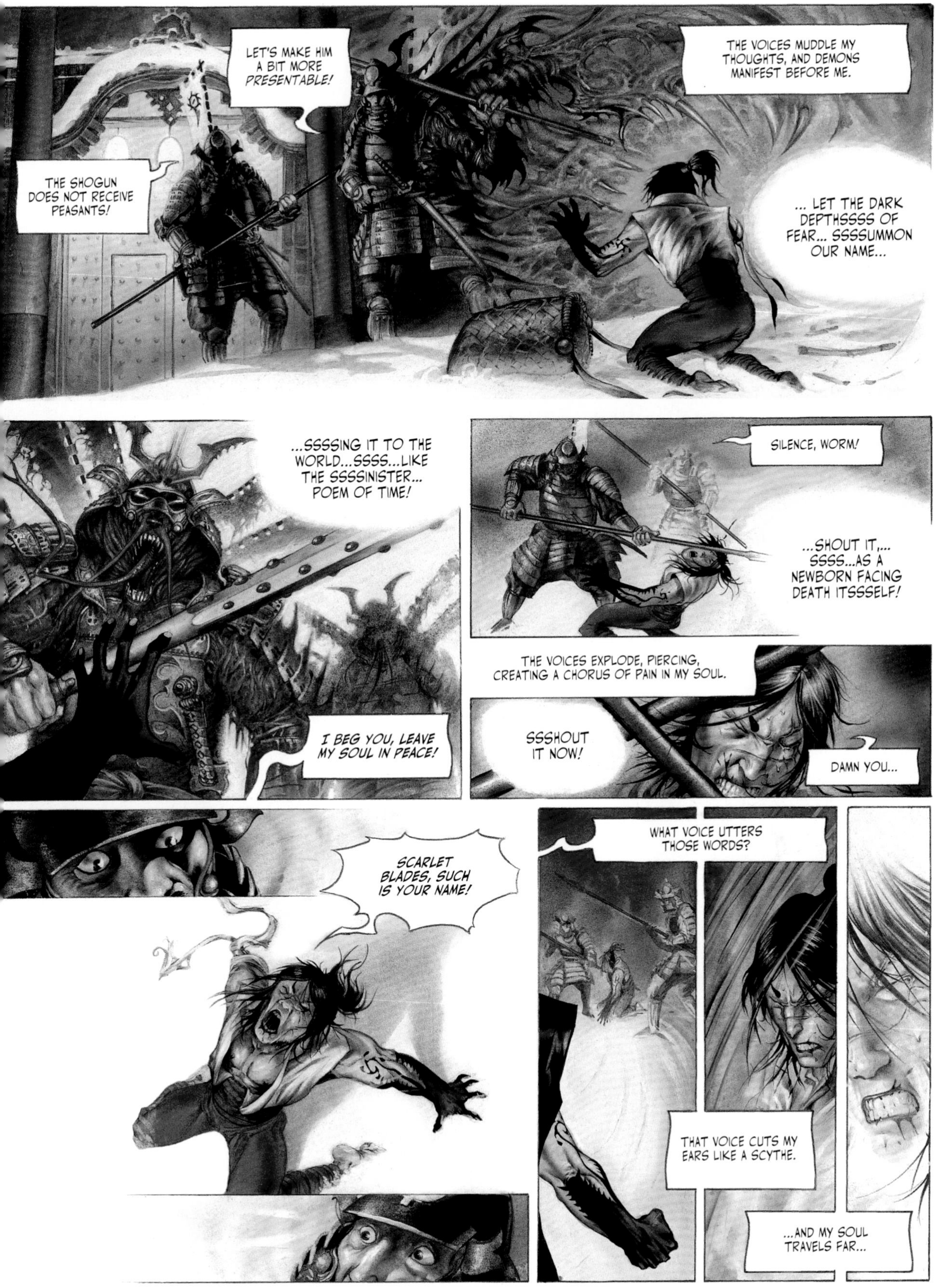

THE SHOGUN DOES NOT RECEIVE PEASANTS!
LET'S MAKE HIM A BIT MORE PRESENTABLE!
THE VOICES MUDDLE MY THOUGHTS, AND DEMONS MANIFEST BEFORE ME.
... LET THE DARK DEPTHSSSS OF FEAR... SSSSUMMON OUR NAME...
...SSSSING IT TO THE WORLD...SSSS...LIKE THE SSSSINISTER... POEM OF TIME!
I BEG YOU, LEAVE MY SOUL IN PEACE!
SILENCE, WORM!
...SHOUT IT,... SSSS...AS A NEWBORN FACING DEATH ITSSSELF!
THE VOICES EXPLODE, PIERCING, CREATING A CHORUS OF PAIN IN MY SOUL.
SSSHOUT IT NOW!
DAMN YOU...
SCARLET BLADES, SUCH IS YOUR NAME!
WHAT VOICE UTTERS THOSE WORDS?
THAT VOICE CUTS MY EARS LIKE A SCYTHE.
...AND MY SOUL TRAVELS FAR...

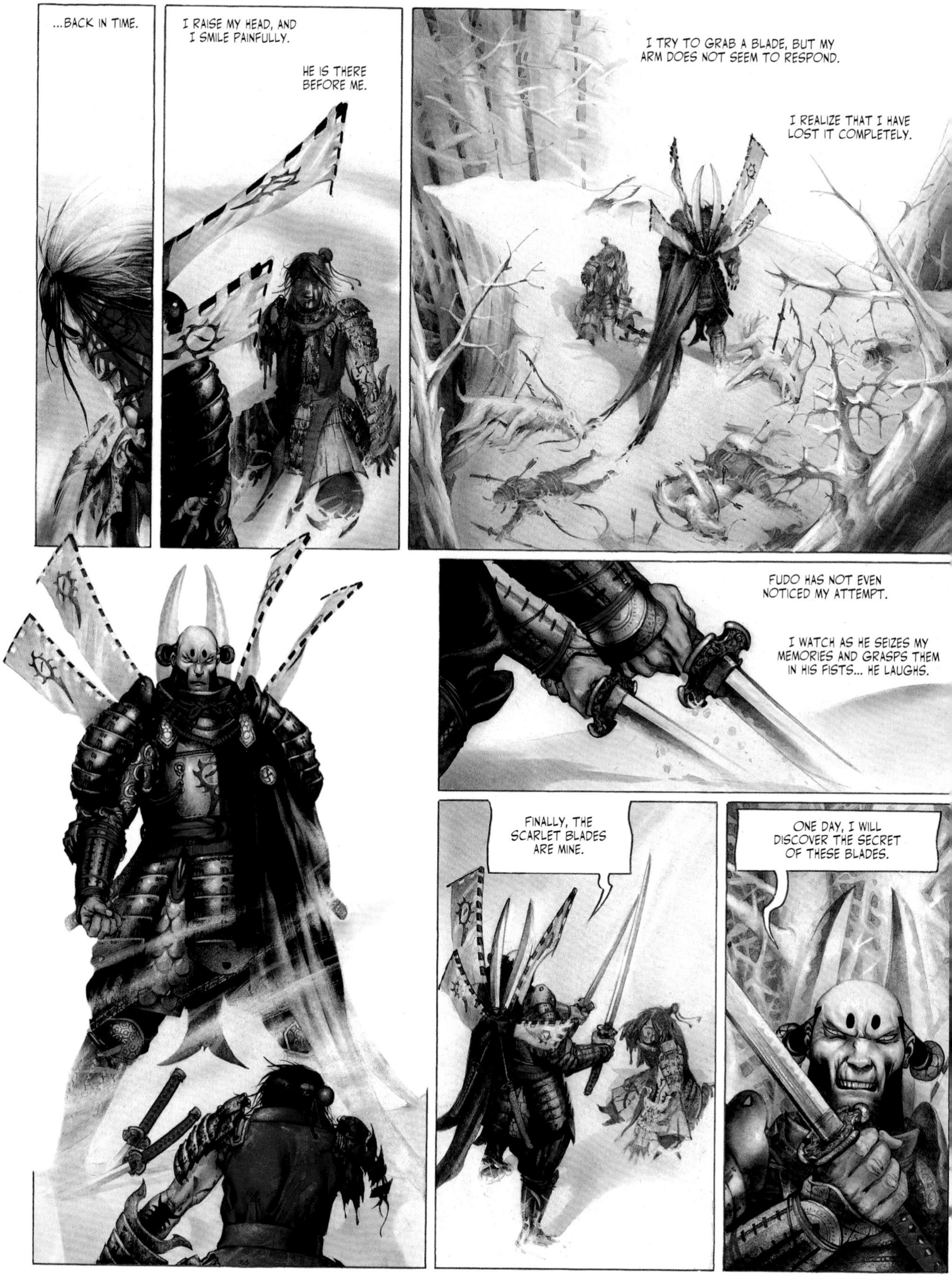
...BACK IN TIME.
I RAISE MY HEAD, AND I SMILE PAINFULLY.
HE IS THERE BEFORE ME.
I TRY TO GRAB A BLADE, BUT MY ARM DOES NOT SEEM TO RESPOND.
I REALIZE THAT I HAVE LOST IT COMPLETELY.
FUDO HAS NOT EVEN NOTICED MY ATTEMPT.
I WATCH AS HE SEIZES MY MEMORIES AND GRASPS THEM IN HIS FISTS... HE LAUGHS.
FINALLY, THE SCARLET BLADES ARE MINE.
ONE DAY, I WILL DISCOVER THE SECRET OF THESE BLADES.

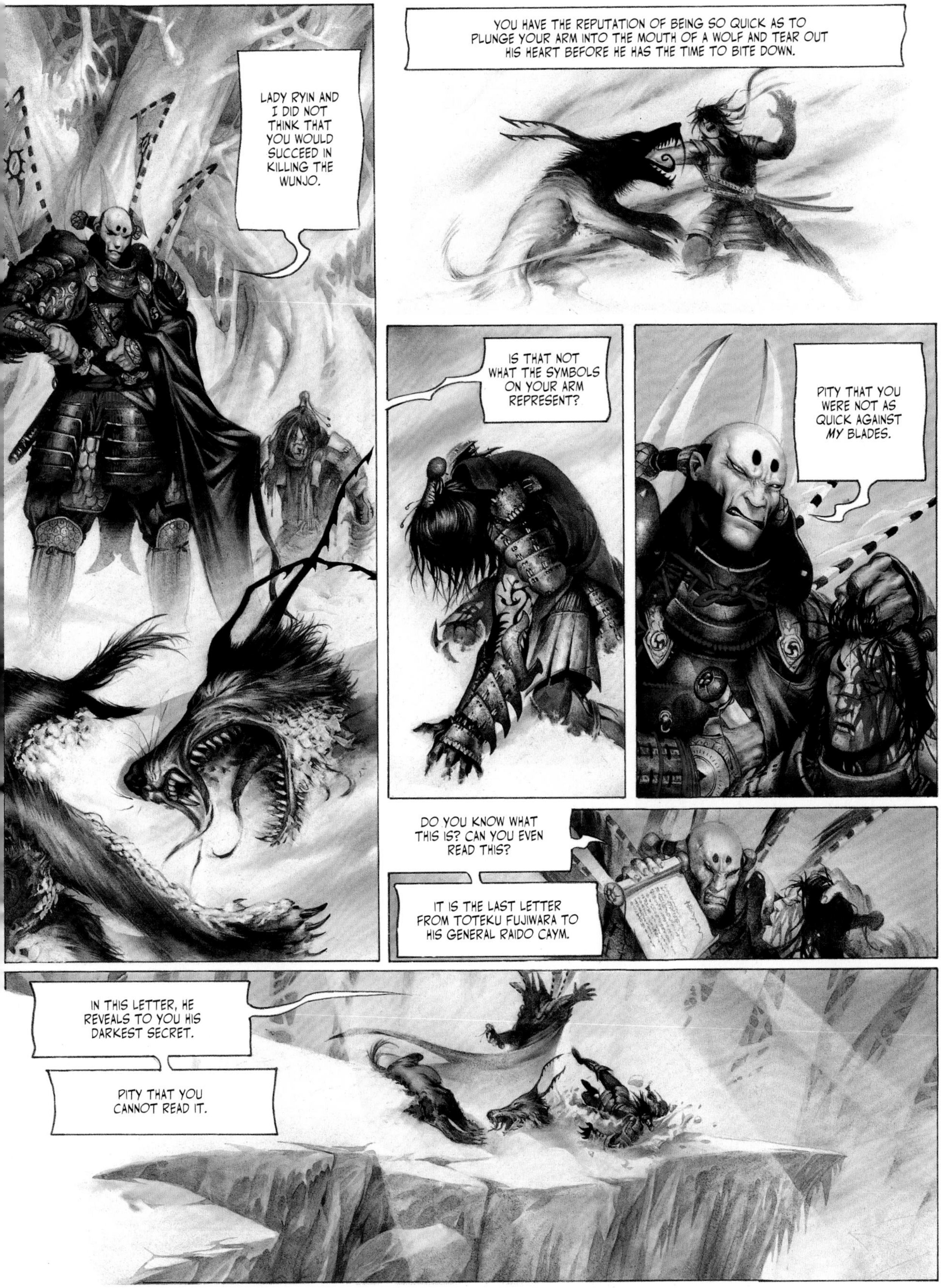
LADY RYIN AND I DID NOT THINK THAT YOU WOULD SUCCEED IN KILLING THE WUNJO.
YOU HAVE THE REPUTATION OF BEING SO QUICK AS TO PLUNGE YOUR ARM INTO THE MOUTH OF A WOLF AND TEAR OUT HIS HEART BEFORE HE HAS THE TIME TO BITE DOWN.
IS THAT NOT WHAT THE SYMBOLS ON YOUR ARM REPRESENT?
PITY THAT YOU WERE NOT AS QUICK AGAINST MY BLADES.
DO YOU KNOW WHAT THIS IS? CAN YOU EVEN READ THIS?
IT IS THE LAST LETTER FROM TOTEKU FUJIWARA TO HIS GENERAL RAIDO CAYM.
IN THIS LETTER, HE REVEALS TO YOU HIS DARKEST SECRET.
PITY THAT YOU CANNOT READ IT.

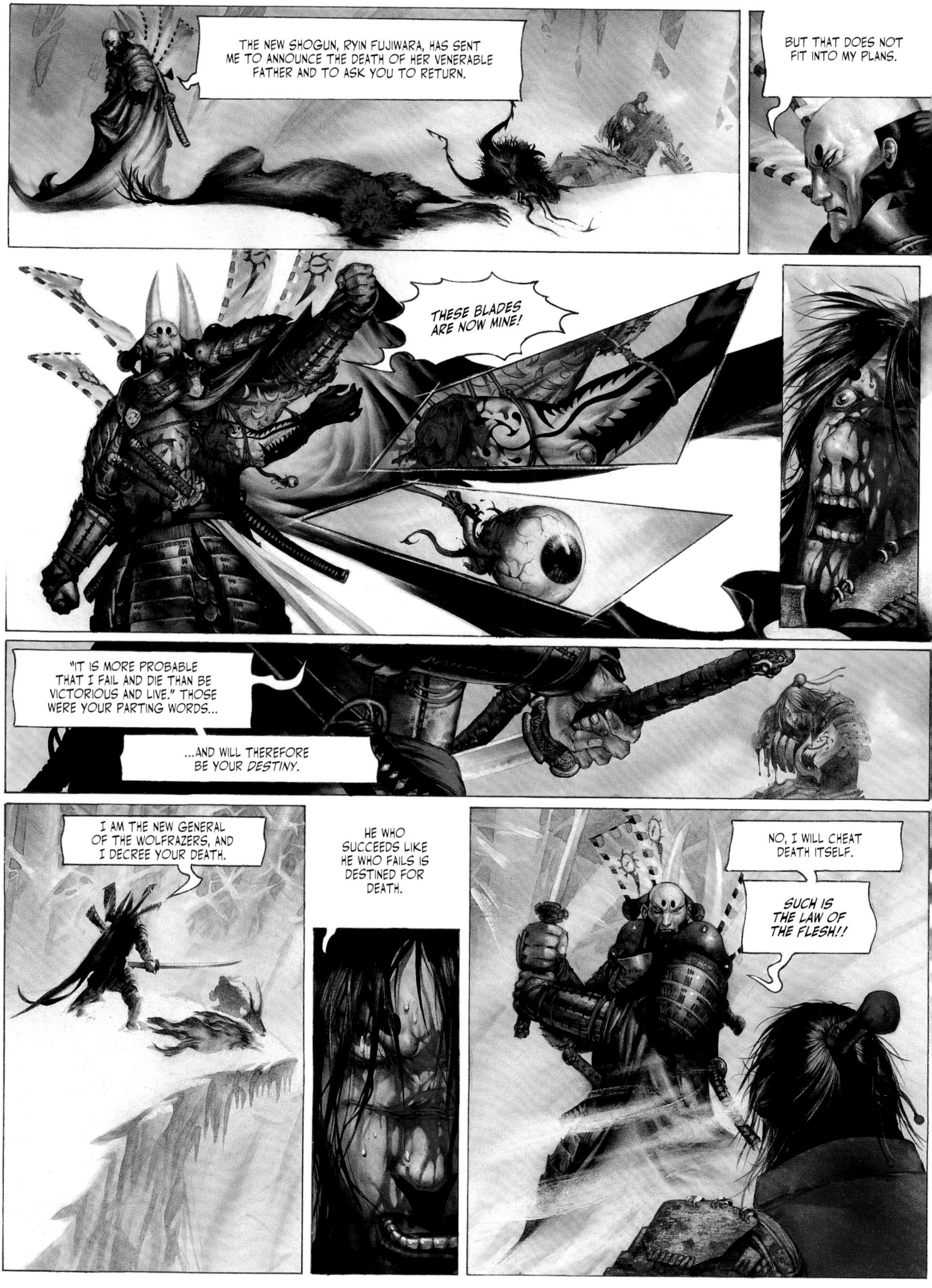
THE NEW SHOGUN, RYIN FUJIWARA, HAS SENT ME TO ANNOUNCE THE DEATH OF HER VENERABLE FATHER AND TO ASK YOU TO RETURN.
BUT THAT DOES NOT FIT INTO MY PLANS.
THESE BLADES ARE NOW MINE!
"IT IS MORE PROBABLE THAT I FAIL AND DIE THAN BE VICTORIOUS AND LIVE." THOSE WERE YOUR PARTING WORDS...
...AND WILL THEREFORE BE YOUR DESTINY.
I AM THE NEW GENERAL OF THE WOLFRAZERS, AND I DECREE YOUR DEATH.
HE WHO SUCCEEDS LIKE HE WHO FAILS IS DESTINED FOR DEATH.
NO, I WILL CHEAT DEATH ITSELF.
SUCH IS THE LAW OF THE FLESH!!

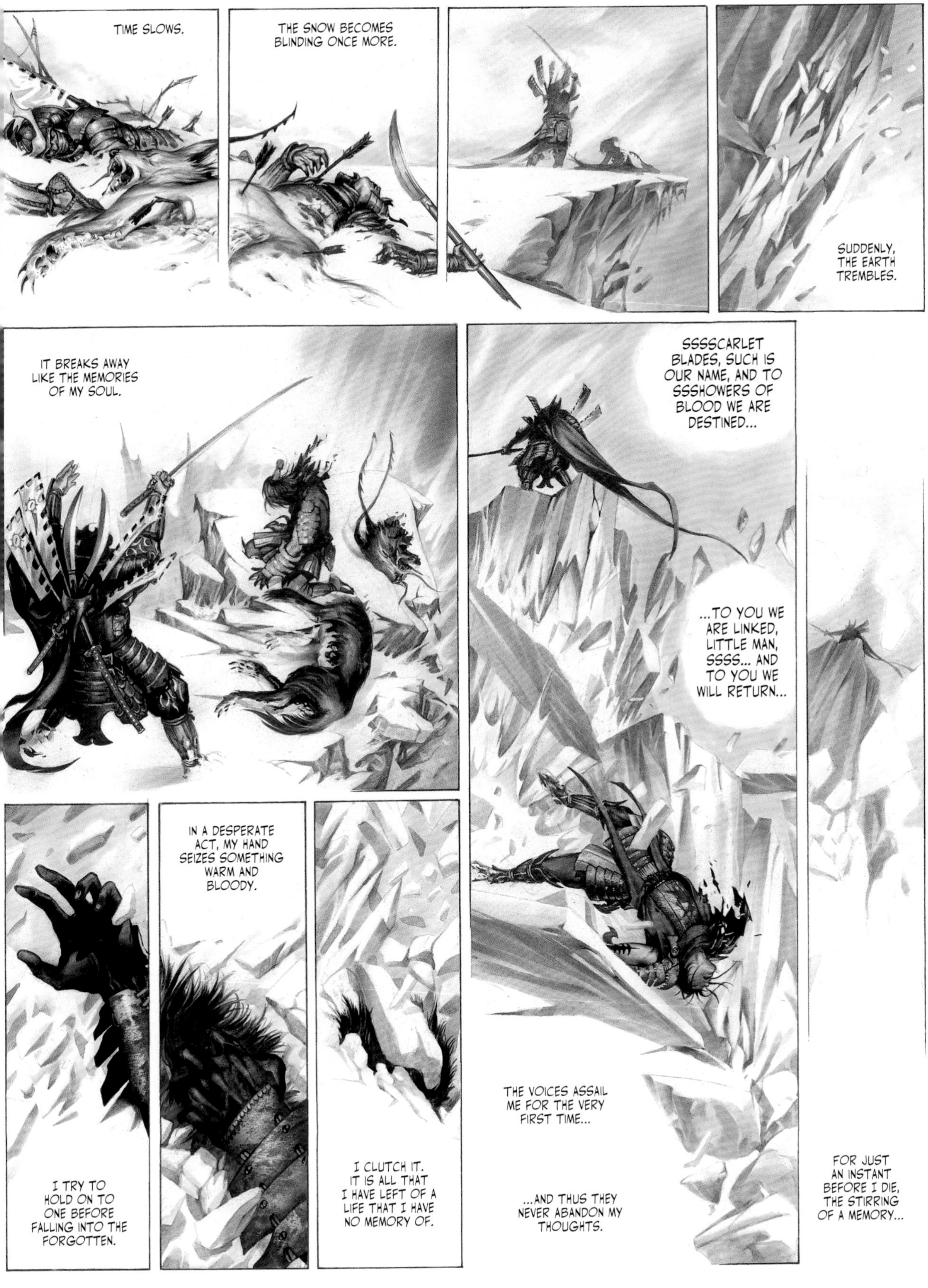
TIME SLOWS.
THE SNOW BECOMES BLINDING ONCE MORE.
SUDDENLY, THE EARTH TREMBLES.
IT BREAKS AWAY LIKE THE MEMORIES OF MY SOUL.
SSSSCARLET BLADES, SUCH IS OUR NAME, AND TO SSSHOWERS OF BLOOD WE ARE DESTINED...
...TO YOU WE ARE LINKED, LITTLE MAN, SSSS... AND TO YOU WE WILL RETURN...
I TRY TO HOLD ON TO ONE BEFORE FALLING INTO THE FORGOTTEN.
IN A DESPERATE ACT, MY HAND SEIZES SOMETHING WARM AND BLOODY.
I CLUTCH IT. IT IS ALL THAT I HAVE LEFT OF A LIFE THAT I HAVE NO MEMORY OF.
THE VOICES ASSAIL ME FOR THE VERY FIRST TIME...
...AND THUS THEY NEVER ABANDON MY THOUGHTS.
FOR JUST AN INSTANT BEFORE I DIE, THE STIRRING OF A MEMORY...

ALL THOSE YEARS PASSED BY LIKE THE FLUTTERING OF A BUTTERFLY'S WINGS...

GENERAL NOBU FUDO!

HIS WORDS STILL RESOUND IN MY EARS.

"THE LAW OF THE FLESH."

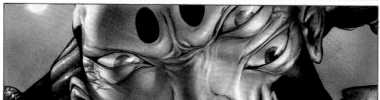

BASTARD, YOU DID NOT COVET ONLY MY BLADES!

FOR YEARS, I CARRIED THIS BURDEN WITHOUT KNOWING WHY.

BASTARD!!

TODAY, I REMEMBER, AND IT NO LONGER MATTERS.

42

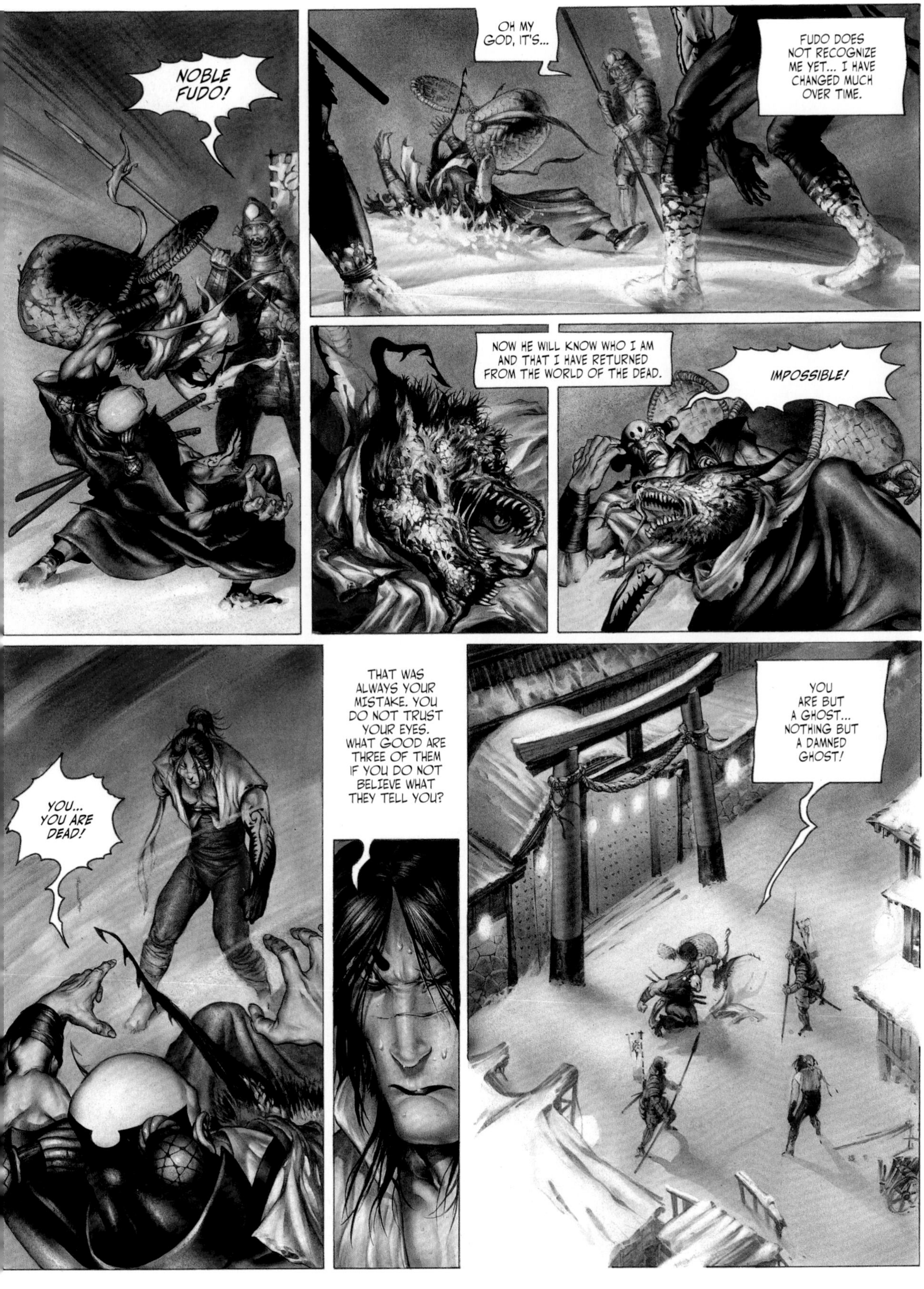
NOBLE FUDO!
OH MY GOD, IT'S...
FUDO DOES NOT RECOGNIZE ME YET... I HAVE CHANGED MUCH OVER TIME.
NOW HE WILL KNOW WHO I AM AND THAT I HAVE RETURNED FROM THE WORLD OF THE DEAD.
IMPOSSIBLE!
YOU... YOU ARE DEAD!
THAT WAS ALWAYS YOUR MISTAKE. YOU DO NOT TRUST YOUR EYES. WHAT GOOD ARE THREE OF THEM IF YOU DO NOT BELIEVE WHAT THEY TELL YOU?
YOU ARE BUT A GHOST... NOTHING BUT A DAMNED GHOST!

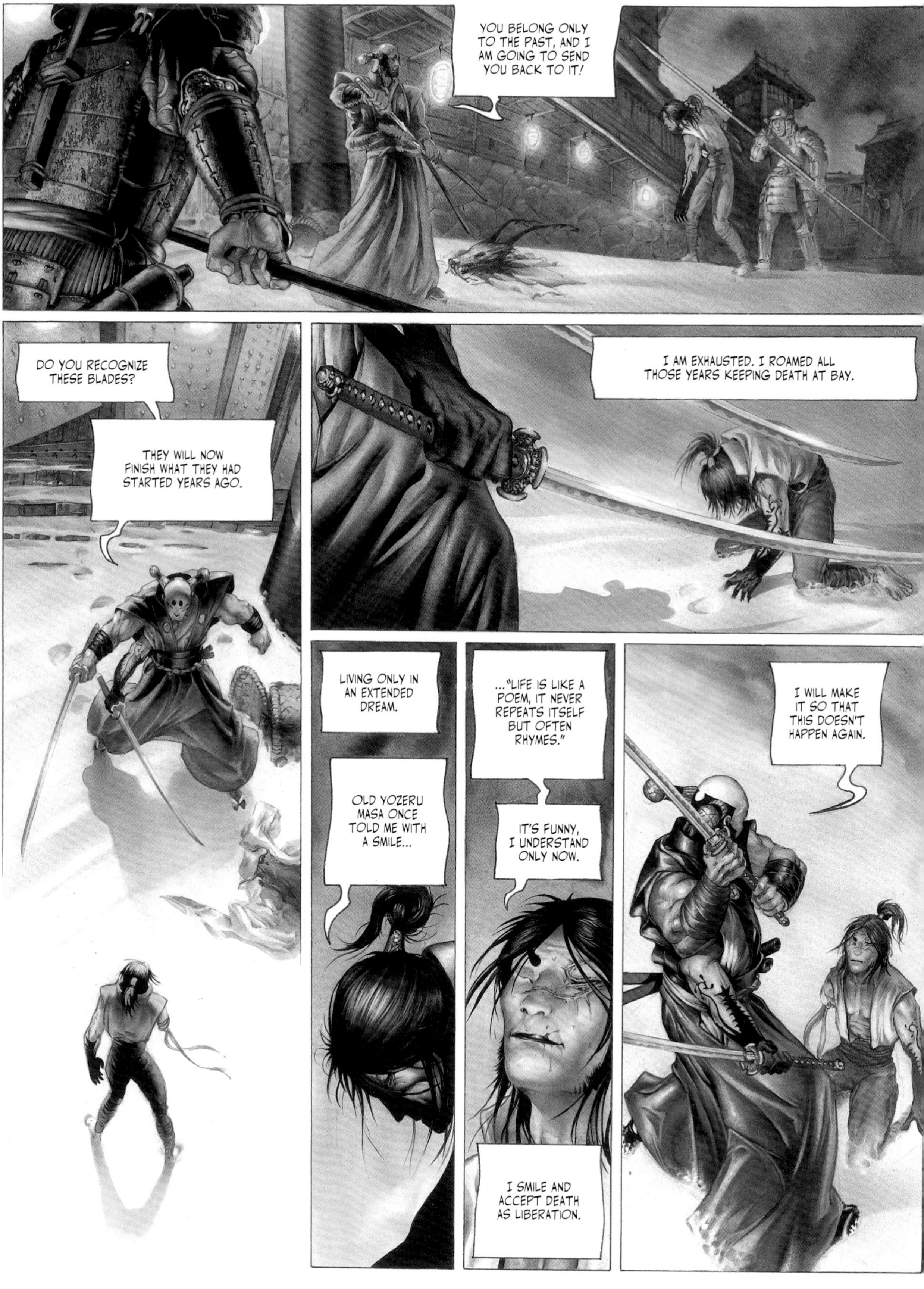
YOU BELONG ONLY TO THE PAST, AND I AM GOING TO SEND YOU BACK TO IT!
DO YOU RECOGNIZE THESE BLADES?
THEY WILL NOW FINISH WHAT THEY HAD STARTED YEARS AGO.
I AM EXHAUSTED. I ROAMED ALL THOSE YEARS KEEPING DEATH AT BAY.
LIVING ONLY IN AN EXTENDED DREAM.
OLD YOZERU MASA ONCE TOLD ME WITH A SMILE...
..."LIFE IS LIKE A POEM, IT NEVER REPEATS ITSELF BUT OFTEN RHYMES."
IT'S FUNNY, I UNDERSTAND ONLY NOW.
I SMILE AND ACCEPT DEATH AS LIBERATION.
I WILL MAKE IT SO THAT THIS DOESN'T HAPPEN AGAIN.

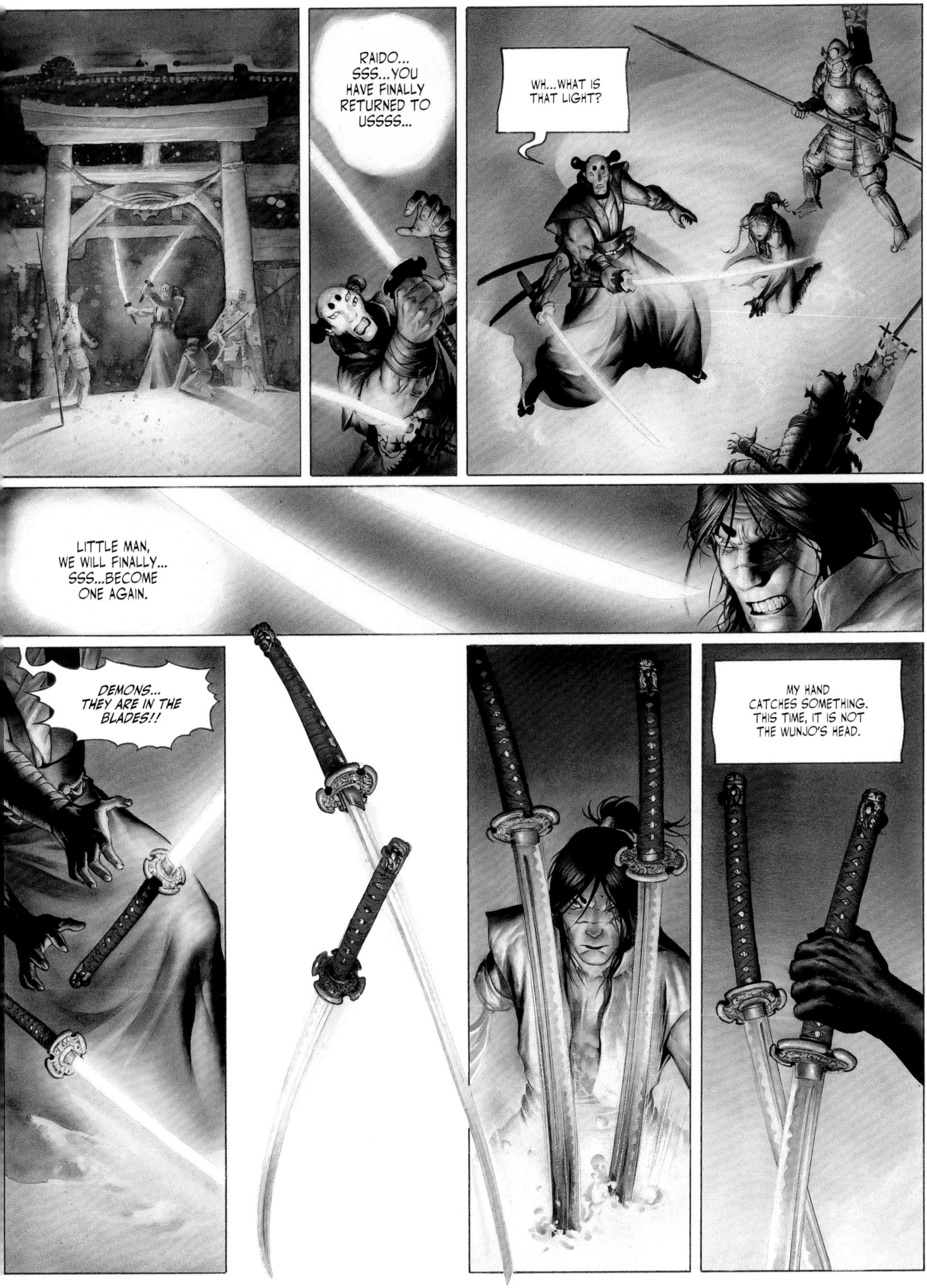
RAIDO... SSS...YOU HAVE FINALLY RETURNED TO USSSS...
WH...WHAT IS THAT LIGHT?
LITTLE MAN, WE WILL FINALLY... SSS...BECOME ONE AGAIN.
DEMONS... THEY ARE IN THE BLADES!!
MY HAND CATCHES SOMETHING. THIS TIME, IT IS NOT THE WUNJO'S HEAD.

NOW MY DEATH WILL BE AN HONORABLE ONE.

RAIDO SAN! HANG ON TIGHT!

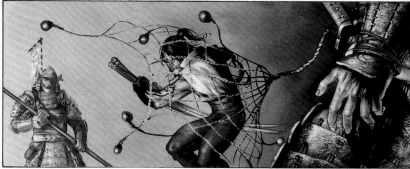

WHO...?

I HOPE THAT I DO NOT REGRET WHAT I AM DOING, MEIKI.

SPUR THE HORSE, OGI... I DO NOT WANT IT TO BE ME WHO REGRETS HAVING ASKED FOR YOUR HELP.

YOU WOULDN'T HAVE DONE IT WITHOUT ME.

I WOULD HAVE DONE IT EITHER WAY.

SOMETHING YET AGAIN PREVENTS MY KARMA FROM BEING FULFILLED...

...AND BRINGS ME BACK TO LIFE.

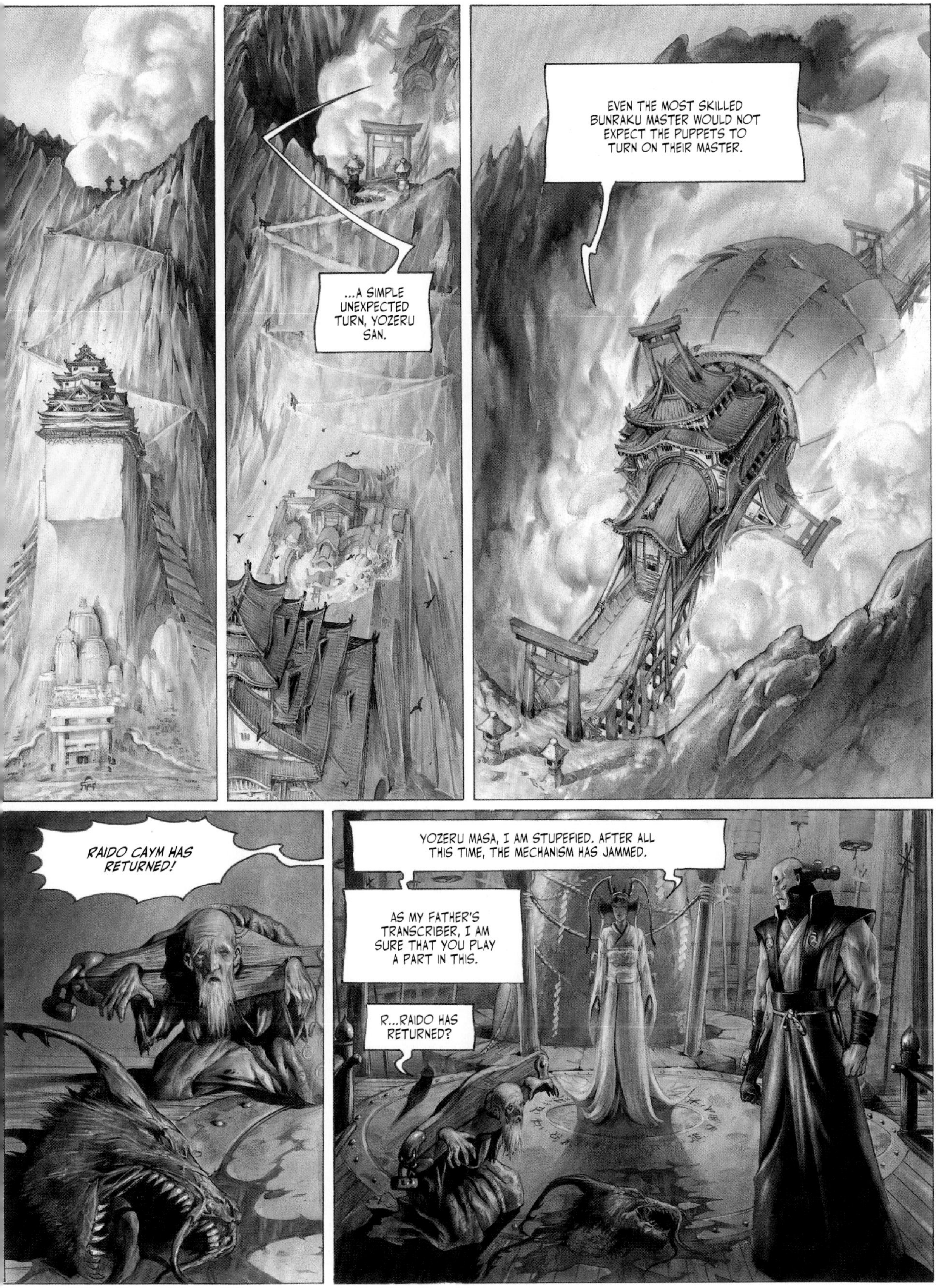
...A SIMPLE UNEXPECTED TURN, YOZERU SAN.
EVEN THE MOST SKILLED BUNRAKU MASTER WOULD NOT EXPECT THE PUPPETS TO TURN ON THEIR MASTER.
RAIDO CAYM HAS RETURNED!
YOZERU MASA, I AM STUPEFIED. AFTER ALL THIS TIME, THE MECHANISM HAS JAMMED.
AS MY FATHER'S TRANSCRIBER, I AM SURE THAT YOU PLAY A PART IN THIS.
R...RAIDO HAS RETURNED?

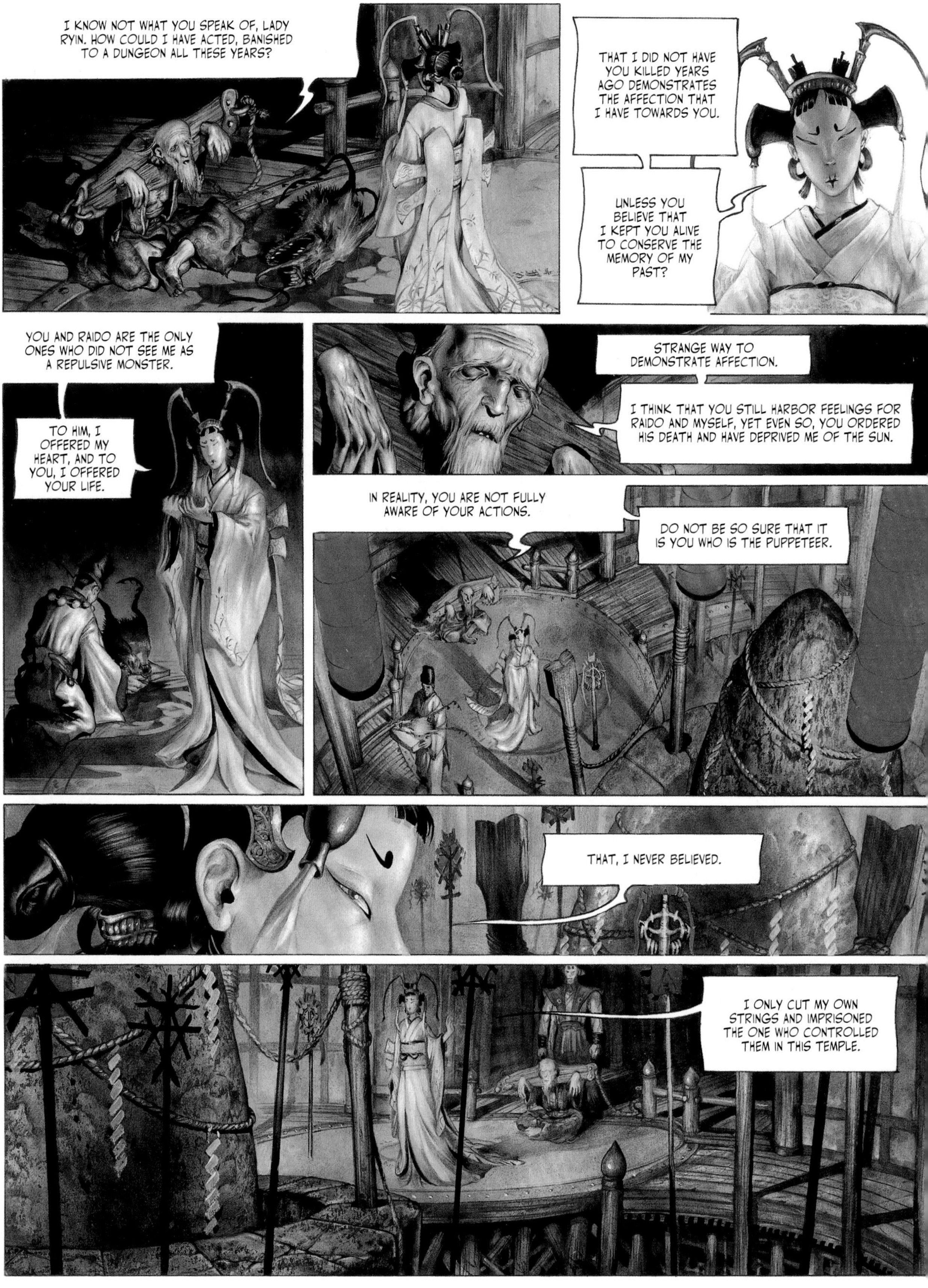
I KNOW NOT WHAT YOU SPEAK OF, LADY RYIN. HOW COULD I HAVE ACTED, BANISHED TO A DUNGEON ALL THESE YEARS?
THAT I DID NOT HAVE YOU KILLED YEARS AGO DEMONSTRATES THE AFFECTION THAT I HAVE TOWARDS YOU.
UNLESS YOU BELIEVE THAT I KEPT YOU ALIVE TO CONSERVE THE MEMORY OF MY PAST?
YOU AND RAIDO ARE THE ONLY ONES WHO DID NOT SEE ME AS A REPULSIVE MONSTER.
TO HIM, I OFFERED MY HEART, AND TO YOU, I OFFERED YOUR LIFE.
STRANGE WAY TO DEMONSTRATE AFFECTION.
I THINK THAT YOU STILL HARBOR FEELINGS FOR RAIDO AND MYSELF, YET EVEN SO, YOU ORDERED HIS DEATH AND HAVE DEPRIVED ME OF THE SUN.
IN REALITY, YOU ARE NOT FULLY AWARE OF YOUR ACTIONS.
DO NOT BE SO SURE THAT IT IS YOU WHO IS THE PUPPETEER.
THAT, I NEVER BELIEVED.
I ONLY CUT MY OWN STRINGS AND IMPRISONED THE ONE WHO CONTROLLED THEM IN THIS TEMPLE.

I AM BUT YOUR LIBERATOR.

YOU SPEAK OF THE GOD OF THE FOREST AS IF HE WERE A CAGED ANIMAL.

YOUR ACTIONS DEFY NATURE.

YOU ARE MISTAKEN. NOBU FUDO IS RIGHT WHEN HE SPEAKS OF HIS LAW OF THE FLESH.

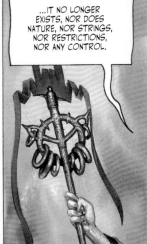

...IT NO LONGER EXISTS, NOR DOES NATURE, NOR STRINGS, NOR RESTRICTIONS, NOR ANY CONTROL.

THE PAST IS NO LONGER IMPORTANT...

WHAT EXISTS ARE OUR LIMBS, WARM WITH LIFE...

...AND FREE FOR ALL ETERNITY.

THIS IS THE ERA OF THE FLESH... HA HA HA HA!

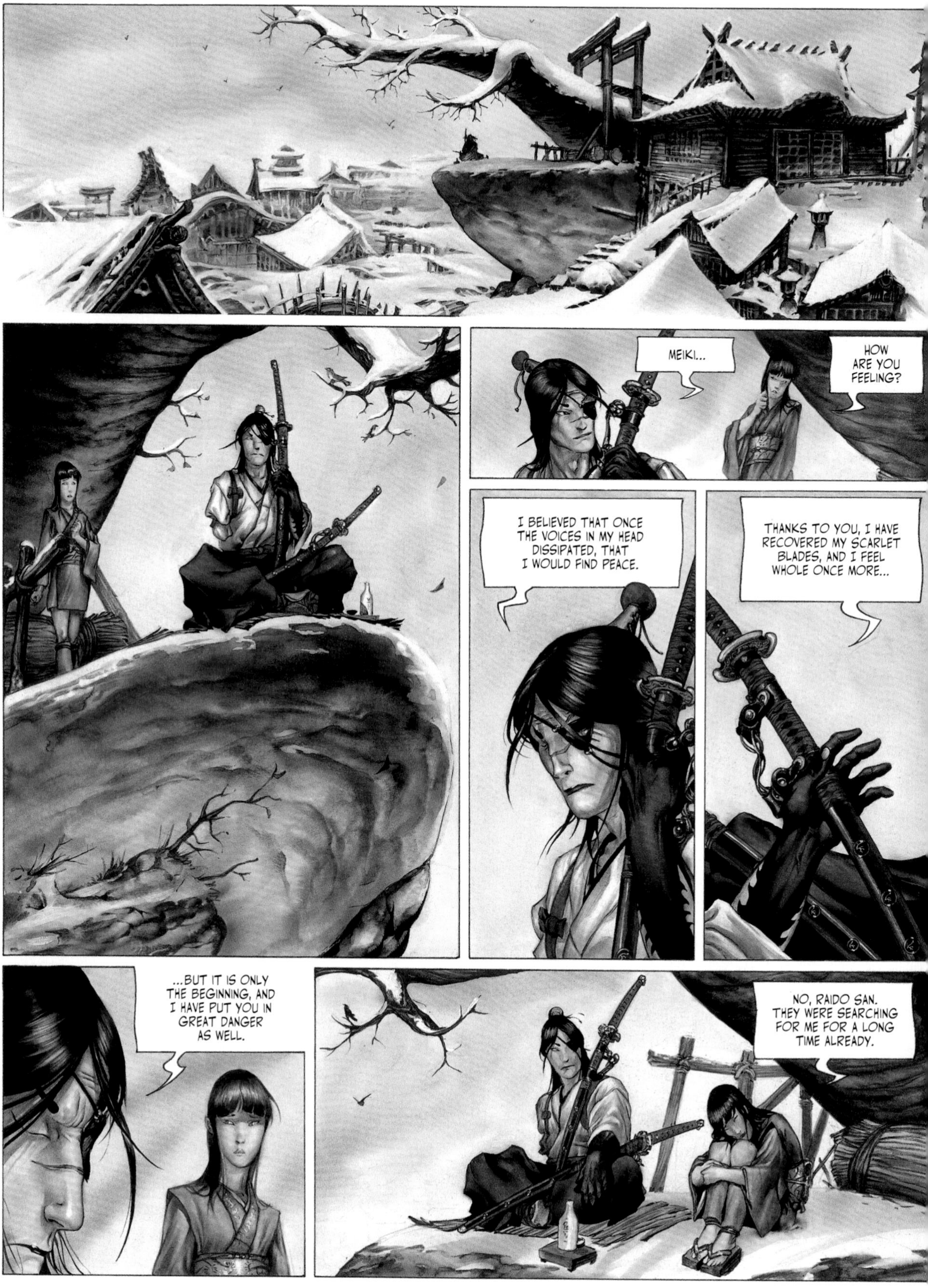
MEIKI...
HOW ARE YOU FEELING?
I BELIEVED THAT ONCE THE VOICES IN MY HEAD DISSIPATED, THAT I WOULD FIND PEACE.
THANKS TO YOU, I HAVE RECOVERED MY SCARLET BLADES, AND I FEEL WHOLE ONCE MORE...
...BUT IT IS ONLY THE BEGINNING, AND I HAVE PUT YOU IN GREAT DANGER AS WELL.
NO, RAIDO SAN. THEY WERE SEARCHING FOR ME FOR A LONG TIME ALREADY.

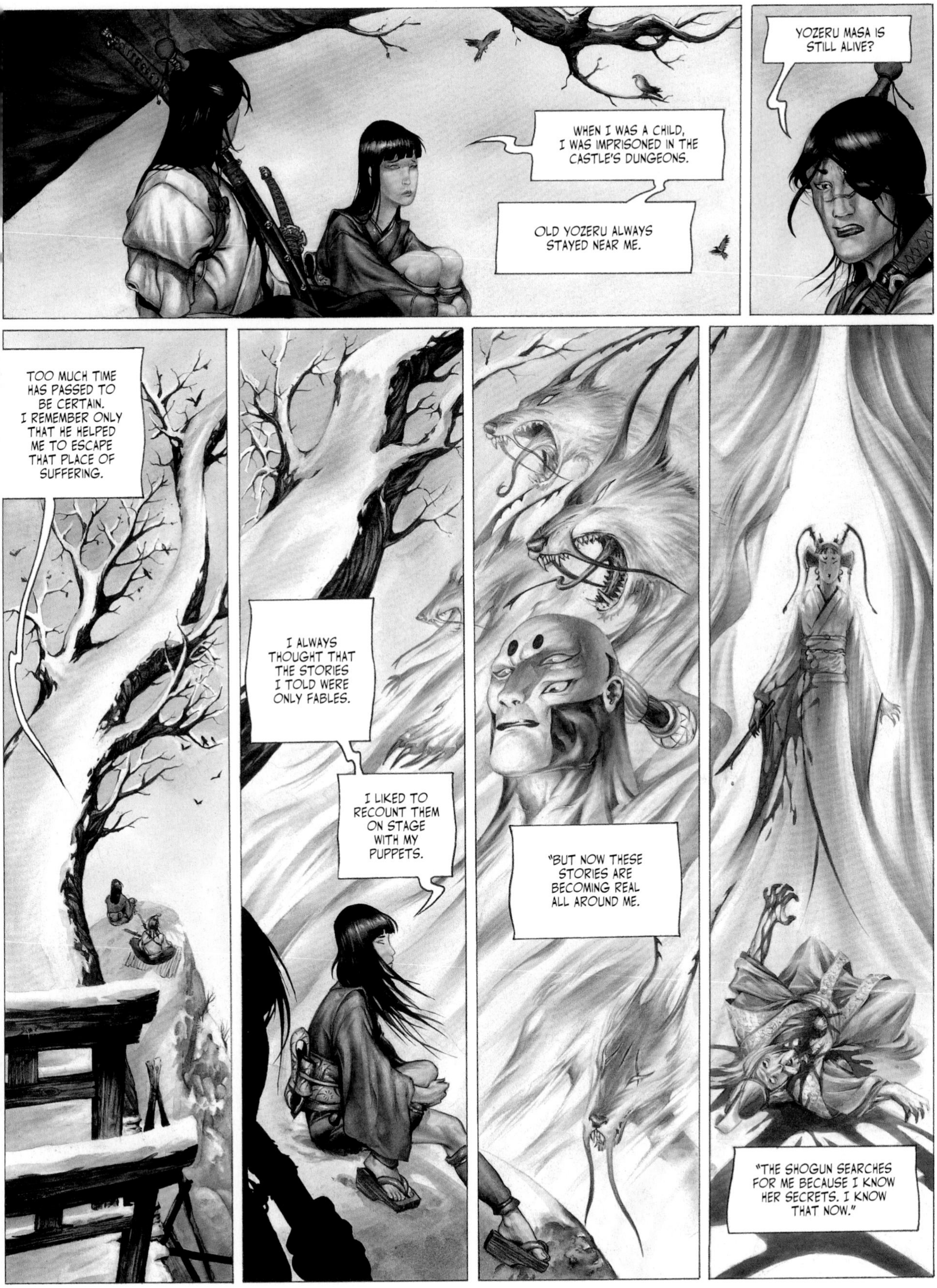
WHEN I WAS A CHILD, I WAS IMPRISONED IN THE CASTLE'S DUNGEONS.
OLD YOZERU ALWAYS STAYED NEAR ME.
YOZERU MASA IS STILL ALIVE?
TOO MUCH TIME HAS PASSED TO BE CERTAIN. I REMEMBER ONLY THAT HE HELPED ME TO ESCAPE THAT PLACE OF SUFFERING.
I ALWAYS THOUGHT THAT THE STORIES I TOLD WERE ONLY FABLES.
I LIKED TO RECOUNT THEM ON STAGE WITH MY PUPPETS.
"BUT NOW THESE STORIES ARE BECOMING REAL ALL AROUND ME.
"THE SHOGUN SEARCHES FOR ME BECAUSE I KNOW HER SECRETS. I KNOW THAT NOW."

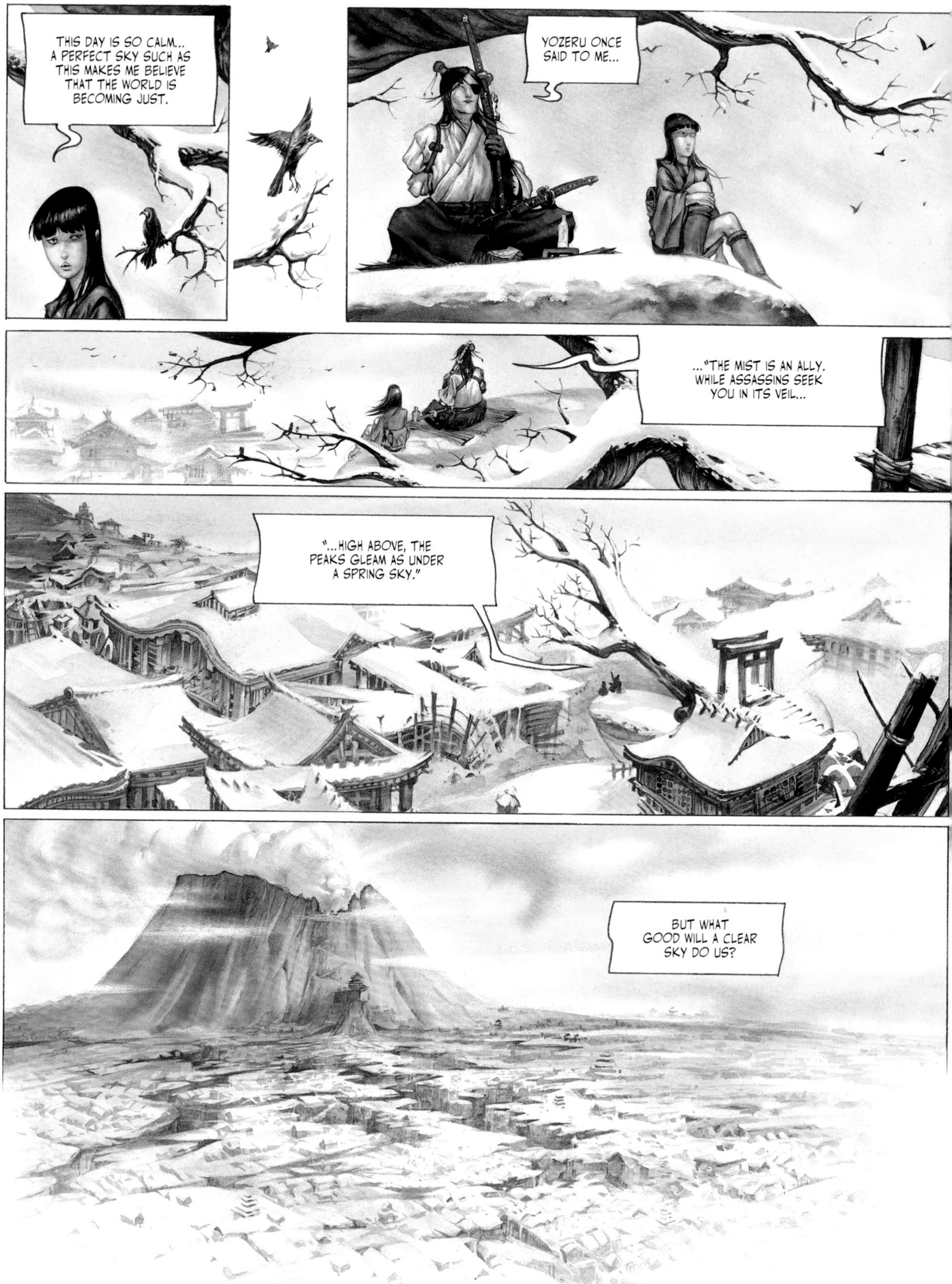
THIS DAY IS SO CALM... A PERFECT SKY SUCH AS THIS MAKES ME BELIEVE THAT THE WORLD IS BECOMING JUST.
YOZERU ONCE SAID TO ME...
..."THE MIST IS AN ALLY. WHILE ASSASSINS SEEK YOU IN ITS VEIL...
"...HIGH ABOVE, THE PEAKS GLEAM AS UNDER A SPRING SKY."
BUT WHAT GOOD WILL A CLEAR SKY DO US?

CHAPTER TWO:
Like Leaves in the Wind

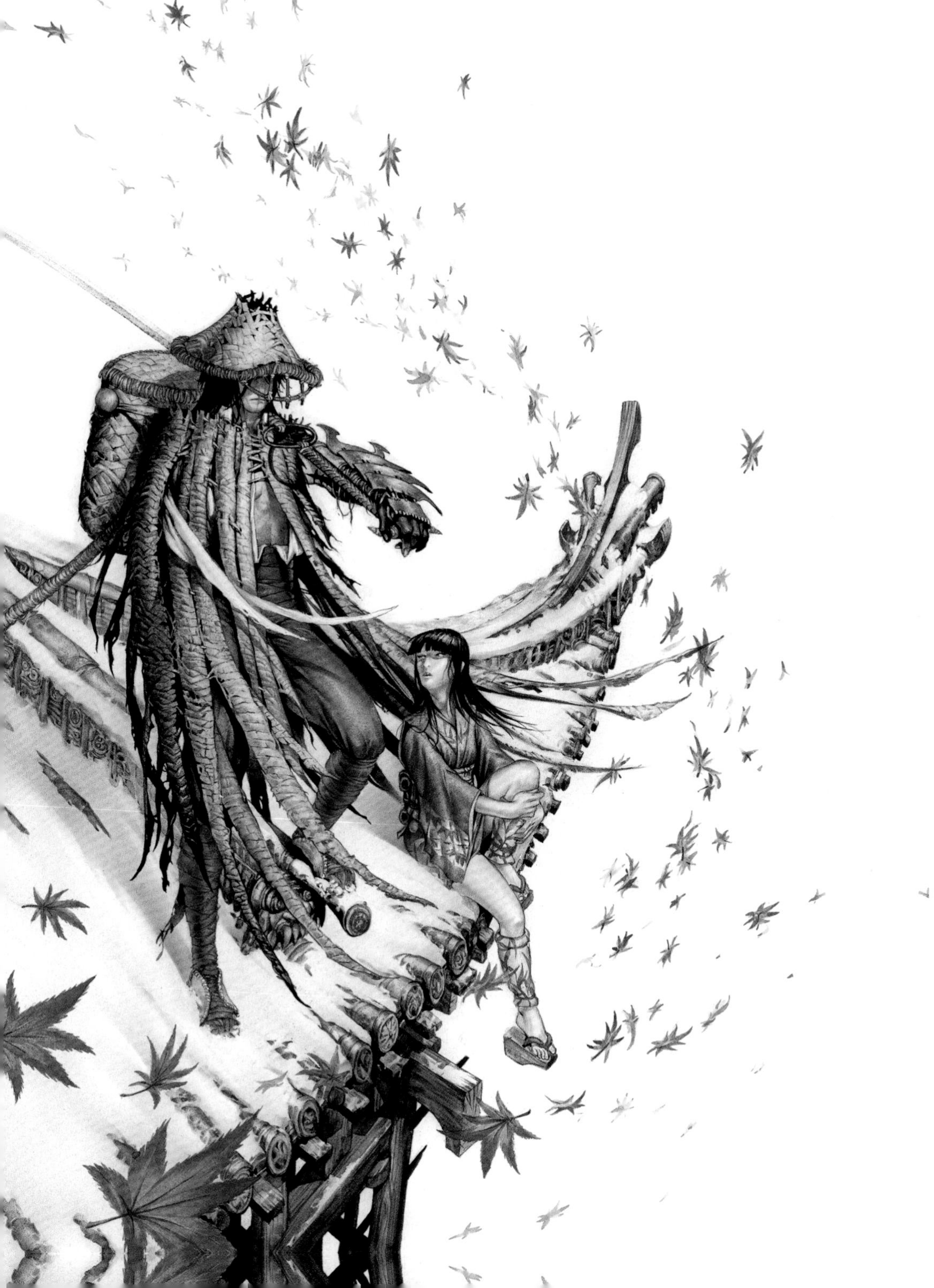

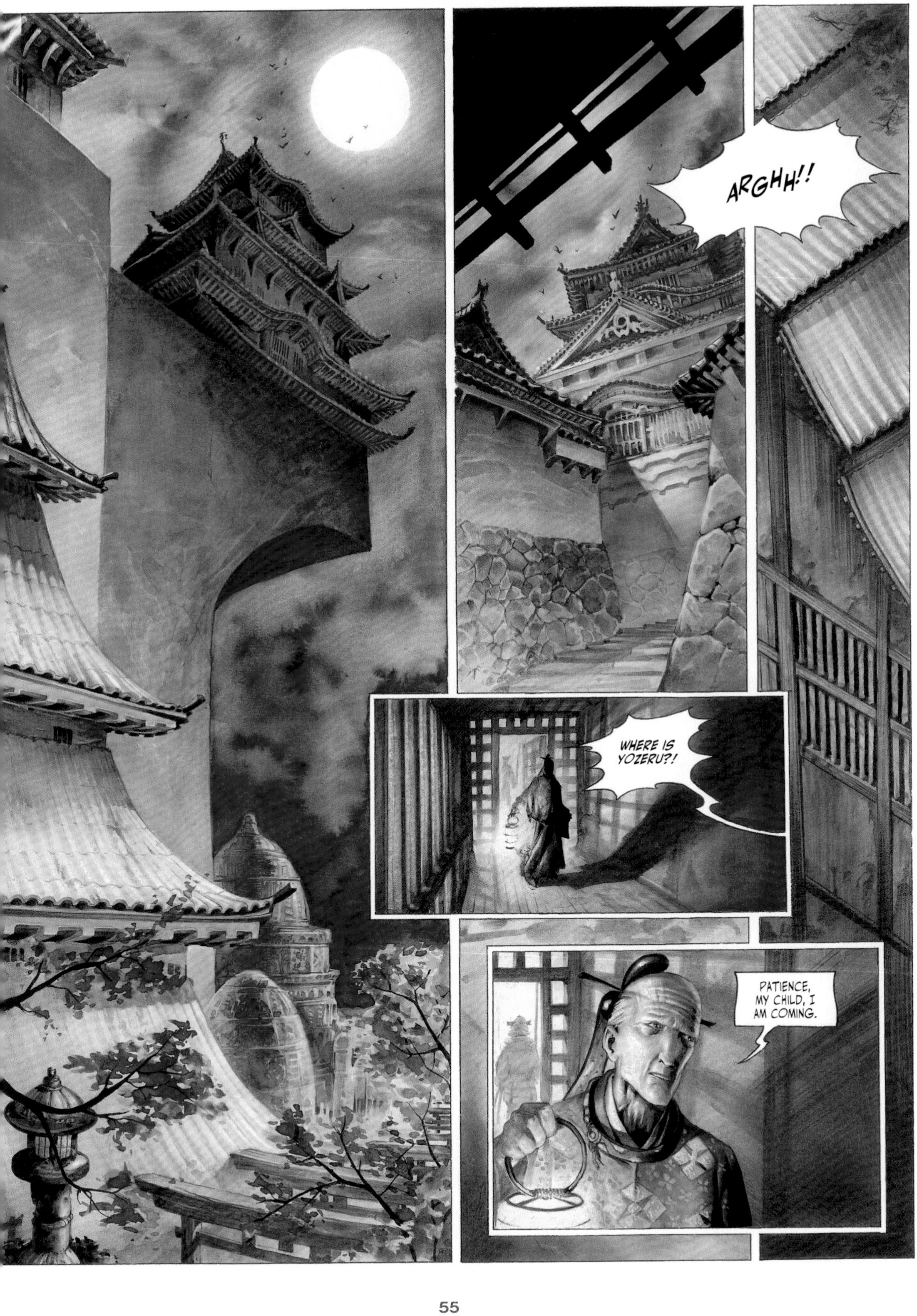
ARGHH!!
WHERE IS YOZERU?!
PATIENCE, MY CHILD, I AM COMING.

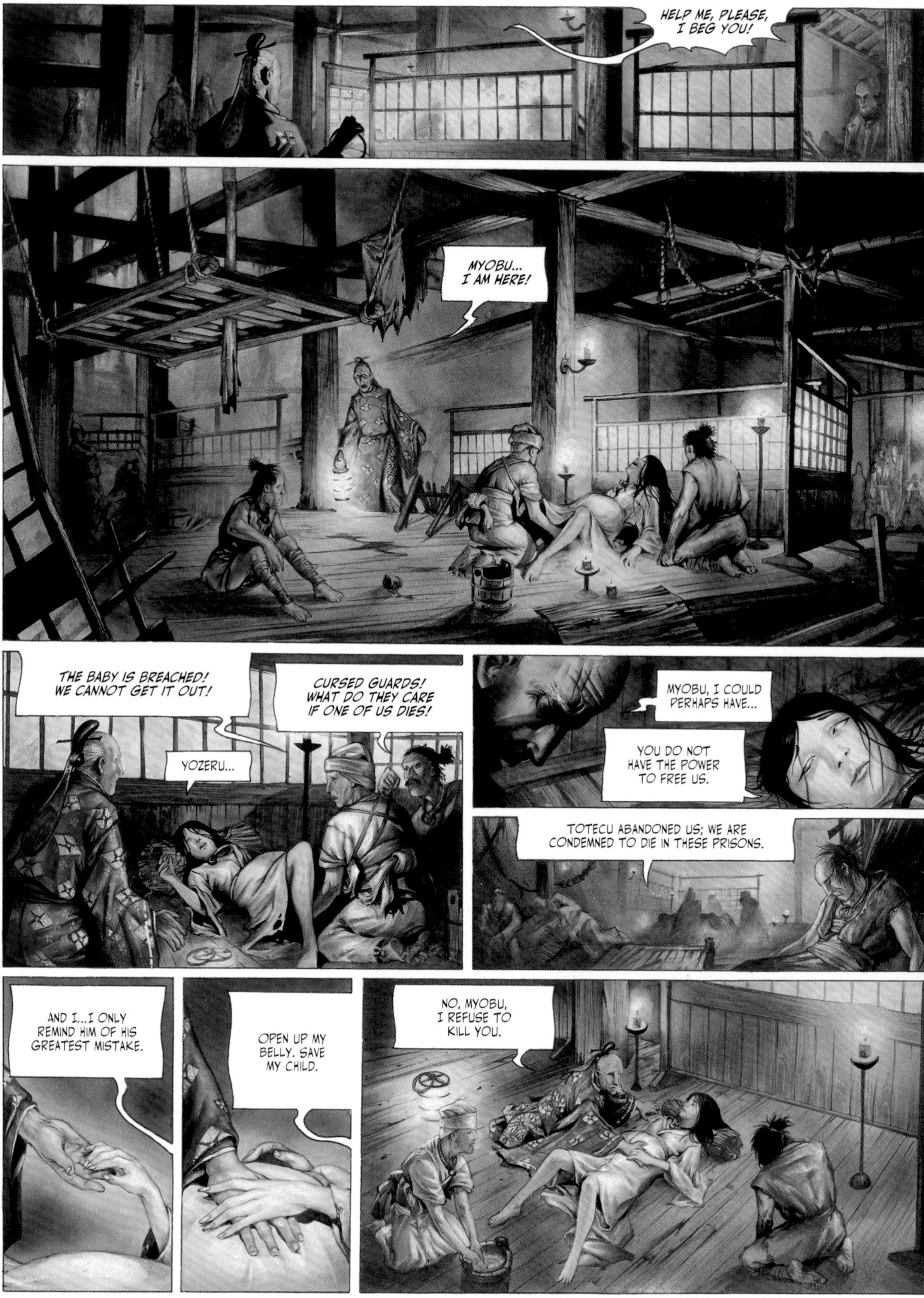
HELP ME, PLEASE, I BEG YOU!
MYOBU... I AM HERE!
THE BABY IS BREACHED! WE CANNOT GET IT OUT!
CURSED GUARDS! WHAT DO THEY CARE IF ONE OF US DIES!
YOZERU...
MYOBU, I COULD PERHAPS HAVE...
YOU DO NOT HAVE THE POWER TO FREE US.
TOTECU ABANDONED US; WE ARE CONDEMNED TO DIE IN THESE PRISONS.
AND I...I ONLY REMIND HIM OF HIS GREATEST MISTAKE.
OPEN UP MY BELLY. SAVE MY CHILD.
NO, MYOBU, I REFUSE TO KILL YOU.

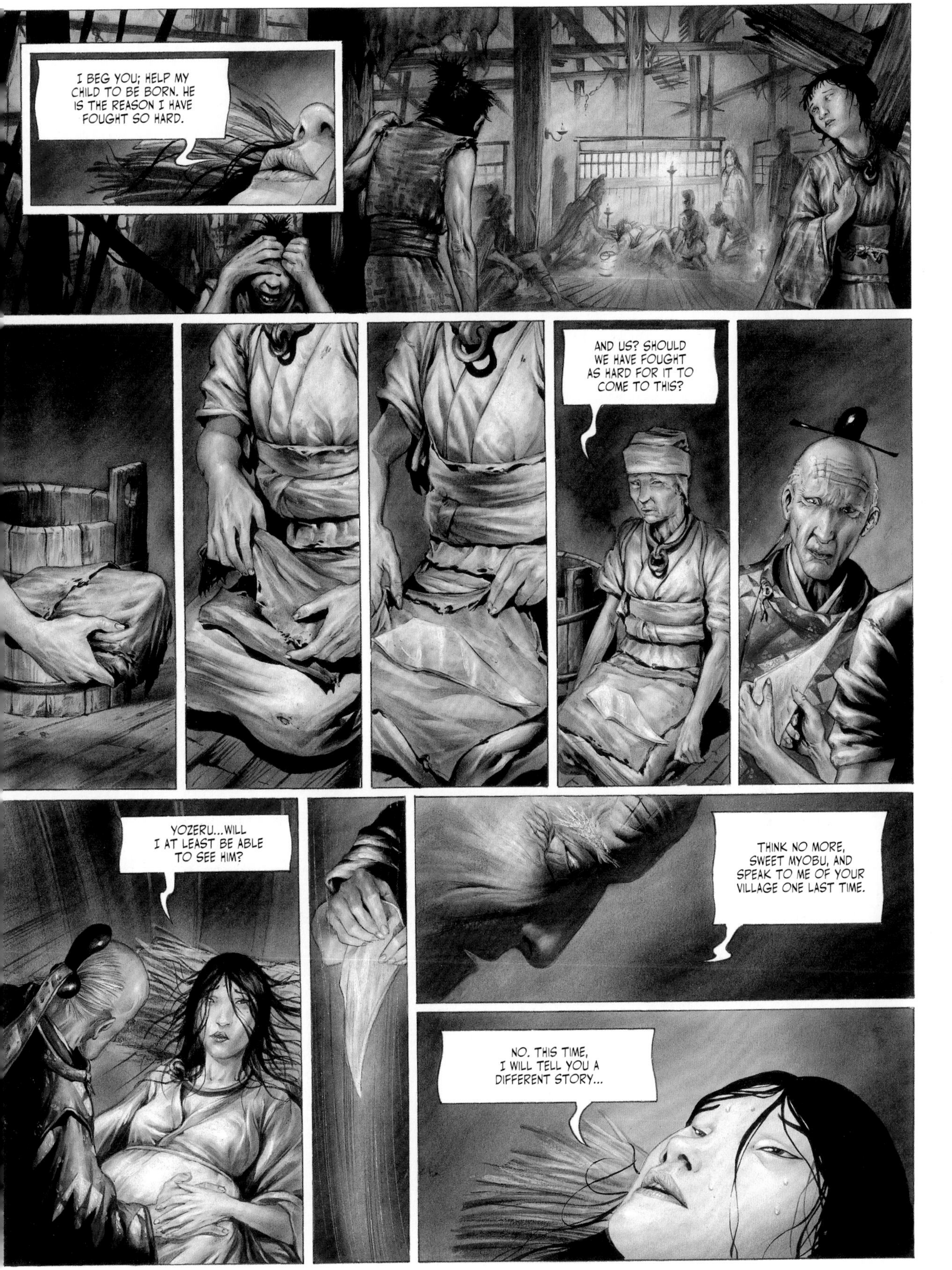
I BEG YOU; HELP MY CHILD TO BE BORN. HE IS THE REASON I HAVE FOUGHT SO HARD.
AND US? SHOULD WE HAVE FOUGHT AS HARD FOR IT TO COME TO THIS?
YOZERU...WILL I AT LEAST BE ABLE TO SEE HIM?
THINK NO MORE, SWEET MYOBU, AND SPEAK TO ME OF YOUR VILLAGE ONE LAST TIME.
NO. THIS TIME, I WILL TELL YOU A DIFFERENT STORY...

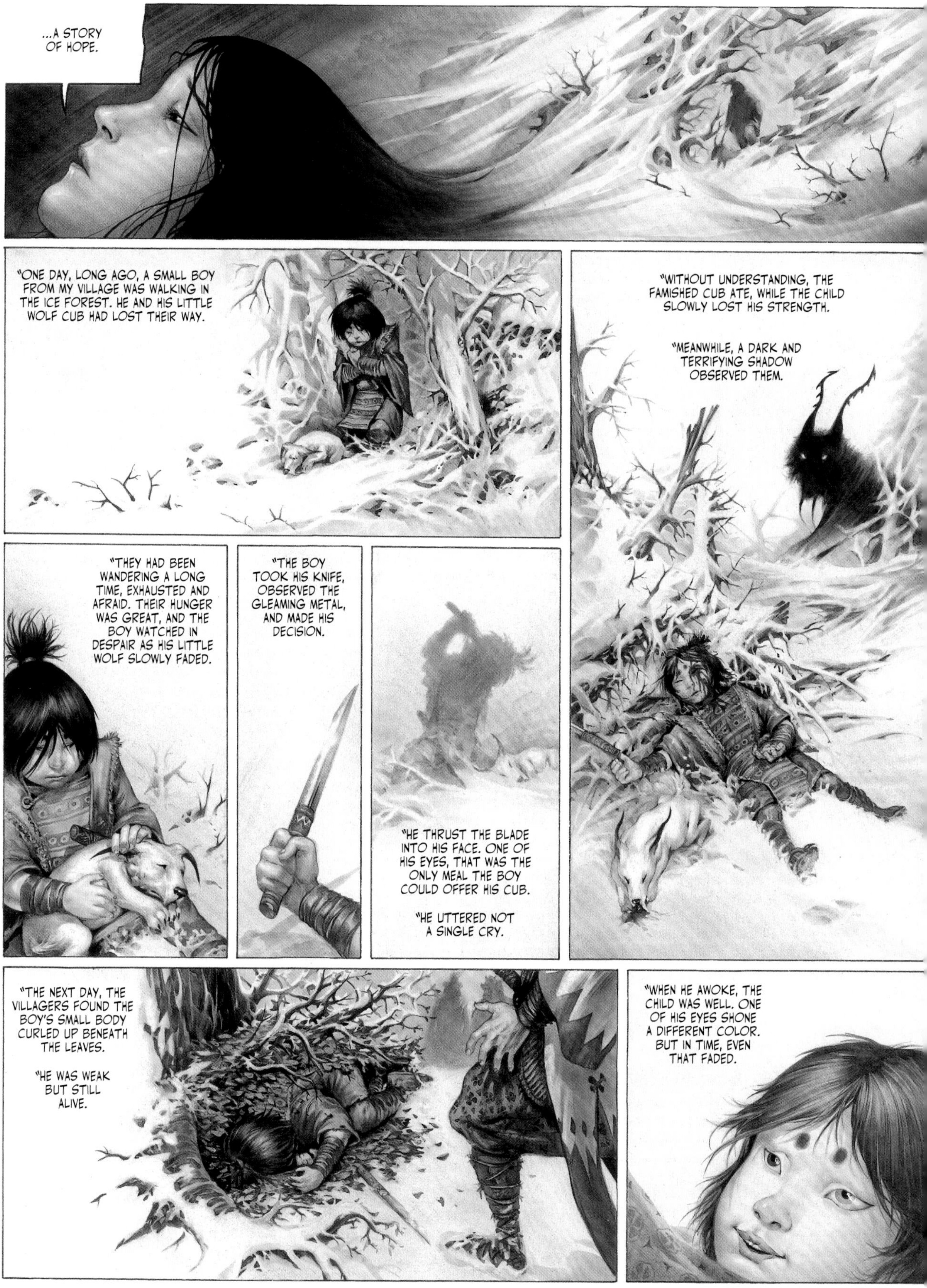

...A STORY OF HOPE.
"ONE DAY, LONG AGO, A SMALL BOY FROM MY VILLAGE WAS WALKING IN THE ICE FOREST. HE AND HIS LITTLE WOLF CUB HAD LOST THEIR WAY.
"THEY HAD BEEN WANDERING A LONG TIME, EXHAUSTED AND AFRAID. THEIR HUNGER WAS GREAT, AND THE BOY WATCHED IN DESPAIR AS HIS LITTLE WOLF SLOWLY FADED.
"THE BOY TOOK HIS KNIFE, OBSERVED THE GLEAMING METAL, AND MADE HIS DECISION.
"HE THRUST THE BLADE INTO HIS FACE. ONE OF HIS EYES, THAT WAS THE ONLY MEAL THE BOY COULD OFFER HIS CUB.
"HE UTTERED NOT A SINGLE CRY.
"WITHOUT UNDERSTANDING, THE FAMISHED CUB ATE, WHILE THE CHILD SLOWLY LOST HIS STRENGTH.
"MEANWHILE, A DARK AND TERRIFYING SHADOW OBSERVED THEM.
"THE NEXT DAY, THE VILLAGERS FOUND THE BOY'S SMALL BODY CURLED UP BENEATH THE LEAVES.
"HE WAS WEAK BUT STILL ALIVE.
"WHEN HE AWOKE, THE CHILD WAS WELL. ONE OF HIS EYES SHONE A DIFFERENT COLOR. BUT IN TIME, EVEN THAT FADED.

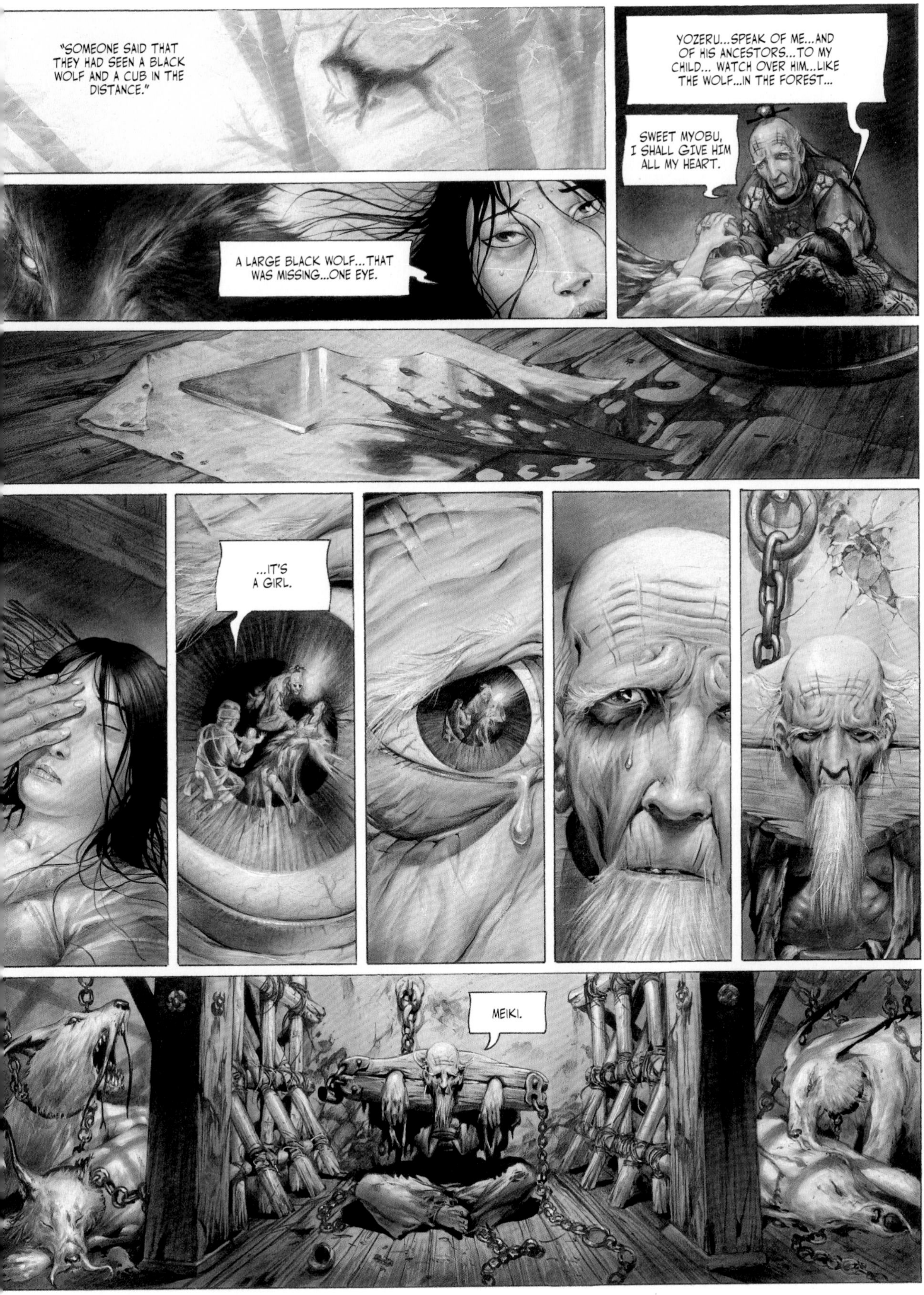
"SOMEONE SAID THAT THEY HAD SEEN A BLACK WOLF AND A CUB IN THE DISTANCE."
YOZERU...SPEAK OF ME...AND OF HIS ANCESTORS...TO MY CHILD... WATCH OVER HIM...LIKE THE WOLF...IN THE FOREST...
SWEET MYOBU, I SHALL GIVE HIM ALL MY HEART.
A LARGE BLACK WOLF...THAT WAS MISSING...ONE EYE.
...IT'S A GIRL.
MEIKI.

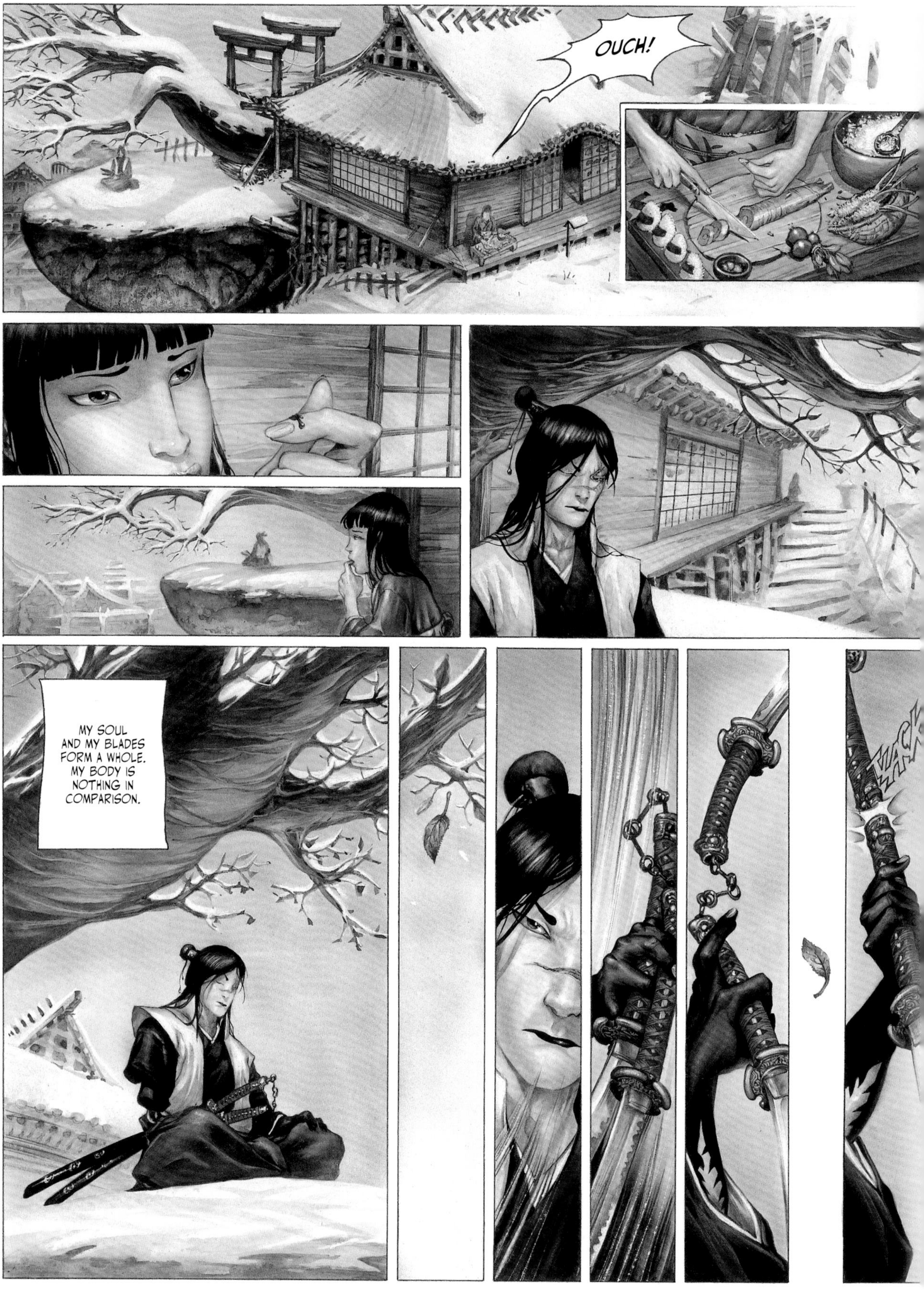
OUCH!
MY SOUL AND MY BLADES FORM A WHOLE. MY BODY IS NOTHING IN COMPARISON.

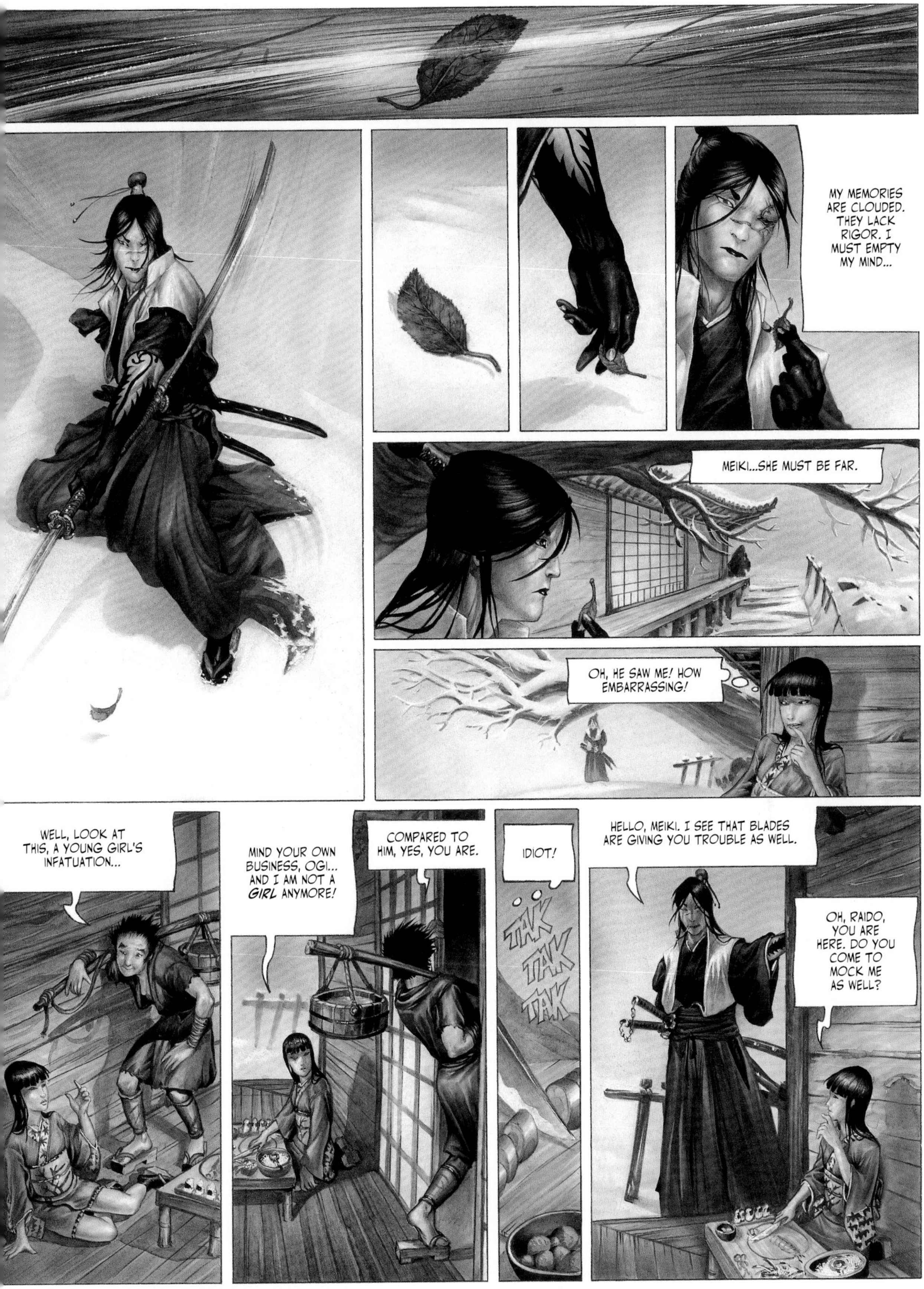
MY MEMORIES ARE CLOUDED. THEY LACK RIGOR. I MUST EMPTY MY MIND...
MEIKI...SHE MUST BE FAR.
OH, HE SAW ME! HOW EMBARRASSING!
WELL, LOOK AT THIS, A YOUNG GIRL'S INFATUATION...
MIND YOUR OWN BUSINESS, OGI... AND I AM NOT A GIRL ANYMORE!
COMPARED TO HIM, YES, YOU ARE.
IDIOT!
TAK TAK TAK
HELLO, MEIKI. I SEE THAT BLADES ARE GIVING YOU TROUBLE AS WELL.
OH, RAIDO, YOU ARE HERE. DO YOU COME TO MOCK ME AS WELL?

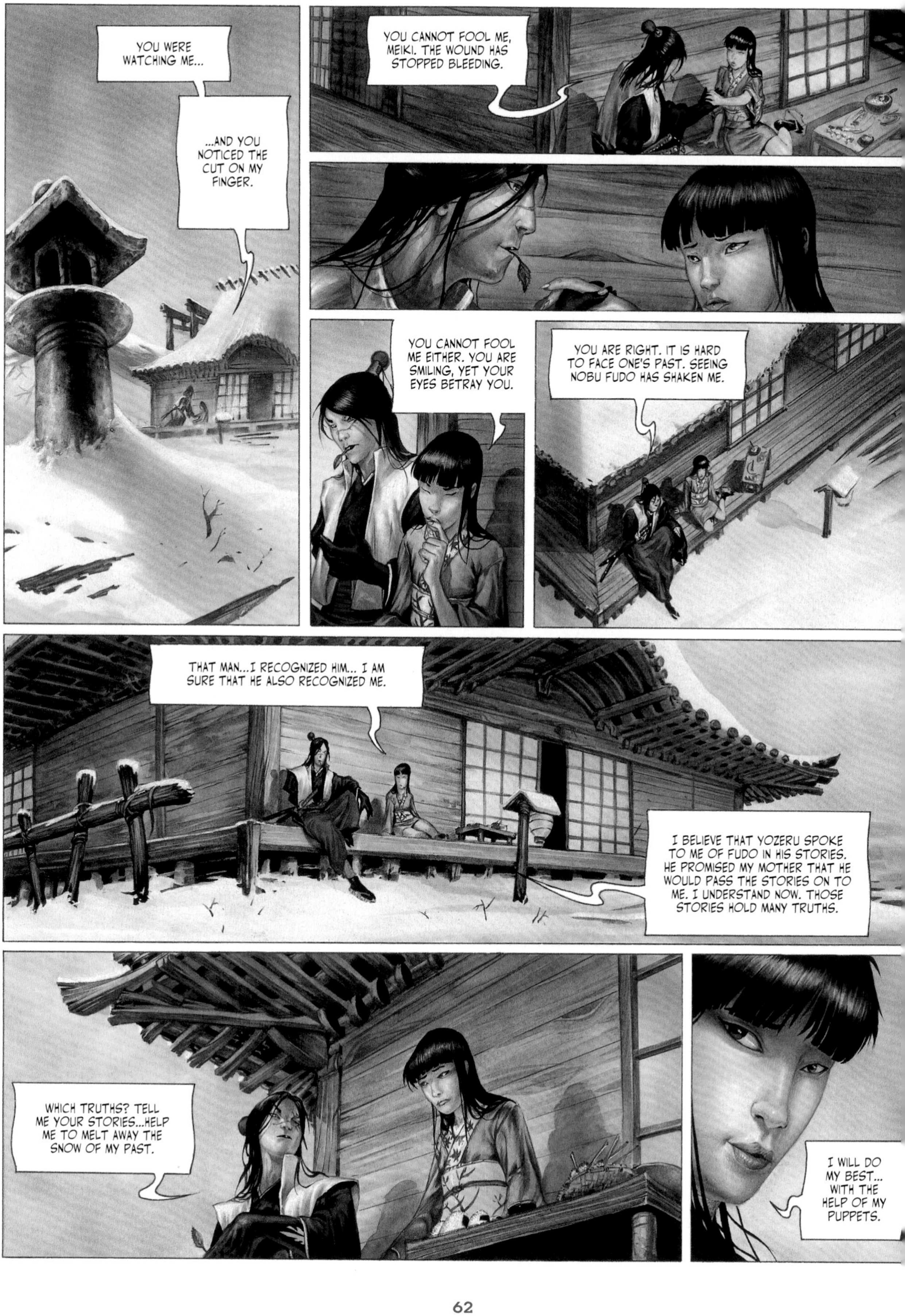
YOU WERE WATCHING ME...
...AND YOU NOTICED THE CUT ON MY FINGER.
YOU CANNOT FOOL ME, MEIKI. THE WOUND HAS STOPPED BLEEDING.
YOU CANNOT FOOL ME EITHER. YOU ARE SMILING, YET YOUR EYES BETRAY YOU.
YOU ARE RIGHT. IT IS HARD TO FACE ONE'S PAST. SEEING NOBU FUDO HAS SHAKEN ME.
THAT MAN...I RECOGNIZED HIM... I AM SURE THAT HE ALSO RECOGNIZED ME.
I BELIEVE THAT YOZERU SPOKE TO ME OF FUDO IN HIS STORIES. HE PROMISED MY MOTHER THAT HE WOULD PASS THE STORIES ON TO ME. I UNDERSTAND NOW. THOSE STORIES HOLD MANY TRUTHS.
WHICH TRUTHS? TELL ME YOUR STORIES...HELP ME TO MELT AWAY THE SNOW OF MY PAST.
I WILL DO MY BEST... WITH THE HELP OF MY PUPPETS.

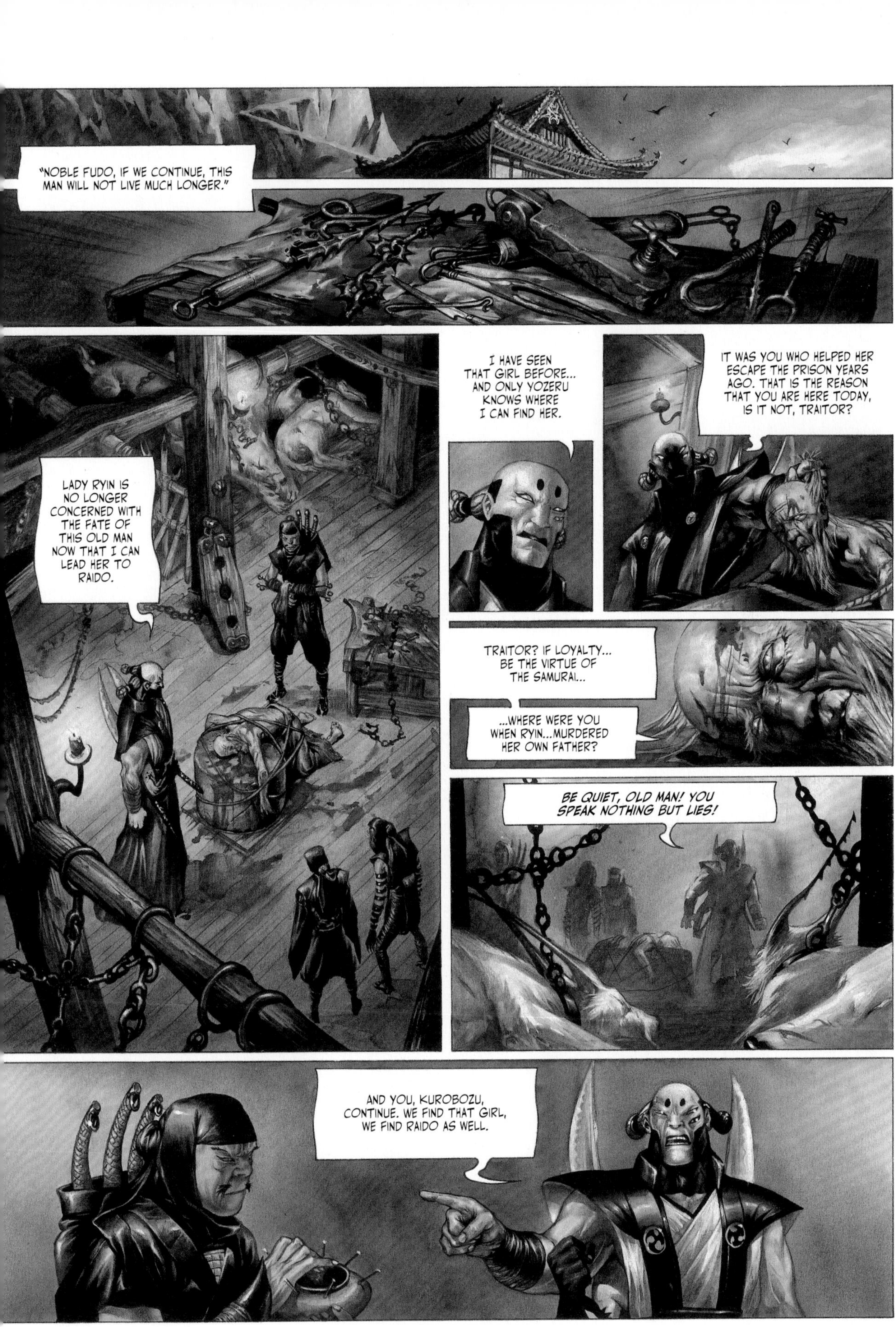

"NOBLE FUDO, IF WE CONTINUE, THIS MAN WILL NOT LIVE MUCH LONGER."
LADY RYIN IS NO LONGER CONCERNED WITH THE FATE OF THIS OLD MAN NOW THAT I CAN LEAD HER TO RAIDO.
I HAVE SEEN THAT GIRL BEFORE... AND ONLY YOZERU KNOWS WHERE I CAN FIND HER.
IT WAS YOU WHO HELPED HER ESCAPE THE PRISON YEARS AGO. THAT IS THE REASON THAT YOU ARE HERE TODAY, IS IT NOT, TRAITOR?
TRAITOR? IF LOYALTY... BE THE VIRTUE OF THE SAMURAI...
...WHERE WERE YOU WHEN RYIN...MURDERED HER OWN FATHER?
BE QUIET, OLD MAN! YOU SPEAK NOTHING BUT LIES!
AND YOU, KUROBOZU, CONTINUE. WE FIND THAT GIRL, WE FIND RAIDO AS WELL.

IF THOSE ARE MY LORD'S ORDERS, I HAVE SOMETHING HERE MORE POTENT THAN A THOUSAND TORTURES.

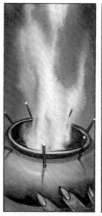

SMELL THIS, OLD MAN...AND REVEAL YOUR SECRETS.

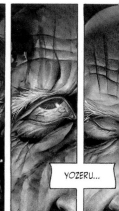

YOZERU...

YOZERU...THAT CHILD, DID HE SEE THE BLACK WOLF AGAIN?

OH, I AM SORRY, LITTLE MEIKI. I WAS LOST IN THOUGHT...

WHERE WAS I?

LISTEN! LISTEN!

AMATERASU HAS ABANDONED US! THE GUARDS, THEY SAID THAT NOBU FUDO HAS RETURNED! IT SEEMS THAT GENERAL RAIDO IS DEAD!

LADY RYIN HAS ORDERED ALL THE YOUNG GIRLS FROM THE PRISON TO THE TEMPLE'S PATH!

THEY ARE ALL DOOMED!

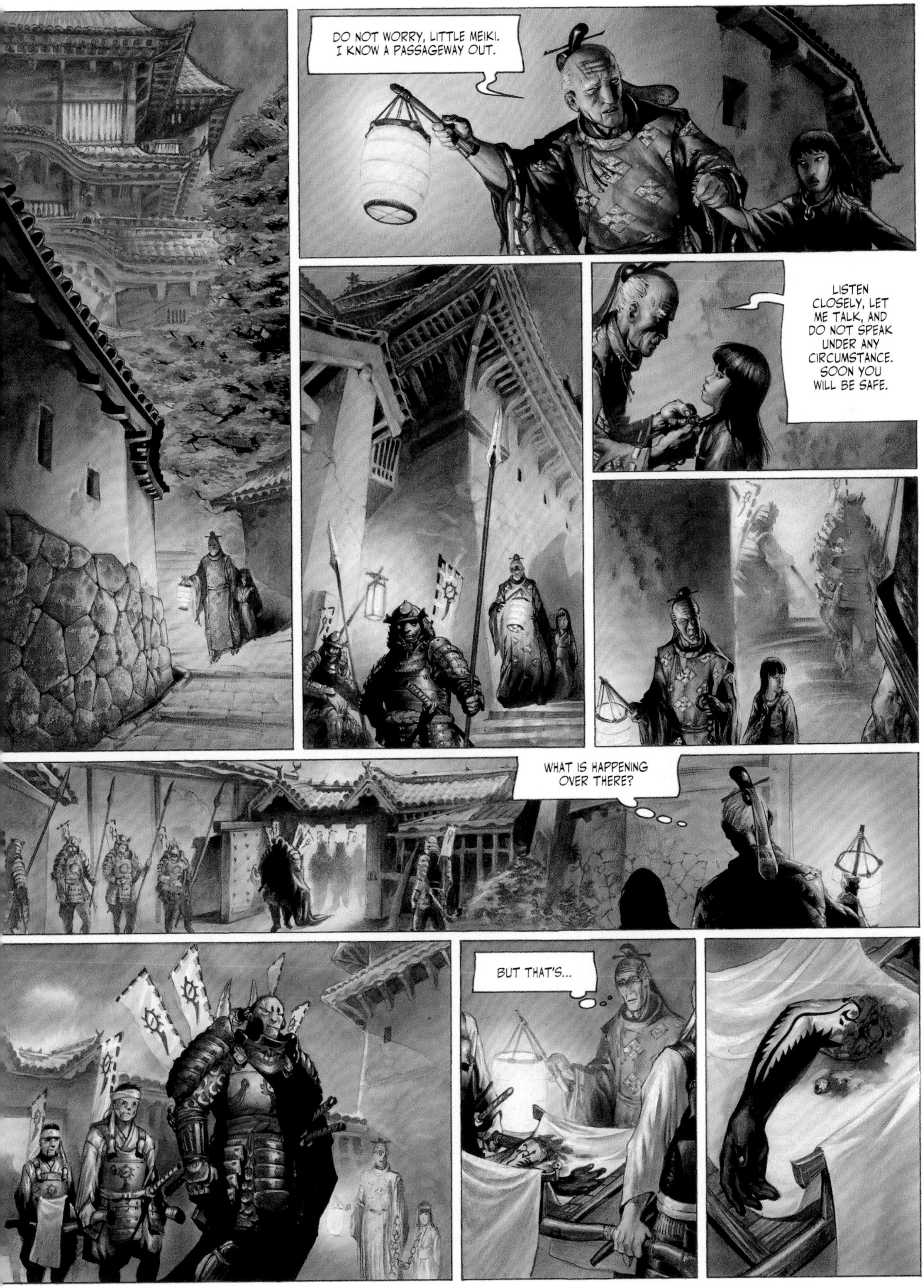
DO NOT WORRY, LITTLE MEIKI. I KNOW A PASSAGEWAY OUT.
LISTEN CLOSELY, LET ME TALK, AND DO NOT SPEAK UNDER ANY CIRCUMSTANCE. SOON YOU WILL BE SAFE.
WHAT IS HAPPENING OVER THERE?
BUT THAT'S...

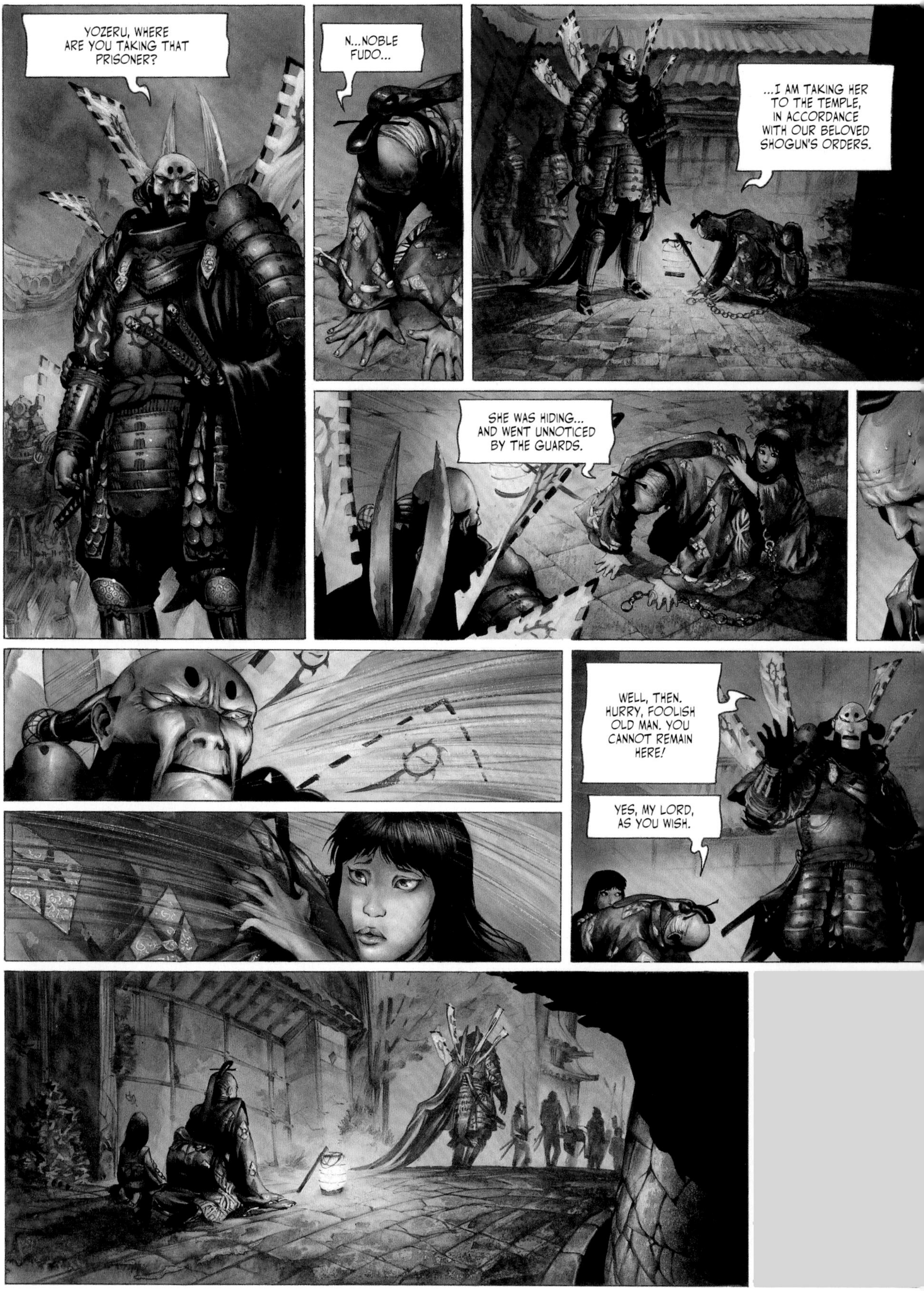
YOZERU, WHERE ARE YOU TAKING THAT PRISONER?
N...NOBLE FUDO...
...I AM TAKING HER TO THE TEMPLE, IN ACCORDANCE WITH OUR BELOVED SHOGUN'S ORDERS.
SHE WAS HIDING... AND WENT UNNOTICED BY THE GUARDS.
WELL, THEN. HURRY, FOOLISH OLD MAN. YOU CANNOT REMAIN HERE!
YES, MY LORD, AS YOU WISH.

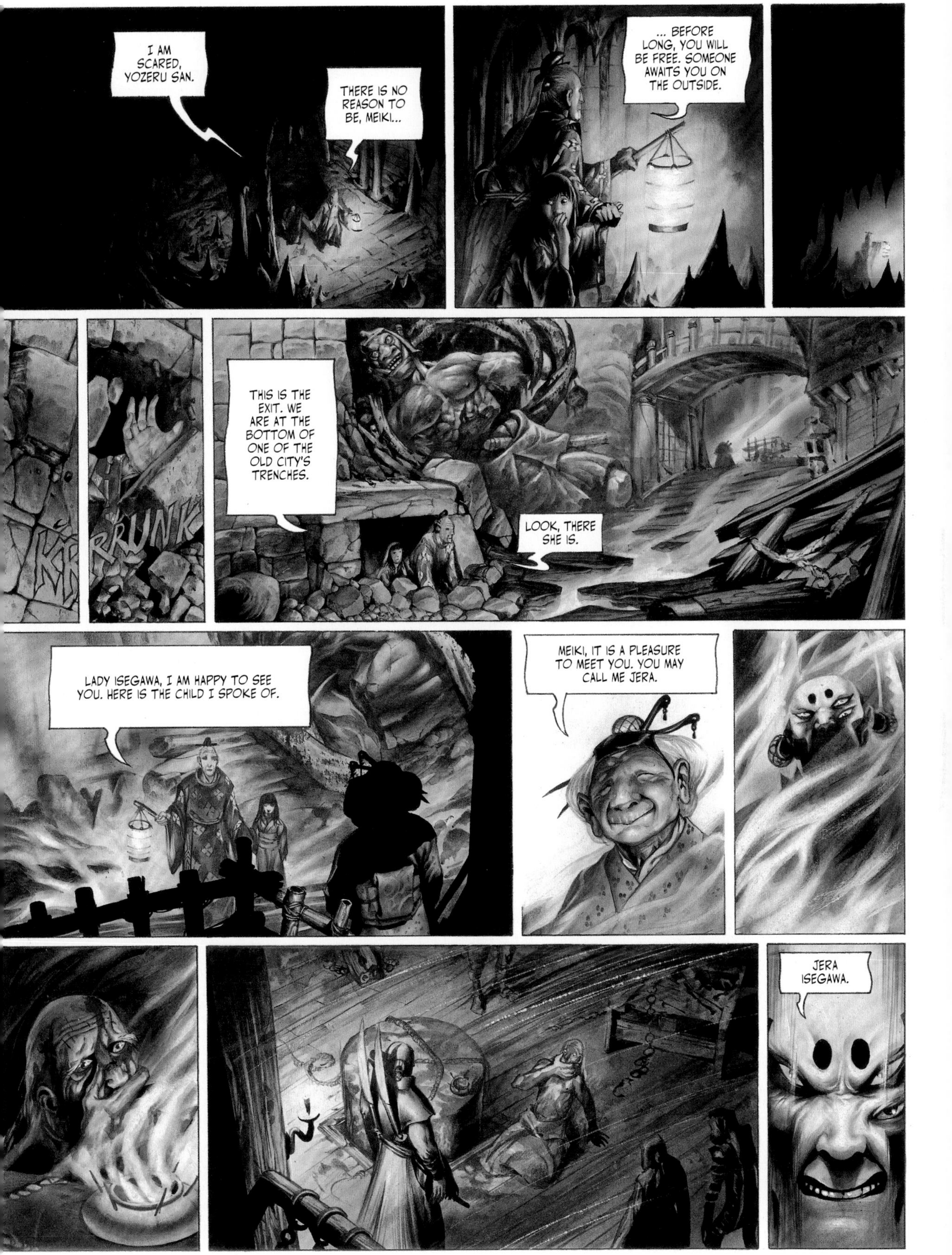
I AM SCARED, YOZERU SAN.
THERE IS NO REASON TO BE, MEIKI...
... BEFORE LONG, YOU WILL BE FREE. SOMEONE AWAITS YOU ON THE OUTSIDE.
KRRRUNK
THIS IS THE EXIT. WE ARE AT THE BOTTOM OF ONE OF THE OLD CITY'S TRENCHES.
LOOK, THERE SHE IS.
LADY ISEGAWA, I AM HAPPY TO SEE YOU. HERE IS THE CHILD I SPOKE OF.
MEIKI, IT IS A PLEASURE TO MEET YOU. YOU MAY CALL ME JERA.
JERA ISEGAWA.

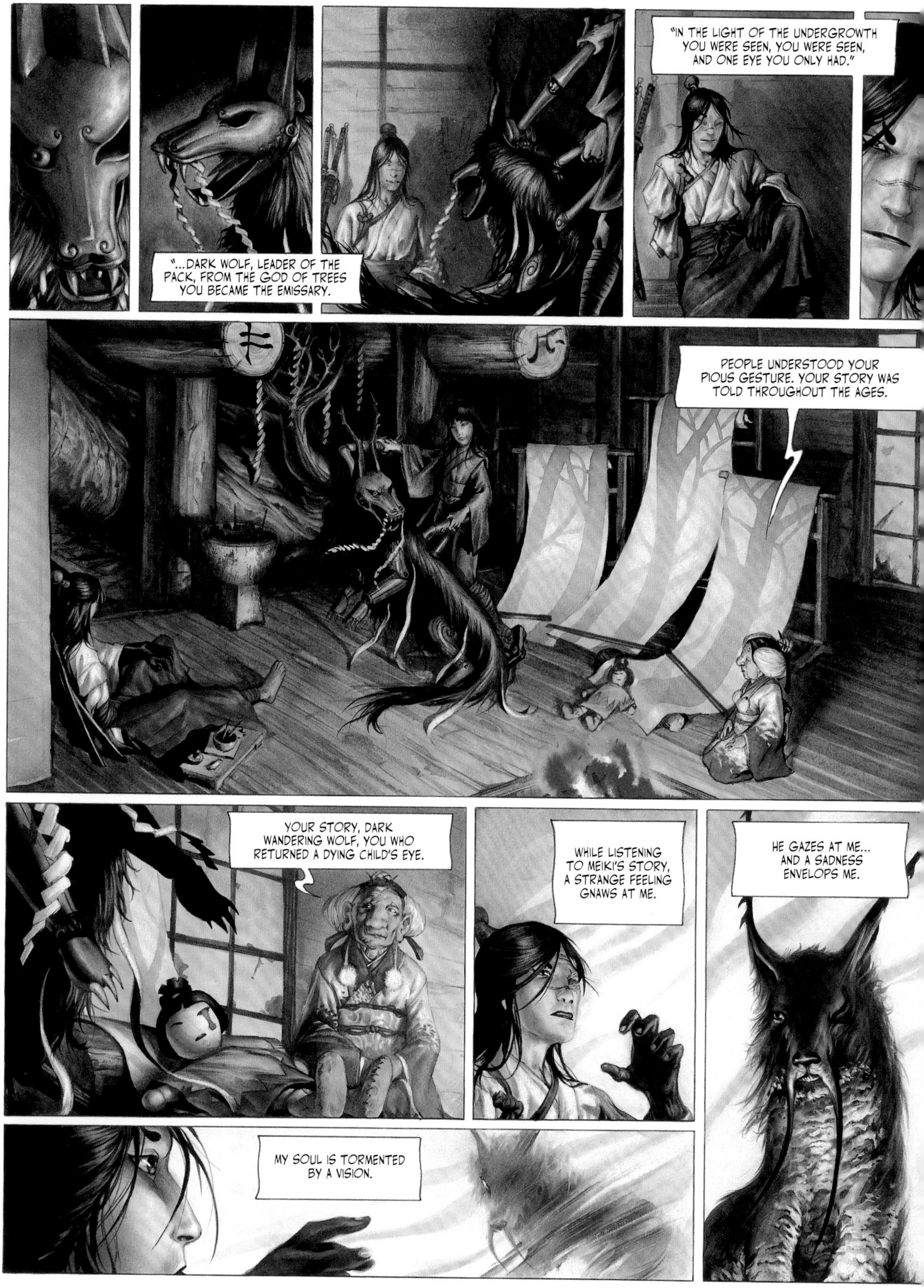
"...DARK WOLF, LEADER OF THE PACK, FROM THE GOD OF TREES YOU BECAME THE EMISSARY.
"IN THE LIGHT OF THE UNDERGROWTH YOU WERE SEEN, YOU WERE SEEN, AND ONE EYE YOU ONLY HAD."
PEOPLE UNDERSTOOD YOUR PIOUS GESTURE. YOUR STORY WAS TOLD THROUGHOUT THE AGES.
YOUR STORY, DARK WANDERING WOLF, YOU WHO RETURNED A DYING CHILD'S EYE.
WHILE LISTENING TO MEIKI'S STORY, A STRANGE FEELING GNAWS AT ME.
HE GAZES AT ME... AND A SADNESS ENVELOPS ME.
MY SOUL IS TORMENTED BY A VISION.

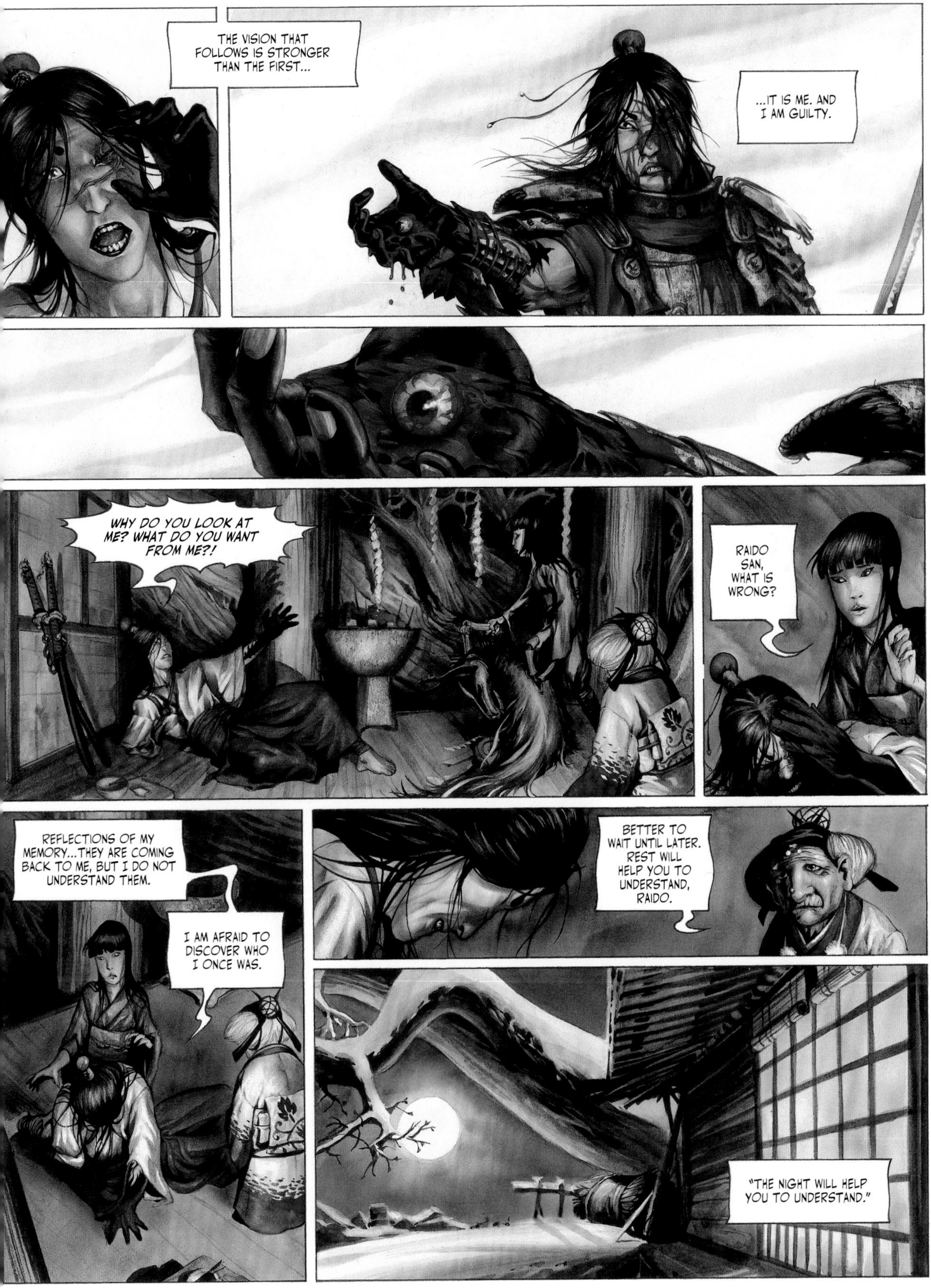
THE VISION THAT FOLLOWS IS STRONGER THAN THE FIRST...
...IT IS ME. AND I AM GUILTY.
WHY DO YOU LOOK AT ME? WHAT DO YOU WANT FROM ME?!
RAIDO SAN, WHAT IS WRONG?
REFLECTIONS OF MY MEMORY...THEY ARE COMING BACK TO ME, BUT I DO NOT UNDERSTAND THEM.
I AM AFRAID TO DISCOVER WHO I ONCE WAS.
BETTER TO WAIT UNTIL LATER. REST WILL HELP YOU TO UNDERSTAND, RAIDO.
"THE NIGHT WILL HELP YOU TO UNDERSTAND."

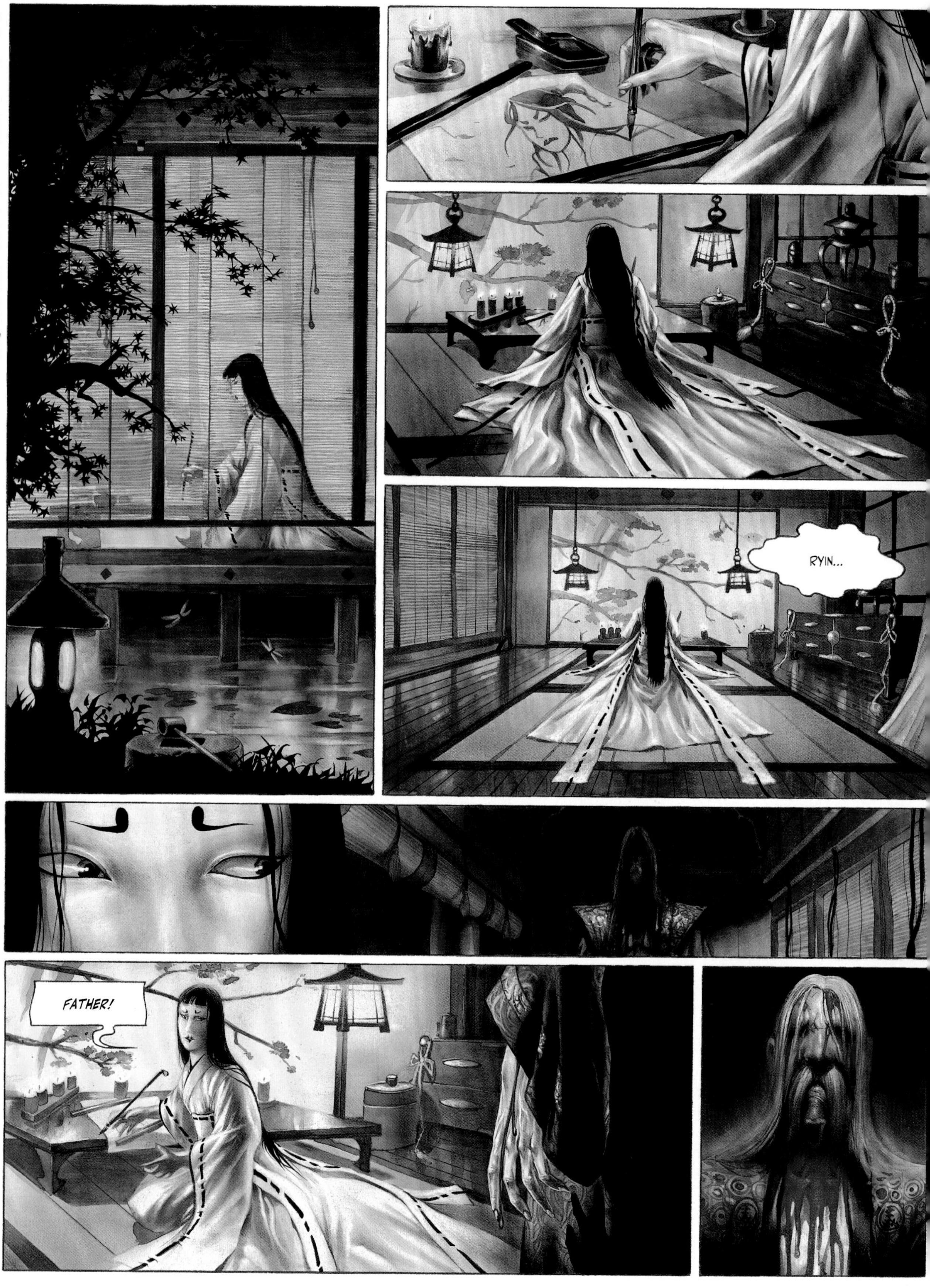
RYIN...
FATHER!

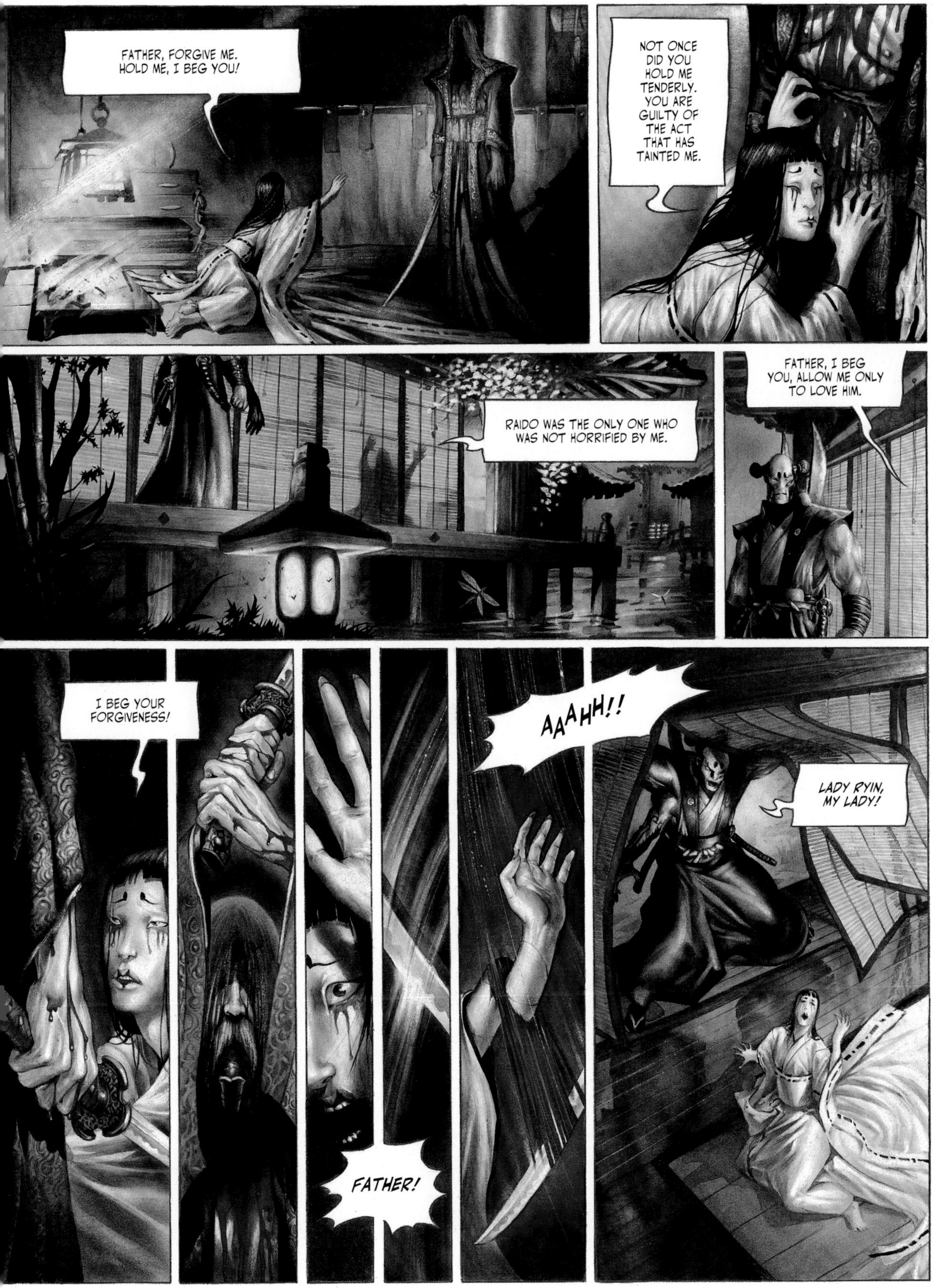
FATHER, FORGIVE ME. HOLD ME, I BEG YOU!
NOT ONCE DID YOU HOLD ME TENDERLY. YOU ARE GUILTY OF THE ACT THAT HAS TAINTED ME.
RAIDO WAS THE ONLY ONE WHO WAS NOT HORRIFIED BY ME.
FATHER, I BEG YOU, ALLOW ME ONLY TO LOVE HIM.
I BEG YOUR FORGIVENESS!
FATHER!
AAAHH!!
LADY RYIN, MY LADY!

DO YOU SEE IT, FUDO? DO YOU SEE IT TOO?

MY LADY...I BELIEVE WHAT YOU SAY, BUT MY EYES SEE NOTHING.

THAT HAND...THAT IS NOT MY HAND!

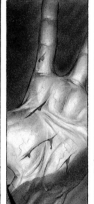

NOBLE FUDO, I TRUST THAT YOU WILL NOT MENTION WHAT HAS JUST HAPPENED.

FURTHERMORE... I HAVE ORDERS FOR YOU.

...YOU MAY DISPOSE OF JERA ISEGAWA AND THE YOUNG GIRL AS YOU SEE FIT.

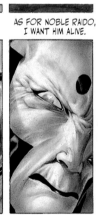

AS FOR NOBLE RAIDO, I WANT HIM ALIVE.

WILL YOU DO THAT FOR ME?

YES...MY LADY.

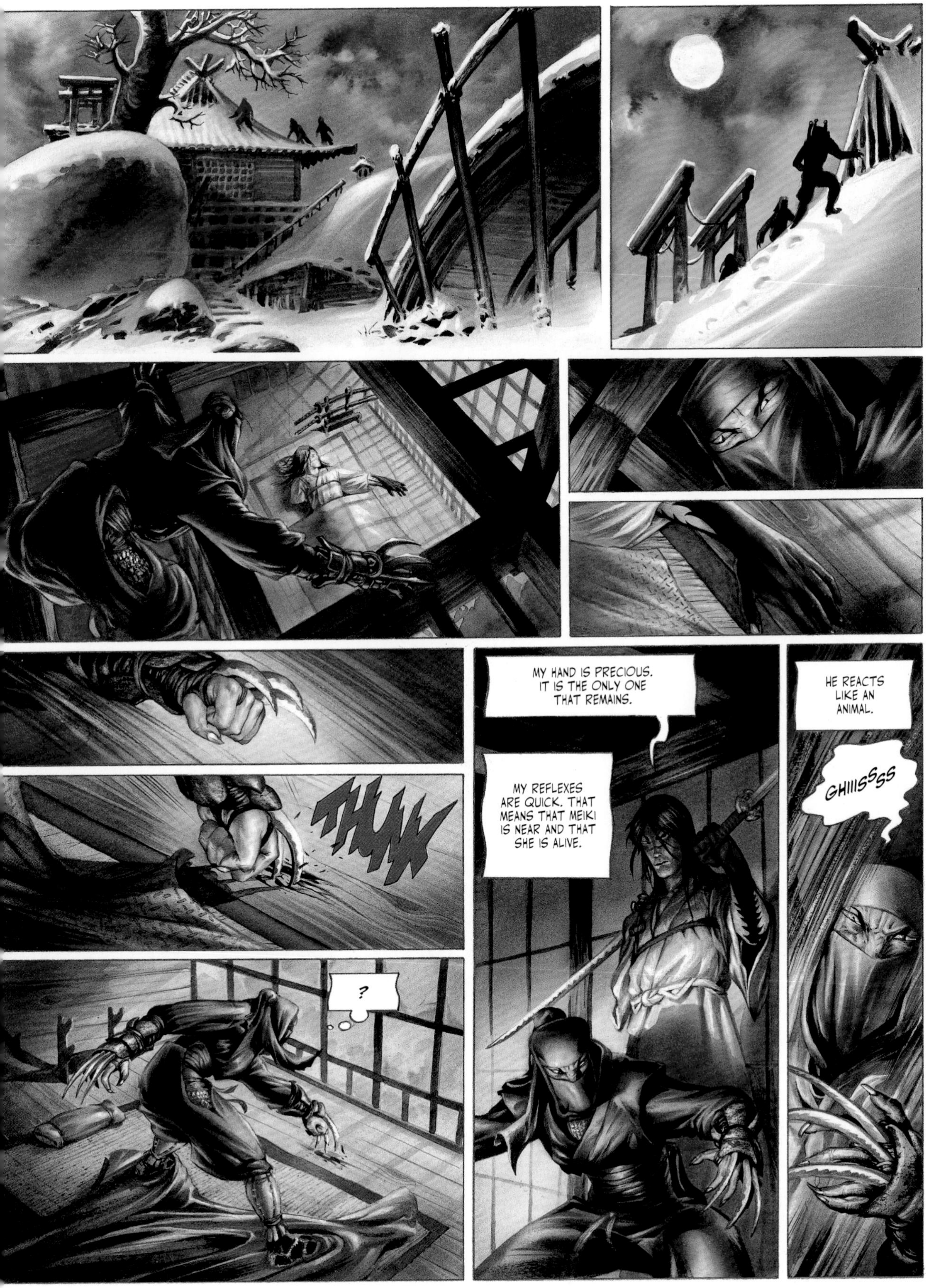
THUK
?
MY HAND IS PRECIOUS. IT IS THE ONLY ONE THAT REMAINS.
MY REFLEXES ARE QUICK. THAT MEANS THAT MEIKI IS NEAR AND THAT SHE IS ALIVE.
HE REACTS LIKE AN ANIMAL.
GHIIISSSS

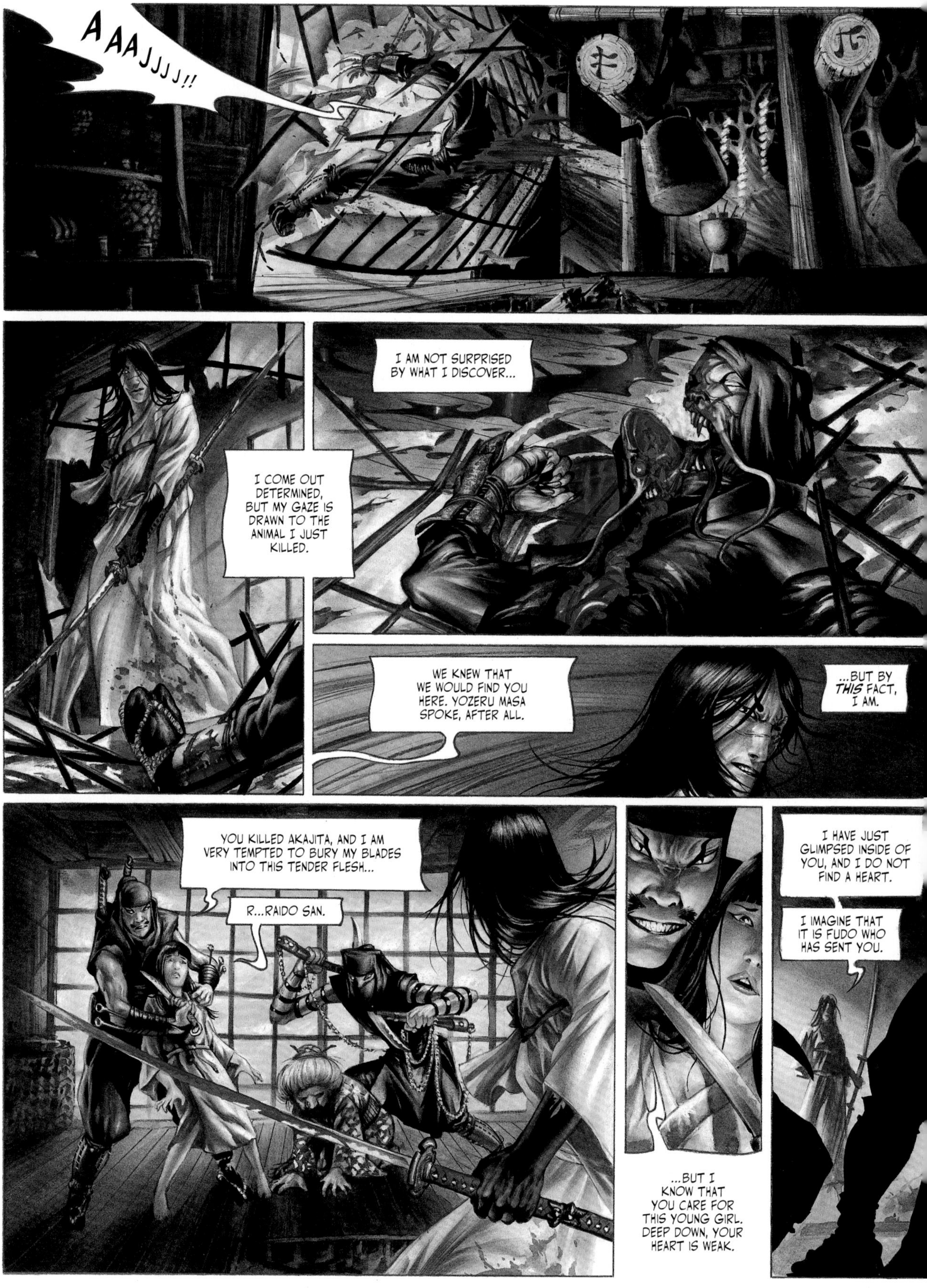
AAAJJJJ!!
I AM NOT SURPRISED BY WHAT I DISCOVER...
I COME OUT DETERMINED, BUT MY GAZE IS DRAWN TO THE ANIMAL I JUST KILLED.
WE KNEW THAT WE WOULD FIND YOU HERE. YOZERU MASA SPOKE, AFTER ALL.
...BUT BY *THIS* FACT, I AM.
YOU KILLED AKAJITA, AND I AM VERY TEMPTED TO BURY MY BLADES INTO THIS TENDER FLESH...
R...RAIDO SAN.
...BUT I KNOW THAT YOU CARE FOR THIS YOUNG GIRL. DEEP DOWN, YOUR HEART IS WEAK.
I HAVE JUST GLIMPSED INSIDE OF YOU, AND I DO NOT FIND A HEART.
I IMAGINE THAT IT IS FUDO WHO HAS SENT YOU.

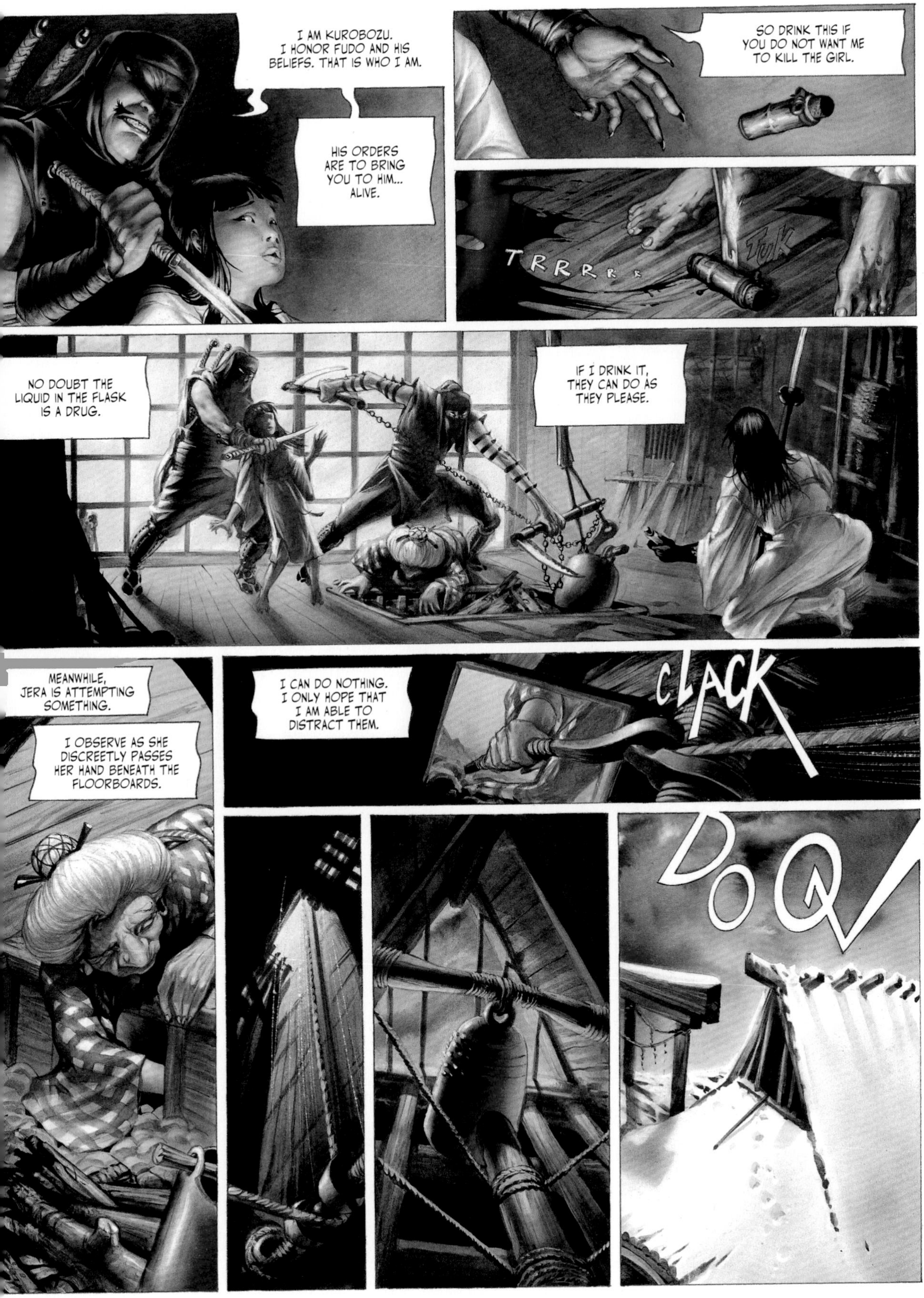
I AM KUROBOZU. I HONOR FUDO AND HIS BELIEFS. THAT IS WHO I AM.
HIS ORDERS ARE TO BRING YOU TO HIM... ALIVE.
SO DRINK THIS IF YOU DO NOT WANT ME TO KILL THE GIRL.
TRRRRR
TUK
NO DOUBT THE LIQUID IN THE FLASK IS A DRUG.
IF I DRINK IT, THEY CAN DO AS THEY PLEASE.
MEANWHILE, JERA IS ATTEMPTING SOMETHING.
I OBSERVE AS SHE DISCREETLY PASSES HER HAND BENEATH THE FLOORBOARDS.
I CAN DO NOTHING. I ONLY HOPE THAT I AM ABLE TO DISTRACT THEM.
CLACK
DOQ

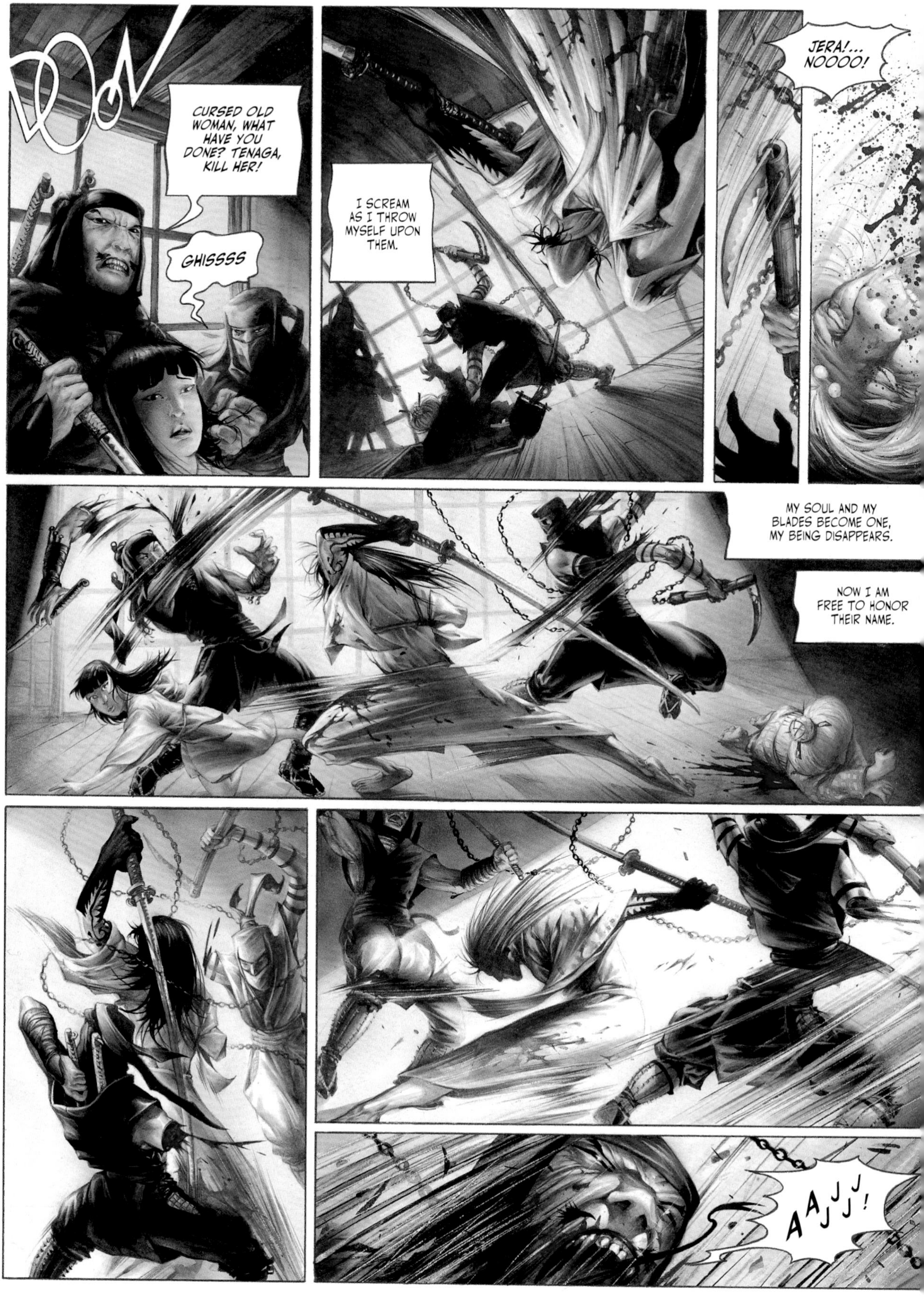
DOOM
CURSED OLD WOMAN, WHAT HAVE YOU DONE? TENAGA, KILL HER!
GHISSSS
I SCREAM AS I THROW MYSELF UPON THEM.
JERA!... NOOOO!
MY SOUL AND MY BLADES BECOME ONE, MY BEING DISAPPEARS.
NOW I AM FREE TO HONOR THEIR NAME.
AAJJJJ!

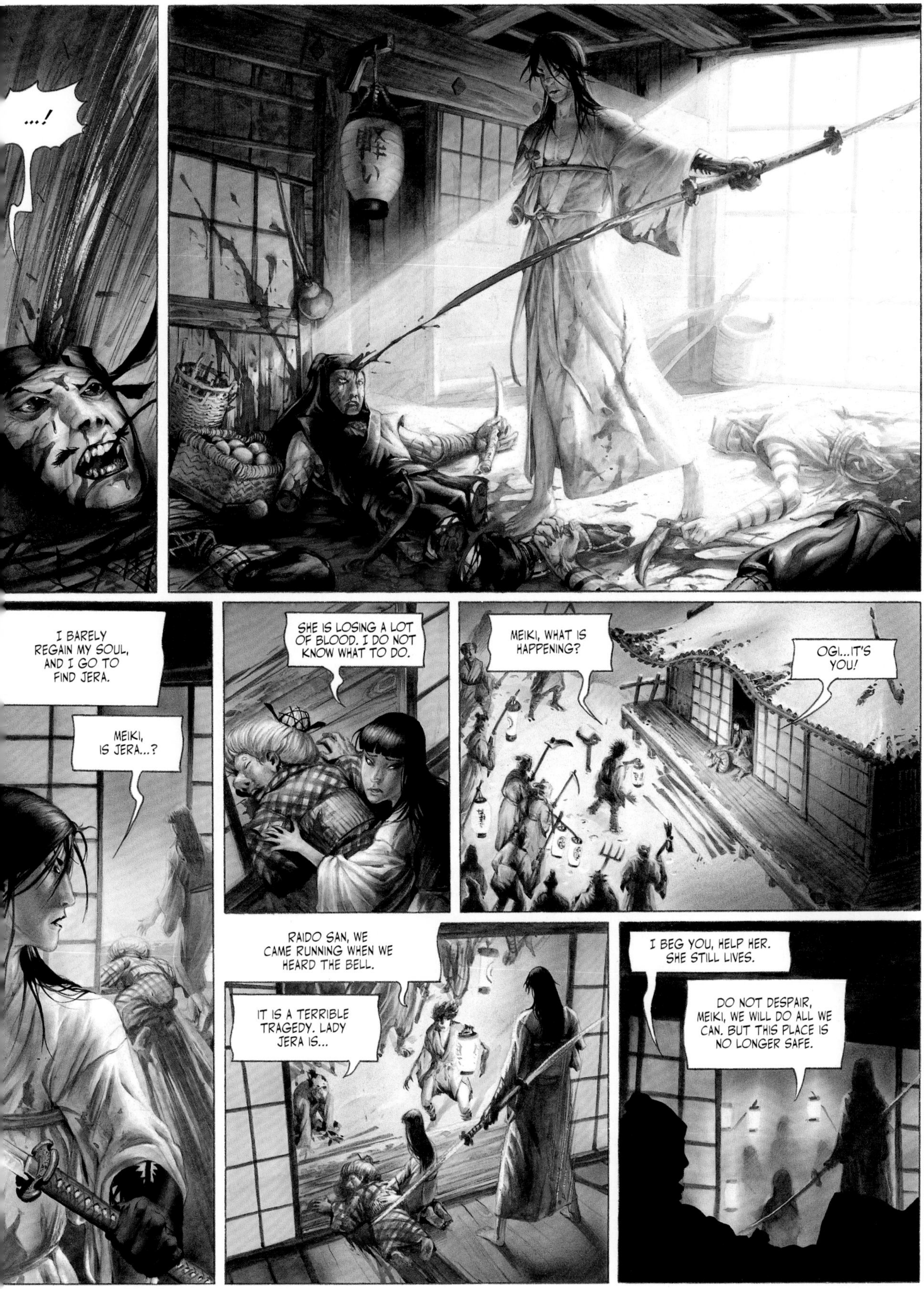
...!
I BARELY REGAIN MY SOUL, AND I GO TO FIND JERA.
MEIKI, IS JERA...?
SHE IS LOSING A LOT OF BLOOD. I DO NOT KNOW WHAT TO DO.
MEIKI, WHAT IS HAPPENING?
OGI...IT'S YOU!
RAIDO SAN, WE CAME RUNNING WHEN WE HEARD THE BELL.
IT IS A TERRIBLE TRAGEDY. LADY JERA IS...
I BEG YOU, HELP HER. SHE STILL LIVES.
DO NOT DESPAIR, MEIKI, WE WILL DO ALL WE CAN. BUT THIS PLACE IS NO LONGER SAFE.

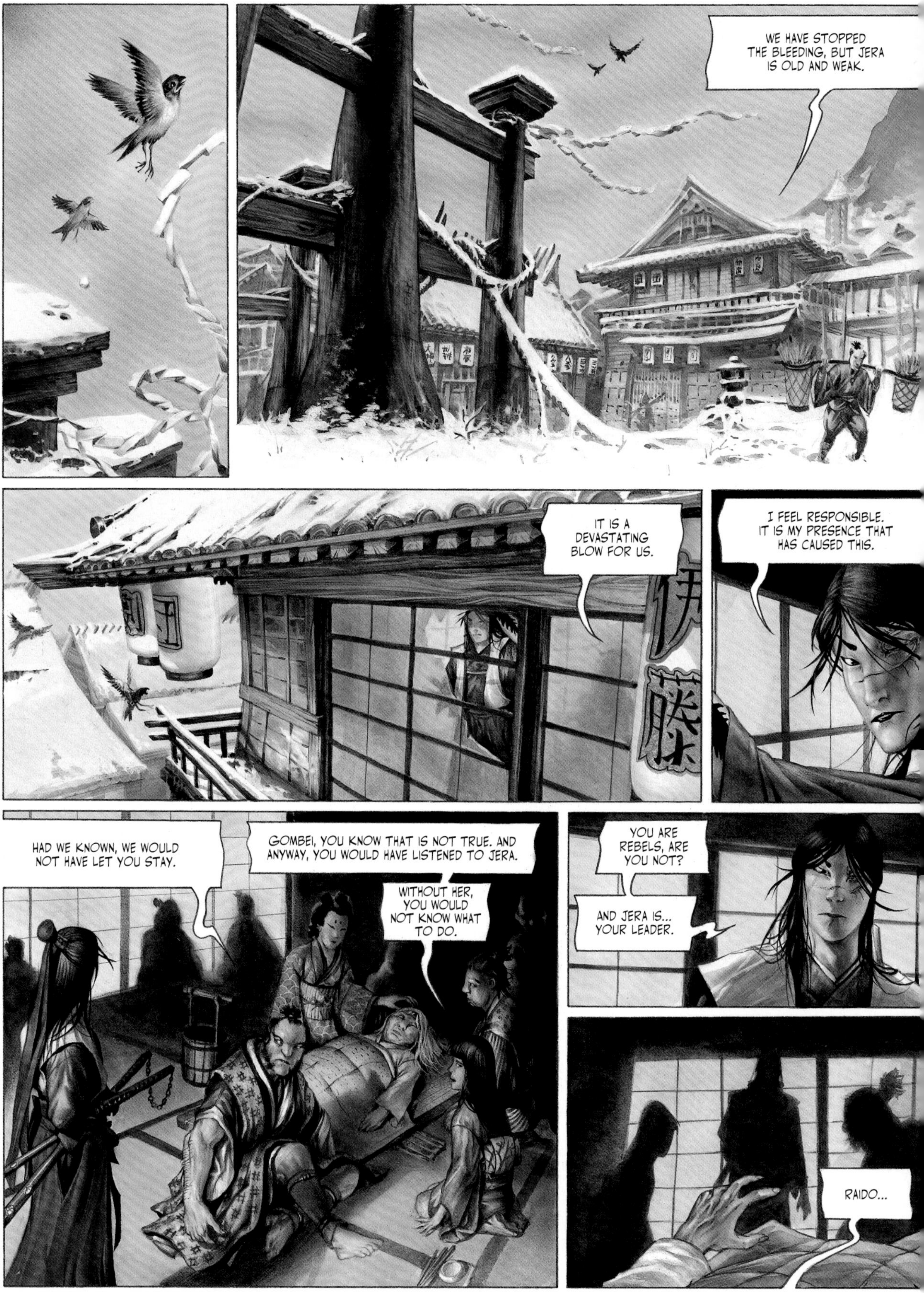
WE HAVE STOPPED THE BLEEDING, BUT JERA IS OLD AND WEAK.
IT IS A DEVASTATING BLOW FOR US.
I FEEL RESPONSIBLE. IT IS MY PRESENCE THAT HAS CAUSED THIS.
HAD WE KNOWN, WE WOULD NOT HAVE LET YOU STAY.
GOMBEI, YOU KNOW THAT IS NOT TRUE. AND ANYWAY, YOU WOULD HAVE LISTENED TO JERA.
WITHOUT HER, YOU WOULD NOT KNOW WHAT TO DO.
YOU ARE REBELS, ARE YOU NOT?
AND JERA IS... YOUR LEADER.
RAIDO...

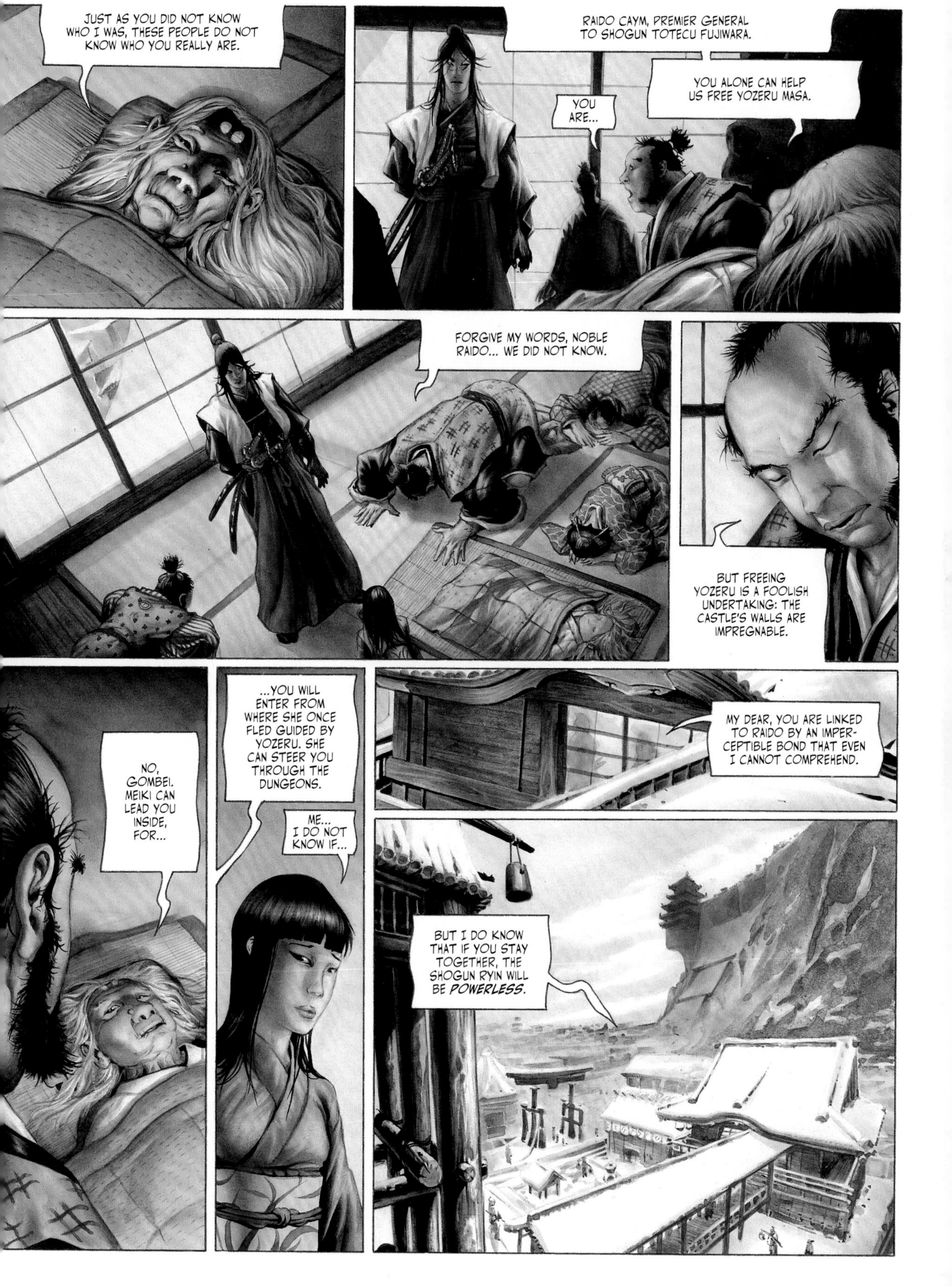
JUST AS YOU DID NOT KNOW WHO I WAS, THESE PEOPLE DO NOT KNOW WHO YOU REALLY ARE.
RAIDO CAYM, PREMIER GENERAL TO SHOGUN TOTECU FUJIWARA.
YOU ARE...
YOU ALONE CAN HELP US FREE YOZERU MASA.
FORGIVE MY WORDS, NOBLE RAIDO... WE DID NOT KNOW.
BUT FREEING YOZERU IS A FOOLISH UNDERTAKING: THE CASTLE'S WALLS ARE IMPREGNABLE.
NO, GOMBEI. MEIKI CAN LEAD YOU INSIDE, FOR...
...YOU WILL ENTER FROM WHERE SHE ONCE FLED GUIDED BY YOZERU. SHE CAN STEER YOU THROUGH THE DUNGEONS.
ME... I DO NOT KNOW IF...
MY DEAR, YOU ARE LINKED TO RAIDO BY AN IMPERCEPTIBLE BOND THAT EVEN I CANNOT COMPREHEND.
BUT I DO KNOW THAT IF YOU STAY TOGETHER, THE SHOGUN RYIN WILL BE *POWERLESS*.

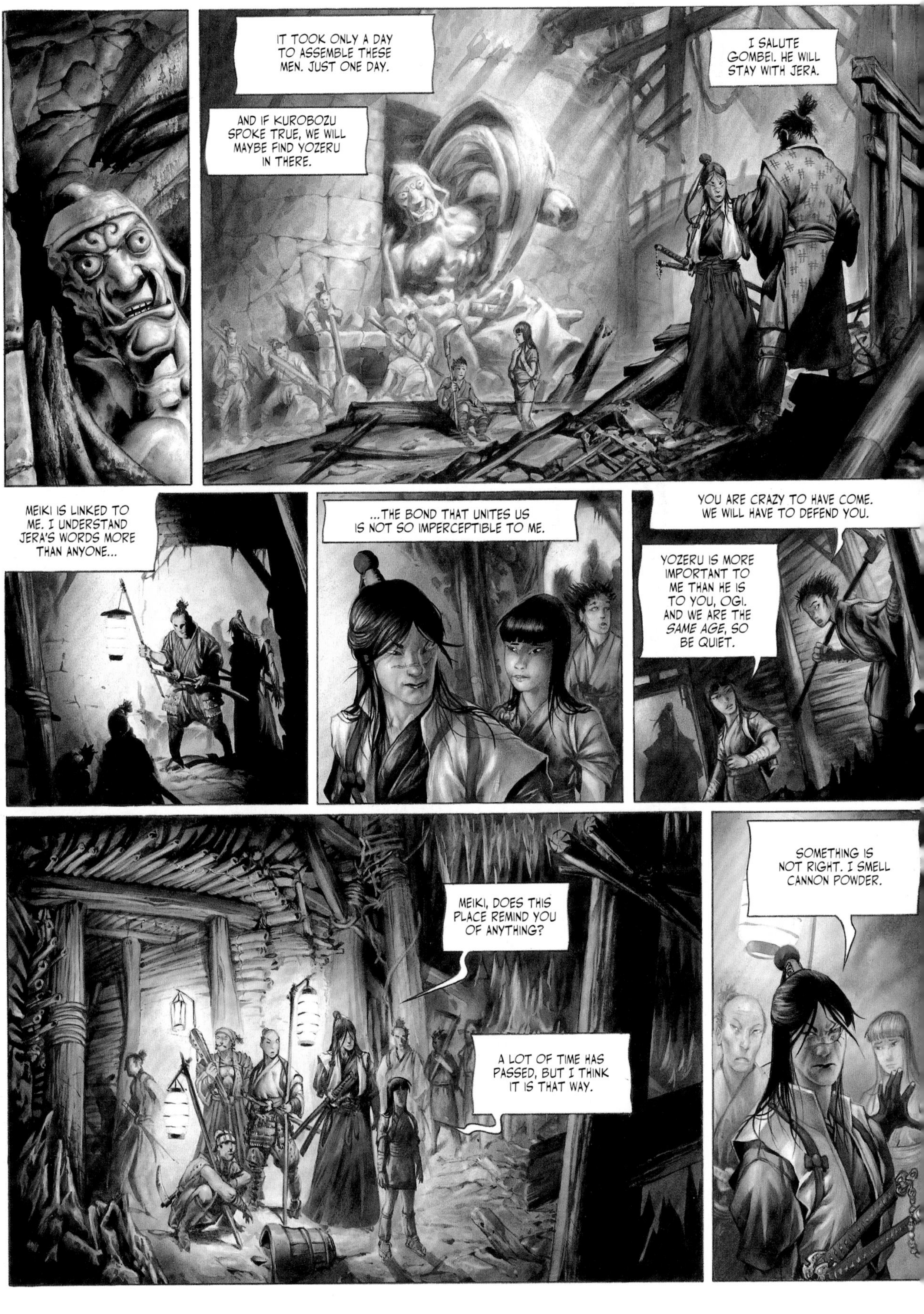

IT TOOK ONLY A DAY TO ASSEMBLE THESE MEN. JUST ONE DAY.
AND IF KUROBOZU SPOKE TRUE, WE WILL MAYBE FIND YOZERU IN THERE.
I SALUTE GOMBEI. HE WILL STAY WITH JERA.
MEIKI IS LINKED TO ME. I UNDERSTAND JERA'S WORDS MORE THAN ANYONE...
...THE BOND THAT UNITES US IS NOT SO IMPERCEPTIBLE TO ME.
YOU ARE CRAZY TO HAVE COME. WE WILL HAVE TO DEFEND YOU.
YOZERU IS MORE IMPORTANT TO ME THAN HE IS TO YOU, OGI. AND WE ARE THE *SAME AGE*, SO BE QUIET.
MEIKI, DOES THIS PLACE REMIND YOU OF ANYTHING?
A LOT OF TIME HAS PASSED, BUT I THINK IT IS THAT WAY.
SOMETHING IS NOT RIGHT. I SMELL CANNON POWDER.

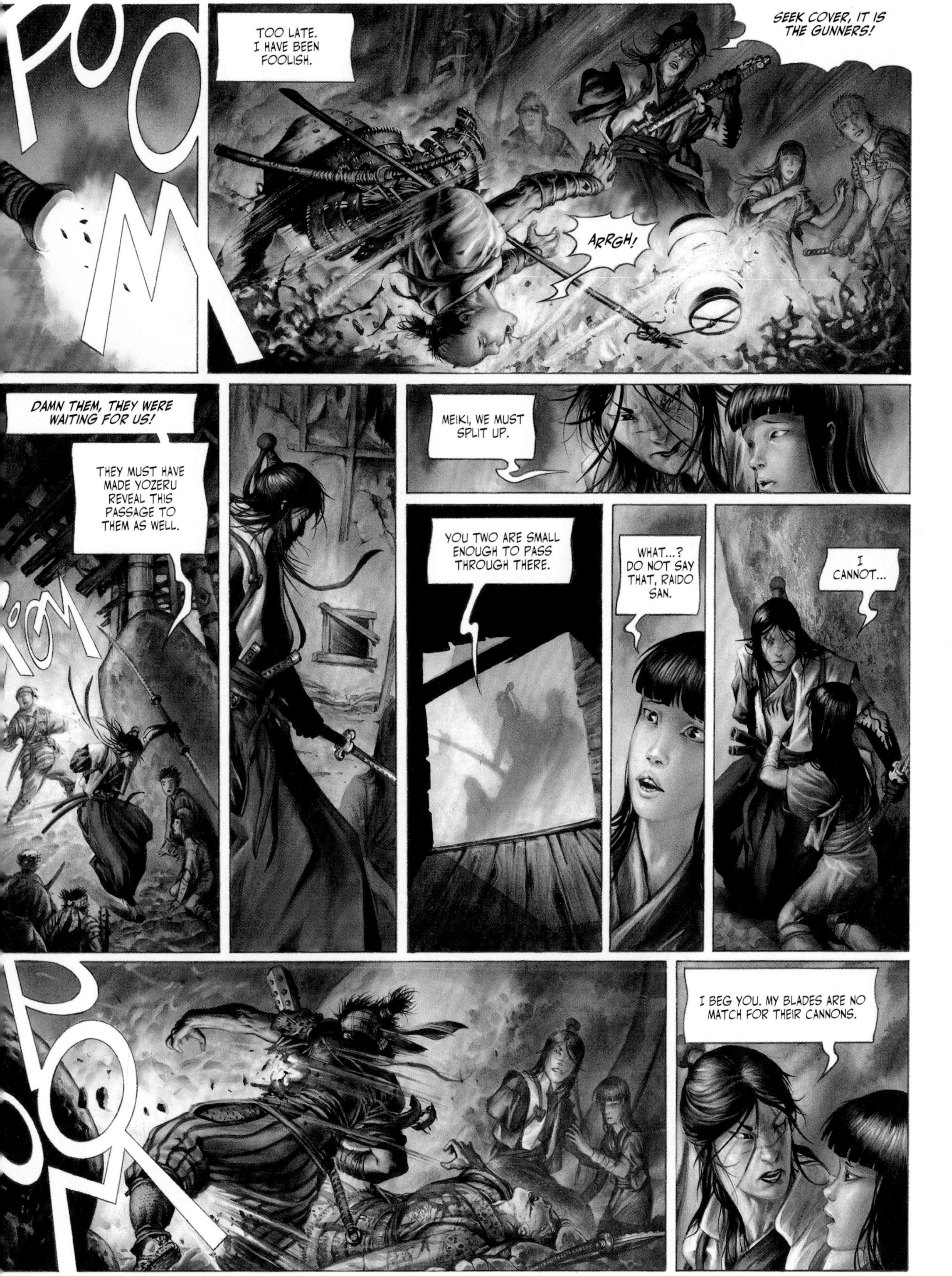
POOM
TOO LATE. I HAVE BEEN FOOLISH.
SEEK COVER, IT IS THE GUNNERS!
ARRGH!
DAMN THEM, THEY WERE WAITING FOR US!
THEY MUST HAVE MADE YOZERU REVEAL THIS PASSAGE TO THEM AS WELL.
MEIKI, WE MUST SPLIT UP.
YOU TWO ARE SMALL ENOUGH TO PASS THROUGH THERE.
WHAT...? DO NOT SAY THAT, RAIDO SAN.
I CANNOT...
I BEG YOU. MY BLADES ARE NO MATCH FOR THEIR CANNONS.

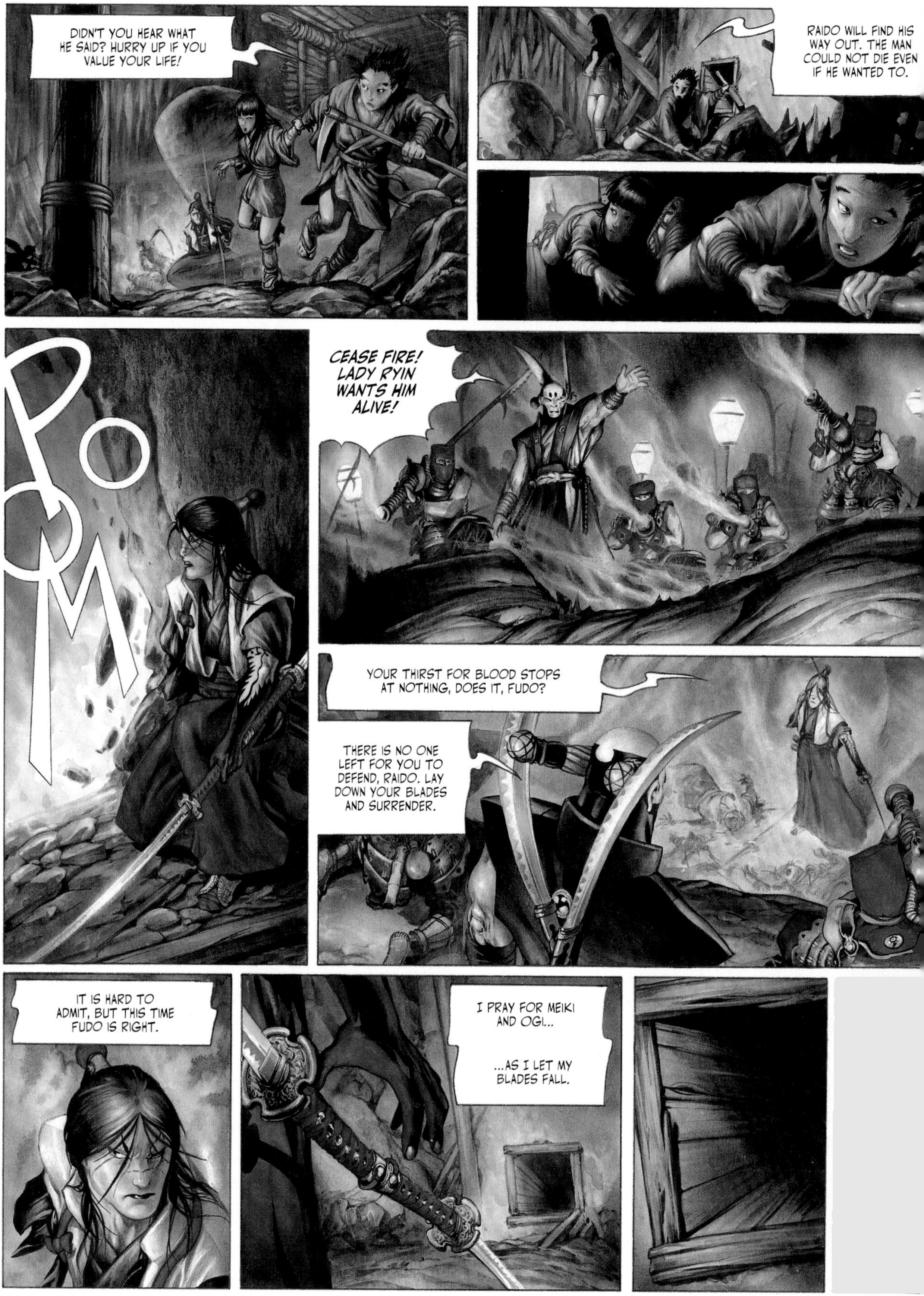
DIDN'T YOU HEAR WHAT HE SAID? HURRY UP IF YOU VALUE YOUR LIFE!
RAIDO WILL FIND HIS WAY OUT. THE MAN COULD NOT DIE EVEN IF HE WANTED TO.
POM
CEASE FIRE! LADY RYIN WANTS HIM ALIVE!
YOUR THIRST FOR BLOOD STOPS AT NOTHING, DOES IT, FUDO?
THERE IS NO ONE LEFT FOR YOU TO DEFEND, RAIDO. LAY DOWN YOUR BLADES AND SURRENDER.
IT IS HARD TO ADMIT, BUT THIS TIME FUDO IS RIGHT.
I PRAY FOR MEIKI AND OGI...
...AS I LET MY BLADES FALL.

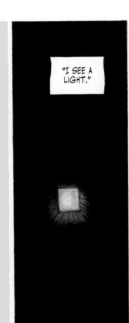

"I SEE A LIGHT."

FINALLY...WE HAVE BEEN CRAWLING IN HERE FOR HOURS. LET US HOPE THAT IS THE EXIT.

THE EXIT? OGI, WE CAME FOR YOZERU, AND WE MUST ALSO HELP RAIDO.

MEIKI, SOMETIMES I GET THE IMPRESSION THAT YOU DO NOT REALIZE...

...AND ANYWAY, IT'S NOT THE EXIT, ARE YOU HAPPY...?!

OUCH!

YIKES! M...MEIKI, IT... IT'S...

DO NOT BE AFRAID, OGI, THEY ARE CHAINED.

IT IS STRANGE... THEY DO NOT SEEM SO TERRIBLE...

BUT THERE... THERE IS A MAN!

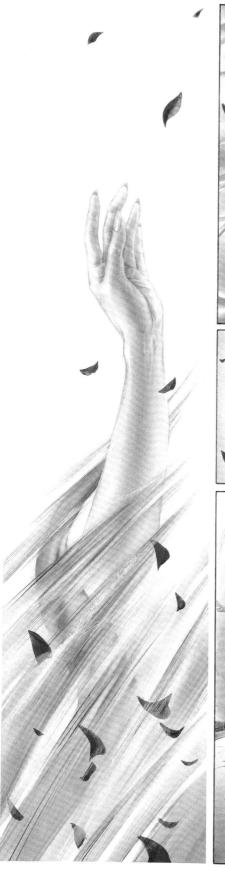

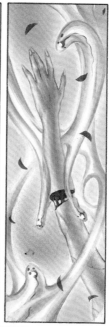

MY LONG WAIT ALREADY FADES INTO MEMORY...

...NOW THAT YOU ARE HERE WITH ME, RAIDO SAN.

IS IT POSSIBLE THAT YOU STILL DO NOT RECOGNIZE ME?

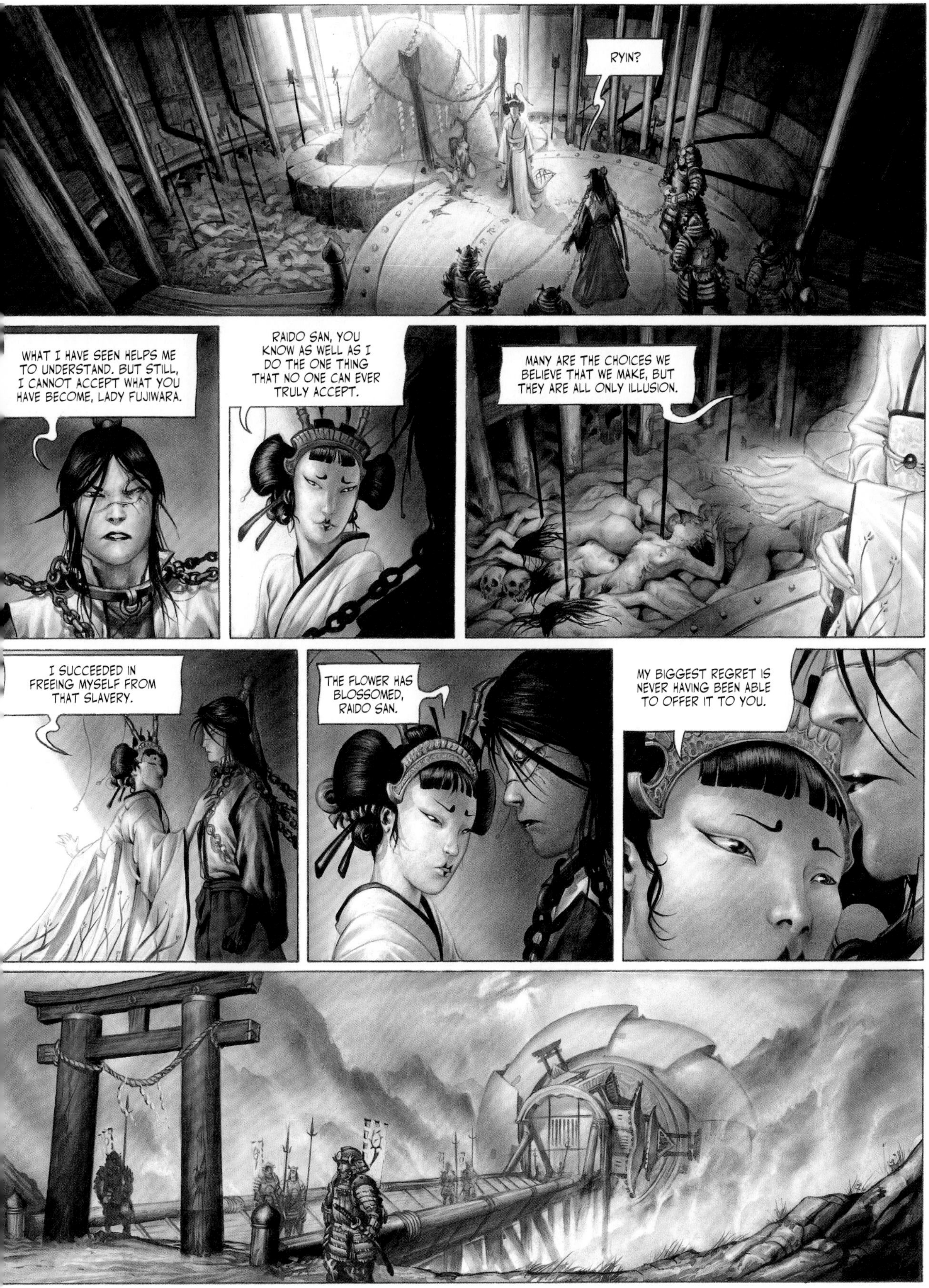
RYIN?
WHAT I HAVE SEEN HELPS ME TO UNDERSTAND. BUT STILL, I CANNOT ACCEPT WHAT YOU HAVE BECOME, LADY FUJIWARA.
RAIDO SAN, YOU KNOW AS WELL AS I DO THE ONE THING THAT NO ONE CAN EVER TRULY ACCEPT.
MANY ARE THE CHOICES WE BELIEVE THAT WE MAKE, BUT THEY ARE ALL ONLY ILLUSION.
I SUCCEEDED IN FREEING MYSELF FROM THAT SLAVERY.
THE FLOWER HAS BLOSSOMED, RAIDO SAN.
MY BIGGEST REGRET IS NEVER HAVING BEEN ABLE TO OFFER IT TO YOU.

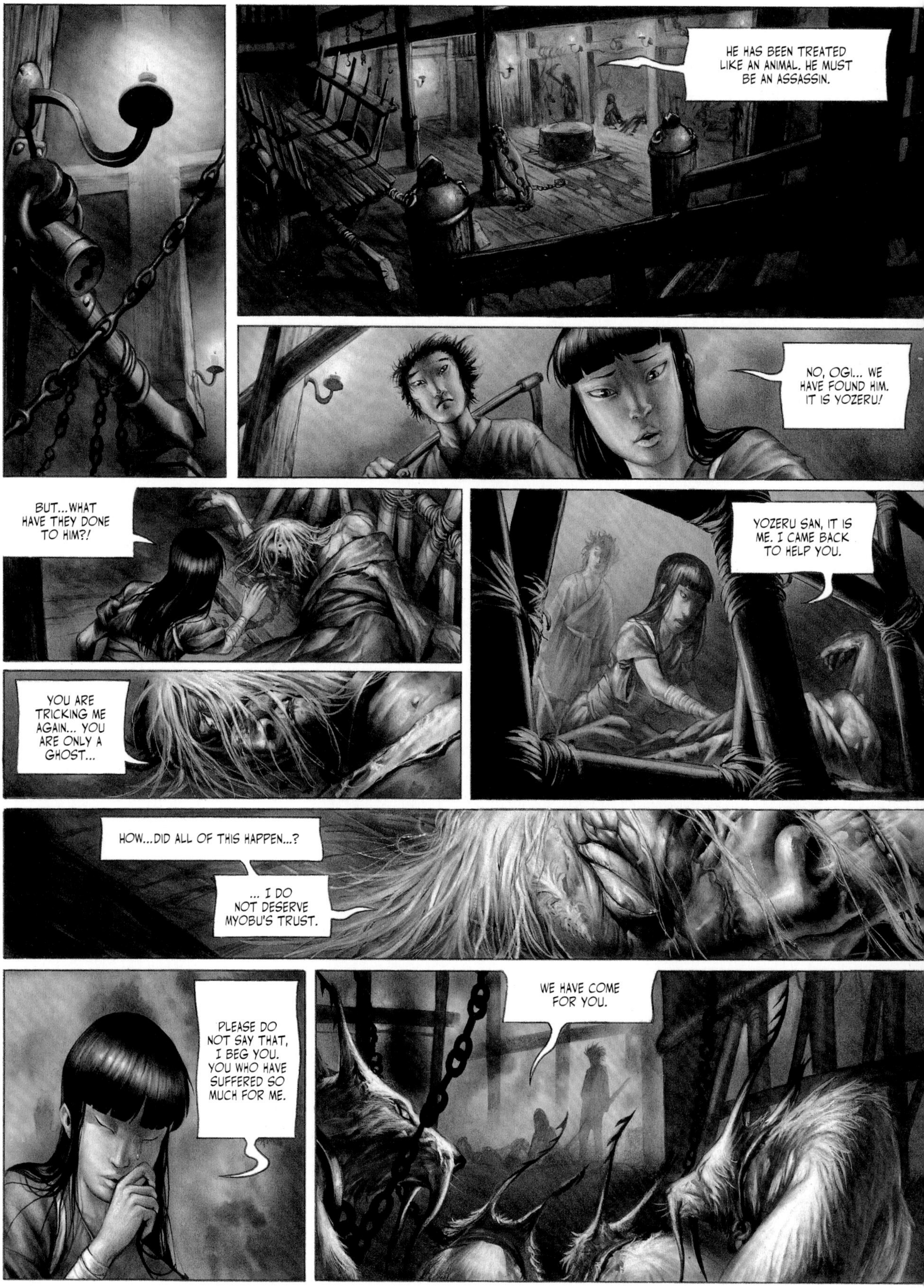
HE HAS BEEN TREATED LIKE AN ANIMAL. HE MUST BE AN ASSASSIN.
NO, OGI... WE HAVE FOUND HIM. IT IS YOZERU!
BUT...WHAT HAVE THEY DONE TO HIM?!
YOU ARE TRICKING ME AGAIN... YOU ARE ONLY A GHOST...
YOZERU SAN, IT IS ME. I CAME BACK TO HELP YOU.
HOW...DID ALL OF THIS HAPPEN...?
... I DO NOT DESERVE MYOBU'S TRUST.
PLEASE DO NOT SAY THAT, I BEG YOU. YOU WHO HAVE SUFFERED SO MUCH FOR ME.
WE HAVE COME FOR YOU.

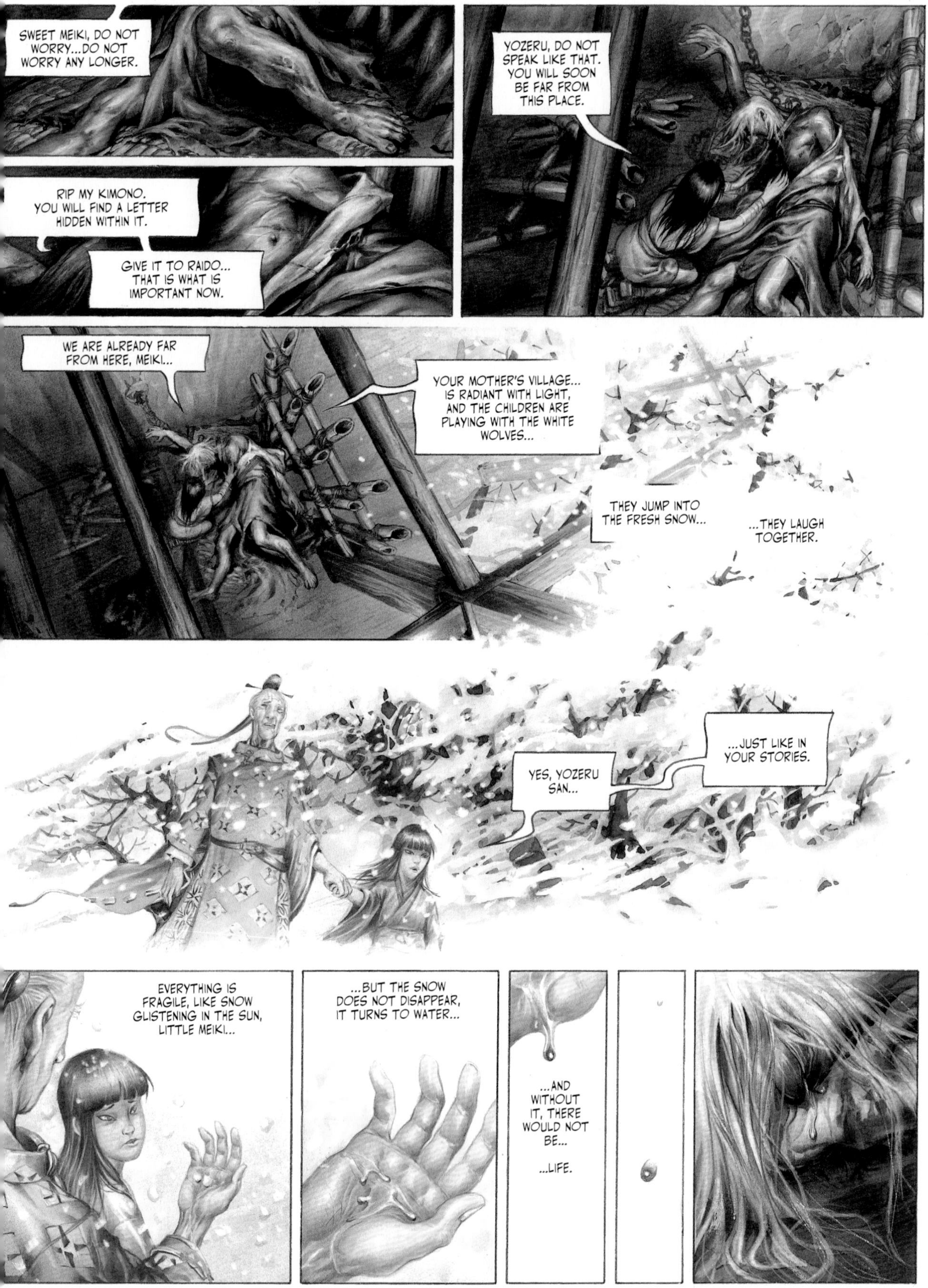
SWEET MEIKI, DO NOT WORRY...DO NOT WORRY ANY LONGER.
YOZERU, DO NOT SPEAK LIKE THAT. YOU WILL SOON BE FAR FROM THIS PLACE.
RIP MY KIMONO. YOU WILL FIND A LETTER HIDDEN WITHIN IT.
GIVE IT TO RAIDO... THAT IS WHAT IS IMPORTANT NOW.
WE ARE ALREADY FAR FROM HERE, MEIKI...
YOUR MOTHER'S VILLAGE... IS RADIANT WITH LIGHT, AND THE CHILDREN ARE PLAYING WITH THE WHITE WOLVES...
THEY JUMP INTO THE FRESH SNOW...
...THEY LAUGH TOGETHER.
YES, YOZERU SAN...
...JUST LIKE IN YOUR STORIES.
EVERYTHING IS FRAGILE, LIKE SNOW GLISTENING IN THE SUN, LITTLE MEIKI...
...BUT THE SNOW DOES NOT DISAPPEAR, IT TURNS TO WATER...
...AND WITHOUT IT, THERE WOULD NOT BE...
...LIFE.

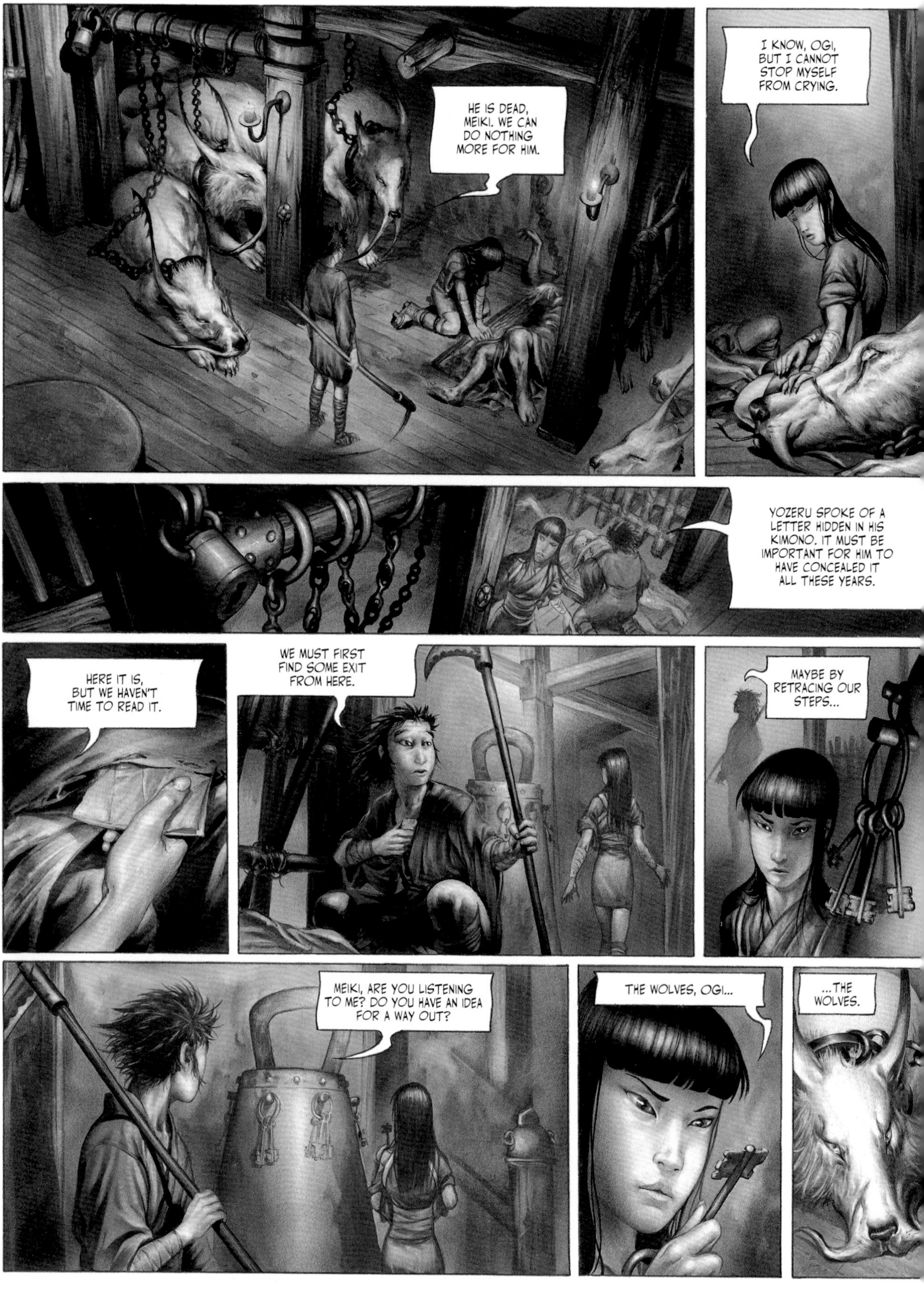
HE IS DEAD, MEIKI. WE CAN DO NOTHING MORE FOR HIM.
I KNOW, OGI, BUT I CANNOT STOP MYSELF FROM CRYING.
YOZERU SPOKE OF A LETTER HIDDEN IN HIS KIMONO. IT MUST BE IMPORTANT FOR HIM TO HAVE CONCEALED IT ALL THESE YEARS.
HERE IT IS, BUT WE HAVEN'T TIME TO READ IT.
WE MUST FIRST FIND SOME EXIT FROM HERE.
MAYBE BY RETRACING OUR STEPS...
MEIKI, ARE YOU LISTENING TO ME? DO YOU HAVE AN IDEA FOR A WAY OUT?
THE WOLVES, OGI...
...THE WOLVES.

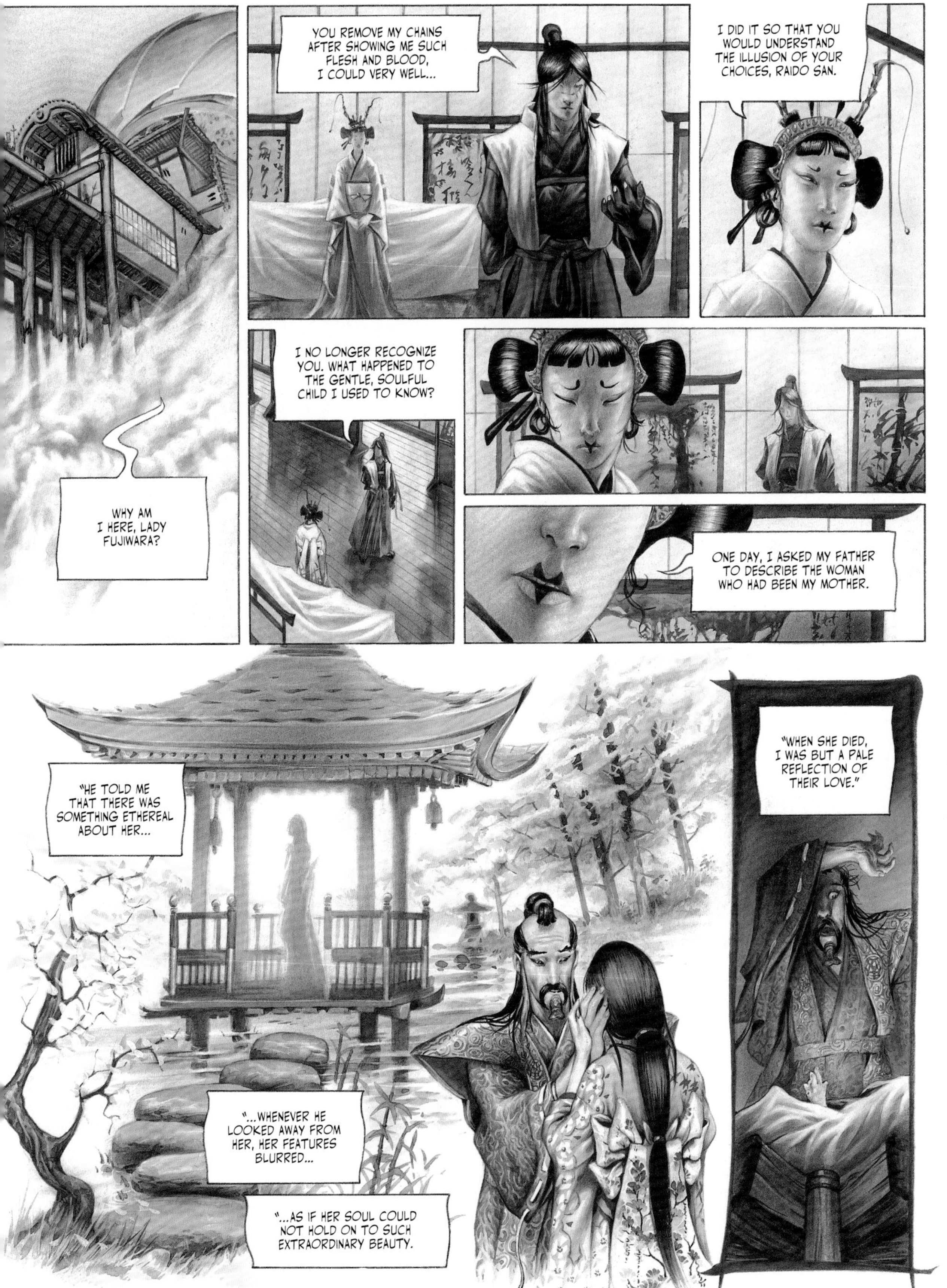
WHY AM I HERE, LADY FUJIWARA?
YOU REMOVE MY CHAINS AFTER SHOWING ME SUCH FLESH AND BLOOD, I COULD VERY WELL...
I DID IT SO THAT YOU WOULD UNDERSTAND THE ILLUSION OF YOUR CHOICES, RAIDO SAN.
I NO LONGER RECOGNIZE YOU. WHAT HAPPENED TO THE GENTLE, SOULFUL CHILD I USED TO KNOW?
ONE DAY, I ASKED MY FATHER TO DESCRIBE THE WOMAN WHO HAD BEEN MY MOTHER.
"HE TOLD ME THAT THERE WAS SOMETHING ETHEREAL ABOUT HER...
"...WHENEVER HE LOOKED AWAY FROM HER, HER FEATURES BLURRED...
"...AS IF HER SOUL COULD NOT HOLD ON TO SUCH EXTRAORDINARY BEAUTY.
"WHEN SHE DIED, I WAS BUT A PALE REFLECTION OF THEIR LOVE."

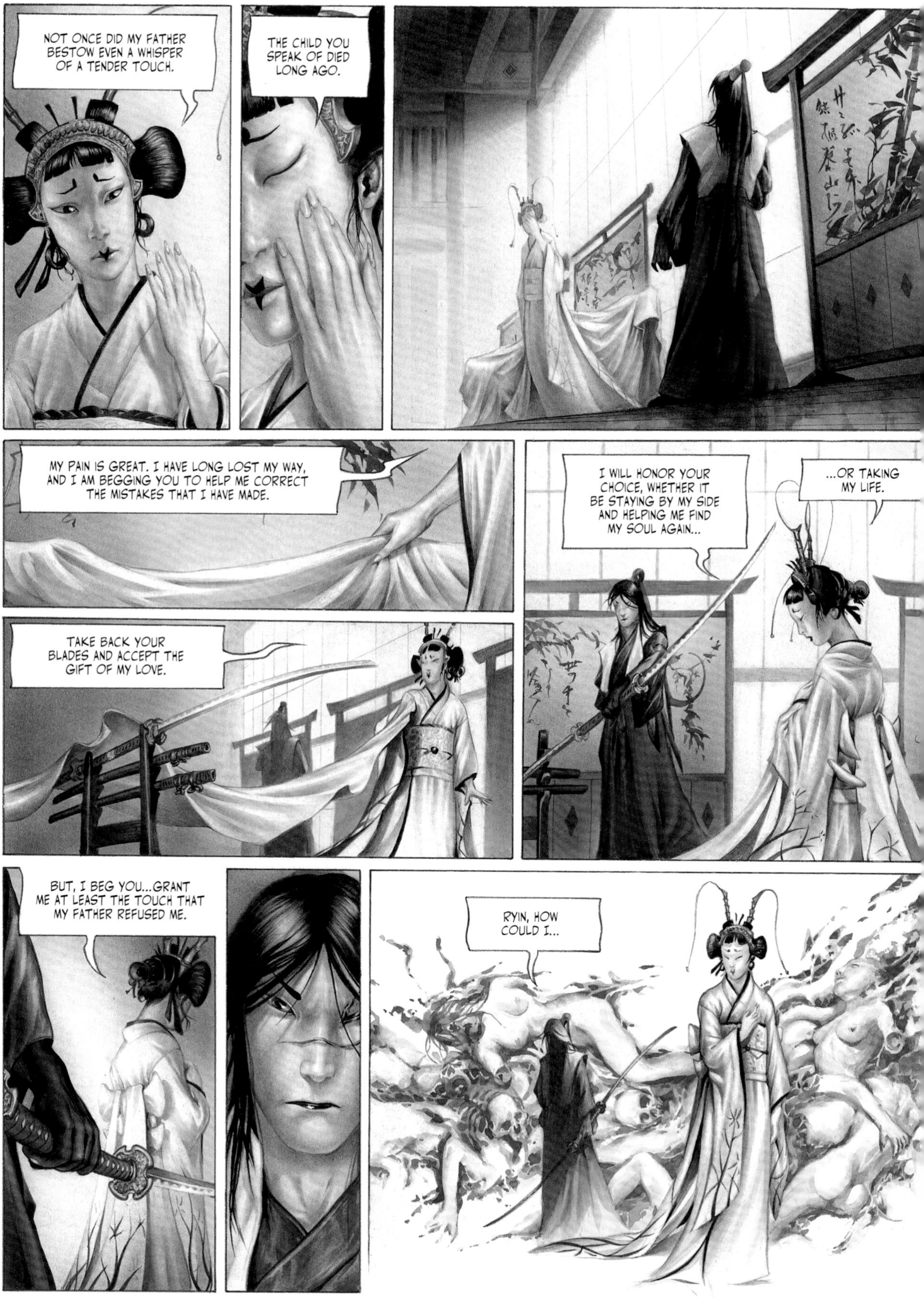
NOT ONCE DID MY FATHER BESTOW EVEN A WHISPER OF A TENDER TOUCH.
THE CHILD YOU SPEAK OF DIED LONG AGO.
MY PAIN IS GREAT. I HAVE LONG LOST MY WAY, AND I AM BEGGING YOU TO HELP ME CORRECT THE MISTAKES THAT I HAVE MADE.
TAKE BACK YOUR BLADES AND ACCEPT THE GIFT OF MY LOVE.
I WILL HONOR YOUR CHOICE, WHETHER IT BE STAYING BY MY SIDE AND HELPING ME FIND MY SOUL AGAIN...
...OR TAKING MY LIFE.
BUT, I BEG YOU...GRANT ME AT LEAST THE TOUCH THAT MY FATHER REFUSED ME.
RYIN, HOW COULD I...

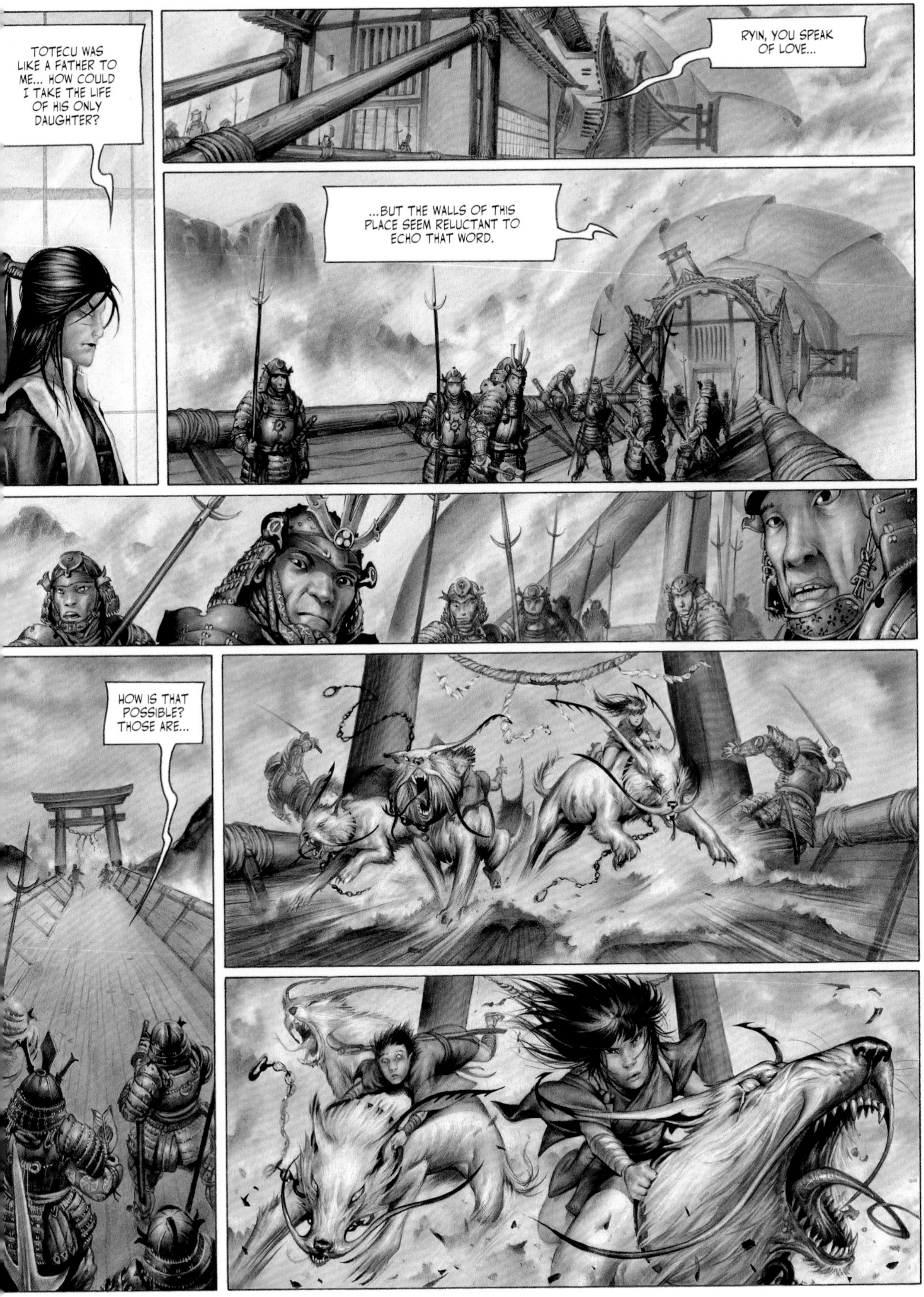
TOTECU WAS LIKE A FATHER TO ME... HOW COULD I TAKE THE LIFE OF HIS ONLY DAUGHTER?
RYIN, YOU SPEAK OF LOVE...
...BUT THE WALLS OF THIS PLACE SEEM RELUCTANT TO ECHO THAT WORD.
HOW IS THAT POSSIBLE? THOSE ARE...

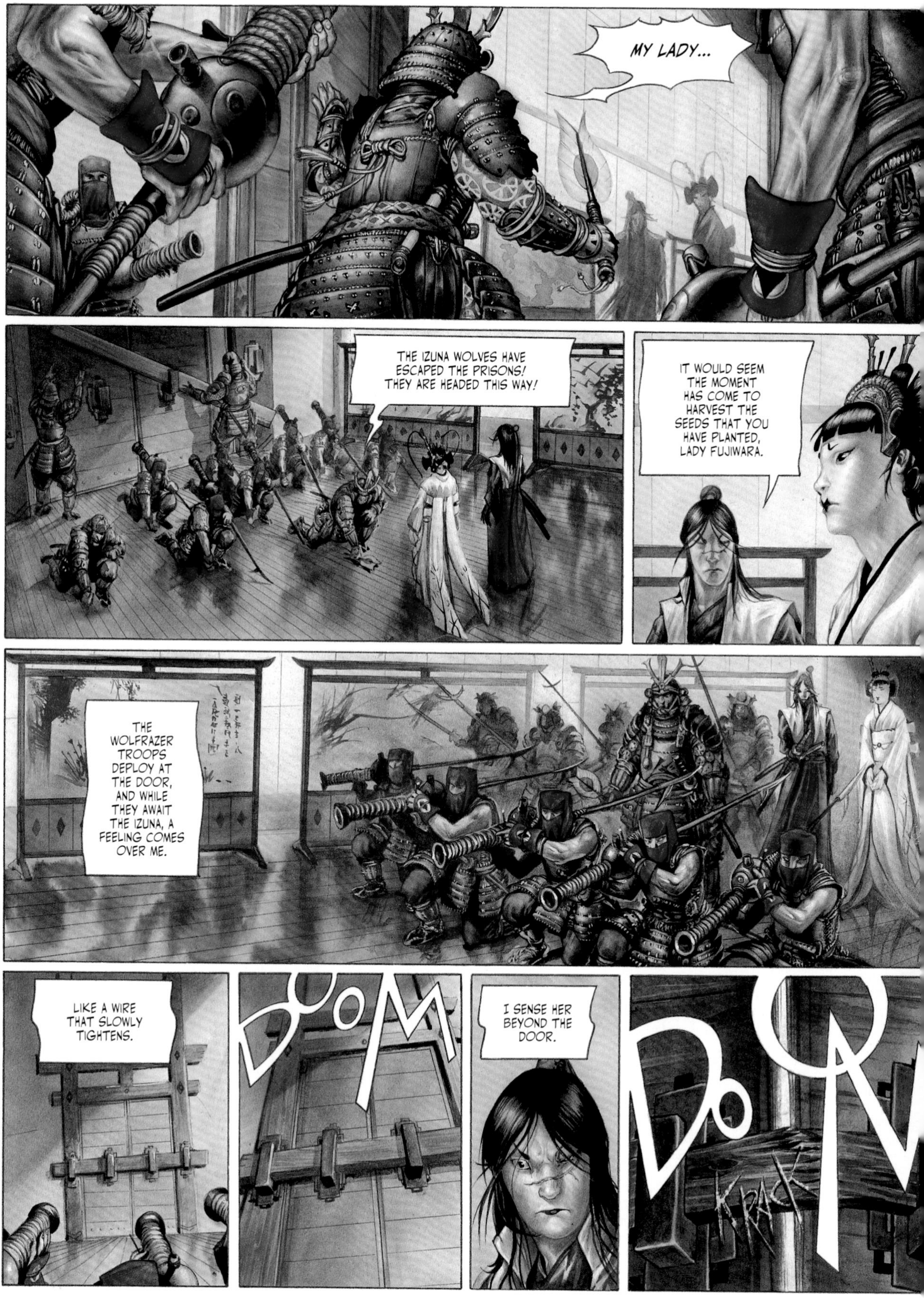
MY LADY...
THE IZUNA WOLVES HAVE ESCAPED THE PRISONS! THEY ARE HEADED THIS WAY!
IT WOULD SEEM THE MOMENT HAS COME TO HARVEST THE SEEDS THAT YOU HAVE PLANTED, LADY FUJIWARA.
THE WOLFRAZER TROOPS DEPLOY AT THE DOOR, AND WHILE THEY AWAIT THE IZUNA, A FEELING COMES OVER ME.
LIKE A WIRE THAT SLOWLY TIGHTENS.
DOOM
I SENSE HER BEYOND THE DOOR.
DOOM
KRACK

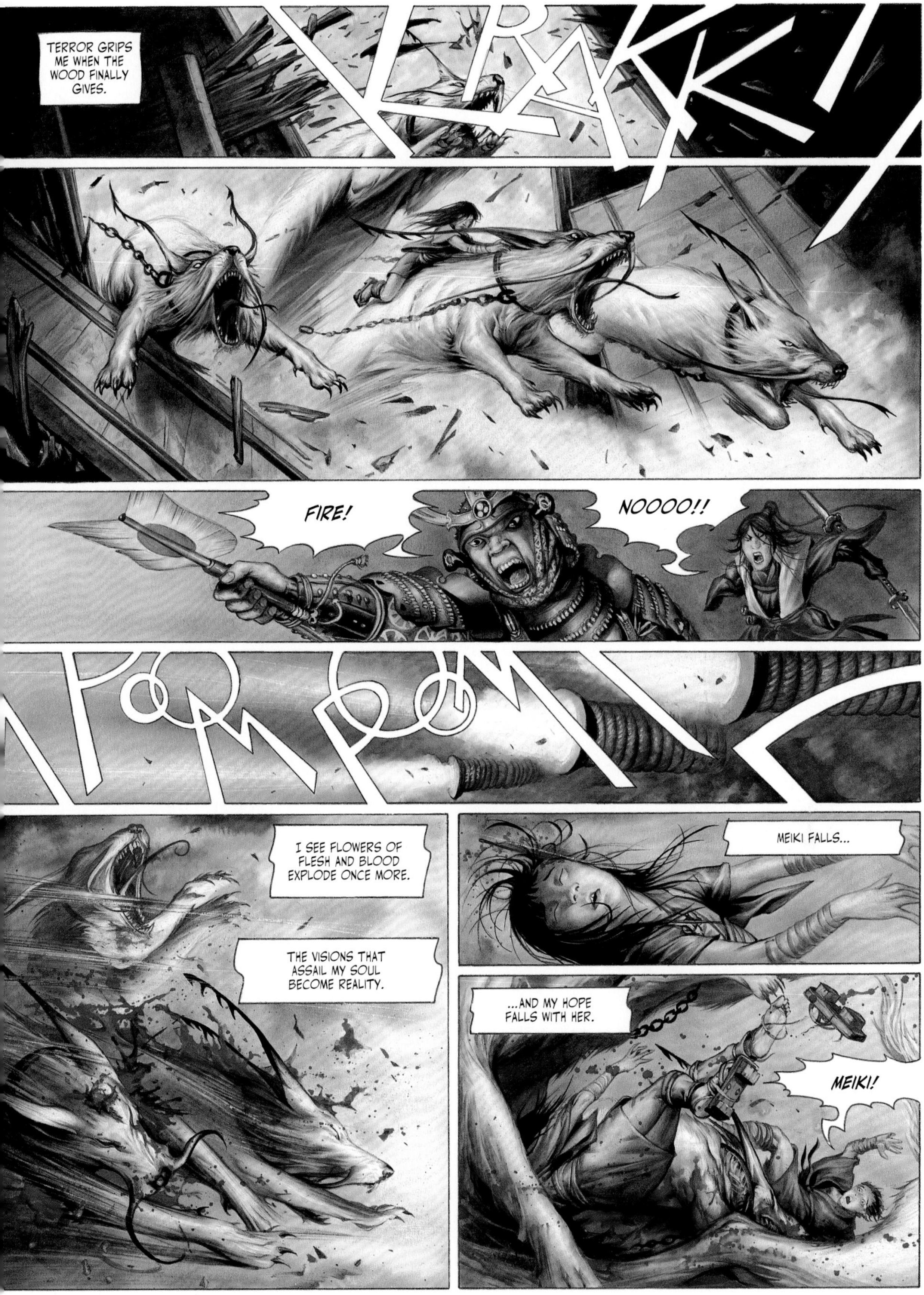
TERROR GRIPS ME WHEN THE WOOD FINALLY GIVES.
FIRE!
NOOOO!!
I SEE FLOWERS OF FLESH AND BLOOD EXPLODE ONCE MORE.
THE VISIONS THAT ASSAIL MY SOUL BECOME REALITY.
MEIKI FALLS...
...AND MY HOPE FALLS WITH HER.
MEIKI!

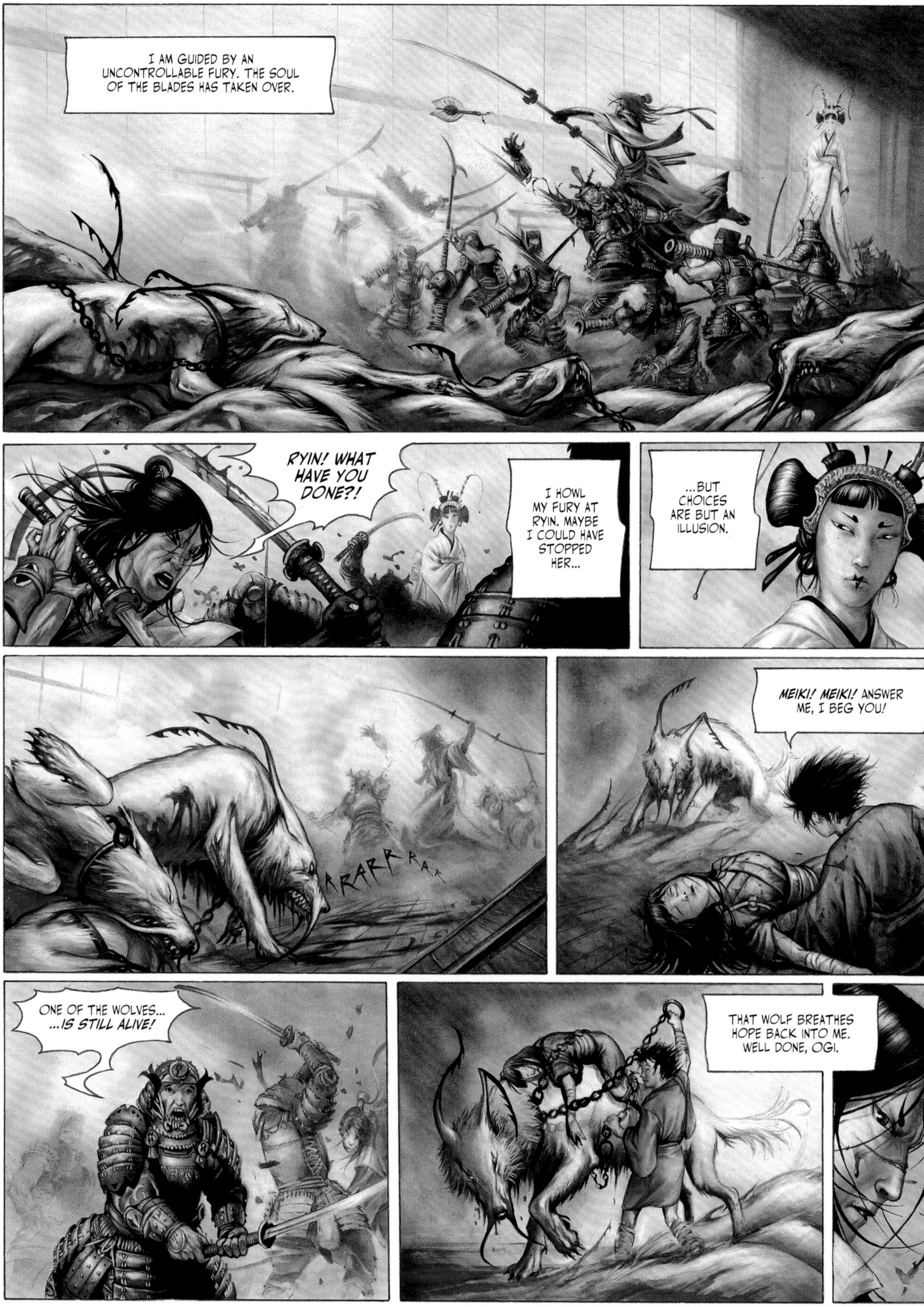
I AM GUIDED BY AN UNCONTROLLABLE FURY. THE SOUL OF THE BLADES HAS TAKEN OVER.
RYIN! WHAT HAVE YOU DONE?!
I HOWL MY FURY AT RYIN. MAYBE I COULD HAVE STOPPED HER...
...BUT CHOICES ARE BUT AN ILLUSION.
RRARRRRRAA
MEIKI! MEIKI! ANSWER ME, I BEG YOU!
ONE OF THE WOLVES... ...IS STILL ALIVE!
THAT WOLF BREATHES HOPE BACK INTO ME. WELL DONE, OGI.

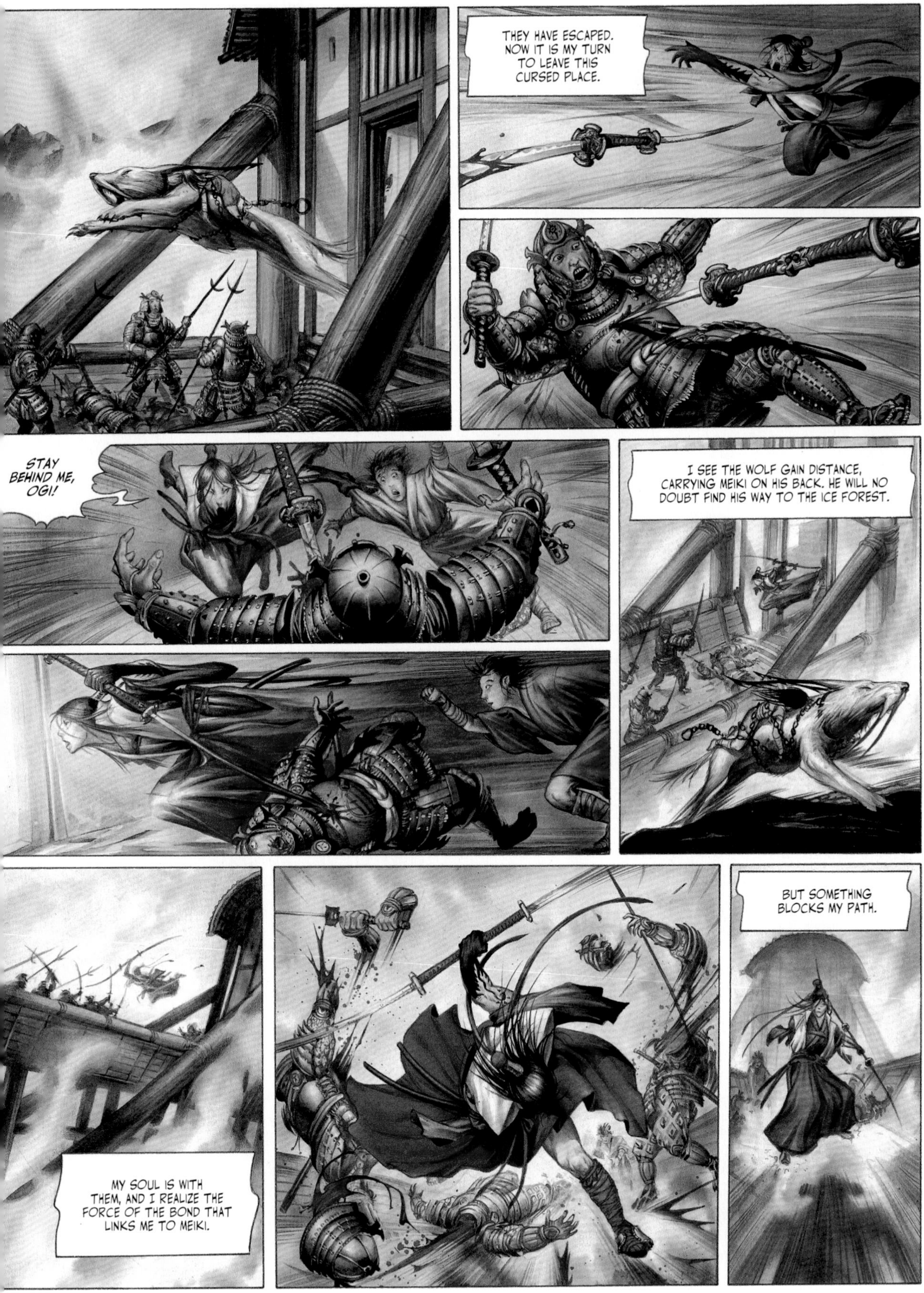
THEY HAVE ESCAPED. NOW IT IS MY TURN TO LEAVE THIS CURSED PLACE.
STAY BEHIND ME, OGI!
I SEE THE WOLF GAIN DISTANCE, CARRYING MEIKI ON HIS BACK. HE WILL NO DOUBT FIND HIS WAY TO THE ICE FOREST.
MY SOUL IS WITH THEM, AND I REALIZE THE FORCE OF THE BOND THAT LINKS ME TO MEIKI.
BUT SOMETHING BLOCKS MY PATH.

YOU ARE NOT *DESERVING* OF THE RESPECT THAT LADY RYIN HAS SHOWN YOU!

FUDO HAS FINALLY FOUND HIS OPPORTUNITY.

TO VANQUISH ME, HE WILL NOT BATTLE HONORABLY...

...HE USES MY OWN ARM AGAINST ME.

I AM DISCONCERTED.

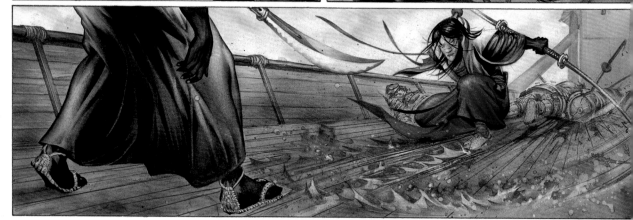

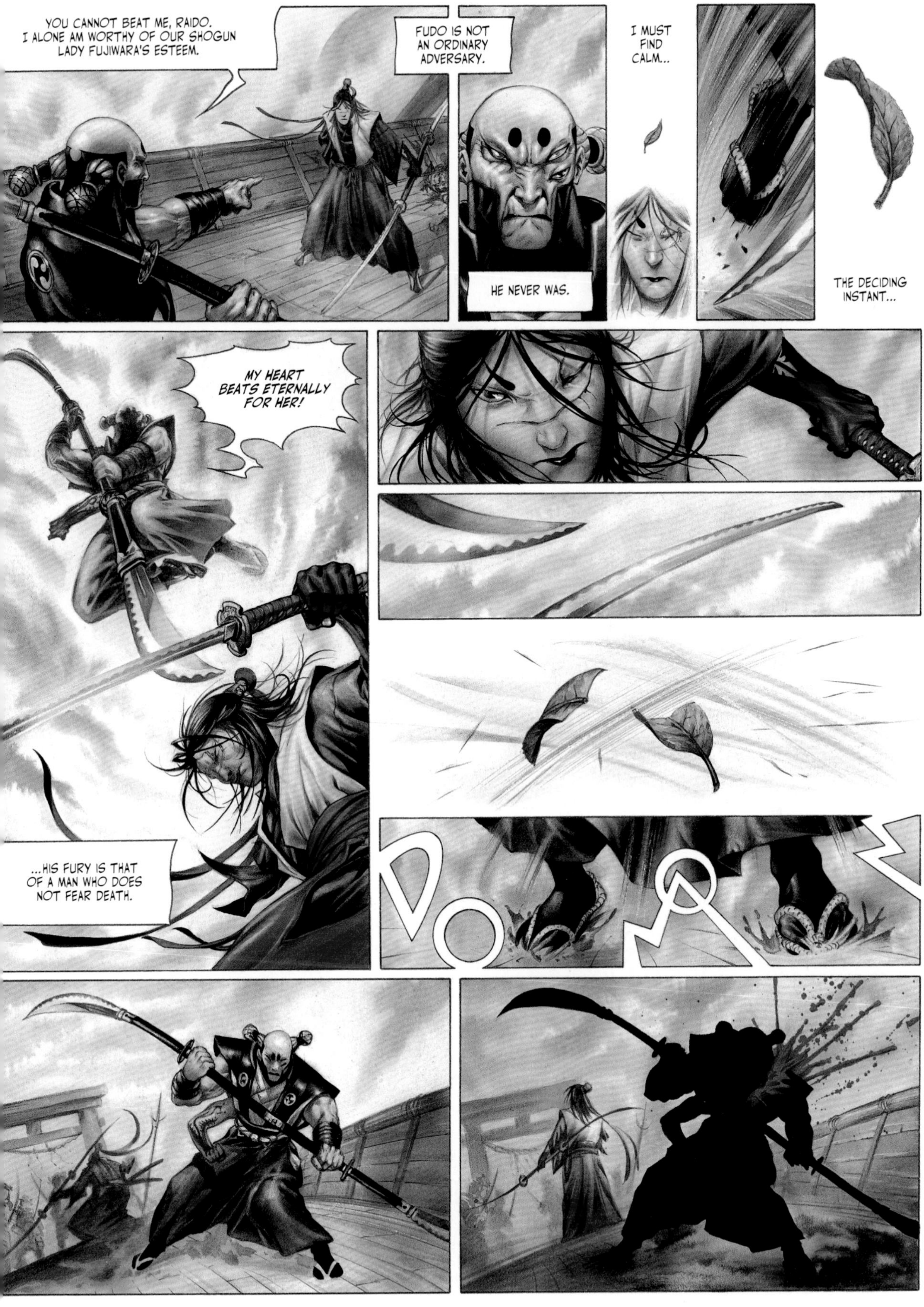

YOU CANNOT BEAT ME, RAIDO. I ALONE AM WORTHY OF OUR SHOGUN LADY FUJIWARA'S ESTEEM.
FUDO IS NOT AN ORDINARY ADVERSARY.
HE NEVER WAS.
I MUST FIND CALM...
THE DECIDING INSTANT...
MY HEART BEATS ETERNALLY FOR HER!
...HIS FURY IS THAT OF A MAN WHO DOES NOT FEAR DEATH.
DOM

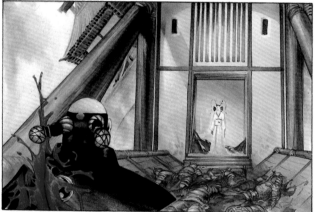

A PROFOUND
SILENCE REMAINS AFTER
FUDO'S DEATH.

THE SOLDIERS
NO LONGER MOVE
TO ATTACK ME.

BEFORE I LEAVE,
I TAKE ONE LAST
LOOK AT RYIN.

FOR AN INSTANT,
I SEE IN HER EYES THE
CHILD SHE ONCE WAS.

NO ONE DARES
TO STOP ME
AS I LEAVE
WITH OGI.

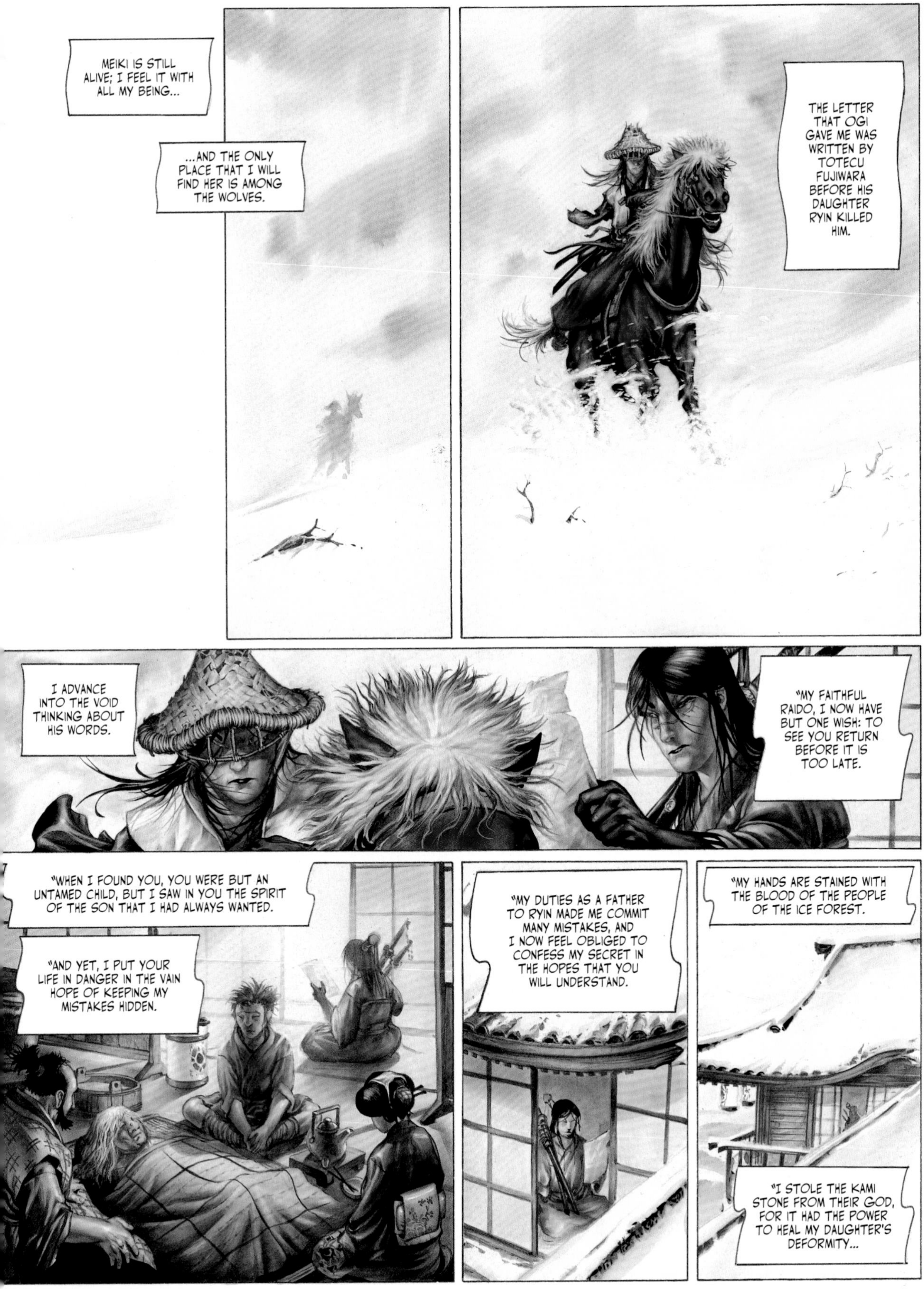
MEIKI IS STILL ALIVE; I FEEL IT WITH ALL MY BEING...
...AND THE ONLY PLACE THAT I WILL FIND HER IS AMONG THE WOLVES.
THE LETTER THAT OGI GAVE ME WAS WRITTEN BY TOTECU FUJIWARA BEFORE HIS DAUGHTER RYIN KILLED HIM.
I ADVANCE INTO THE VOID THINKING ABOUT HIS WORDS.
"MY FAITHFUL RAIDO, I NOW HAVE BUT ONE WISH: TO SEE YOU RETURN BEFORE IT IS TOO LATE.
"WHEN I FOUND YOU, YOU WERE BUT AN UNTAMED CHILD, BUT I SAW IN YOU THE SPIRIT OF THE SON THAT I HAD ALWAYS WANTED.
"AND YET, I PUT YOUR LIFE IN DANGER IN THE VAIN HOPE OF KEEPING MY MISTAKES HIDDEN.
"MY DUTIES AS A FATHER TO RYIN MADE ME COMMIT MANY MISTAKES, AND I NOW FEEL OBLIGED TO CONFESS MY SECRET IN THE HOPES THAT YOU WILL UNDERSTAND.
"MY HANDS ARE STAINED WITH THE BLOOD OF THE PEOPLE OF THE ICE FOREST.
"I STOLE THE KAMI STONE FROM THEIR GOD, FOR IT HAD THE POWER TO HEAL MY DAUGHTER'S DEFORMITY...

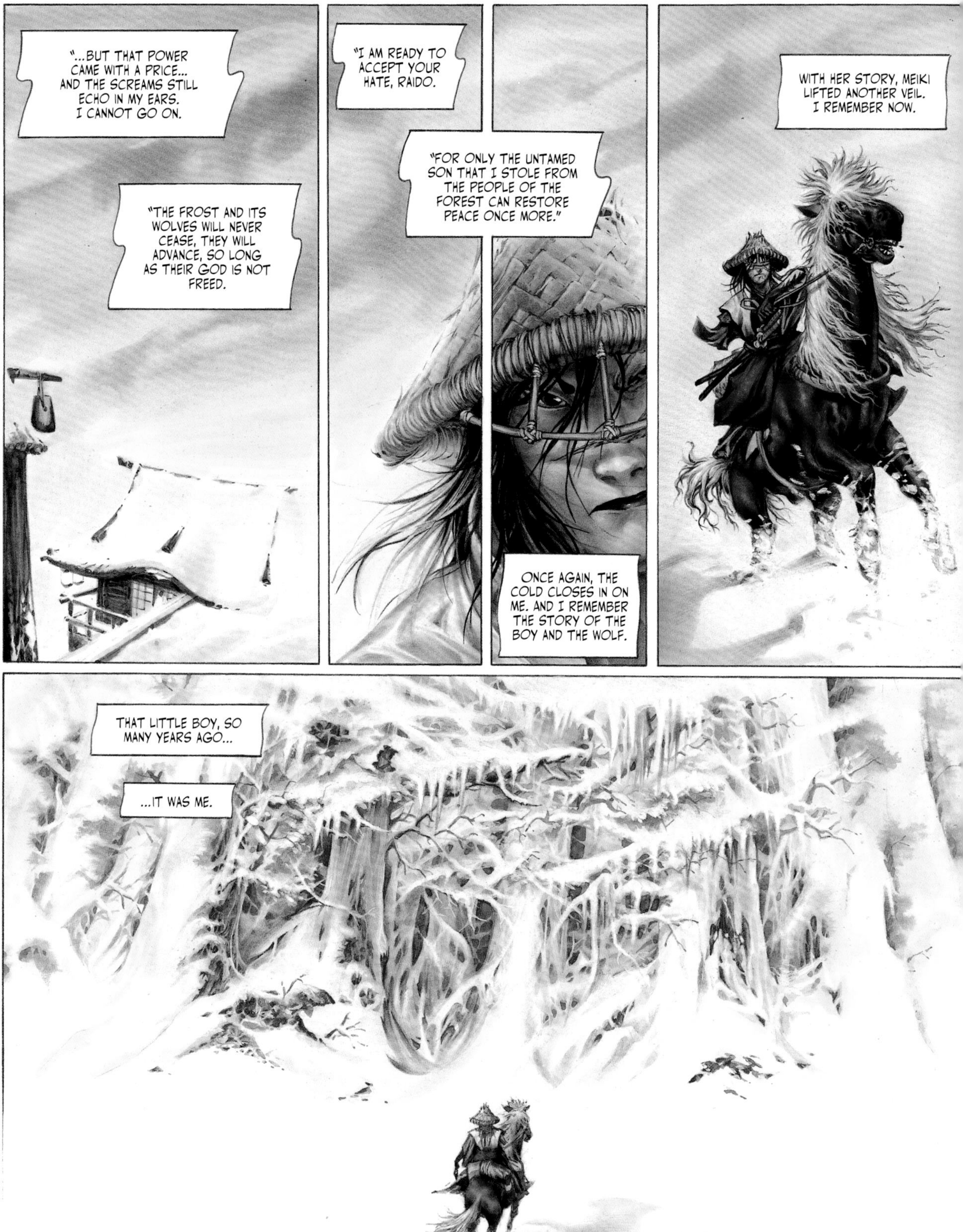
"...BUT THAT POWER CAME WITH A PRICE... AND THE SCREAMS STILL ECHO IN MY EARS. I CANNOT GO ON.
"THE FROST AND ITS WOLVES WILL NEVER CEASE, THEY WILL ADVANCE, SO LONG AS THEIR GOD IS NOT FREED.
"I AM READY TO ACCEPT YOUR HATE, RAIDO.
"FOR ONLY THE UNTAMED SON THAT I STOLE FROM THE PEOPLE OF THE FOREST CAN RESTORE PEACE ONCE MORE."
ONCE AGAIN, THE COLD CLOSES IN ON ME. AND I REMEMBER THE STORY OF THE BOY AND THE WOLF.
WITH HER STORY, MEIKI LIFTED ANOTHER VEIL. I REMEMBER NOW.
THAT LITTLE BOY, SO MANY YEARS AGO...
...IT WAS ME.

CHAPTER THREE:

The Perfect Stroke

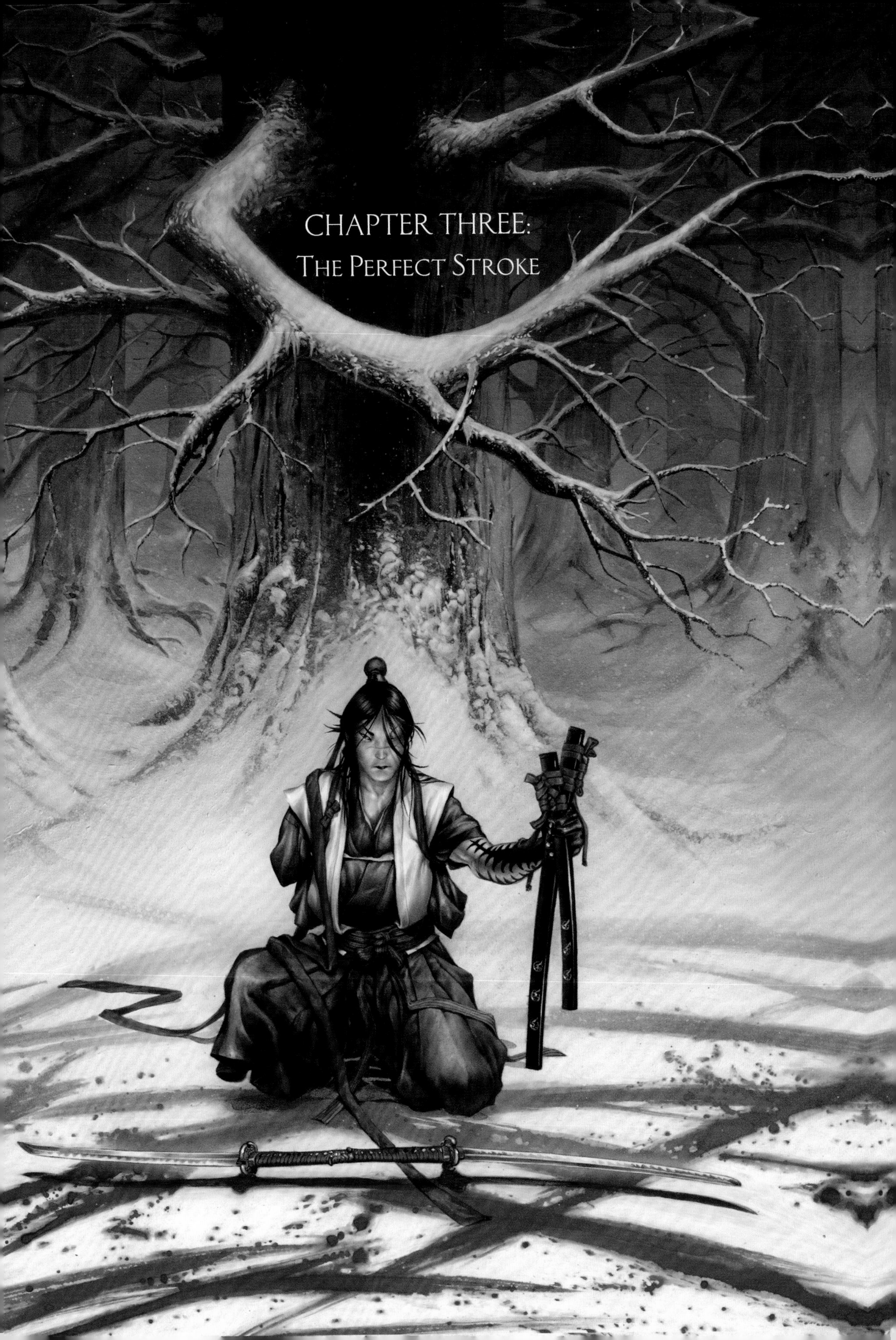

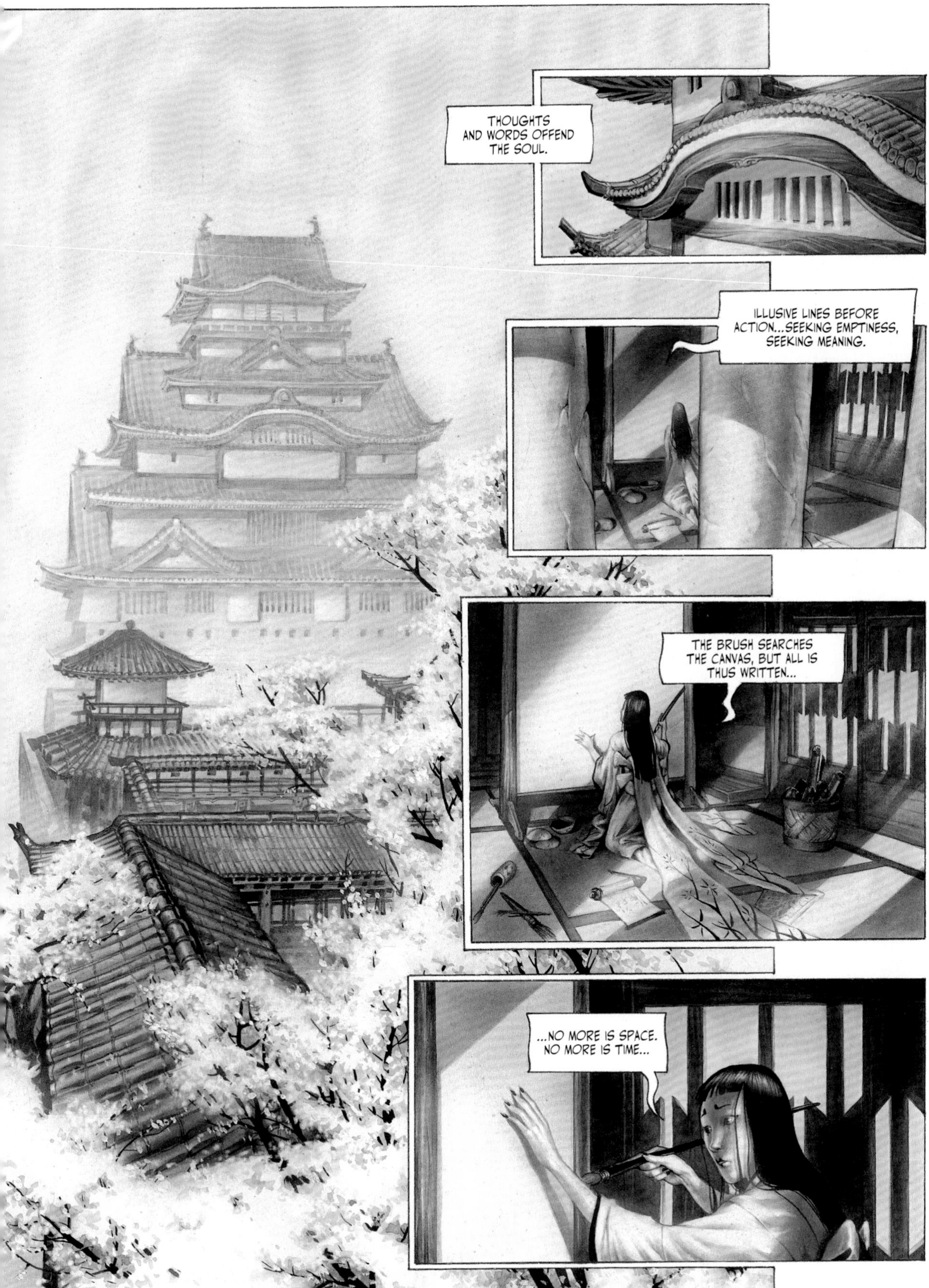
THOUGHTS AND WORDS OFFEND THE SOUL.
ILLUSIVE LINES BEFORE ACTION...SEEKING EMPTINESS, SEEKING MEANING.
THE BRUSH SEARCHES THE CANVAS, BUT ALL IS THUS WRITTEN...
...NO MORE IS SPACE. NO MORE IS TIME...

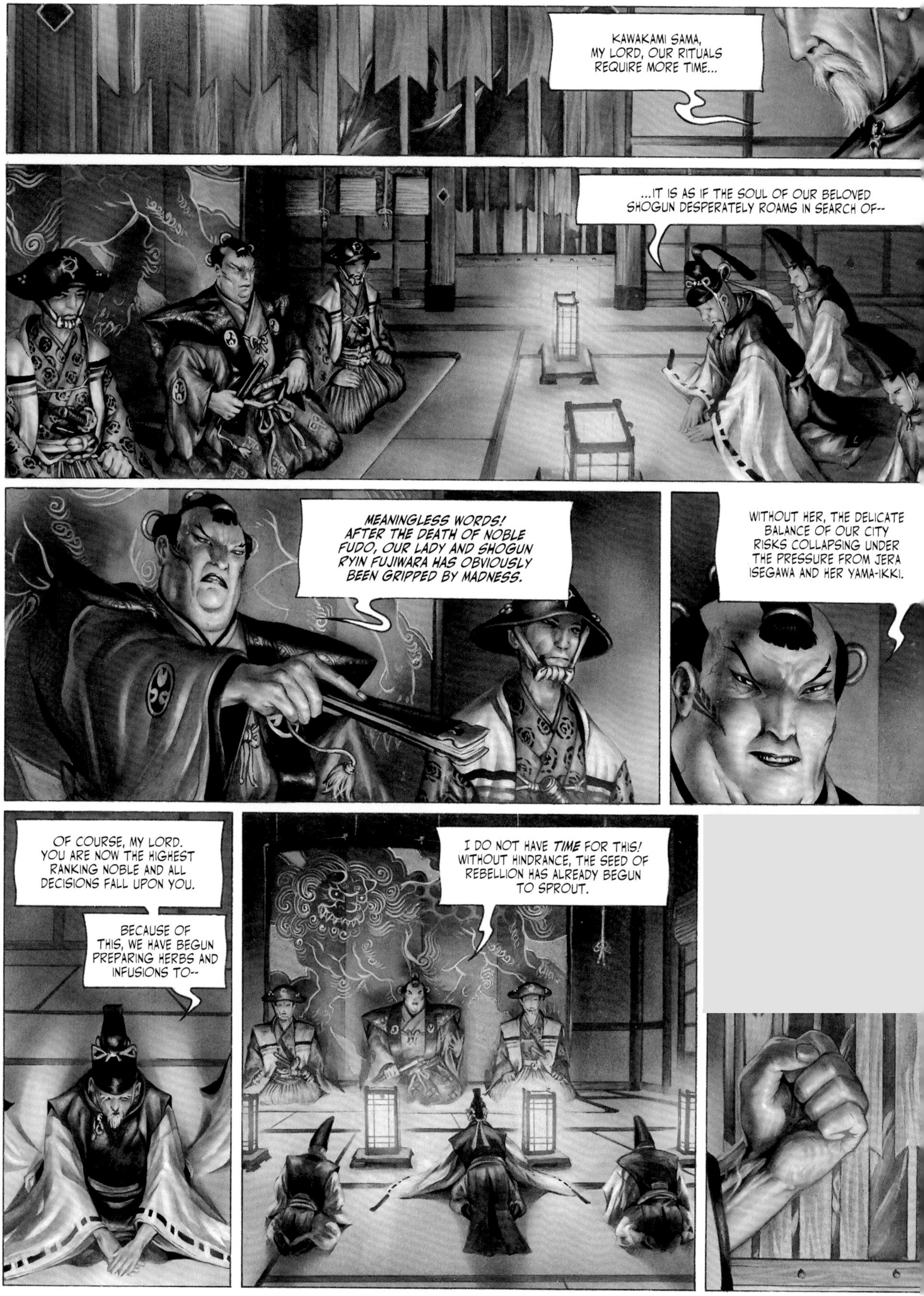
KAWAKAMI SAMA, MY LORD, OUR RITUALS REQUIRE MORE TIME...
...IT IS AS IF THE SOUL OF OUR BELOVED SHOGUN DESPERATELY ROAMS IN SEARCH OF--
MEANINGLESS WORDS! AFTER THE DEATH OF NOBLE FUDO, OUR LADY AND SHOGUN RYIN FUJIWARA HAS OBVIOUSLY BEEN GRIPPED BY MADNESS.
WITHOUT HER, THE DELICATE BALANCE OF OUR CITY RISKS COLLAPSING UNDER THE PRESSURE FROM JERA ISEGAWA AND HER YAMA-IKKI.
OF COURSE, MY LORD. YOU ARE NOW THE HIGHEST RANKING NOBLE AND ALL DECISIONS FALL UPON YOU.
BECAUSE OF THIS, WE HAVE BEGUN PREPARING HERBS AND INFUSIONS TO--
I DO NOT HAVE TIME FOR THIS! WITHOUT HINDRANCE, THE SEED OF REBELLION HAS ALREADY BEGUN TO SPROUT.

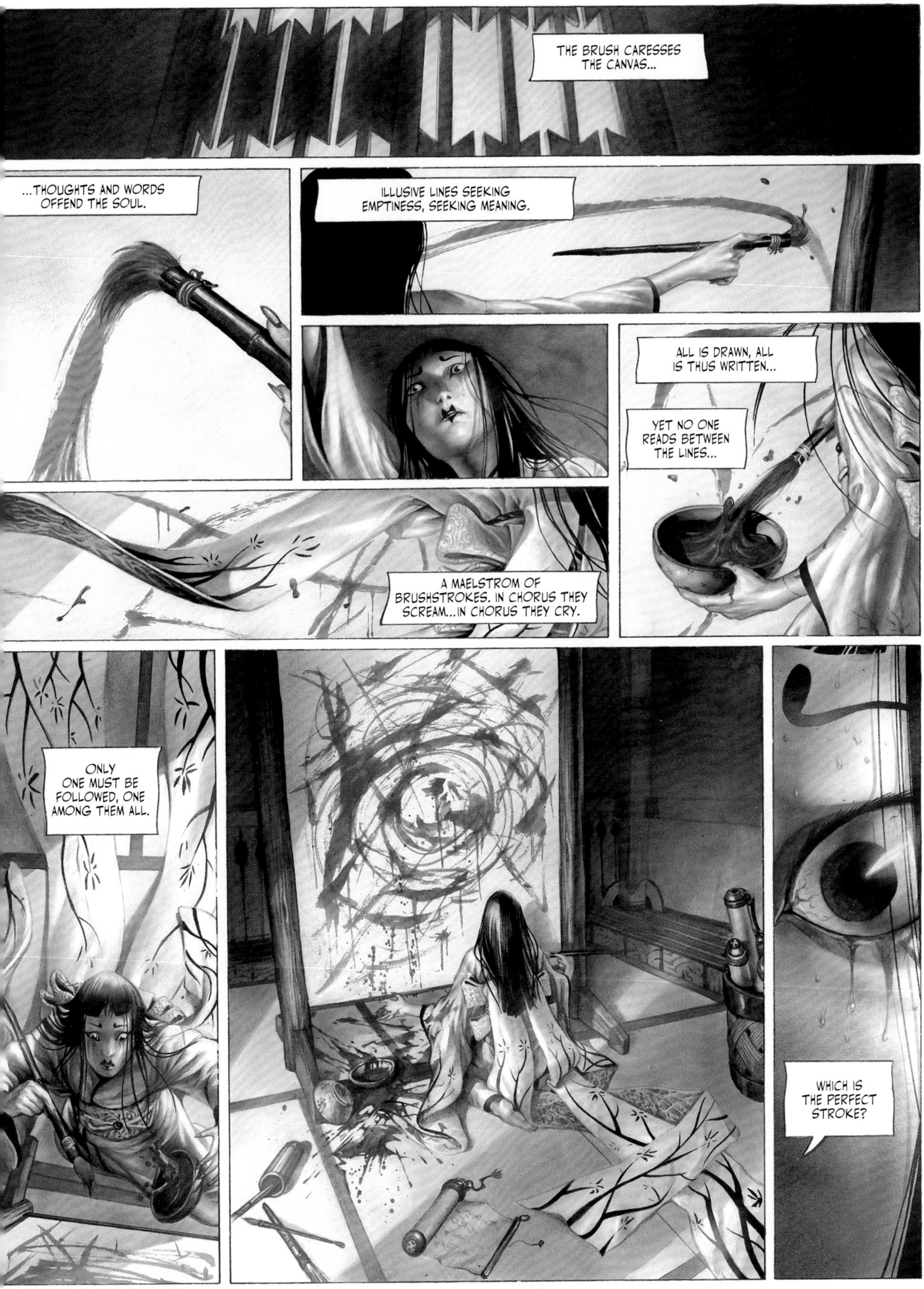
THE BRUSH CARESSES THE CANVAS...
...THOUGHTS AND WORDS OFFEND THE SOUL.
ILLUSIVE LINES SEEKING EMPTINESS, SEEKING MEANING.
ALL IS DRAWN, ALL IS THUS WRITTEN...
YET NO ONE READS BETWEEN THE LINES...
A MAELSTROM OF BRUSHSTROKES. IN CHORUS THEY SCREAM...IN CHORUS THEY CRY.
ONLY ONE MUST BE FOLLOWED, ONE AMONG THEM ALL.
WHICH IS THE PERFECT STROKE?

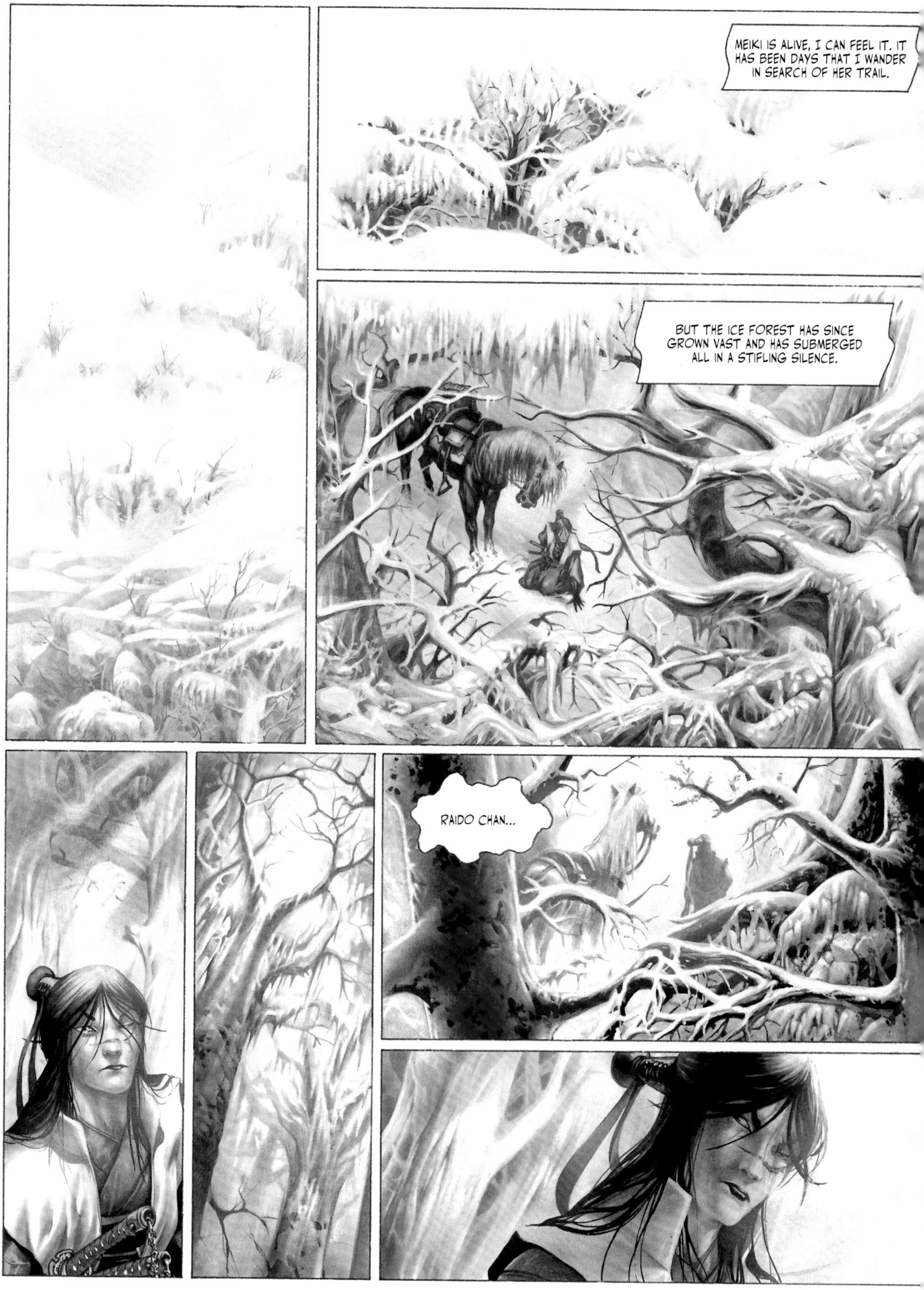
MEIKI IS ALIVE, I CAN FEEL IT. IT HAS BEEN DAYS THAT I WANDER IN SEARCH OF HER TRAIL.
BUT THE ICE FOREST HAS SINCE GROWN VAST AND HAS SUBMERGED ALL IN A STIFLING SILENCE.
RAIDO CHAN...

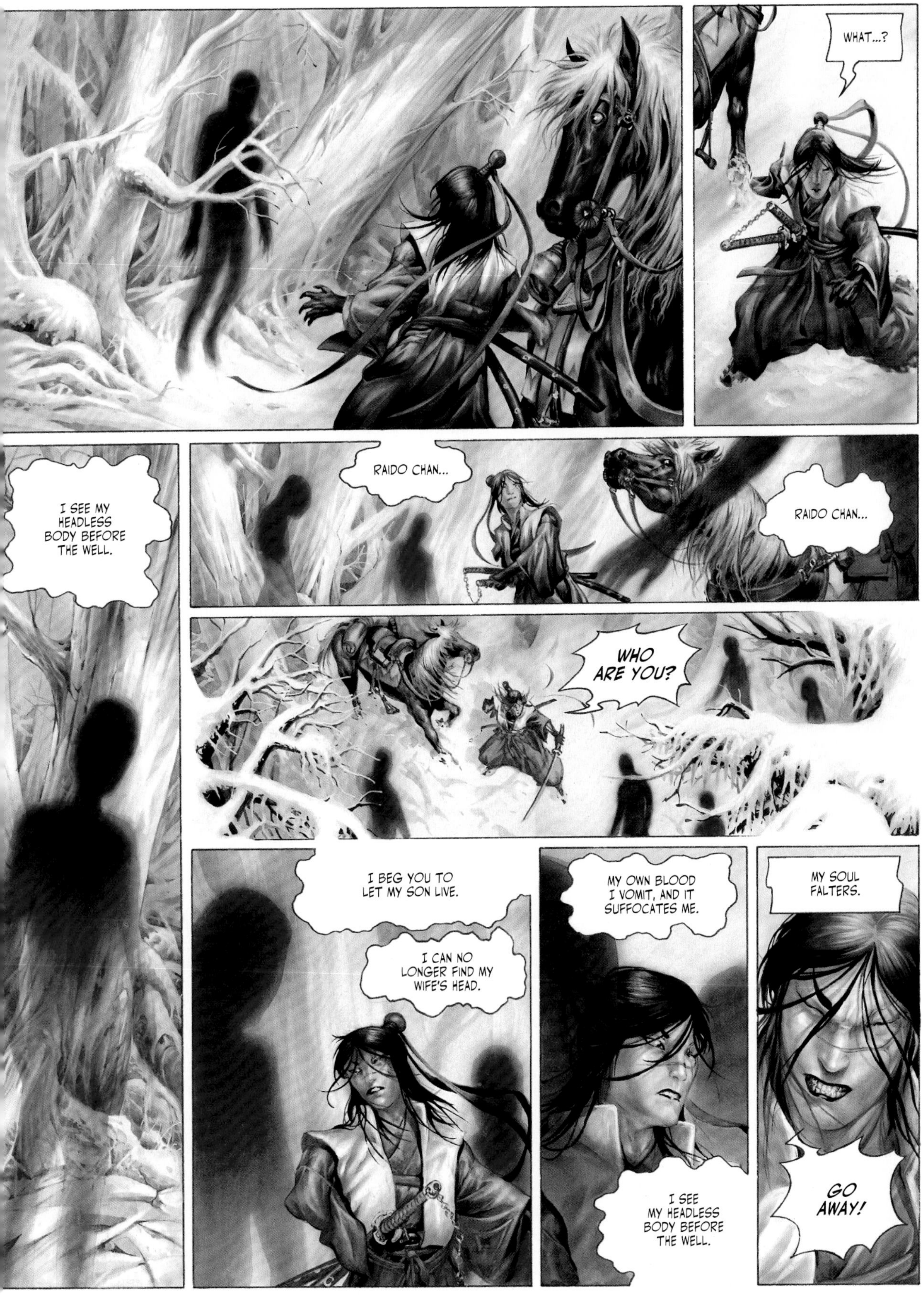
WHAT...?
I SEE MY HEADLESS BODY BEFORE THE WELL.
RAIDO CHAN...
RAIDO CHAN...
WHO ARE YOU?
I BEG YOU TO LET MY SON LIVE.
I CAN NO LONGER FIND MY WIFE'S HEAD.
MY OWN BLOOD I VOMIT, AND IT SUFFOCATES ME.
I SEE MY HEADLESS BODY BEFORE THE WELL.
MY SOUL FALTERS.
GO AWAY!

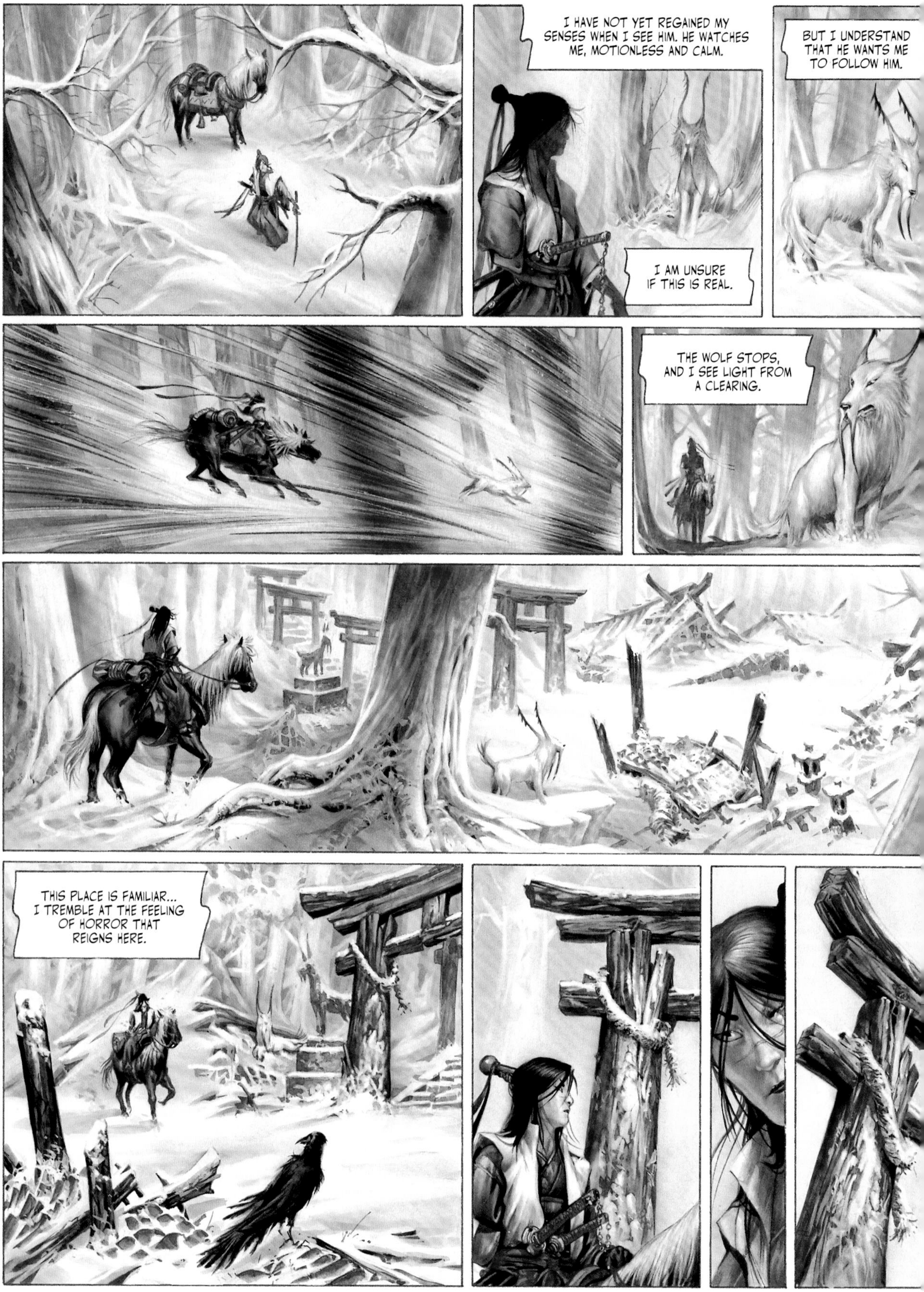
I HAVE NOT YET REGAINED MY SENSES WHEN I SEE HIM. HE WATCHES ME, MOTIONLESS AND CALM.
I AM UNSURE IF THIS IS REAL.
BUT I UNDERSTAND THAT HE WANTS ME TO FOLLOW HIM.
THE WOLF STOPS, AND I SEE LIGHT FROM A CLEARING.
THIS PLACE IS FAMILIAR... I TREMBLE AT THE FEELING OF HORROR THAT REIGNS HERE.

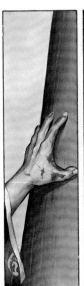
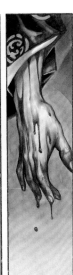

FATHER, LEAN ON ME. I AM STRONG.

I KNOW, RAIDO. BUT I AM THE GUARDIAN OF THE SCARLET BLADES, AND MY STRENGTH MUST NOT LEAVE ME NOW...

...NOW THAT ALL SEEMS LOST.

RAIDO! LOOK OUT!

FATHER!

109

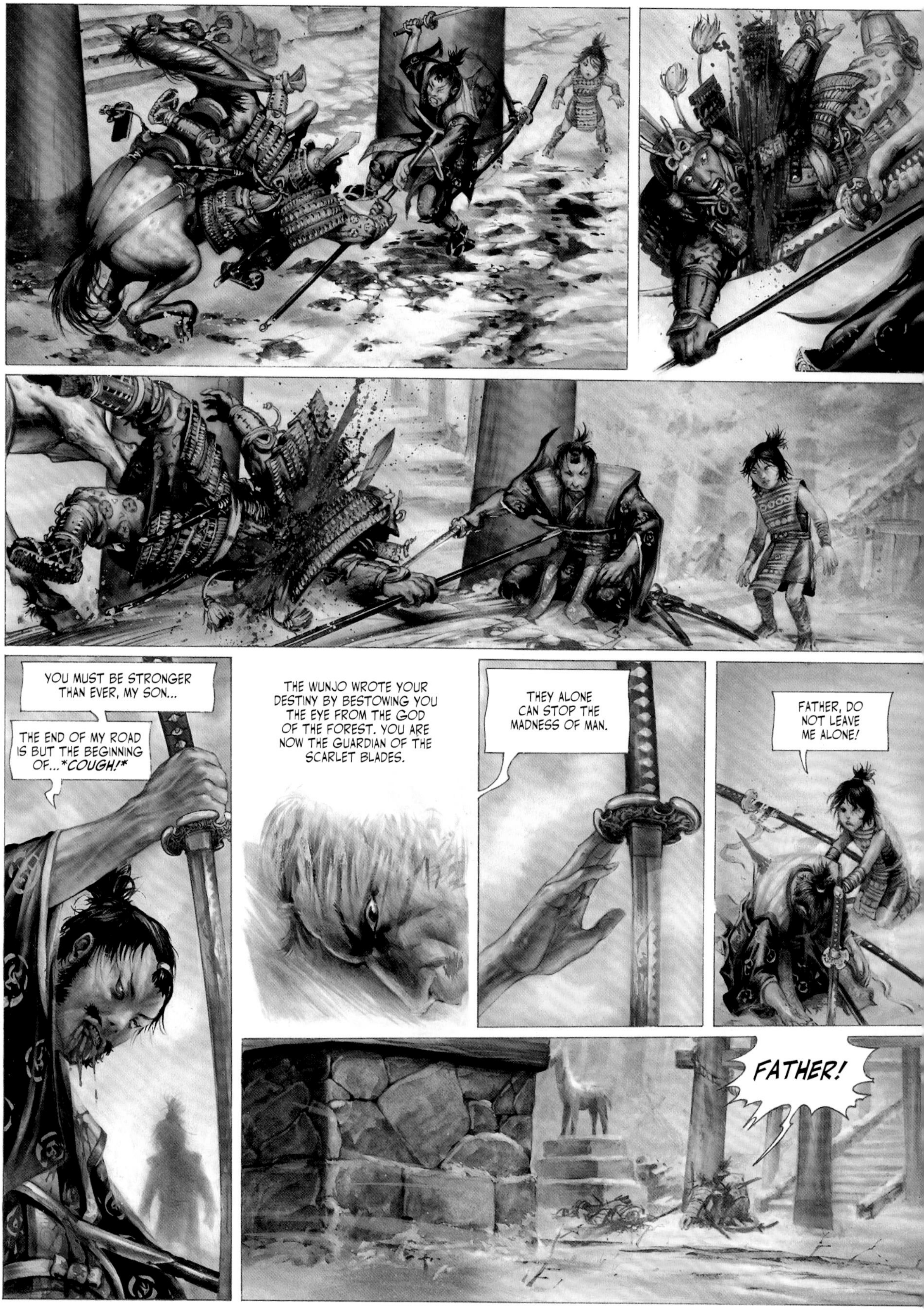

YOU MUST BE STRONGER THAN EVER, MY SON...
THE END OF MY ROAD IS BUT THE BEGINNING OF...*COUGH!*
THE WUNJO WROTE YOUR DESTINY BY BESTOWING YOU THE EYE FROM THE GOD OF THE FOREST. YOU ARE NOW THE GUARDIAN OF THE SCARLET BLADES.
THEY ALONE CAN STOP THE MADNESS OF MAN.
FATHER, DO NOT LEAVE ME ALONE!
FATHER!

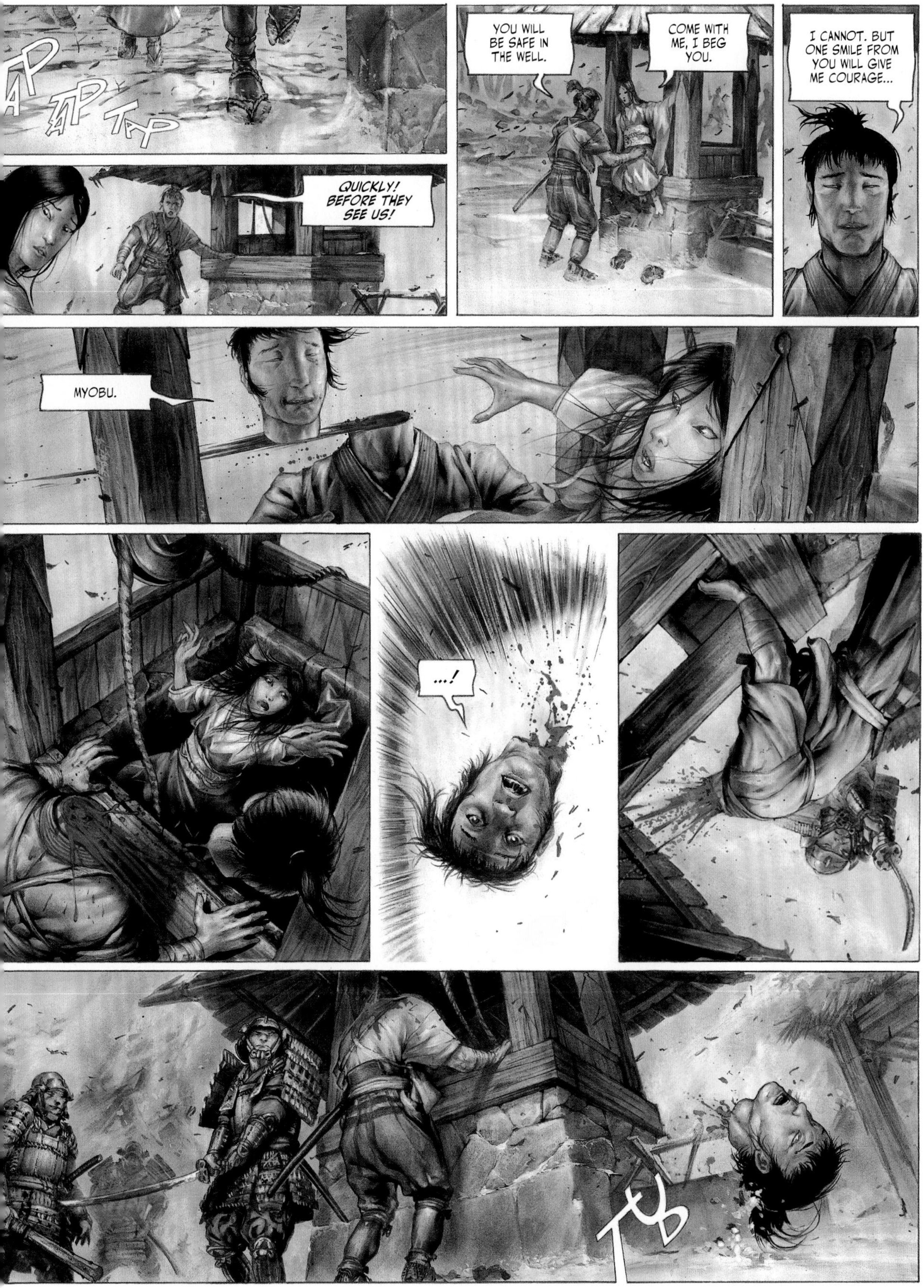

TAP
TAP
TAP
YOU WILL BE SAFE IN THE WELL.
COME WITH ME, I BEG YOU.
I CANNOT. BUT ONE SMILE FROM YOU WILL GIVE ME COURAGE...
QUICKLY! BEFORE THEY SEE US!
MYOBU.
...!
TUB

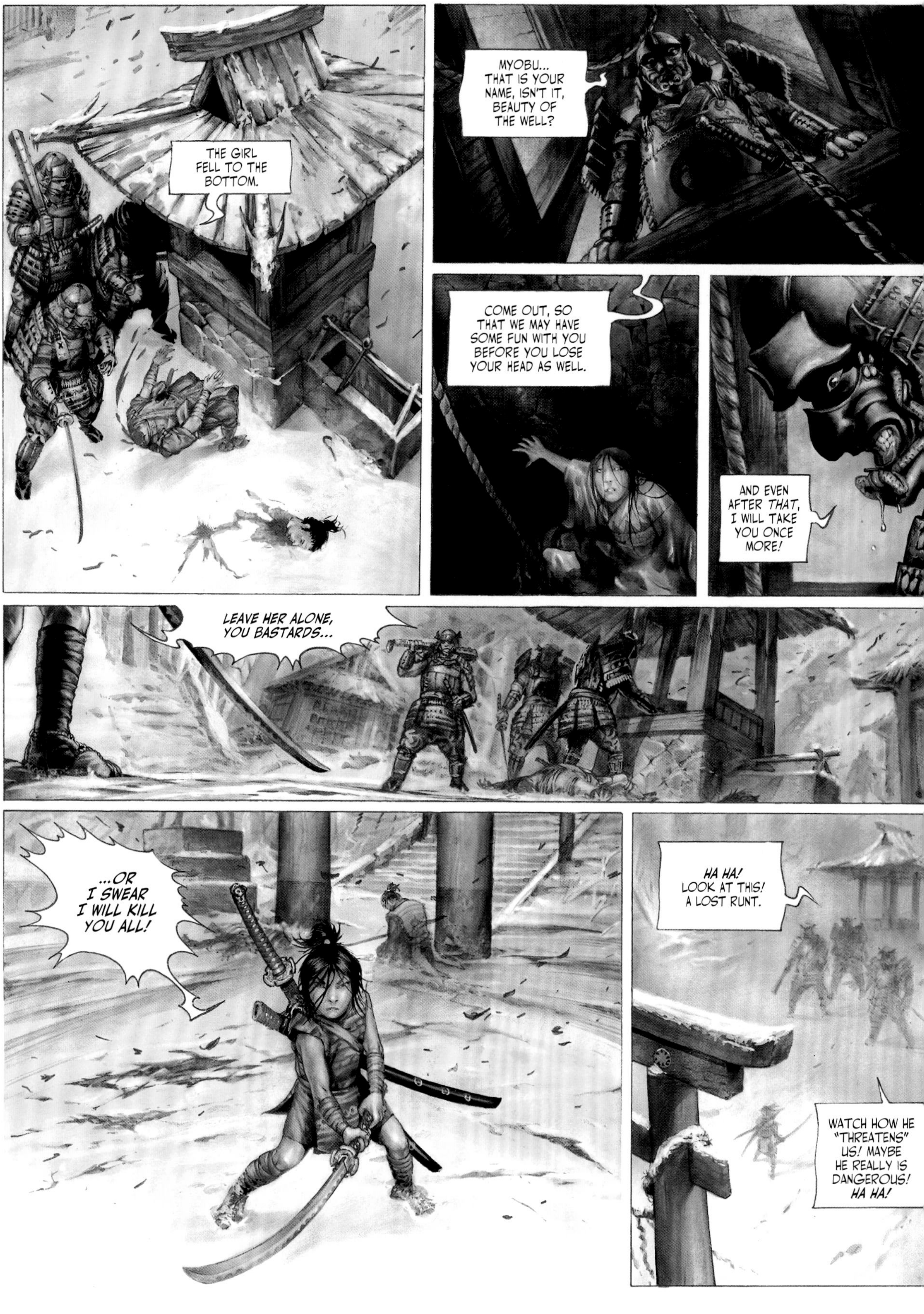
THE GIRL FELL TO THE BOTTOM.
MYOBU... THAT IS YOUR NAME, ISN'T IT, BEAUTY OF THE WELL?
COME OUT, SO THAT WE MAY HAVE SOME FUN WITH YOU BEFORE YOU LOSE YOUR HEAD AS WELL.
AND EVEN AFTER *THAT*, I WILL TAKE YOU ONCE MORE!
LEAVE HER ALONE, YOU BASTARDS...
...OR I SWEAR I WILL KILL YOU ALL!
HA HA! LOOK AT THIS! A LOST RUNT.
WATCH HOW HE "THREATENS" US! MAYBE HE REALLY IS DANGEROUS! *HA HA!*

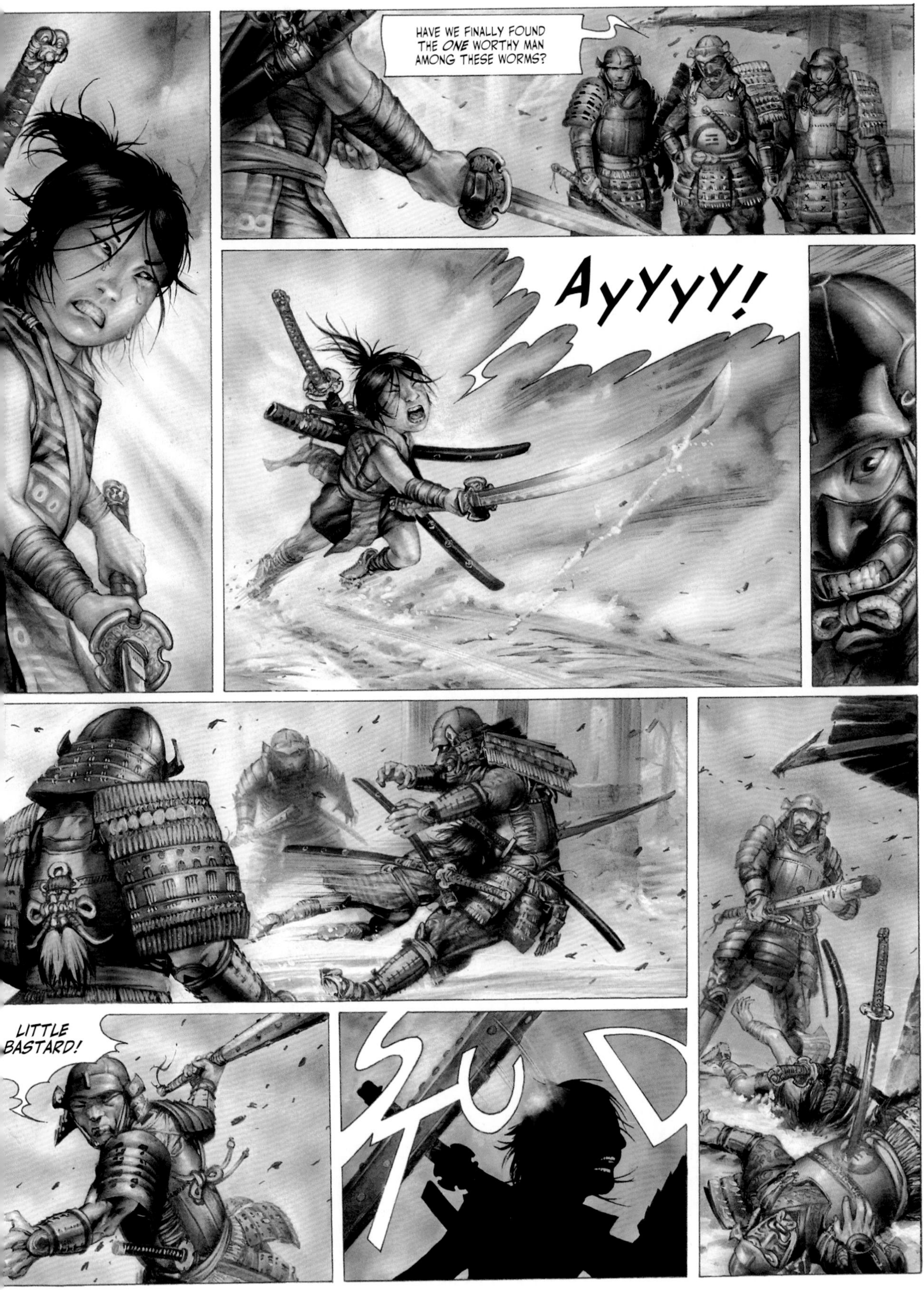
HAVE WE FINALLY FOUND THE *ONE* WORTHY MAN AMONG THESE WORMS?
AyYYY!
LITTLE BASTARD!
STUD

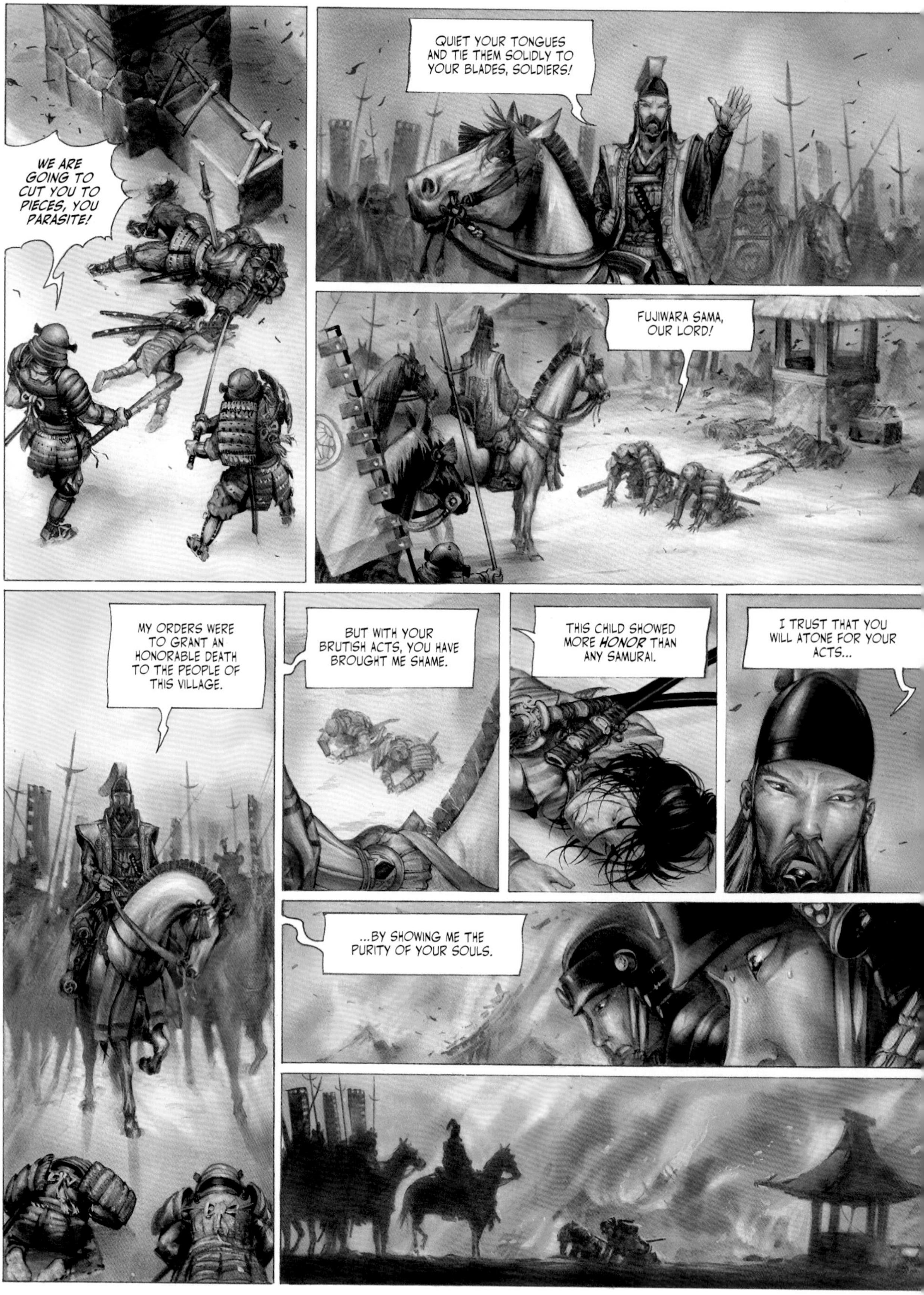
WE ARE GOING TO CUT YOU TO PIECES, YOU PARASITE!
QUIET YOUR TONGUES AND TIE THEM SOLIDLY TO YOUR BLADES, SOLDIERS!
FUJIWARA SAMA, OUR LORD!
MY ORDERS WERE TO GRANT AN HONORABLE DEATH TO THE PEOPLE OF THIS VILLAGE.
BUT WITH YOUR BRUTISH ACTS, YOU HAVE BROUGHT ME SHAME.
THIS CHILD SHOWED MORE HONOR THAN ANY SAMURAI.
I TRUST THAT YOU WILL ATONE FOR YOUR ACTS...
...BY SHOWING ME THE PURITY OF YOUR SOULS.

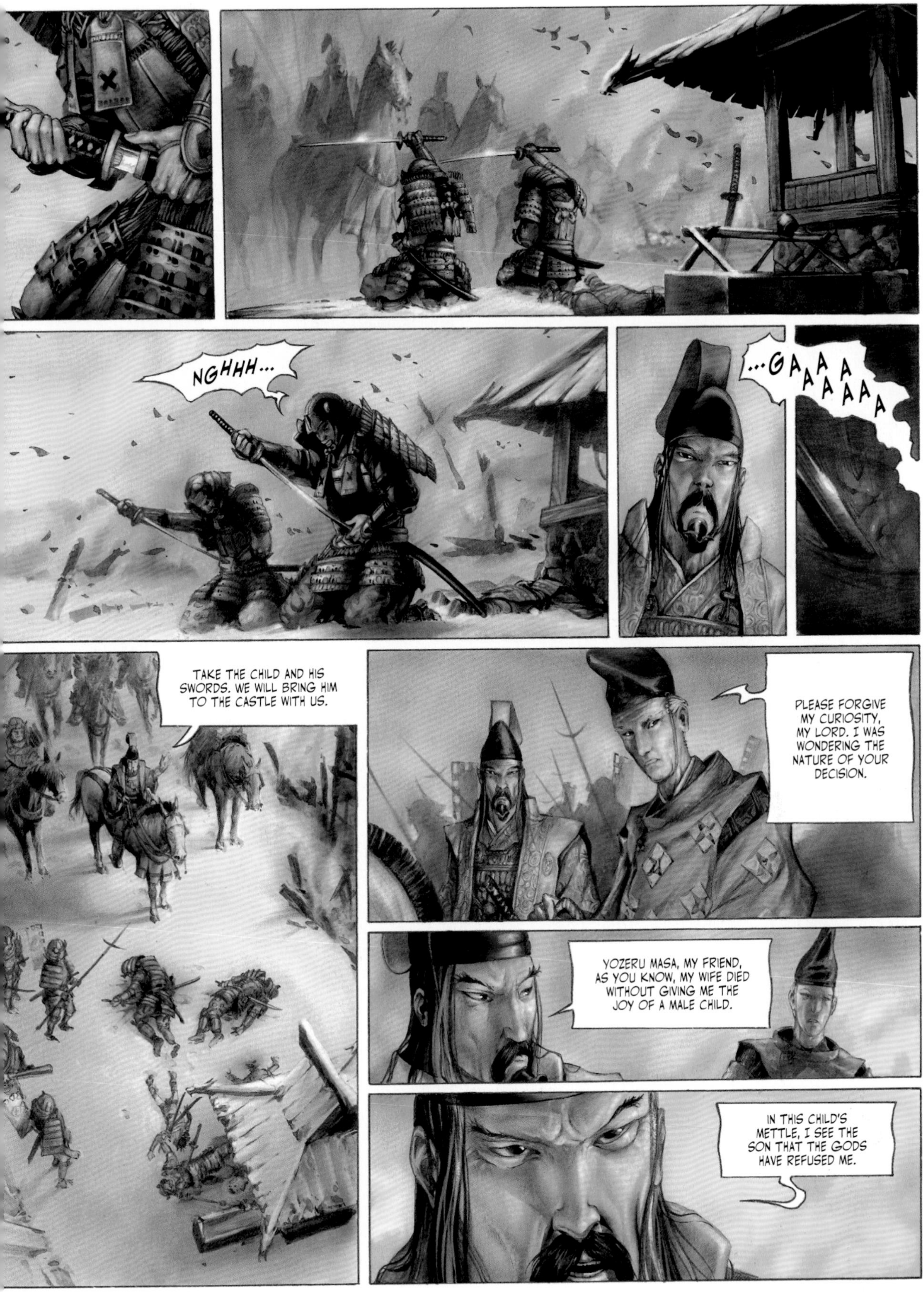
NGHHH...
...GAAAAAAAA
TAKE THE CHILD AND HIS SWORDS. WE WILL BRING HIM TO THE CASTLE WITH US.
PLEASE FORGIVE MY CURIOSITY, MY LORD. I WAS WONDERING THE NATURE OF YOUR DECISION.
YOZERU MASA, MY FRIEND, AS YOU KNOW, MY WIFE DIED WITHOUT GIVING ME THE JOY OF A MALE CHILD.
IN THIS CHILD'S METTLE, I SEE THE SON THAT THE GODS HAVE REFUSED ME.

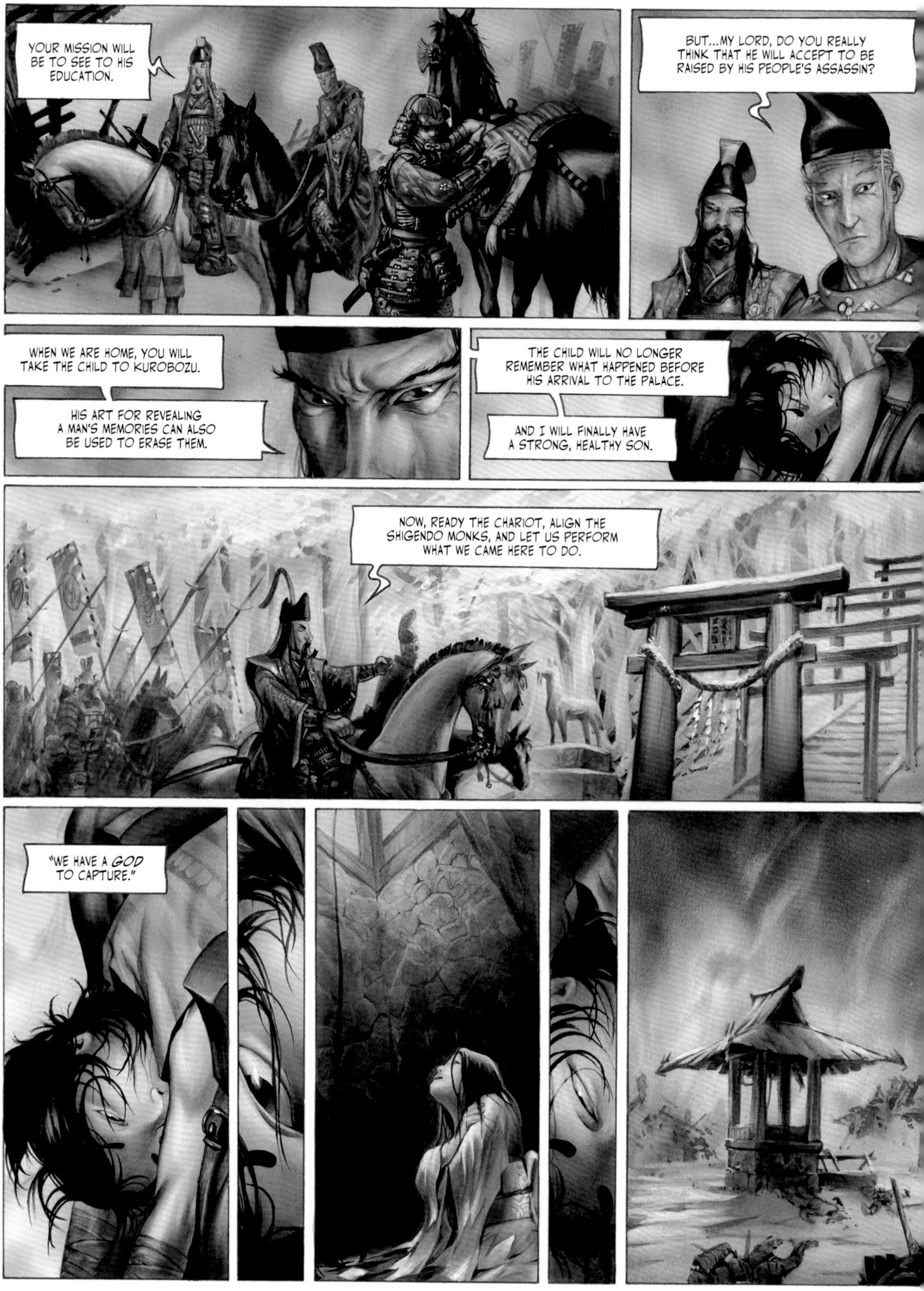
YOUR MISSION WILL BE TO SEE TO HIS EDUCATION.
BUT...MY LORD, DO YOU REALLY THINK THAT HE WILL ACCEPT TO BE RAISED BY HIS PEOPLE'S ASSASSIN?
WHEN WE ARE HOME, YOU WILL TAKE THE CHILD TO KUROBOZU.
HIS ART FOR REVEALING A MAN'S MEMORIES CAN ALSO BE USED TO ERASE THEM.
THE CHILD WILL NO LONGER REMEMBER WHAT HAPPENED BEFORE HIS ARRIVAL TO THE PALACE.
AND I WILL FINALLY HAVE A STRONG, HEALTHY SON.
NOW, READY THE CHARIOT, ALIGN THE SHIGENDO MONKS, AND LET US PERFORM WHAT WE CAME HERE TO DO.
"WE HAVE A *GOD* TO CAPTURE."

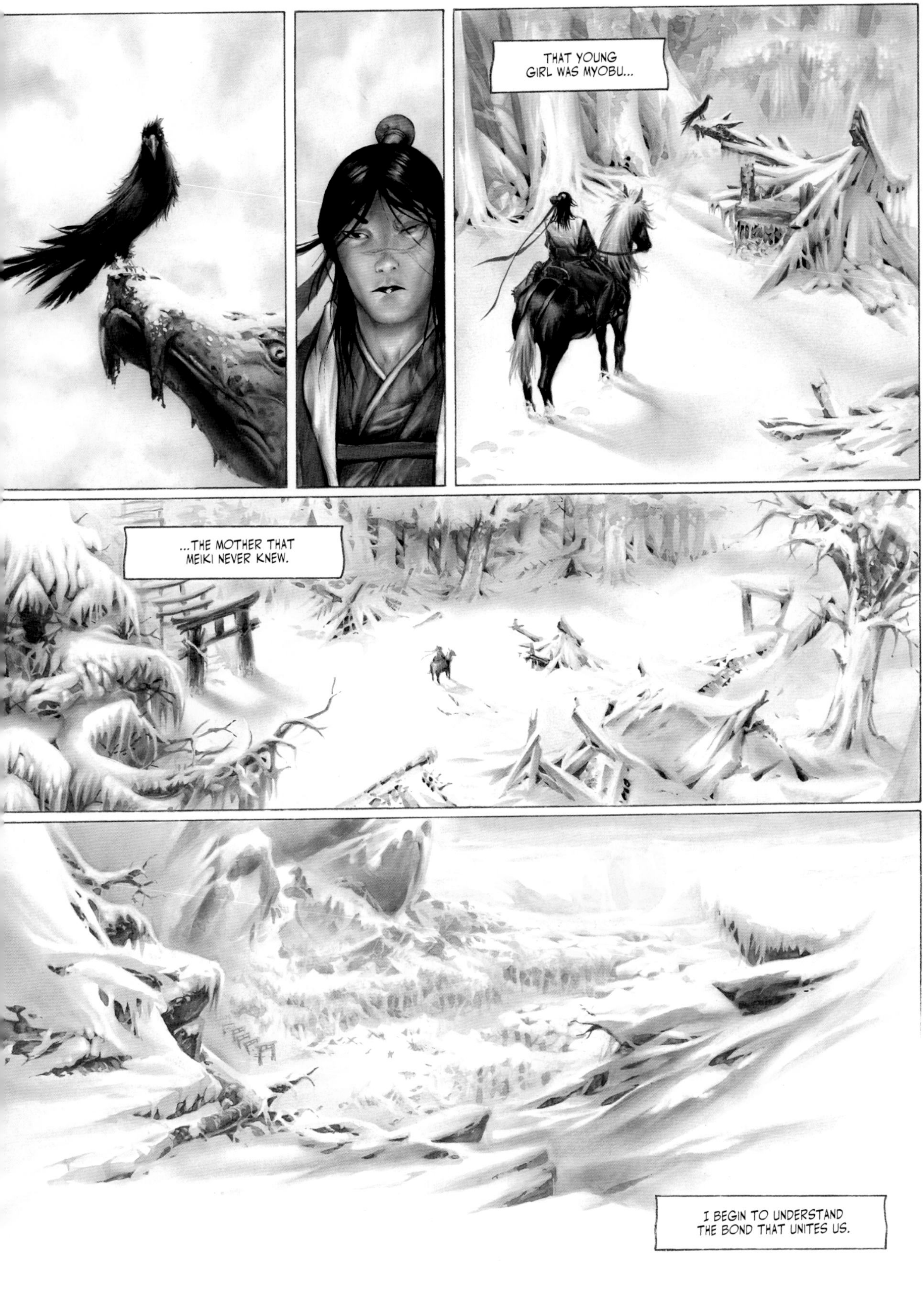
THAT YOUNG GIRL WAS MYOBU...
...THE MOTHER THAT MEIKI NEVER KNEW.
I BEGIN TO UNDERSTAND THE BOND THAT UNITES US.

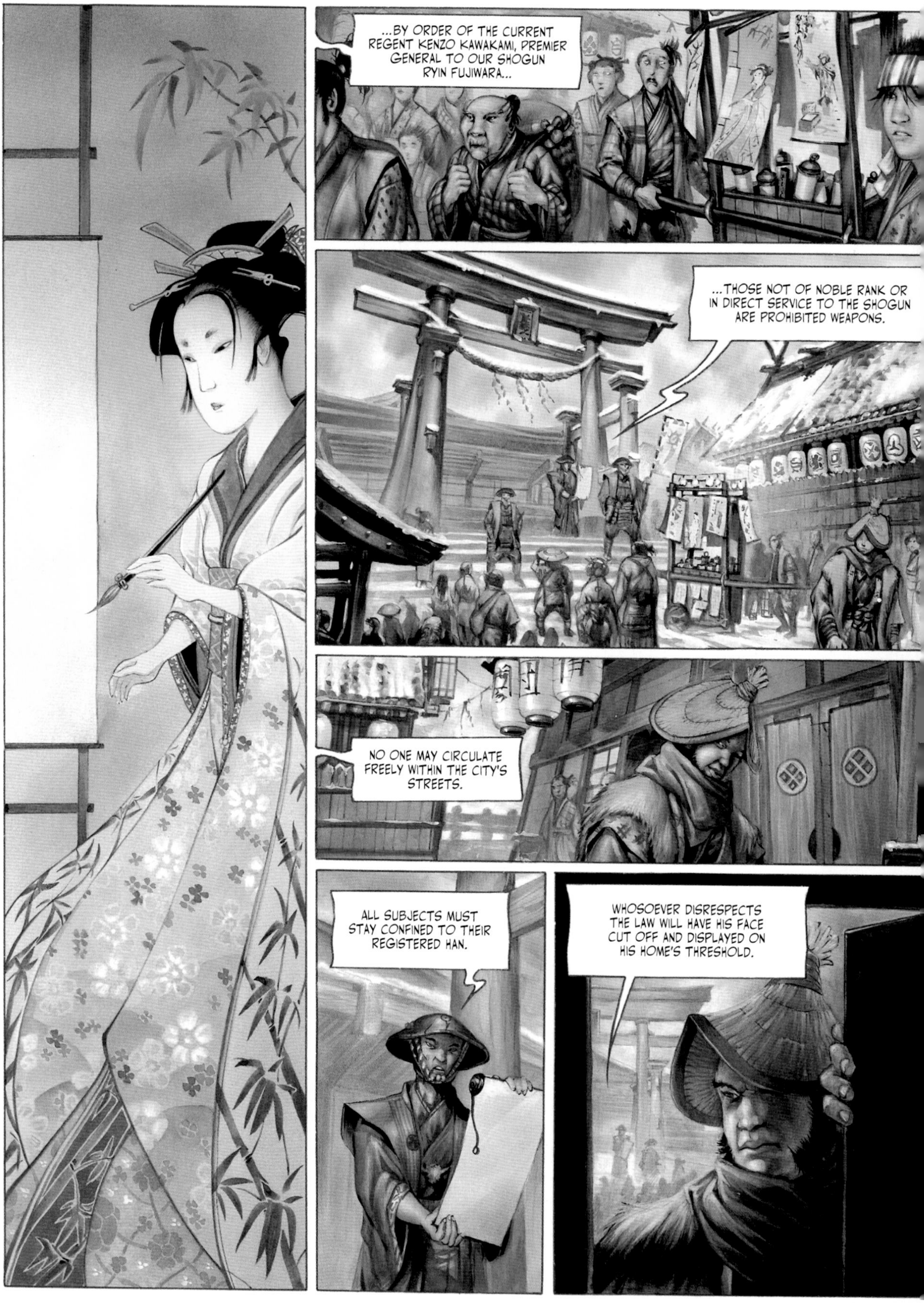
...BY ORDER OF THE CURRENT REGENT KENZO KAWAKAMI, PREMIER GENERAL TO OUR SHOGUN RYIN FUJIWARA...
...THOSE NOT OF NOBLE RANK OR IN DIRECT SERVICE TO THE SHOGUN ARE PROHIBITED WEAPONS.
NO ONE MAY CIRCULATE FREELY WITHIN THE CITY'S STREETS.
ALL SUBJECTS MUST STAY CONFINED TO THEIR REGISTERED HAN.
WHOSOEVER DISRESPECTS THE LAW WILL HAVE HIS FACE CUT OFF AND DISPLAYED ON HIS HOME'S THRESHOLD.

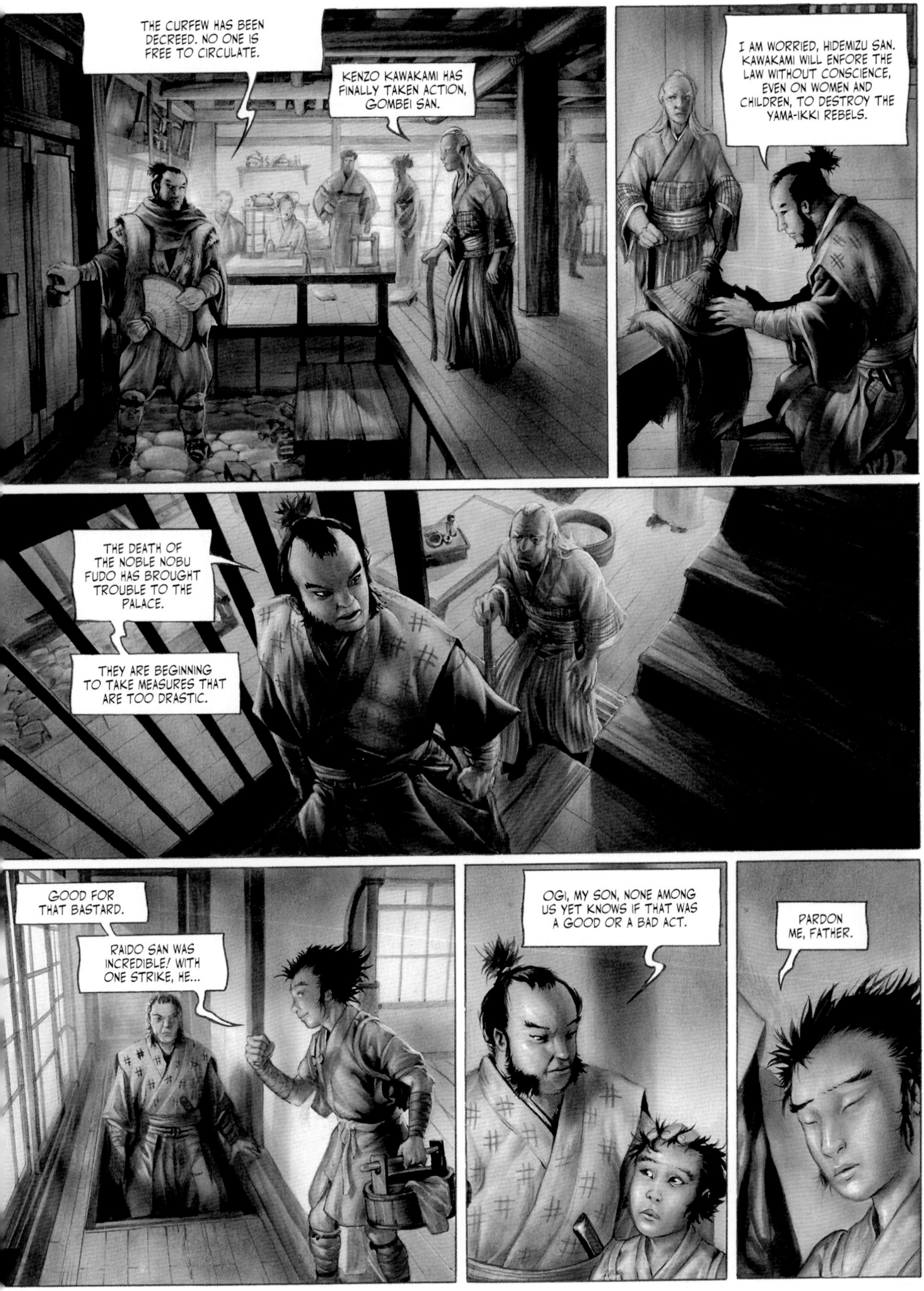

THE CURFEW HAS BEEN DECREED. NO ONE IS FREE TO CIRCULATE.
KENZO KAWAKAMI HAS FINALLY TAKEN ACTION, GOMBEI SAN.
I AM WORRIED, HIDEMIZU SAN. KAWAKAMI WILL ENFORE THE LAW WITHOUT CONSCIENCE, EVEN ON WOMEN AND CHILDREN, TO DESTROY THE YAMA-IKKI REBELS.
THE DEATH OF THE NOBLE NOBU FUDO HAS BROUGHT TROUBLE TO THE PALACE.
THEY ARE BEGINNING TO TAKE MEASURES THAT ARE TOO DRASTIC.
GOOD FOR THAT BASTARD.
RAIDO SAN WAS INCREDIBLE! WITH ONE STRIKE, HE...
OGI, MY SON, NONE AMONG US YET KNOWS IF THAT WAS A GOOD OR A BAD ACT.
PARDON ME, FATHER.

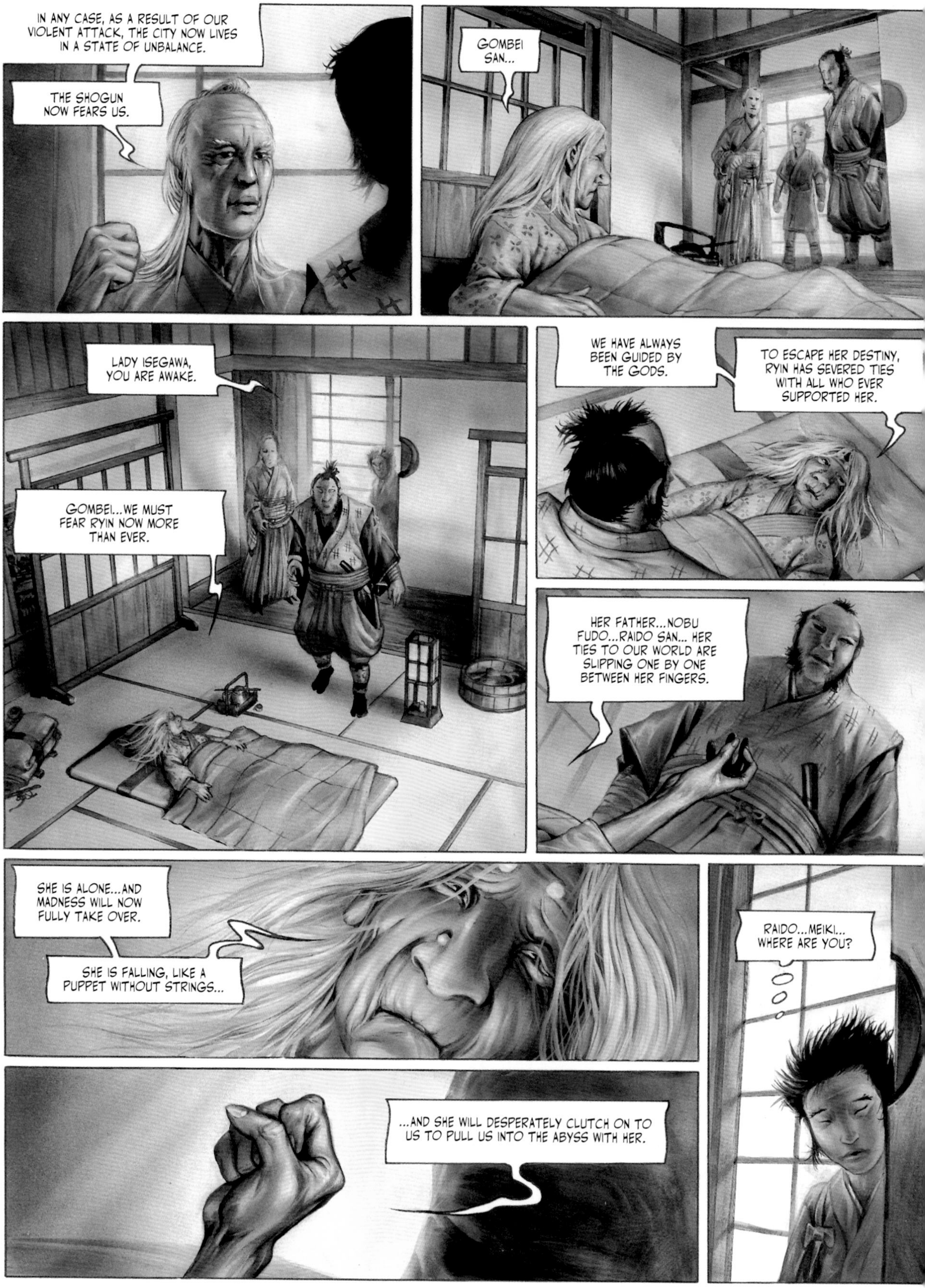
IN ANY CASE, AS A RESULT OF OUR VIOLENT ATTACK, THE CITY NOW LIVES IN A STATE OF UNBALANCE.
THE SHOGUN NOW FEARS US.
GOMBEI SAN...
LADY ISEGAWA, YOU ARE AWAKE.
GOMBEI...WE MUST FEAR RYIN NOW MORE THAN EVER.
WE HAVE ALWAYS BEEN GUIDED BY THE GODS.
TO ESCAPE HER DESTINY, RYIN HAS SEVERED TIES WITH ALL WHO EVER SUPPORTED HER.
HER FATHER...NOBU FUDO...RAIDO SAN... HER TIES TO OUR WORLD ARE SLIPPING ONE BY ONE BETWEEN HER FINGERS.
SHE IS ALONE...AND MADNESS WILL NOW FULLY TAKE OVER.
SHE IS FALLING, LIKE A PUPPET WITHOUT STRINGS...
...AND SHE WILL DESPERATELY CLUTCH ON TO US TO PULL US INTO THE ABYSS WITH HER.
RAIDO...MEIKI... WHERE ARE YOU?

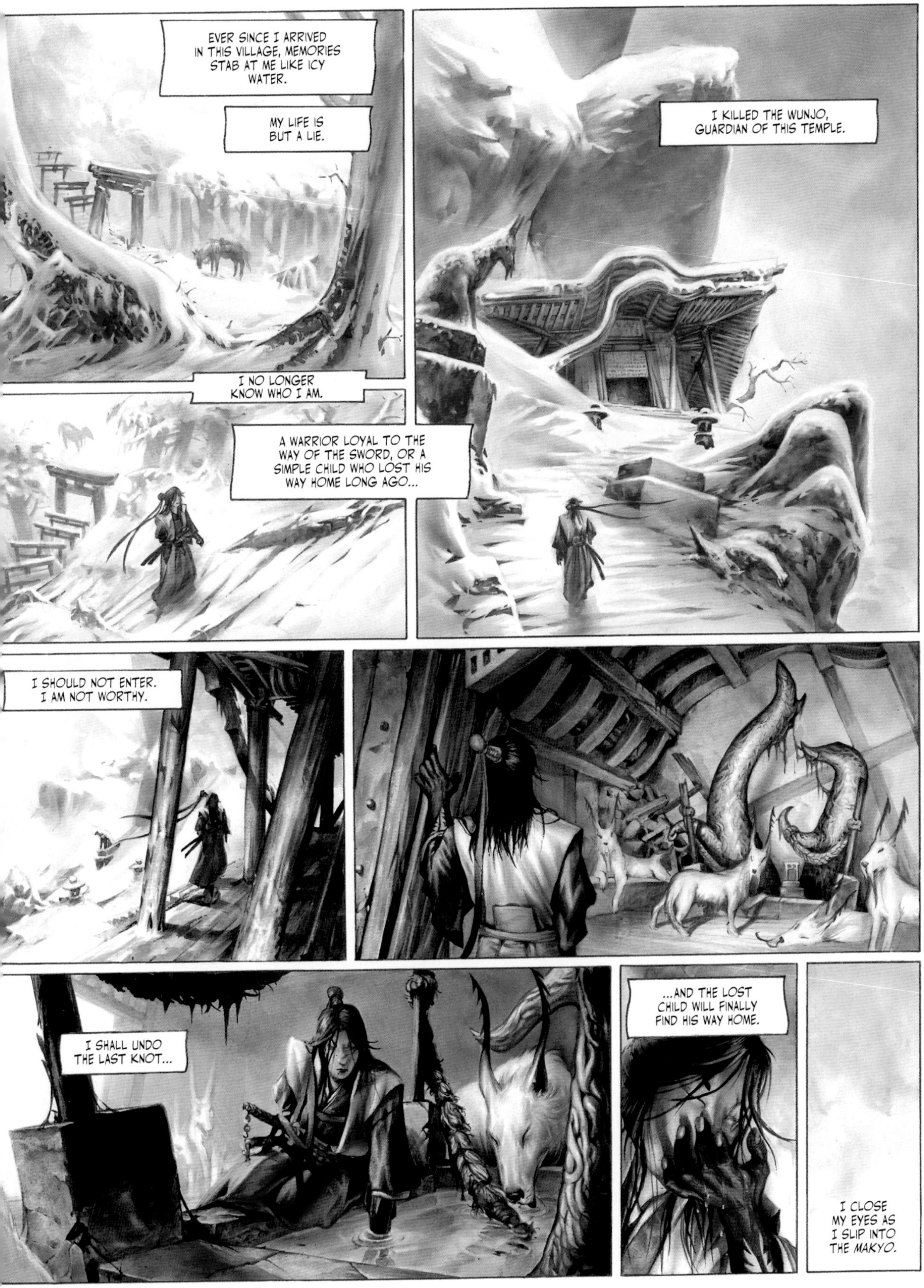
EVER SINCE I ARRIVED IN THIS VILLAGE, MEMORIES STAB AT ME LIKE ICY WATER.
MY LIFE IS BUT A LIE.
I NO LONGER KNOW WHO I AM.
A WARRIOR LOYAL TO THE WAY OF THE SWORD, OR A SIMPLE CHILD WHO LOST HIS WAY HOME LONG AGO...
I KILLED THE WUNJO, GUARDIAN OF THIS TEMPLE.
I SHOULD NOT ENTER. I AM NOT WORTHY.
I SHALL UNDO THE LAST KNOT...
...AND THE LOST CHILD WILL FINALLY FIND HIS WAY HOME.
I CLOSE MY EYES AS I SLIP INTO THE *MAKYO*.

THE COLD
ENVELOPS ME.

MEMORIES SWEEP
THROUGH ME AND
THE LAST VISION
SURFACES.

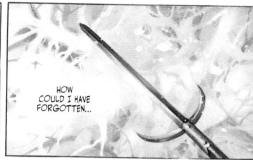

HOW
COULD I HAVE
FORGOTTEN...

...THE EMOTION
FELT BEFORE SUCH
BEAUTY?

A CACOPHONY OF CRIES
AND WAILING RESPOND TO
THE WHISTLING OF BLADES
SLICING THROUGH THE AIR.

IT IS THE ART WITH
WHICH I HONOR MY
LORD AND SHOGUN,
TOTECU FUJIWARA.

BUT ONE BY ONE,
THE FLOWERS OF
THE CHERRY TREE
FALL.

...AND BY NIGHTFALL
NOTHING REMAINS,
SAVE AN EXPANSE
OF PETALS IN THE
STORM'S WAKE.

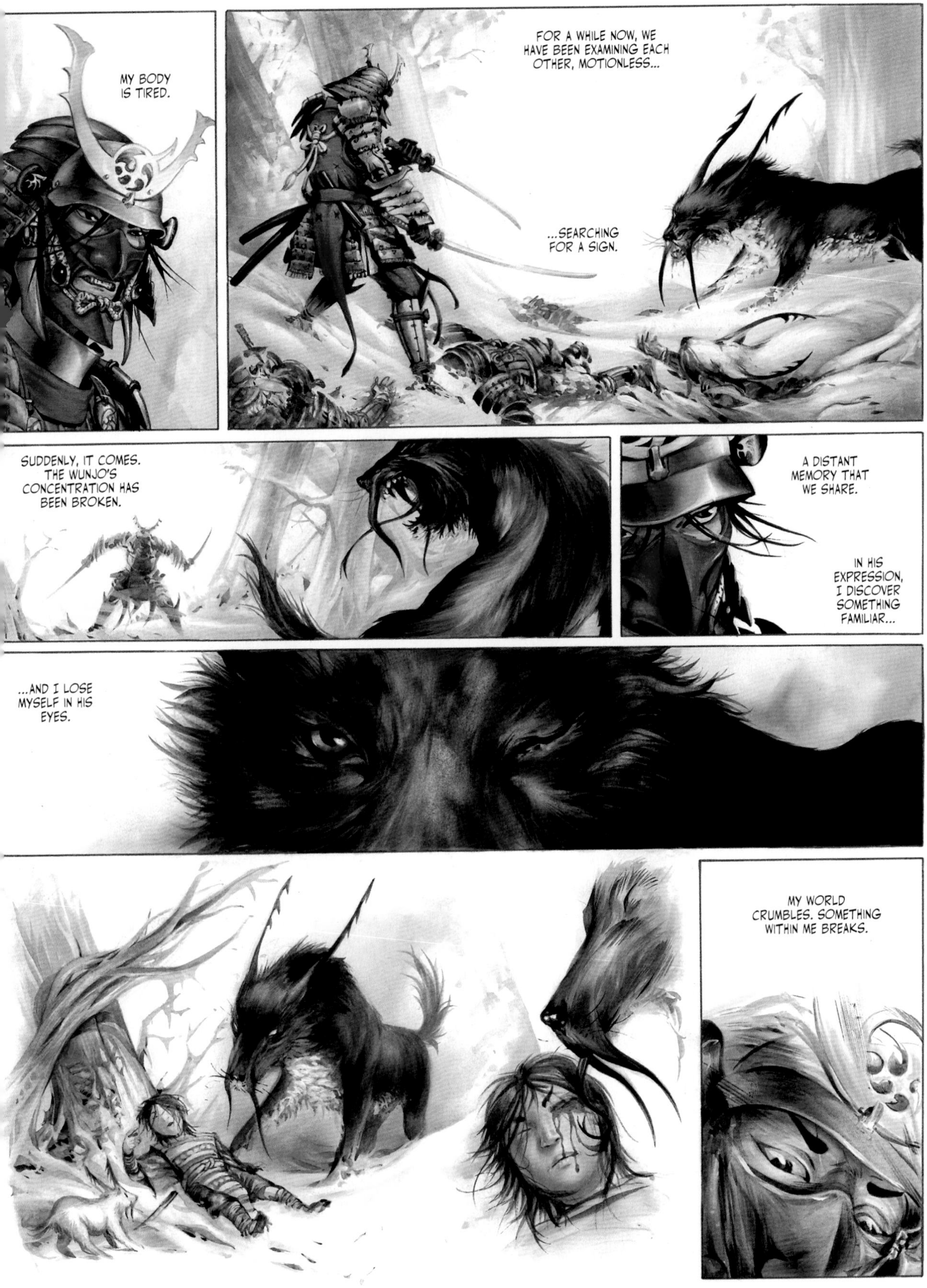
MY BODY IS TIRED.
FOR A WHILE NOW, WE HAVE BEEN EXAMINING EACH OTHER, MOTIONLESS...
...SEARCHING FOR A SIGN.
SUDDENLY, IT COMES. THE WUNJO'S CONCENTRATION HAS BEEN BROKEN.
A DISTANT MEMORY THAT WE SHARE.
IN HIS EXPRESSION, I DISCOVER SOMETHING FAMILIAR...
...AND I LOSE MYSELF IN HIS EYES.
MY WORLD CRUMBLES. SOMETHING WITHIN ME BREAKS.

ONE SOLE MEMORY HAS LED ME ASTRAY INTO THIS ENDLESS LABYRINTH.

NOTHING MAKES SENSE ANYMORE.

I RAISE MY HEAD TO GAZE AT THE WUNJO IN ALL OF HIS COMPASSION AND GLORY.

HE ALREADY IS THE VICTOR...

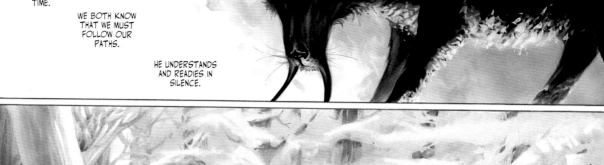

...BUT IT IS IMPOSSIBLE TO TURN BACK TIME.

WE BOTH KNOW THAT WE MUST FOLLOW OUR PATHS.

HE UNDERSTANDS AND READIES IN SILENCE.

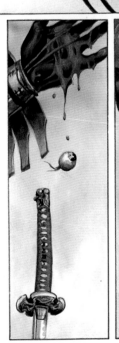

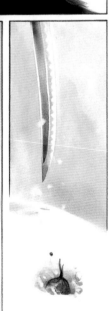

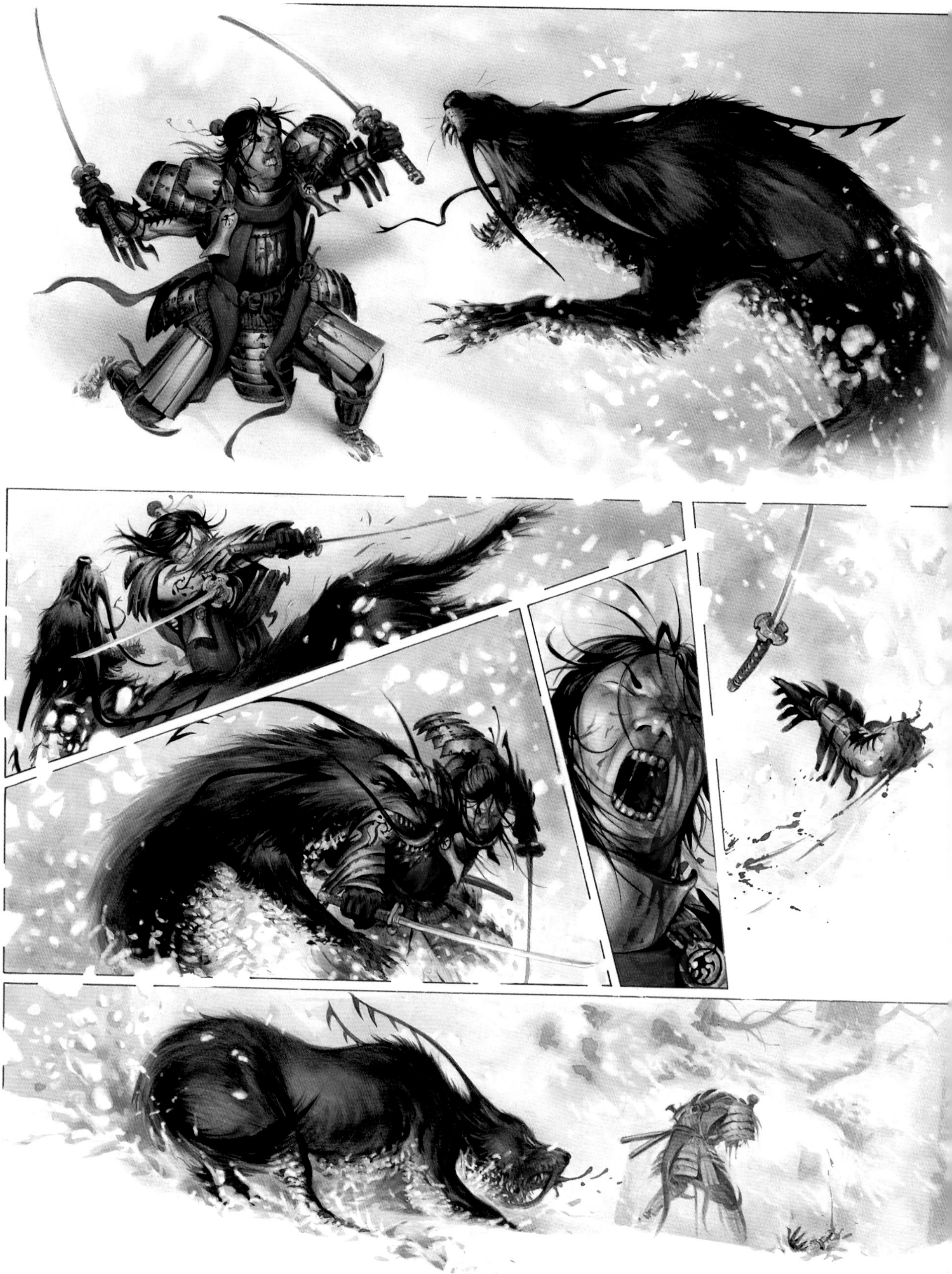

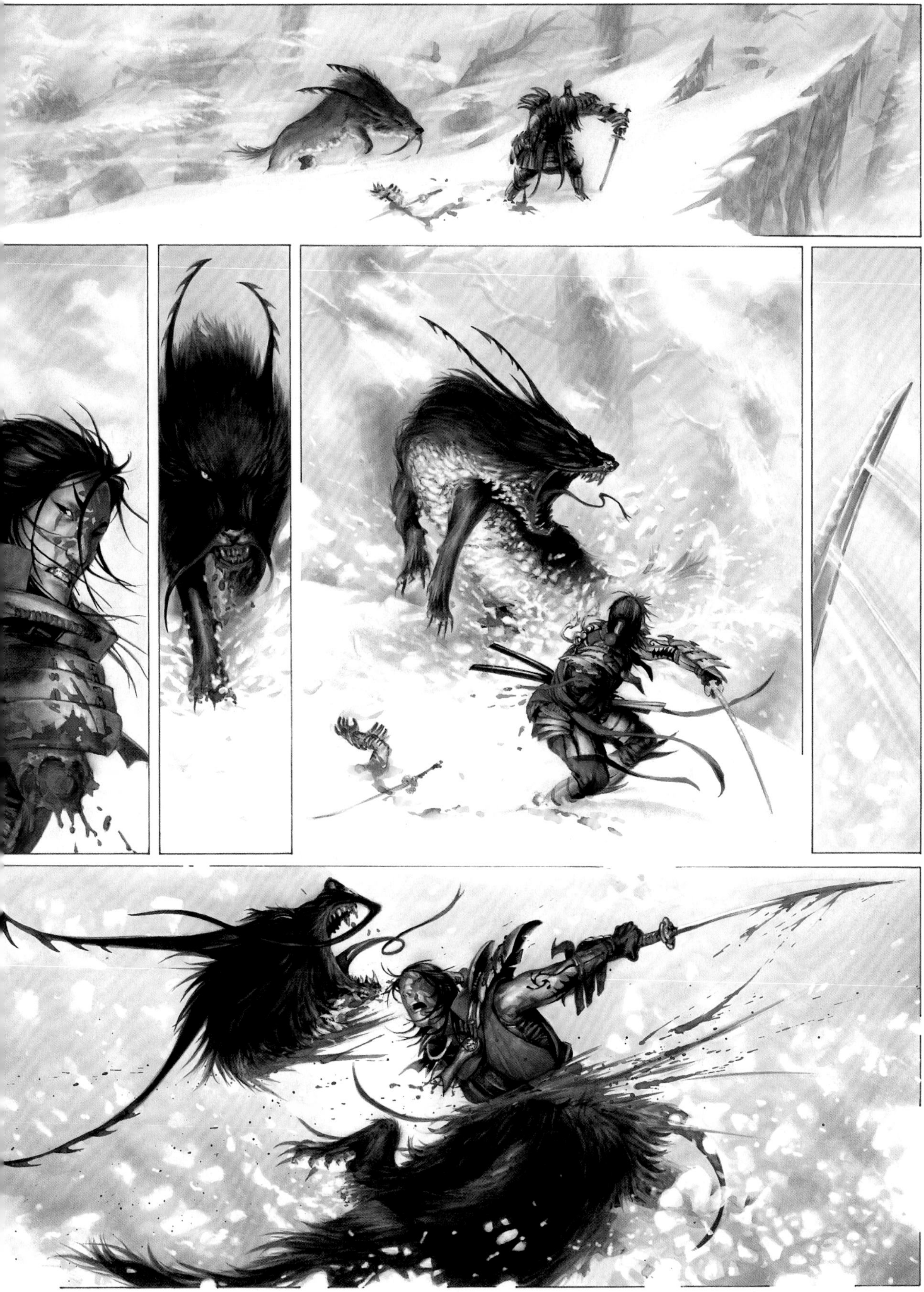

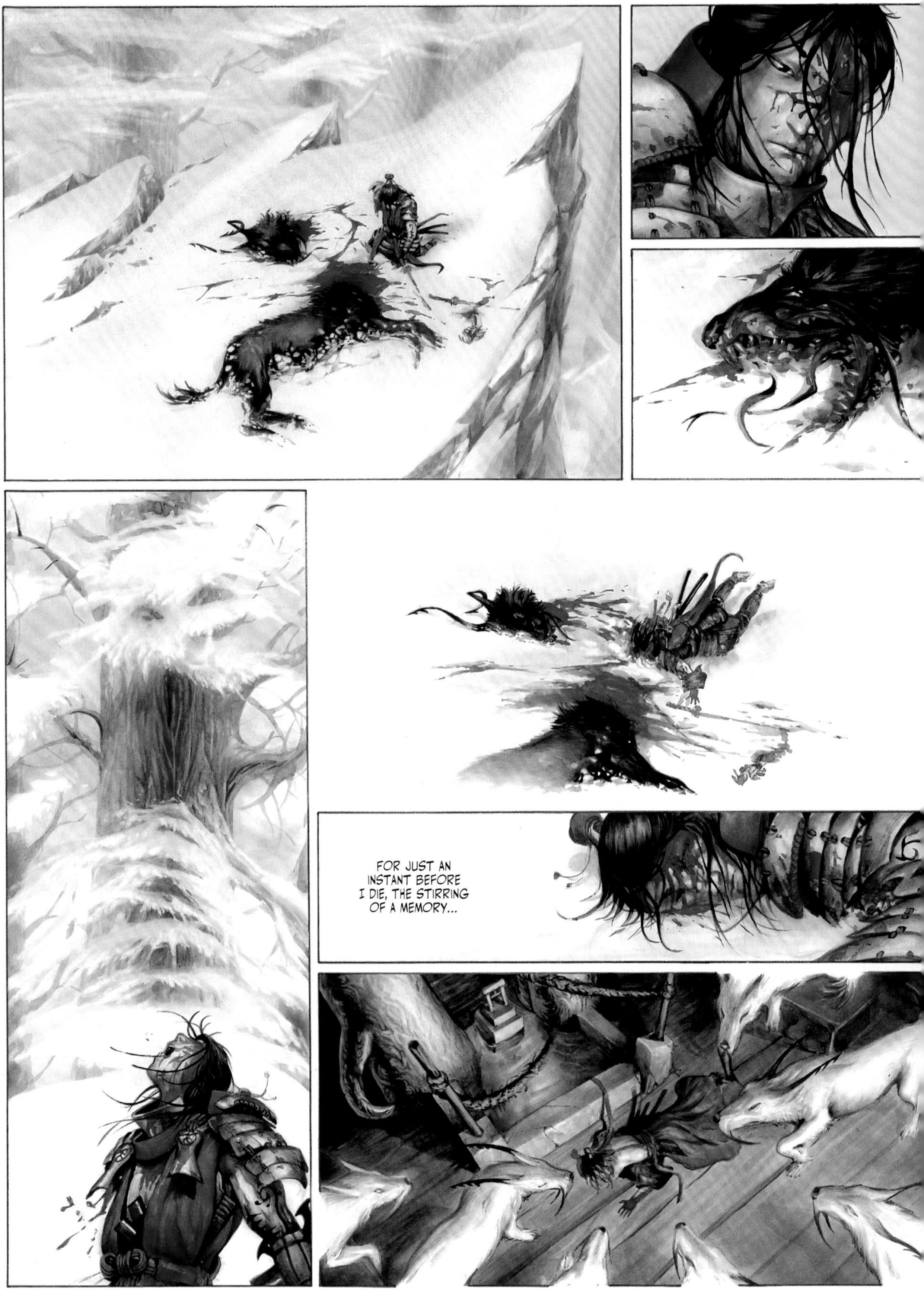
FOR JUST AN
INSTANT BEFORE
I DIE, THE STIRRING
OF A MEMORY...

TLAK TLAK

AH!

DO NOT LOOK, LITTLE SISTER, AND
KEEP RUNNING. WE MUST GET HOME
BEFORE THE GUARDS COME.

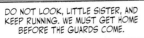

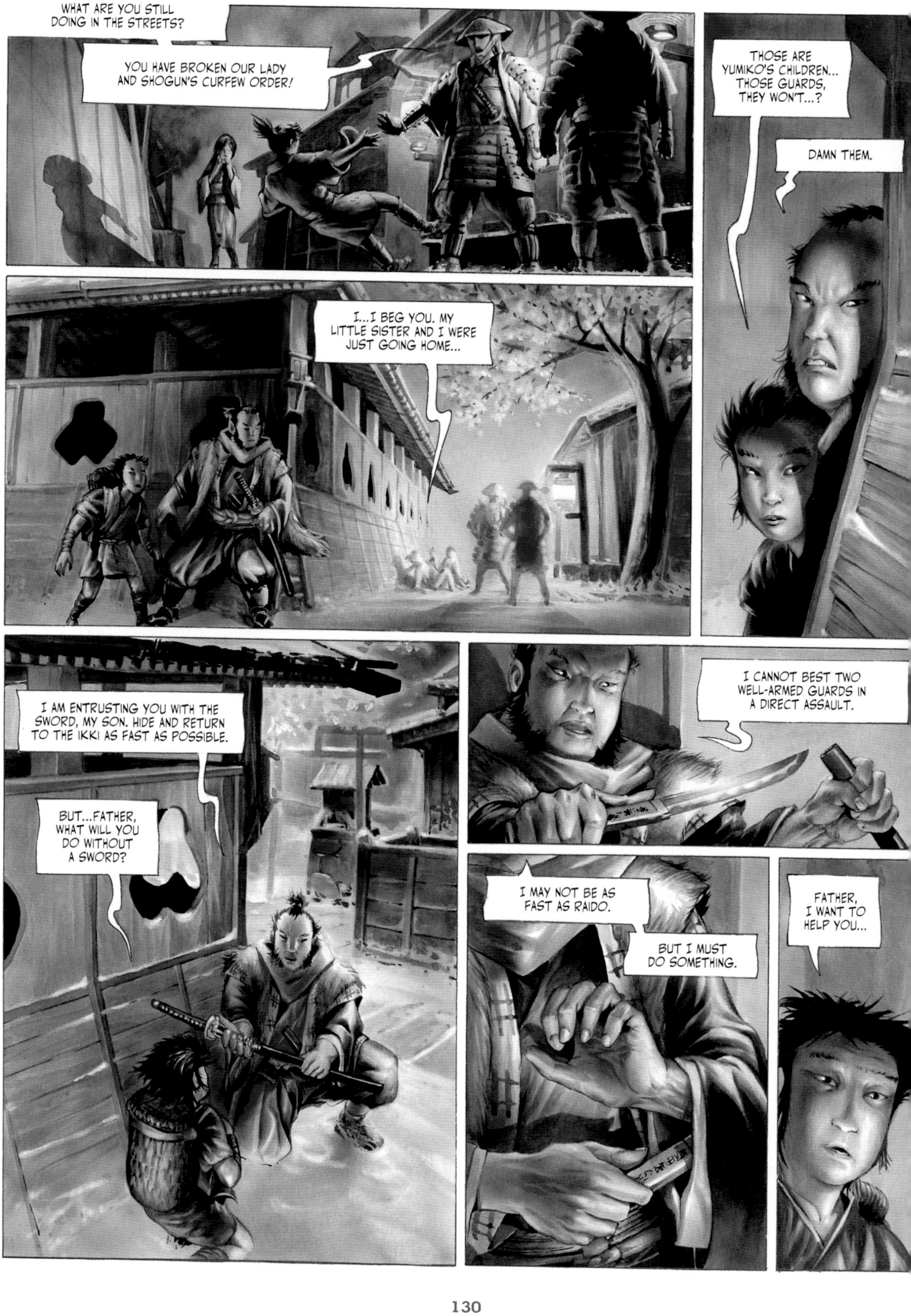
WHAT ARE YOU STILL DOING IN THE STREETS?
YOU HAVE BROKEN OUR LADY AND SHOGUN'S CURFEW ORDER!
I...I BEG YOU. MY LITTLE SISTER AND I WERE JUST GOING HOME...
THOSE ARE YUMIKO'S CHILDREN... THOSE GUARDS, THEY WON'T...?
DAMN THEM.
I AM ENTRUSTING YOU WITH THE SWORD, MY SON. HIDE AND RETURN TO THE IKKI AS FAST AS POSSIBLE.
BUT...FATHER, WHAT WILL YOU DO WITHOUT A SWORD?
I CANNOT BEST TWO WELL-ARMED GUARDS IN A DIRECT ASSAULT.
I MAY NOT BE AS FAST AS RAIDO.
BUT I MUST DO SOMETHING.
FATHER, I WANT TO HELP YOU...

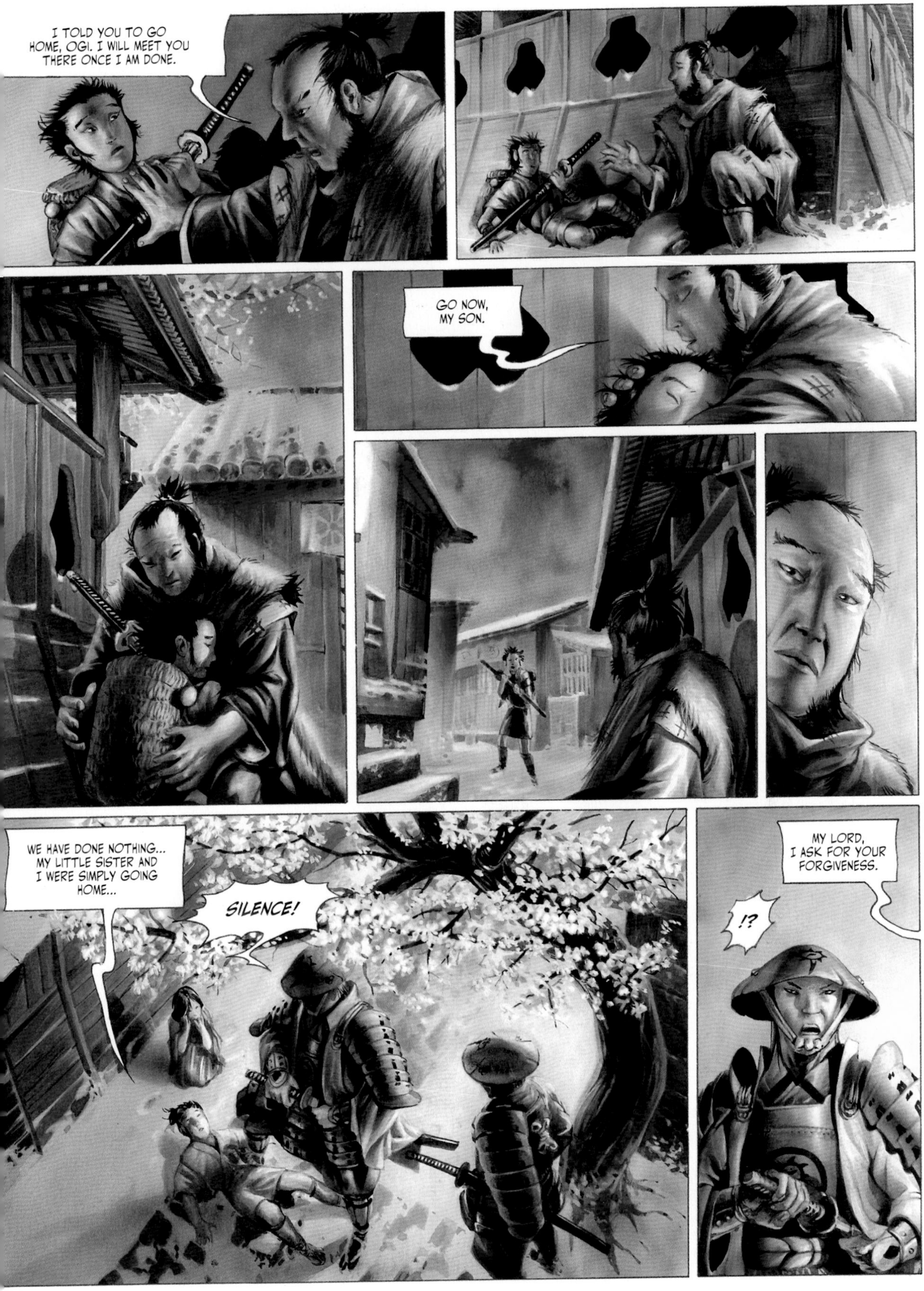
I TOLD YOU TO GO HOME, OGI. I WILL MEET YOU THERE ONCE I AM DONE.
GO NOW, MY SON.
WE HAVE DONE NOTHING... MY LITTLE SISTER AND I WERE SIMPLY GOING HOME...
SILENCE!
MY LORD, I ASK FOR YOUR FORGIVENESS.
!?

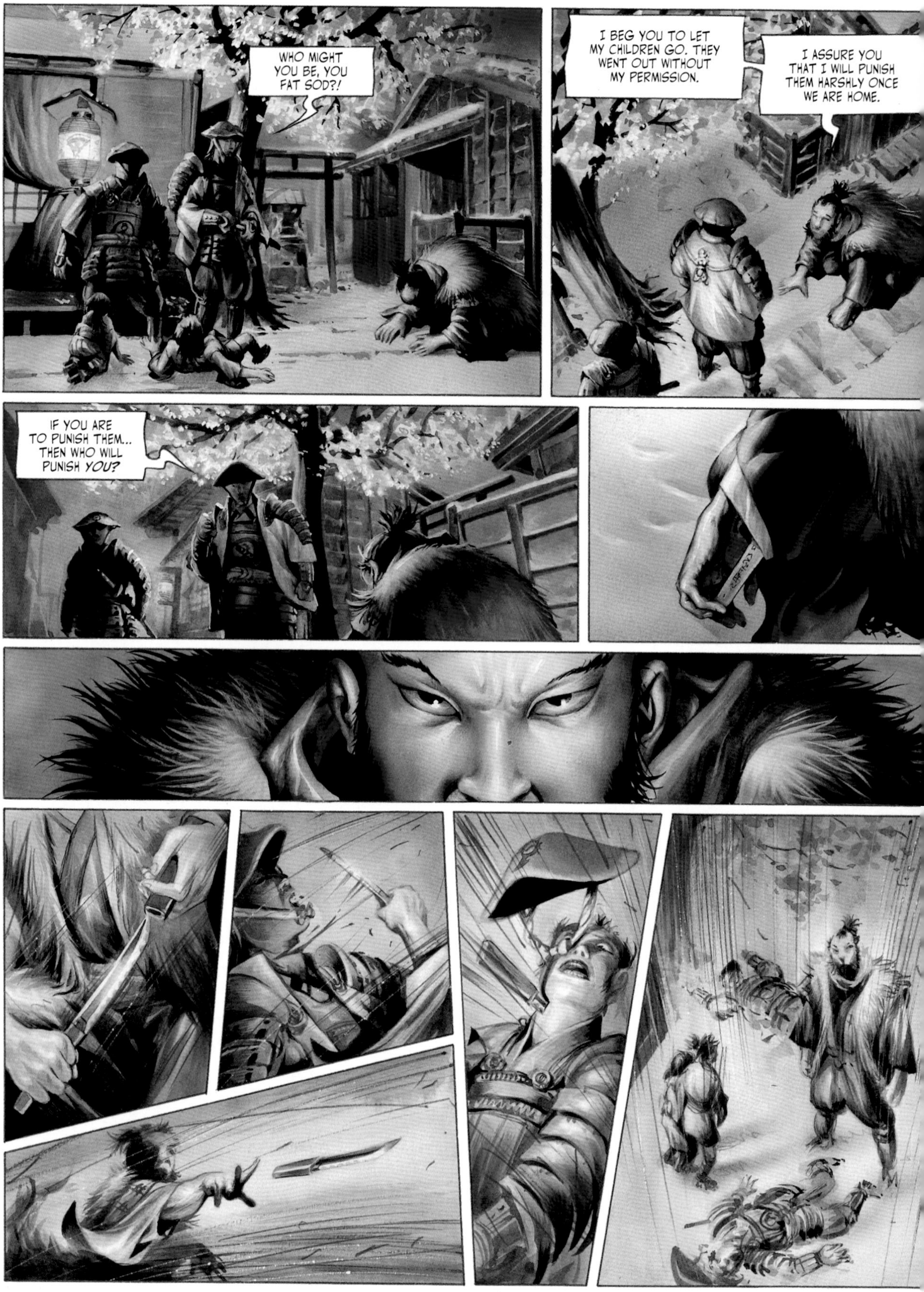
WHO MIGHT YOU BE, YOU FAT SOD?!
I BEG YOU TO LET MY CHILDREN GO. THEY WENT OUT WITHOUT MY PERMISSION.
I ASSURE YOU THAT I WILL PUNISH THEM HARSHLY ONCE WE ARE HOME.
IF YOU ARE TO PUNISH THEM... THEN WHO WILL PUNISH *YOU?*

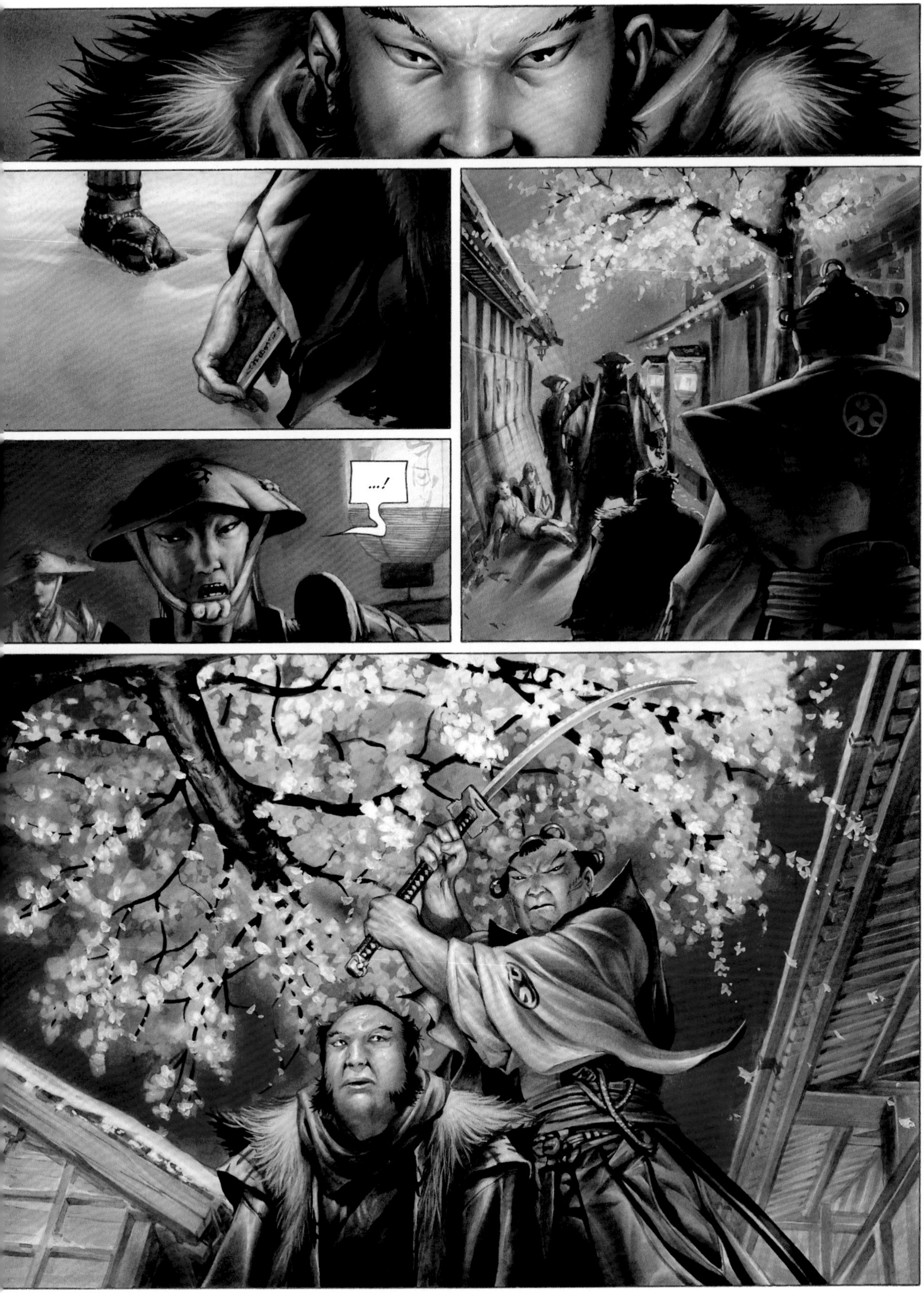

...!

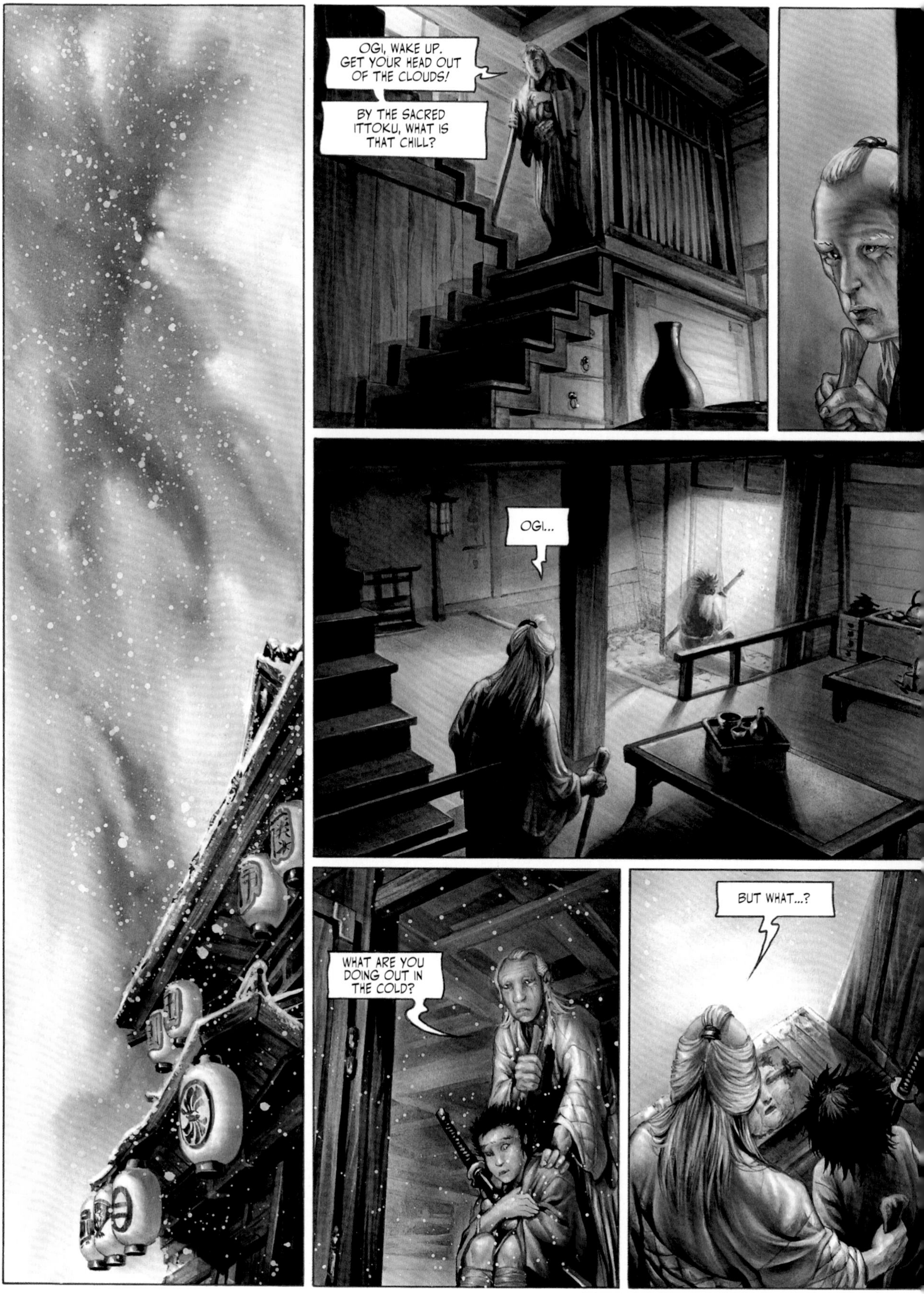
OGI, WAKE UP. GET YOUR HEAD OUT OF THE CLOUDS!
BY THE SACRED ITTOKU, WHAT IS THAT CHILL?
OGI...
WHAT ARE YOU DOING OUT IN THE COLD?
BUT WHAT...?

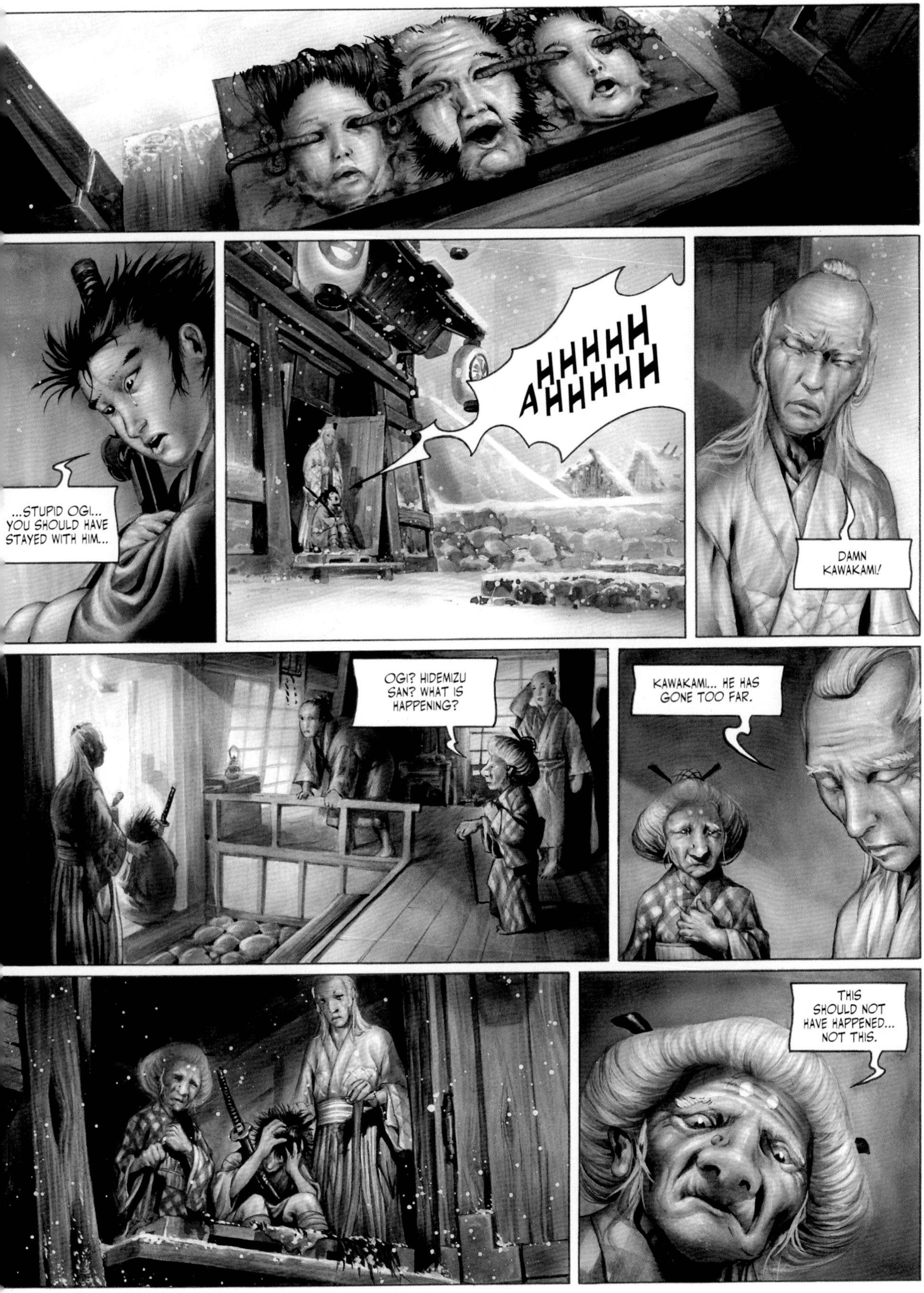
...STUPID OGI... YOU SHOULD HAVE STAYED WITH HIM...
HHHHH AHHHHH
DAMN KAWAKAMI!
OGI? HIDEMIZU SAN? WHAT IS HAPPENING?
KAWAKAMI... HE HAS GONE TOO FAR.
THIS SHOULD NOT HAVE HAPPENED... NOT THIS.

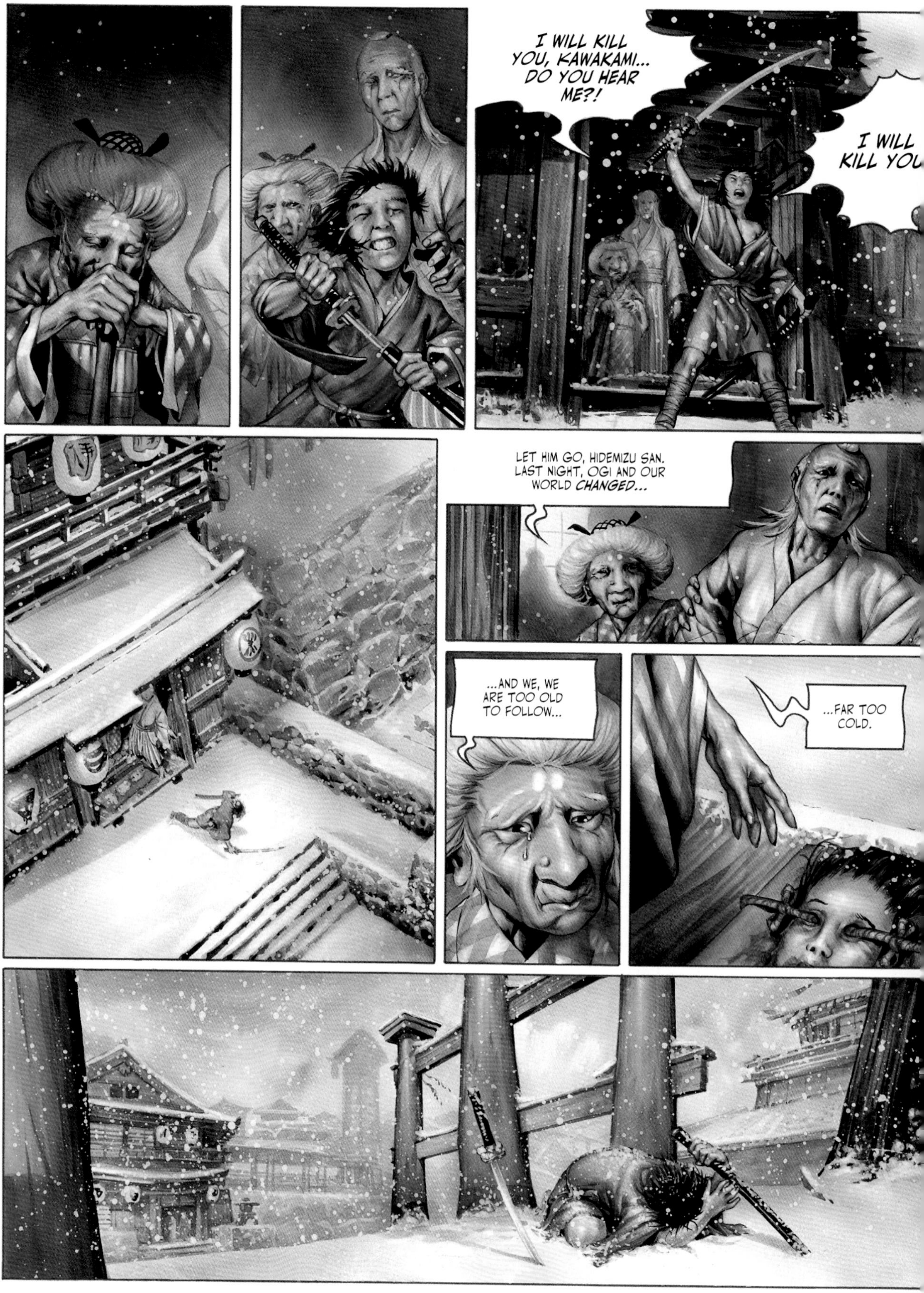
I WILL KILL YOU, KAWAKAMI... DO YOU HEAR ME?!
I WILL KILL YOU
LET HIM GO, HIDEMIZU SAN. LAST NIGHT, OGI AND OUR WORLD CHANGED...
...AND WE, WE ARE TOO OLD TO FOLLOW...
...FAR TOO COLD.

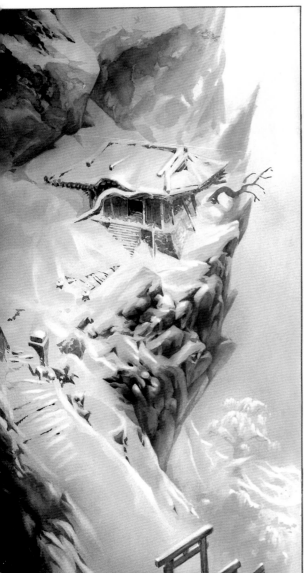

MY THOUGHTS ARE MORE LUCID, AND MY PERCEPTION IS CLEARER.

MY BODY ACHES AFTER THE EFFORT OF THE *MAKYO* PURIFICATION.

I TRY TO RISE, BUT MY LEGS FEEL AS IF I HAVE RACED ACROSS THE WHOLE FOREST.

YET, WHAT ENTERS MY THOUGHTS IN THIS MOMENT IS VERY SIMPLE...

...I FEEL WELL.

IT IS AS IF I HAVE BEEN RELEASED FROM A BURDEN TOO LONG CARRIED.

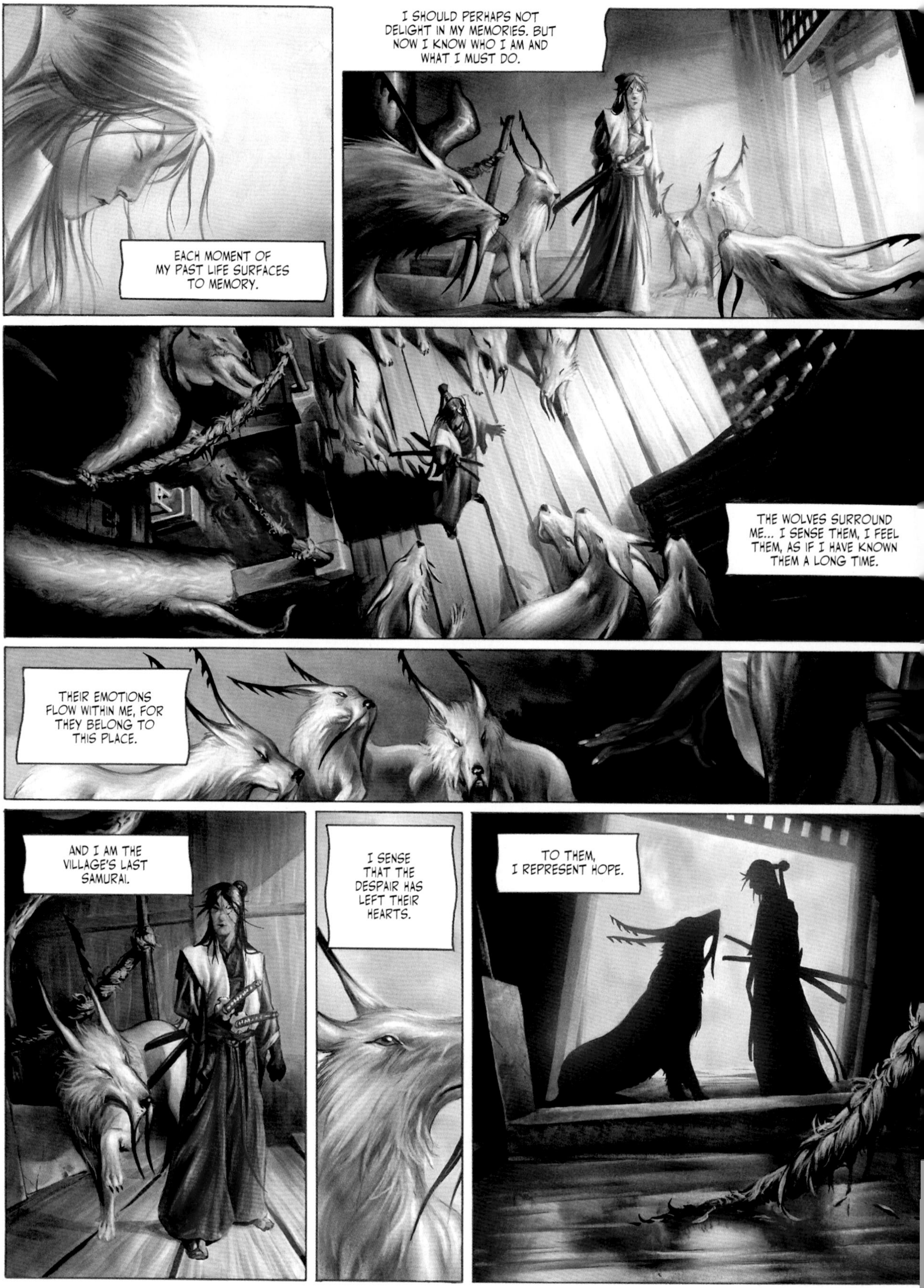
EACH MOMENT OF MY PAST LIFE SURFACES TO MEMORY.
I SHOULD PERHAPS NOT DELIGHT IN MY MEMORIES. BUT NOW I KNOW WHO I AM AND WHAT I MUST DO.
THE WOLVES SURROUND ME... I SENSE THEM, I FEEL THEM, AS IF I HAVE KNOWN THEM A LONG TIME.
THEIR EMOTIONS FLOW WITHIN ME, FOR THEY BELONG TO THIS PLACE.
AND I AM THE VILLAGE'S LAST SAMURAI.
I SENSE THAT THE DESPAIR HAS LEFT THEIR HEARTS.
TO THEM, I REPRESENT HOPE.

MY SOUL RETURNS TO THOUGHTS OF THE YOUNG WOMAN HIDDEN IN THE WELL.

SHE ALSO ESCAPED THE DESTRUCTION OF THE VILLAGE ORDERED BY TOTECU FUJIWARA.

MYOBU... MEIKI'S MOTHER.

SHE AND I ARE ALL WHO REMAIN OF THE PEOPLE WHO HONORED THIS SACRED TEMPLE. OUR PATHS ARE LINKED, MORE SO THAN I EVER IMAGINED.

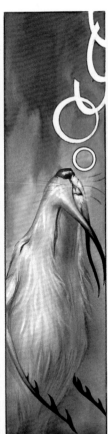

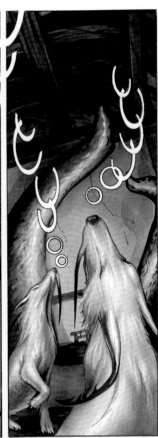

THE SONG OF THE IZUNA INVITES ME TO WALK OUTSIDE WITH THEM.

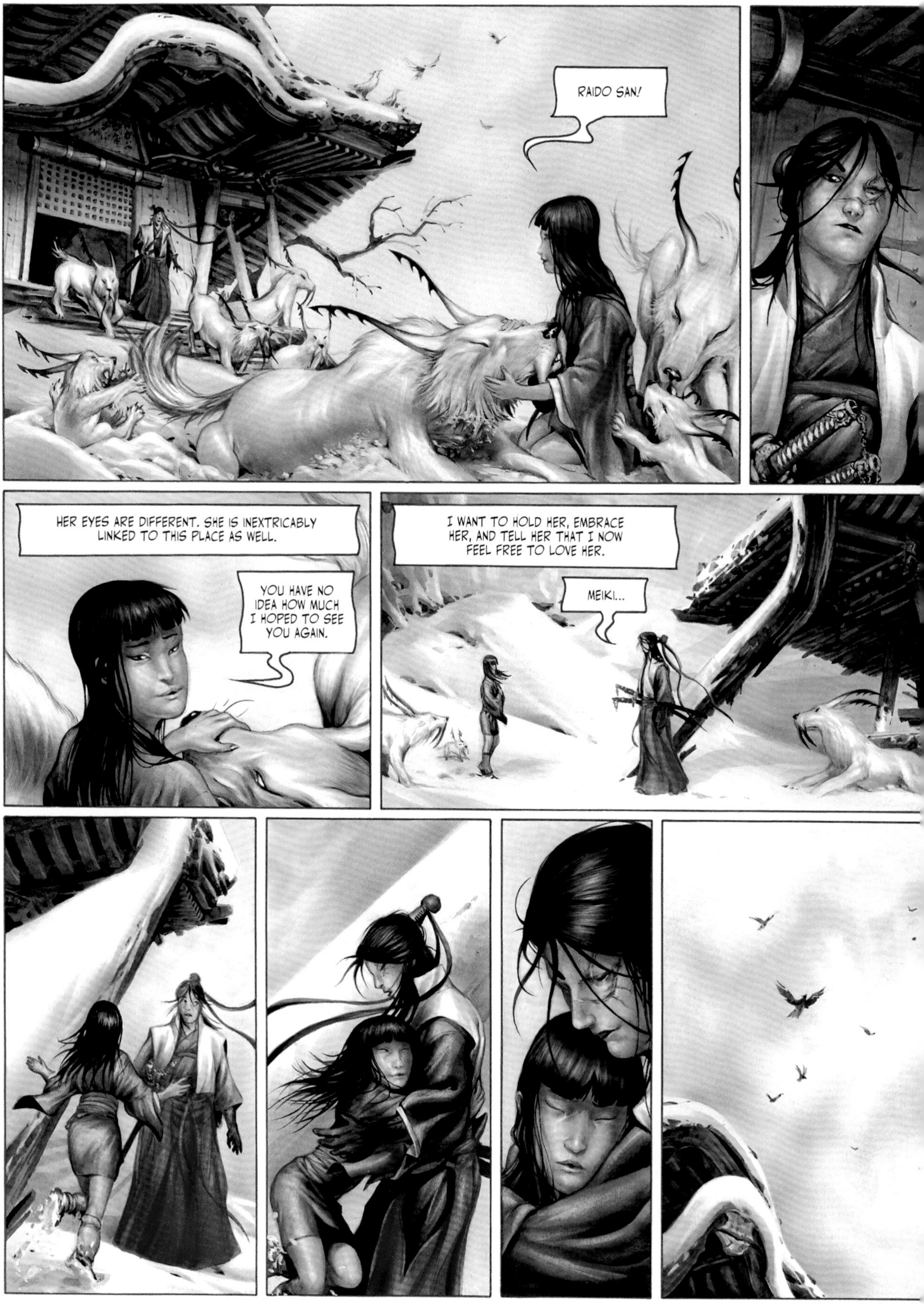
RAIDO SAN!
HER EYES ARE DIFFERENT. SHE IS INEXTRICABLY LINKED TO THIS PLACE AS WELL.
YOU HAVE NO IDEA HOW MUCH I HOPED TO SEE YOU AGAIN.
I WANT TO HOLD HER, EMBRACE HER, AND TELL HER THAT I NOW FEEL FREE TO LOVE HER.
MEIKI...

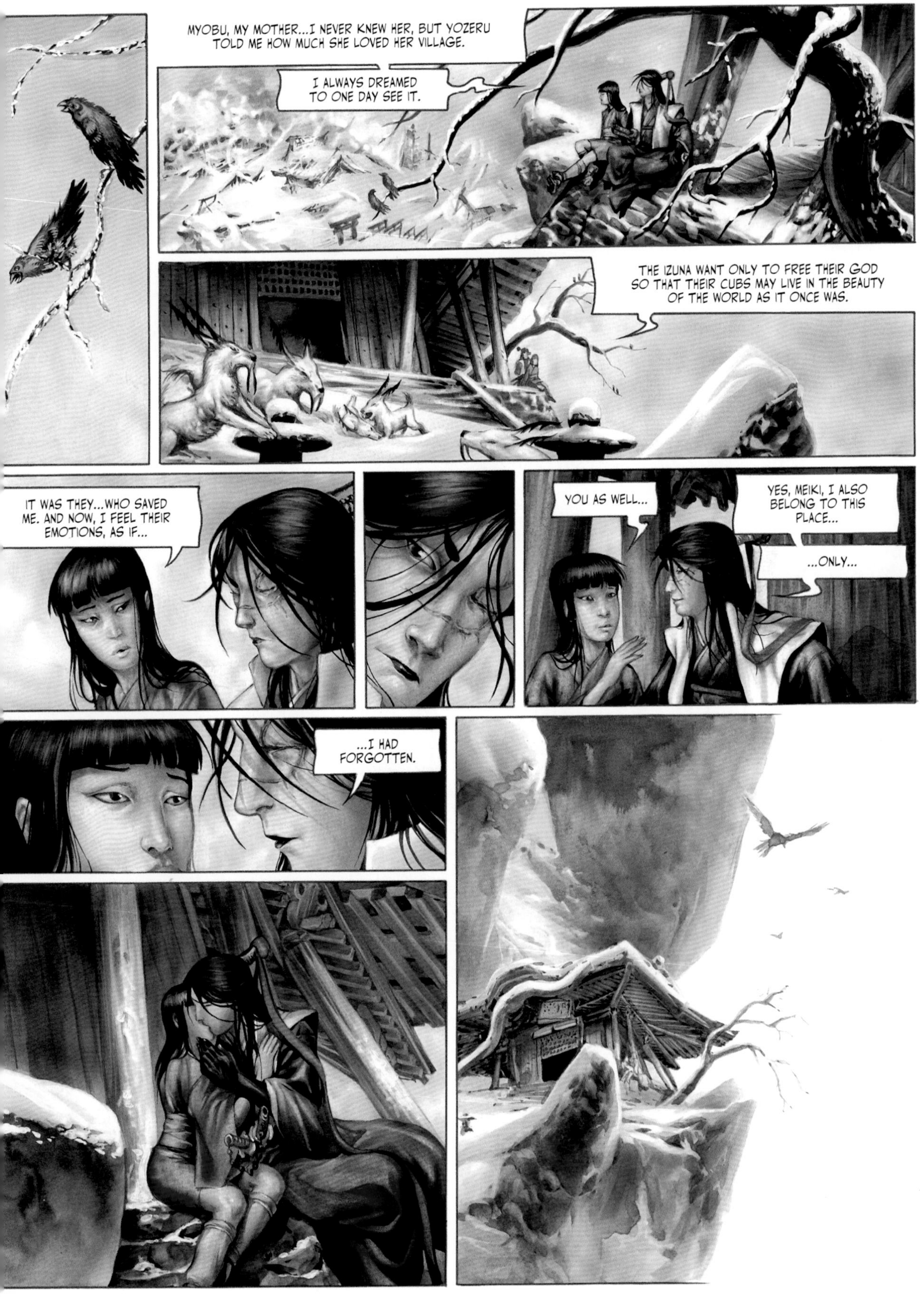

MYOBU, MY MOTHER...I NEVER KNEW HER, BUT YOZERU TOLD ME HOW MUCH SHE LOVED HER VILLAGE.
I ALWAYS DREAMED TO ONE DAY SEE IT.
THE IZUNA WANT ONLY TO FREE THEIR GOD SO THAT THEIR CUBS MAY LIVE IN THE BEAUTY OF THE WORLD AS IT ONCE WAS.
IT WAS THEY...WHO SAVED ME. AND NOW, I FEEL THEIR EMOTIONS, AS IF...
YOU AS WELL...
YES, MEIKI, I ALSO BELONG TO THIS PLACE...
...ONLY...
...I HAD FORGOTTEN.

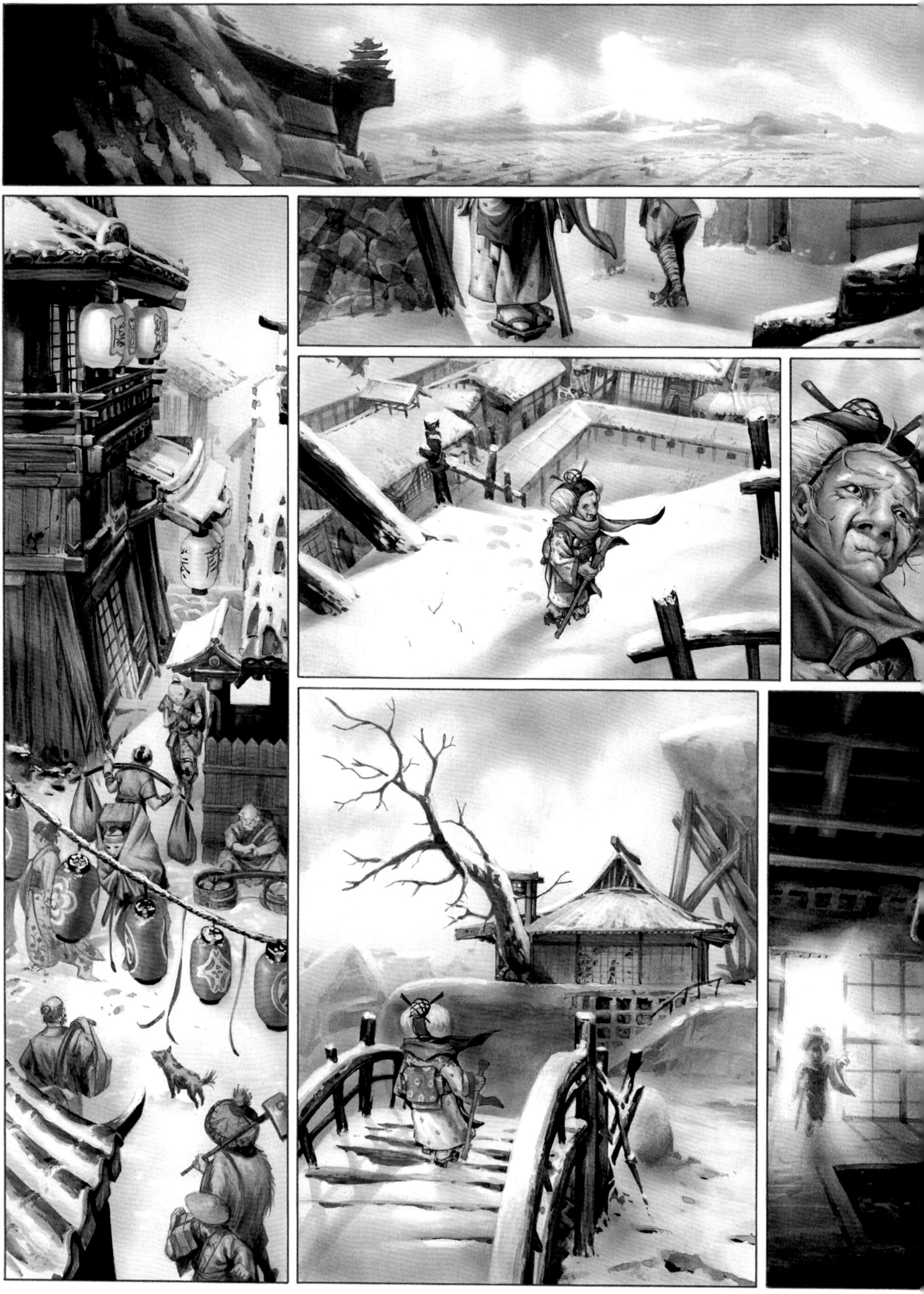

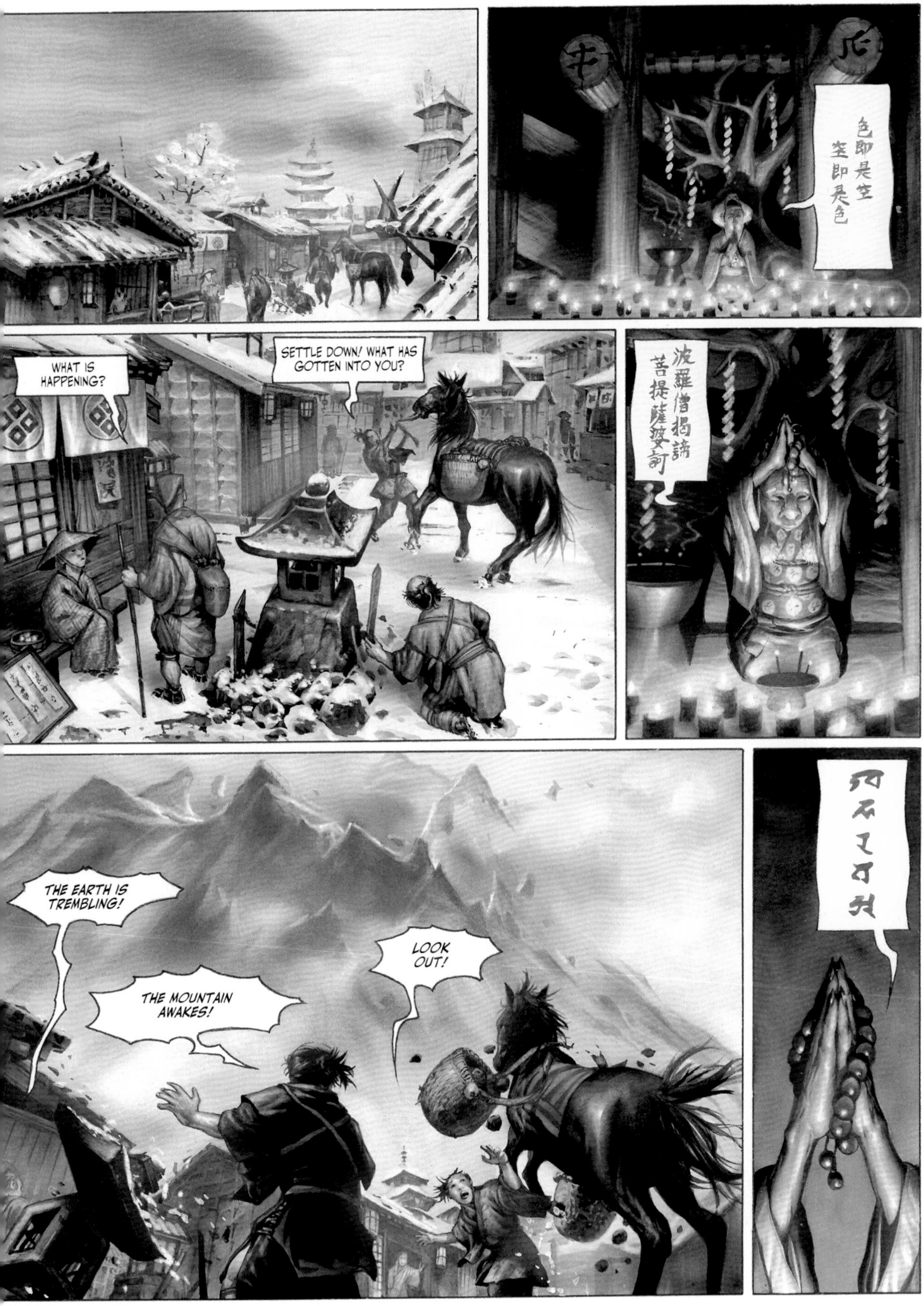

色即是空
空即是色
WHAT IS HAPPENING?
SETTLE DOWN! WHAT HAS GOTTEN INTO YOU?
波羅僧揭諦
菩提薩婆訶
THE EARTH IS TREMBLING!
THE MOUNTAIN AWAKES!
LOOK OUT!

BRROOOUMM

IT'S THE SHUGENDO!

MY LADY...

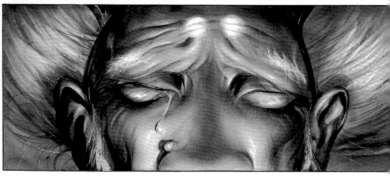

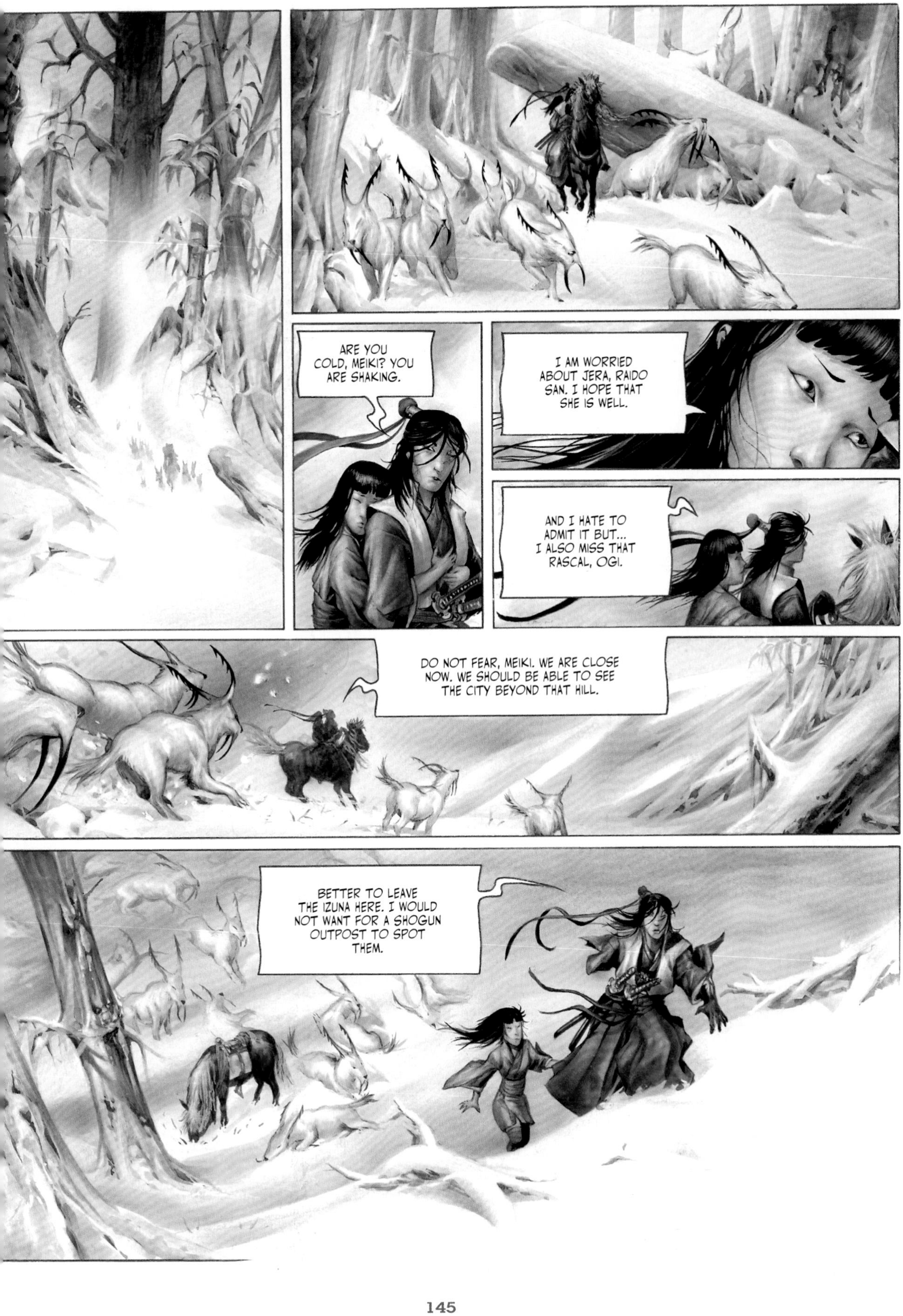

ARE YOU COLD, MEIKI? YOU ARE SHAKING.
I AM WORRIED ABOUT JERA, RAIDO SAN. I HOPE THAT SHE IS WELL.
AND I HATE TO ADMIT IT BUT... I ALSO MISS THAT RASCAL, OGI.
DO NOT FEAR, MEIKI. WE ARE CLOSE NOW. WE SHOULD BE ABLE TO SEE THE CITY BEYOND THAT HILL.
BETTER TO LEAVE THE IZUNA HERE. I WOULD NOT WANT FOR A SHOGUN OUTPOST TO SPOT THEM.

IT IS NOT FOG, MEIKI...
THE MOUNTAIN IS WAKING.

RAIDO SAN,
I AM AFRAID.

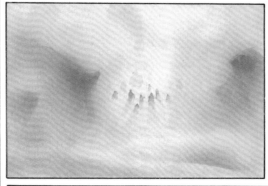

THE GODS ARE ANGRY,
AND THEY SHOUT THEIR
FURY TO THE SKY.

"ALL THESE PEOPLE ARE
LEAVING THE CITY THAT
SPEAKS TO THE SKY."

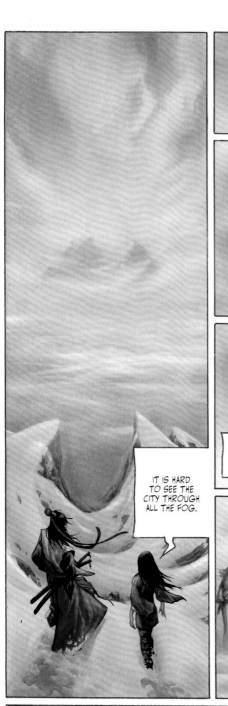

IT IS HARD
TO SEE THE
CITY THROUGH
ALL THE FOG.

THEY LEAVE BEHIND THEIR
HOMES, THEIR SHOPS, ALL
THEIR BELONGINGS.

YOU ARE NOT
ALONE WITH YOUR
FEAR, MEIKI.

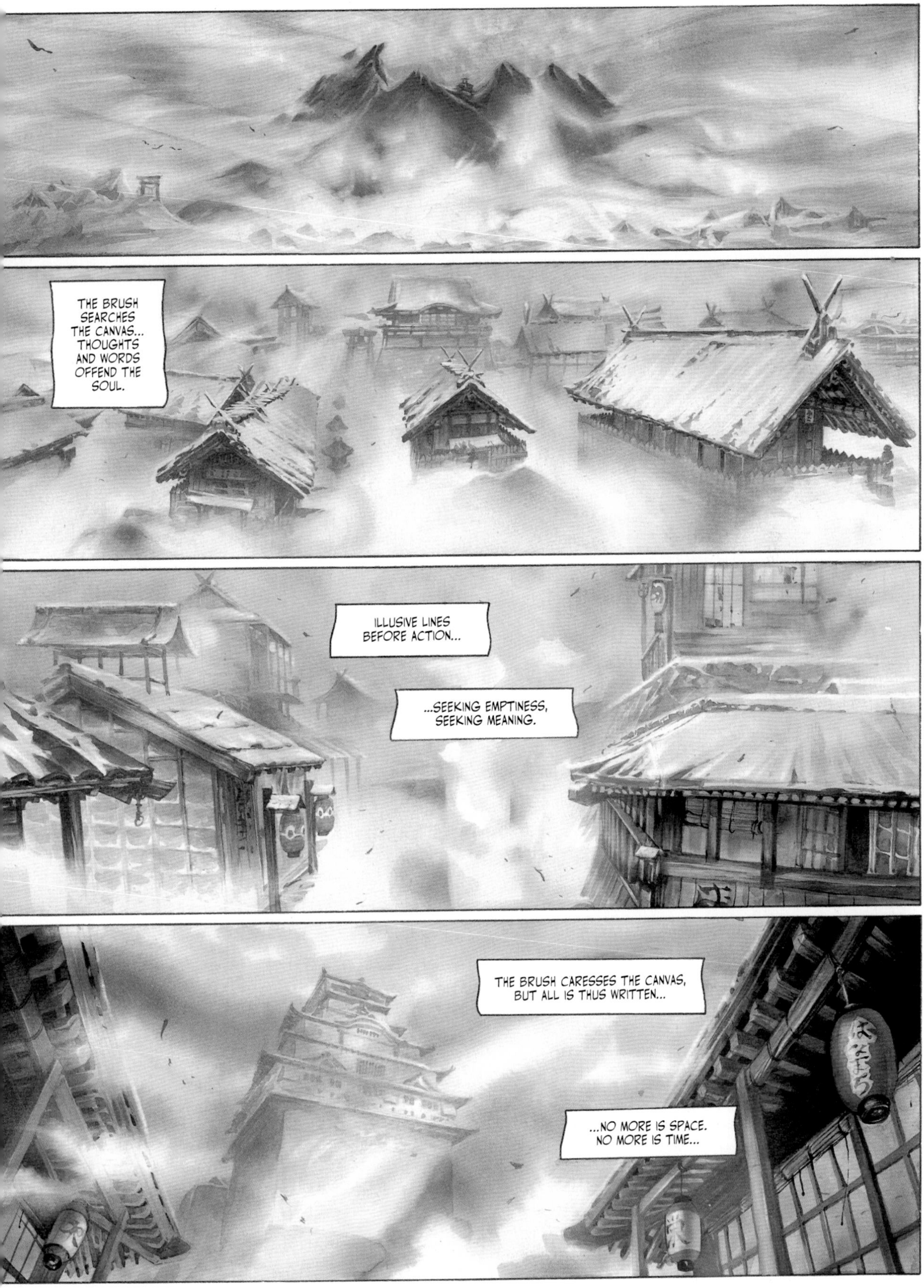
THE BRUSH SEARCHES THE CANVAS... THOUGHTS AND WORDS OFFEND THE SOUL.
ILLUSIVE LINES BEFORE ACTION...
...SEEKING EMPTINESS, SEEKING MEANING.
THE BRUSH CARESSES THE CANVAS, BUT ALL IS THUS WRITTEN...
...NO MORE IS SPACE. NO MORE IS TIME...

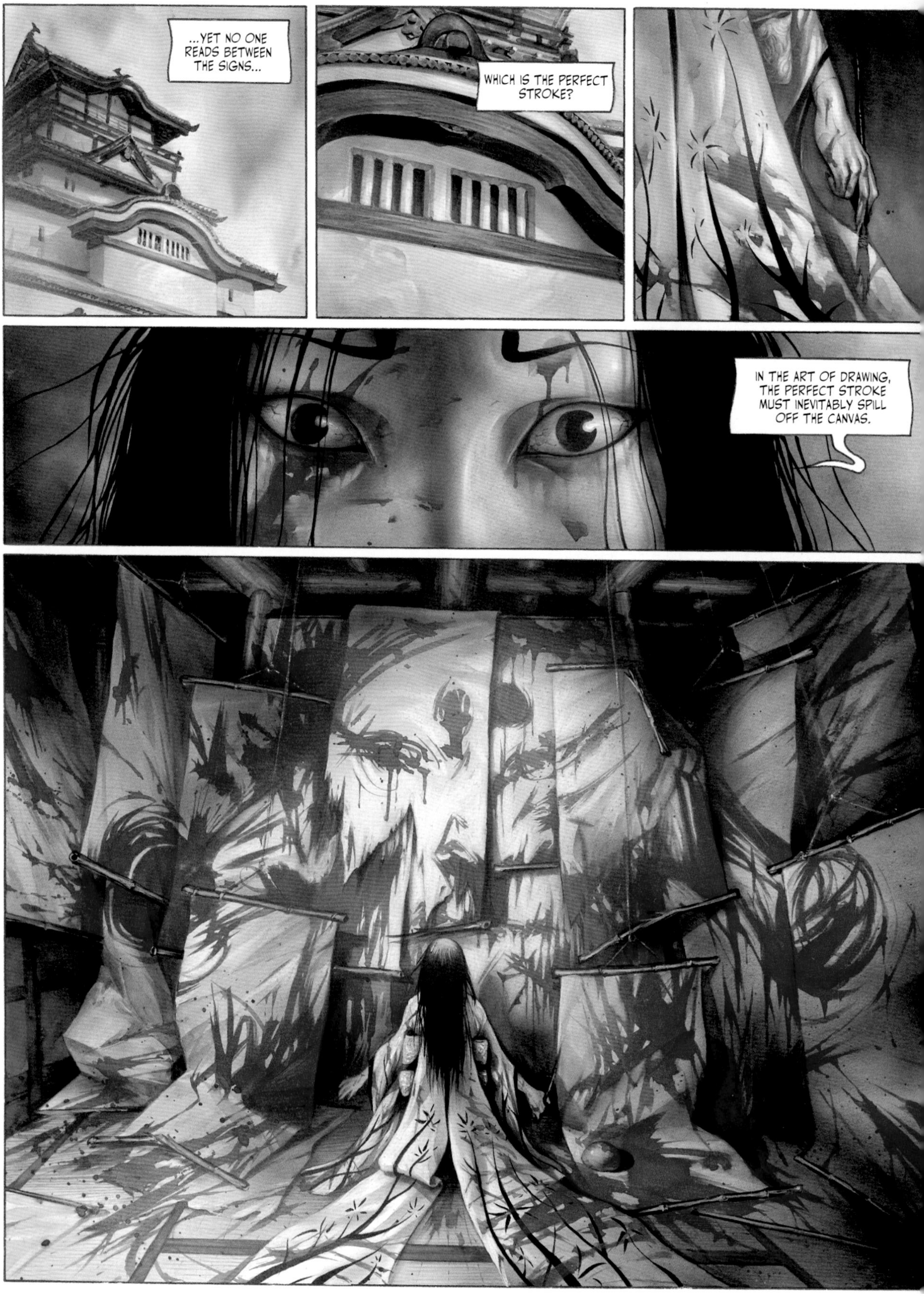
...YET NO ONE READS BETWEEN THE SIGNS...
WHICH IS THE PERFECT STROKE?
IN THE ART OF DRAWING, THE PERFECT STROKE MUST INEVITABLY SPILL OFF THE CANVAS.

CHAPTER FOUR:
The Abomination's Hidden Flower

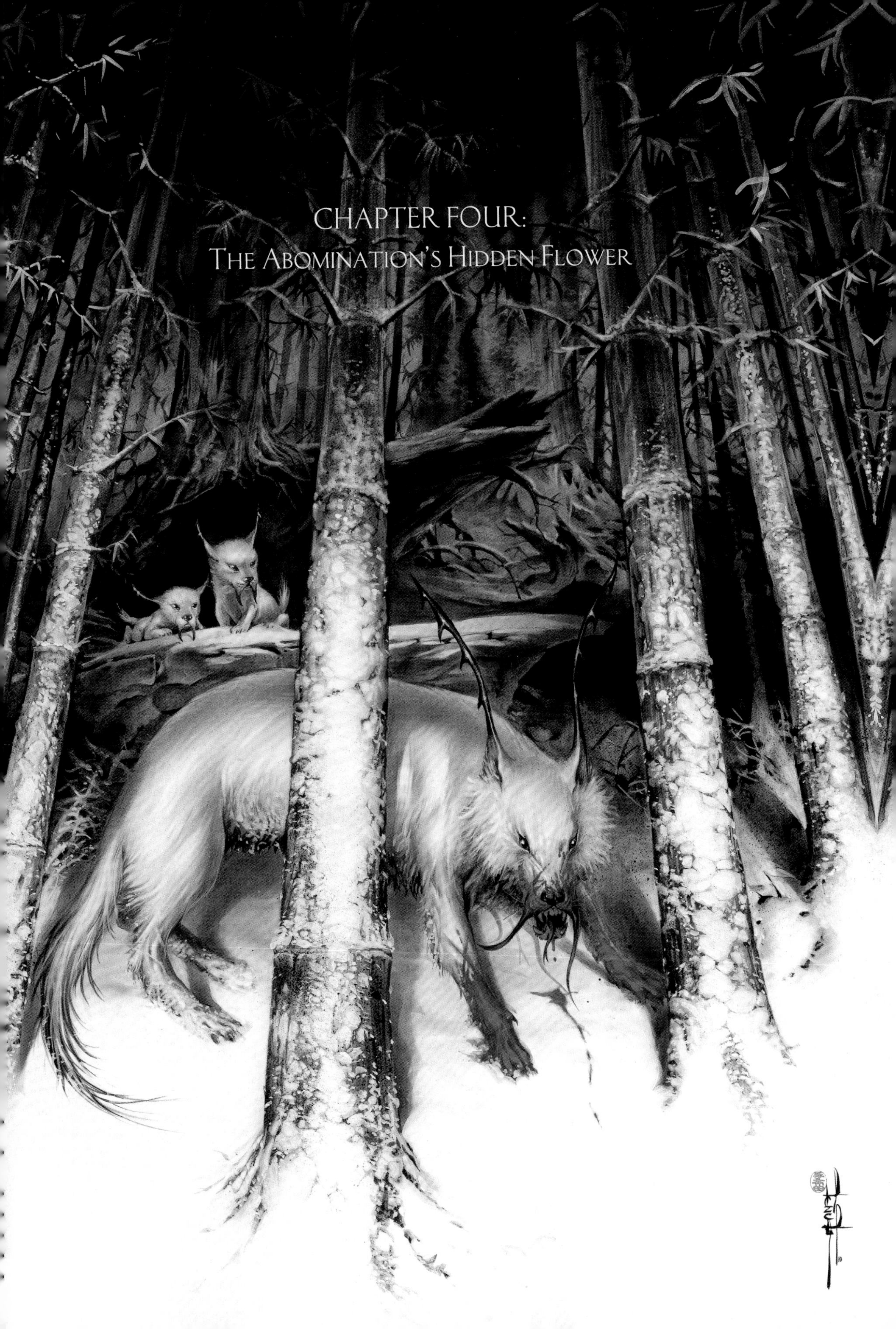

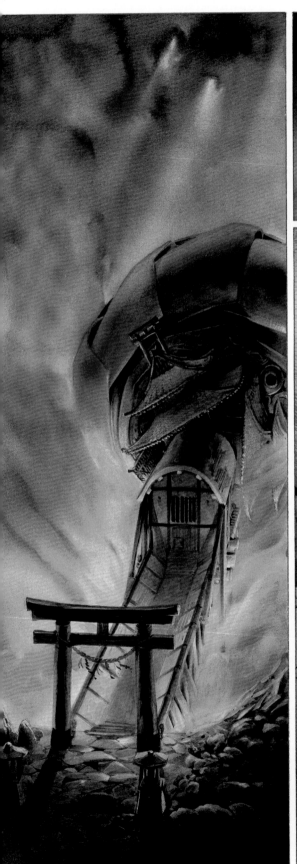

"CLOUDS OF BLOOD, CLOUDS OF RED, WITNESSES STANDING COLDLY BY.

"YOUR WHIRLWINDS SWIRLING LIKE PRYING EYES.

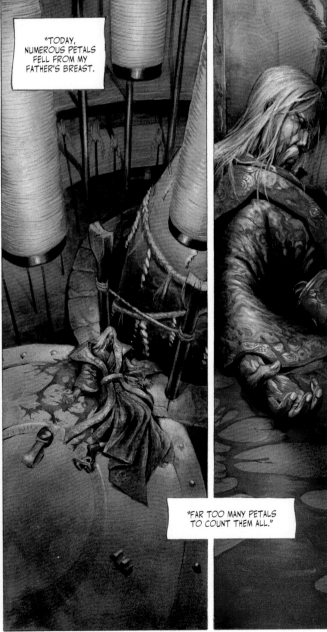

"TODAY, NUMEROUS PETALS FELL FROM MY FATHER'S BREAST.

"FAR TOO MANY PETALS TO COUNT THEM ALL."

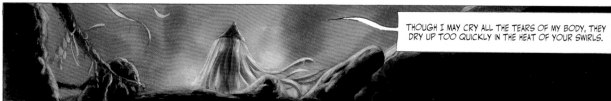

THOUGH I MAY CRY ALL THE TEARS OF MY BODY, THEY DRY UP TOO QUICKLY IN THE HEAT OF YOUR SWIRLS.

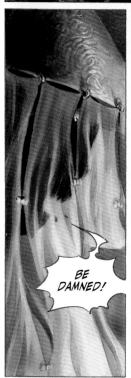

BE DAMNED!

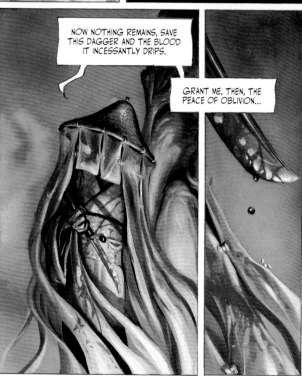

NOW NOTHING REMAINS, SAVE THIS DAGGER AND THE BLOOD IT INCESSANTLY DRIPS.

GRANT ME, THEN, THE PEACE OF OBLIVION...

...AND WITH THIS BLADE, TAKE IN YOUR EMBRACE THE LAST WITHERED FUJIWARA PETAL.

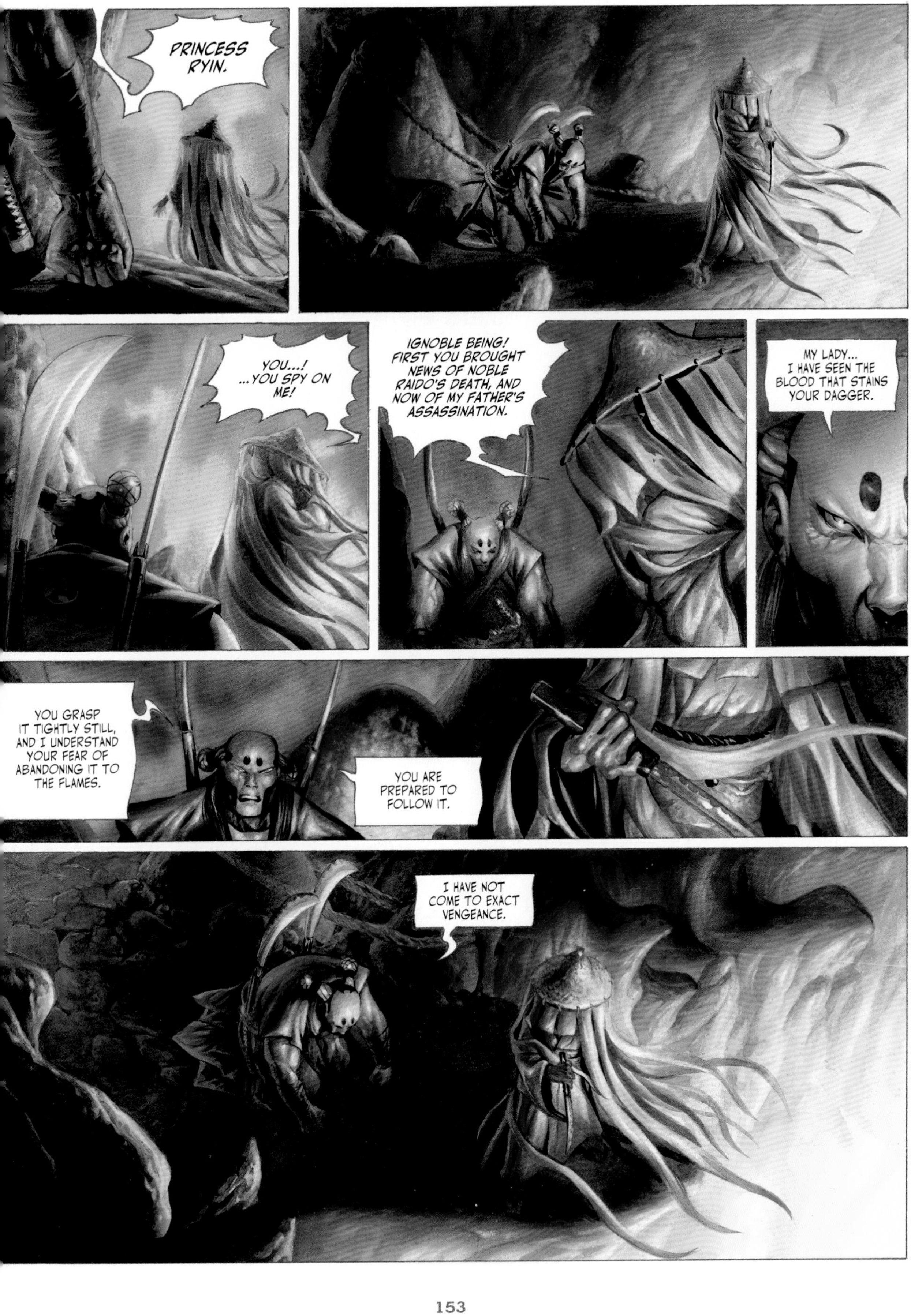
PRINCESS RYIN.
YOU...! ...YOU SPY ON ME!
IGNOBLE BEING! FIRST YOU BROUGHT NEWS OF NOBLE RAIDO'S DEATH, AND NOW OF MY FATHER'S ASSASSINATION.
MY LADY... I HAVE SEEN THE BLOOD THAT STAINS YOUR DAGGER.
YOU GRASP IT TIGHTLY STILL, AND I UNDERSTAND YOUR FEAR OF ABANDONING IT TO THE FLAMES.
YOU ARE PREPARED TO FOLLOW IT.
I HAVE NOT COME TO EXACT VENGEANCE.

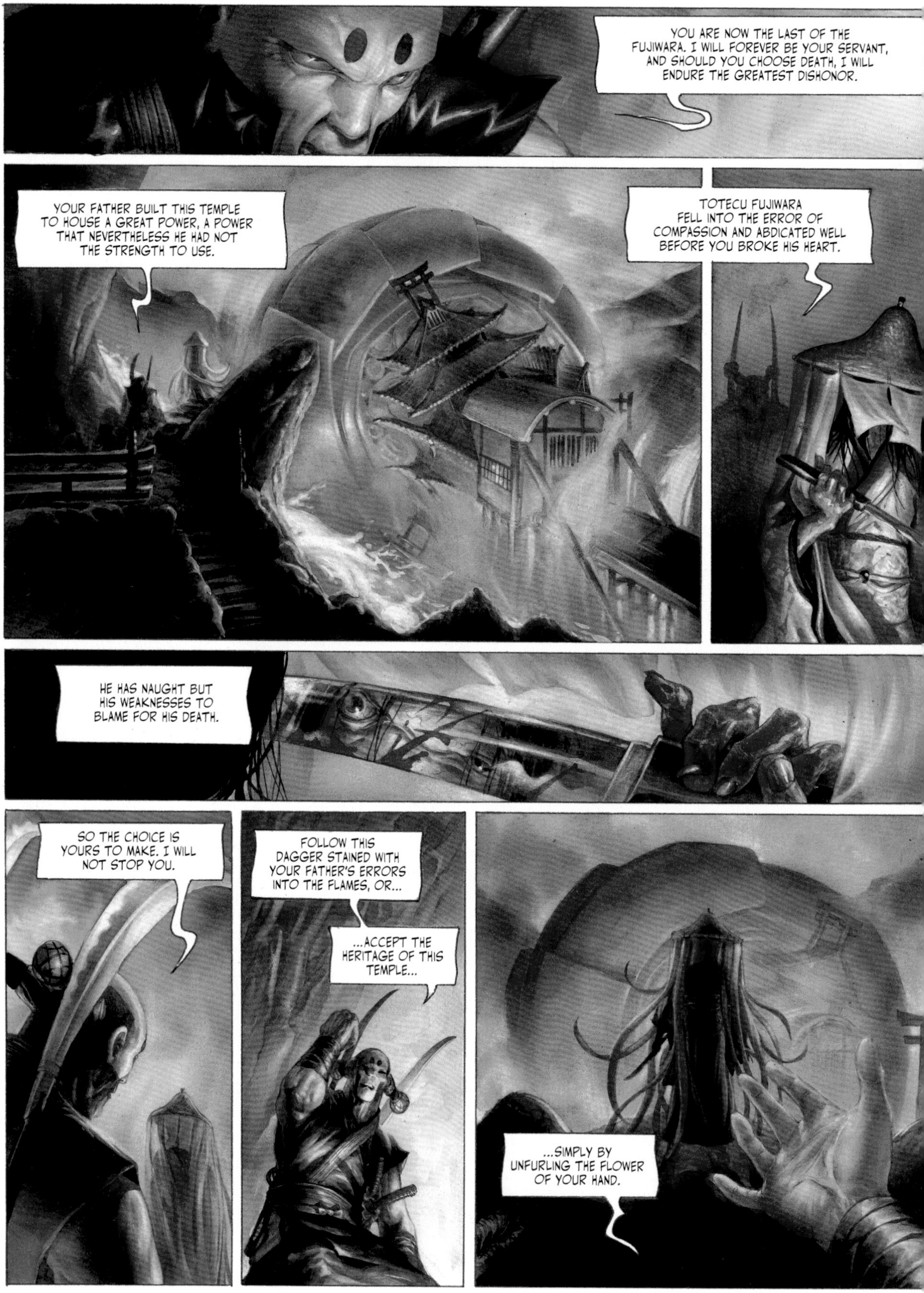
YOU ARE NOW THE LAST OF THE FUJIWARA. I WILL FOREVER BE YOUR SERVANT, AND SHOULD YOU CHOOSE DEATH, I WILL ENDURE THE GREATEST DISHONOR.
YOUR FATHER BUILT THIS TEMPLE TO HOUSE A GREAT POWER, A POWER THAT NEVERTHELESS HE HAD NOT THE STRENGTH TO USE.
TOTECU FUJIWARA FELL INTO THE ERROR OF COMPASSION AND ABDICATED WELL BEFORE YOU BROKE HIS HEART.
HE HAS NAUGHT BUT HIS WEAKNESSES TO BLAME FOR HIS DEATH.
SO THE CHOICE IS YOURS TO MAKE. I WILL NOT STOP YOU.
FOLLOW THIS DAGGER STAINED WITH YOUR FATHER'S ERRORS INTO THE FLAMES, OR...
...ACCEPT THE HERITAGE OF THIS TEMPLE...
...SIMPLY BY UNFURLING THE FLOWER OF YOUR HAND.

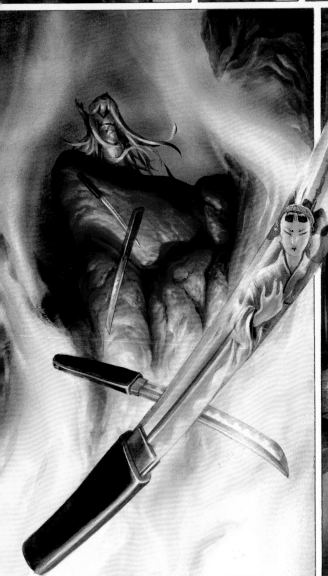

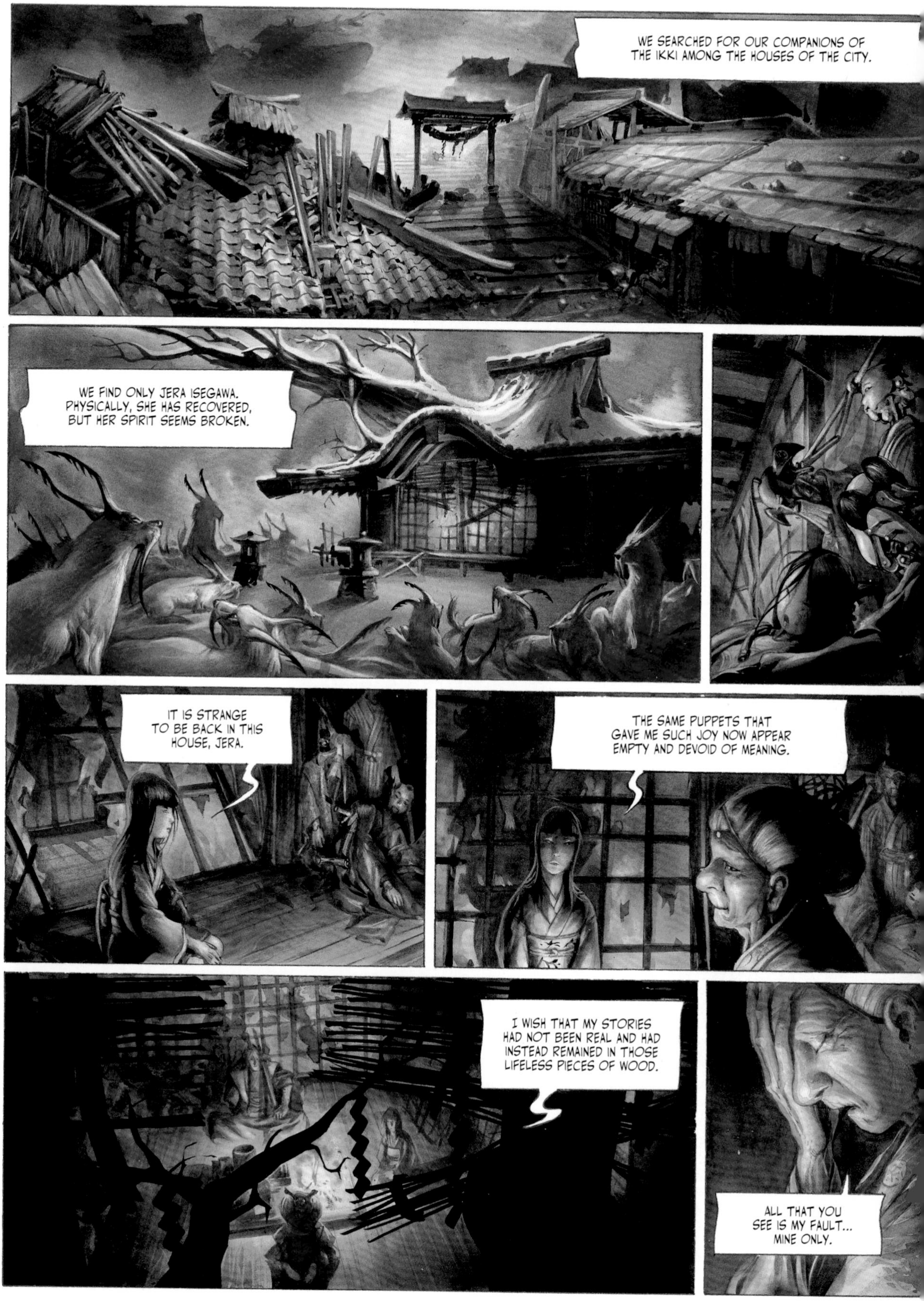
WE SEARCHED FOR OUR COMPANIONS OF THE IKKI AMONG THE HOUSES OF THE CITY.
WE FIND ONLY JERA ISEGAWA. PHYSICALLY, SHE HAS RECOVERED, BUT HER SPIRIT SEEMS BROKEN.
IT IS STRANGE TO BE BACK IN THIS HOUSE, JERA.
THE SAME PUPPETS THAT GAVE ME SUCH JOY NOW APPEAR EMPTY AND DEVOID OF MEANING.
I WISH THAT MY STORIES HAD NOT BEEN REAL AND HAD INSTEAD REMAINED IN THOSE LIFELESS PIECES OF WOOD.
ALL THAT YOU SEE IS MY FAULT... MINE ONLY.

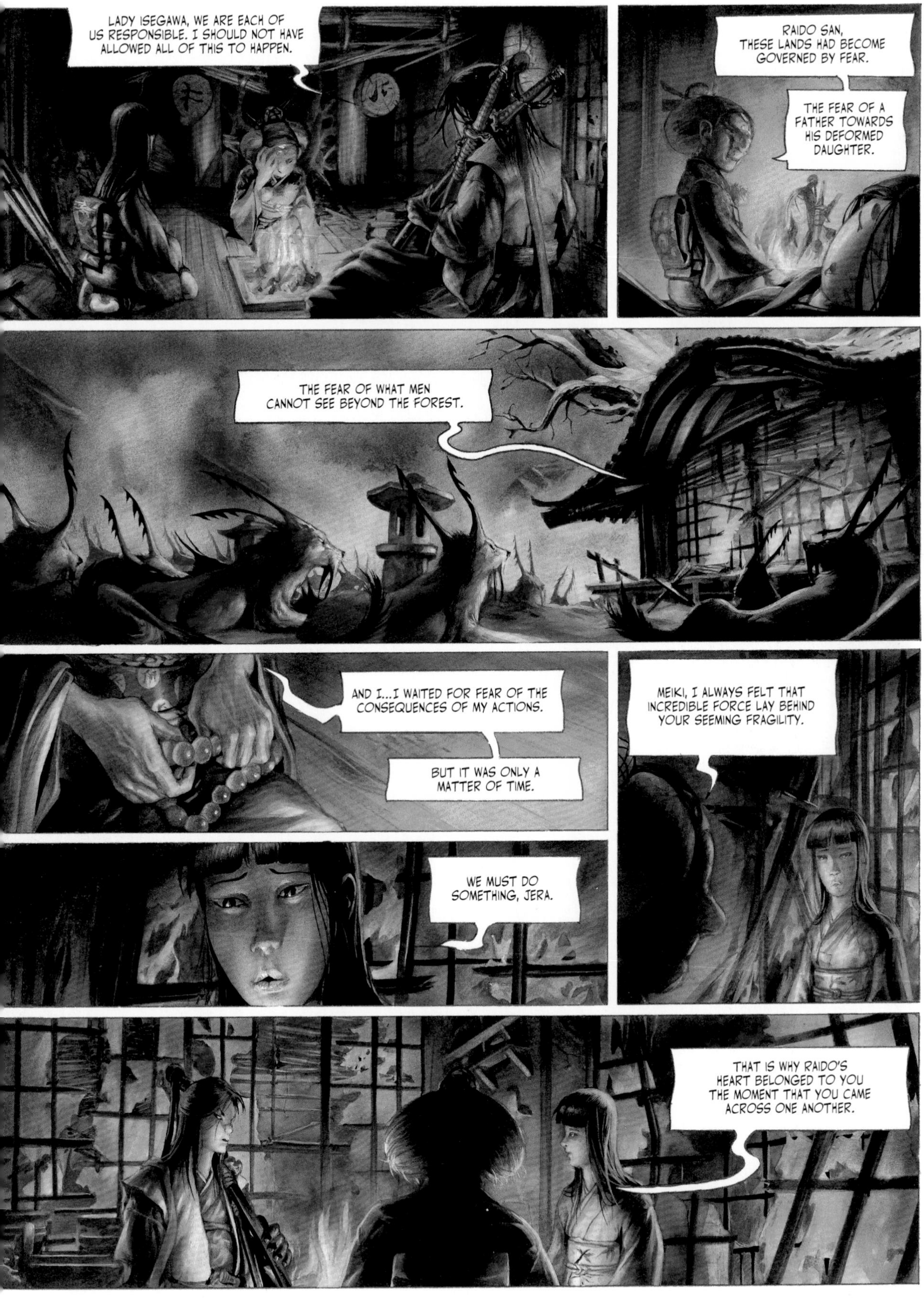
LADY ISEGAWA, WE ARE EACH OF US RESPONSIBLE. I SHOULD NOT HAVE ALLOWED ALL OF THIS TO HAPPEN.
RAIDO SAN, THESE LANDS HAD BECOME GOVERNED BY FEAR.
THE FEAR OF A FATHER TOWARDS HIS DEFORMED DAUGHTER.
THE FEAR OF WHAT MEN CANNOT SEE BEYOND THE FOREST.
AND I...I WAITED FOR FEAR OF THE CONSEQUENCES OF MY ACTIONS.
BUT IT WAS ONLY A MATTER OF TIME.
MEIKI, I ALWAYS FELT THAT INCREDIBLE FORCE LAY BEHIND YOUR SEEMING FRAGILITY.
WE MUST DO SOMETHING, JERA.
THAT IS WHY RAIDO'S HEART BELONGED TO YOU THE MOMENT THAT YOU CAME ACROSS ONE ANOTHER.

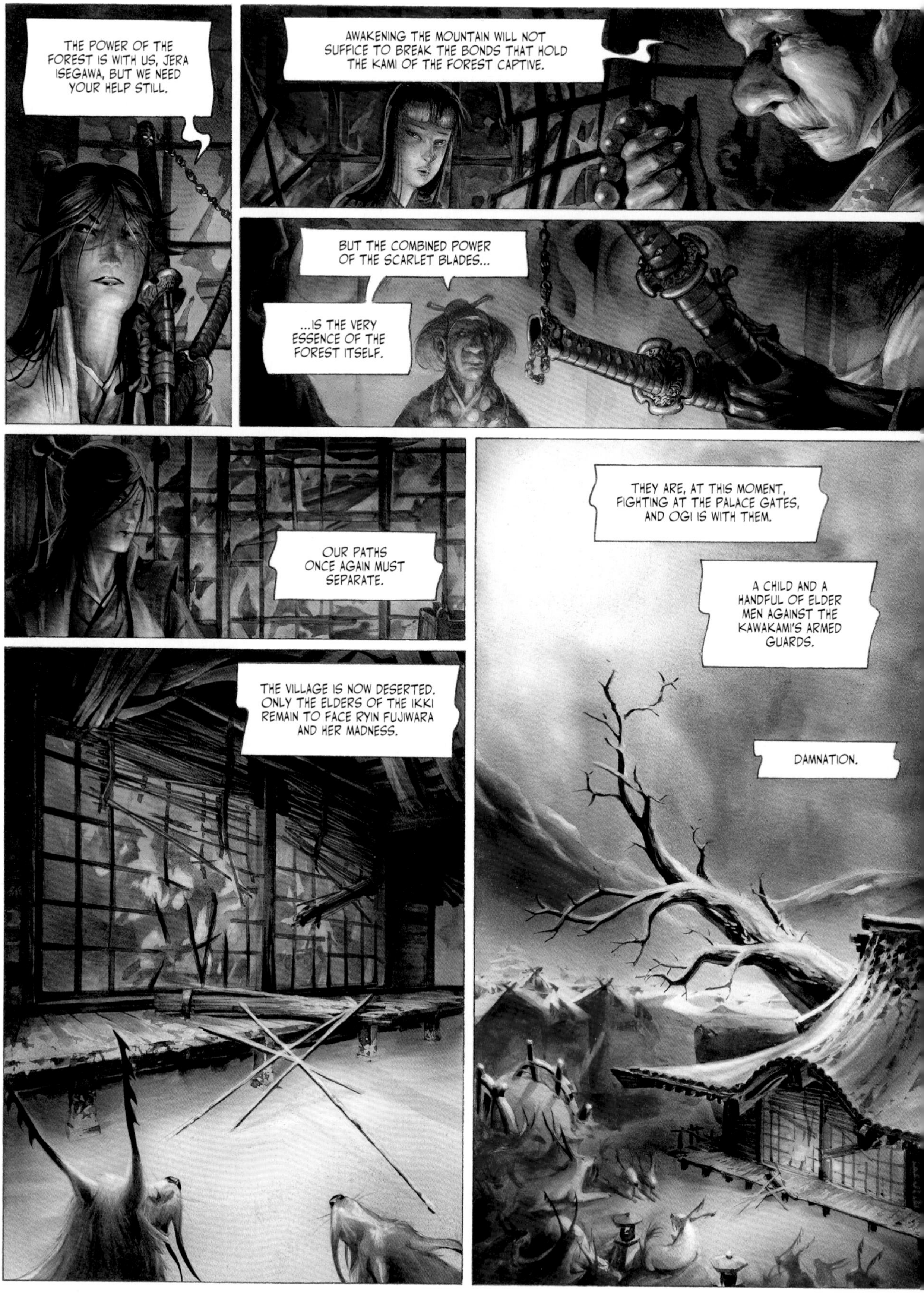
THE POWER OF THE FOREST IS WITH US, JERA ISEGAWA, BUT WE NEED YOUR HELP STILL.
AWAKENING THE MOUNTAIN WILL NOT SUFFICE TO BREAK THE BONDS THAT HOLD THE KAMI OF THE FOREST CAPTIVE.
BUT THE COMBINED POWER OF THE SCARLET BLADES...
...IS THE VERY ESSENCE OF THE FOREST ITSELF.
OUR PATHS ONCE AGAIN MUST SEPARATE.
THEY ARE, AT THIS MOMENT, FIGHTING AT THE PALACE GATES, AND OGI IS WITH THEM.
A CHILD AND A HANDFUL OF ELDER MEN AGAINST THE KAWAKAMI'S ARMED GUARDS.
DAMNATION.
THE VILLAGE IS NOW DESERTED. ONLY THE ELDERS OF THE IKKI REMAIN TO FACE RYIN FUJIWARA AND HER MADNESS.

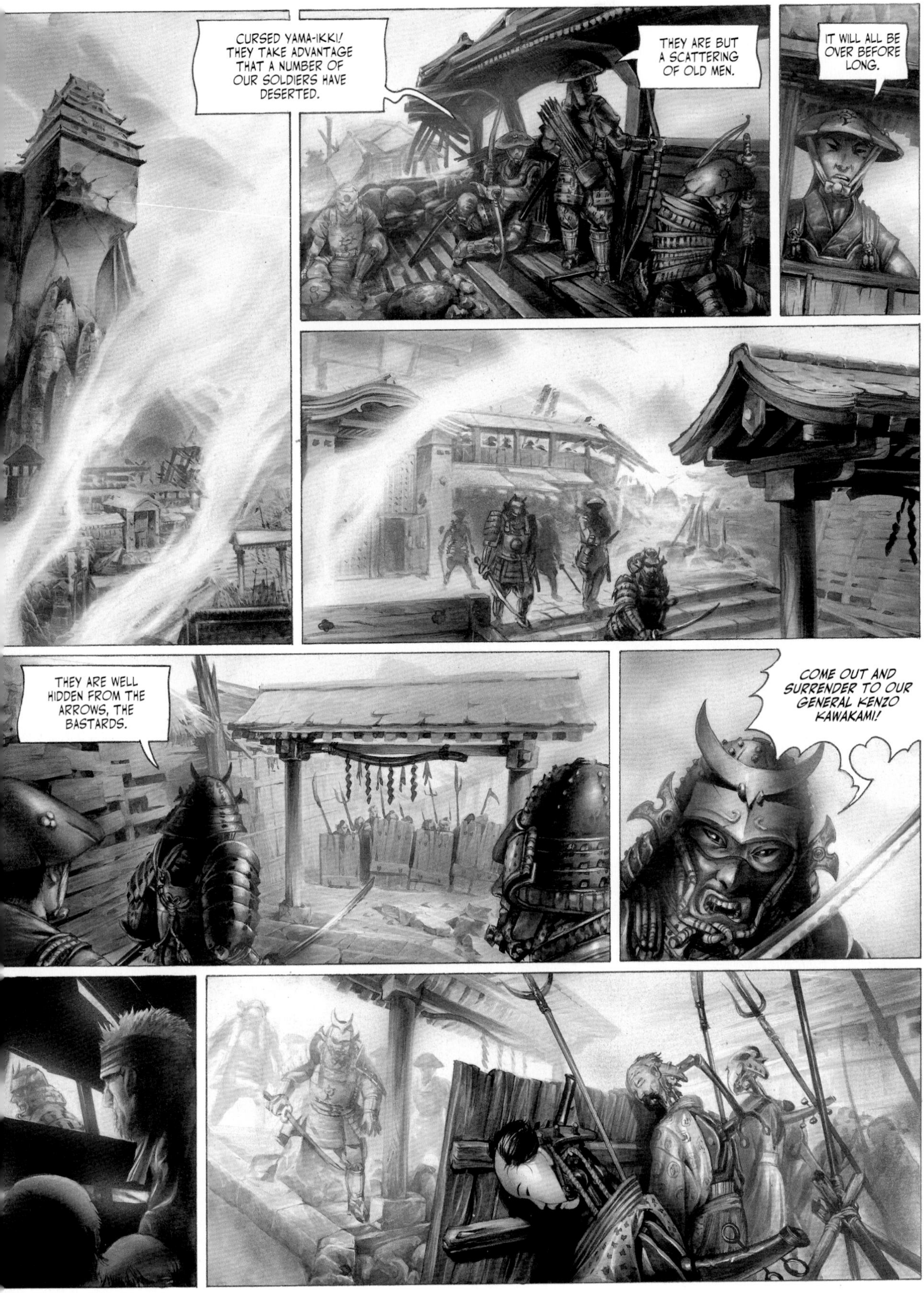
CURSED YAMA-IKKI! THEY TAKE ADVANTAGE THAT A NUMBER OF OUR SOLDIERS HAVE DESERTED.
THEY ARE BUT A SCATTERING OF OLD MEN.
IT WILL ALL BE OVER BEFORE LONG.
THEY ARE WELL HIDDEN FROM THE ARROWS, THE BASTARDS.
COME OUT AND SURRENDER TO OUR GENERAL KENZO KAWAKAMI!

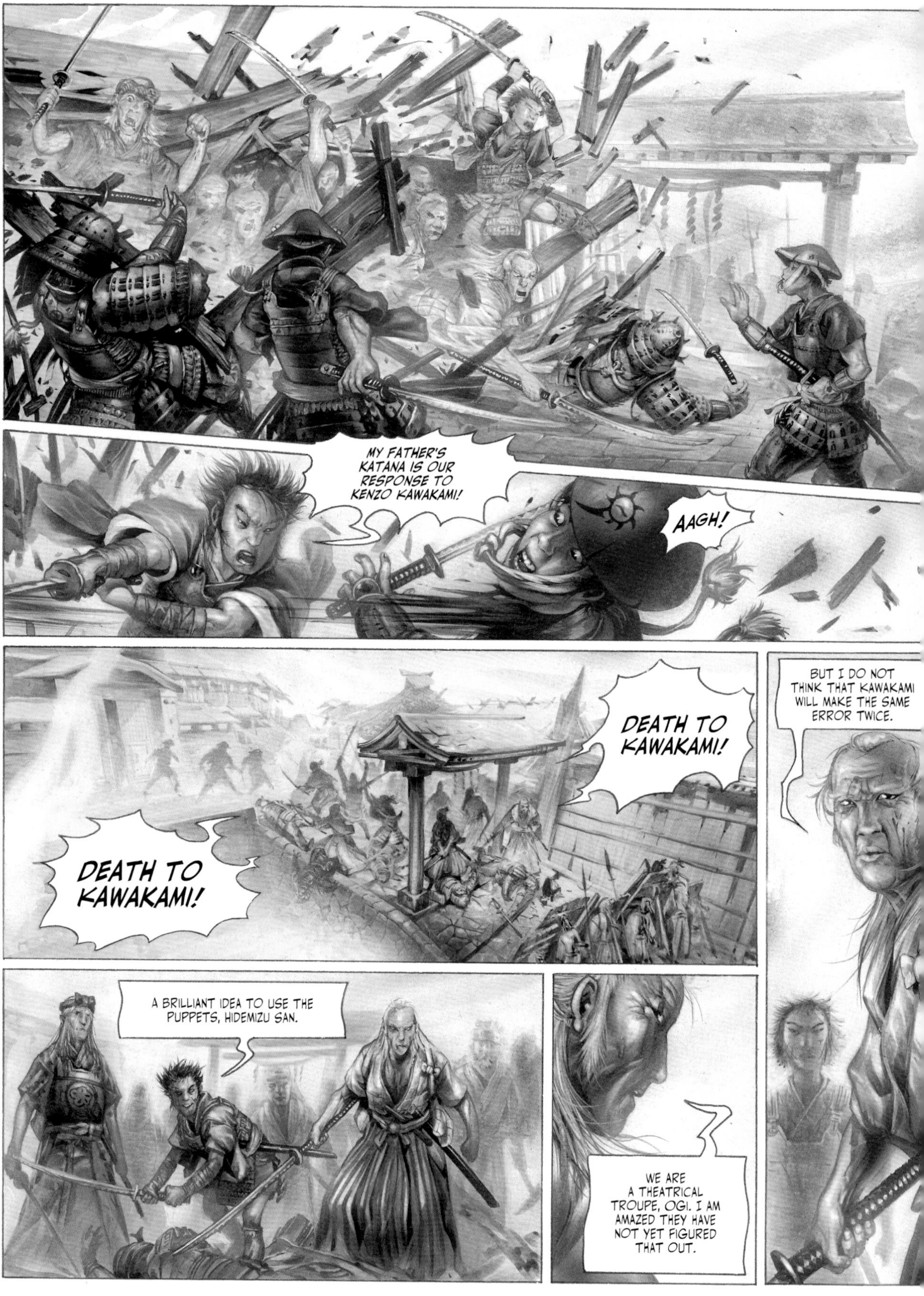
MY FATHER'S KATANA IS OUR RESPONSE TO KENZO KAWAKAMI!
AAGH!
DEATH TO KAWAKAMI!
DEATH TO KAWAKAMI!
BUT I DO NOT THINK THAT KAWAKAMI WILL MAKE THE SAME ERROR TWICE.
A BRILLIANT IDEA TO USE THE PUPPETS, HIDEMIZU SAN.
WE ARE A THEATRICAL TROUPE, OGI. I AM AMAZED THEY HAVE NOT YET FIGURED THAT OUT.

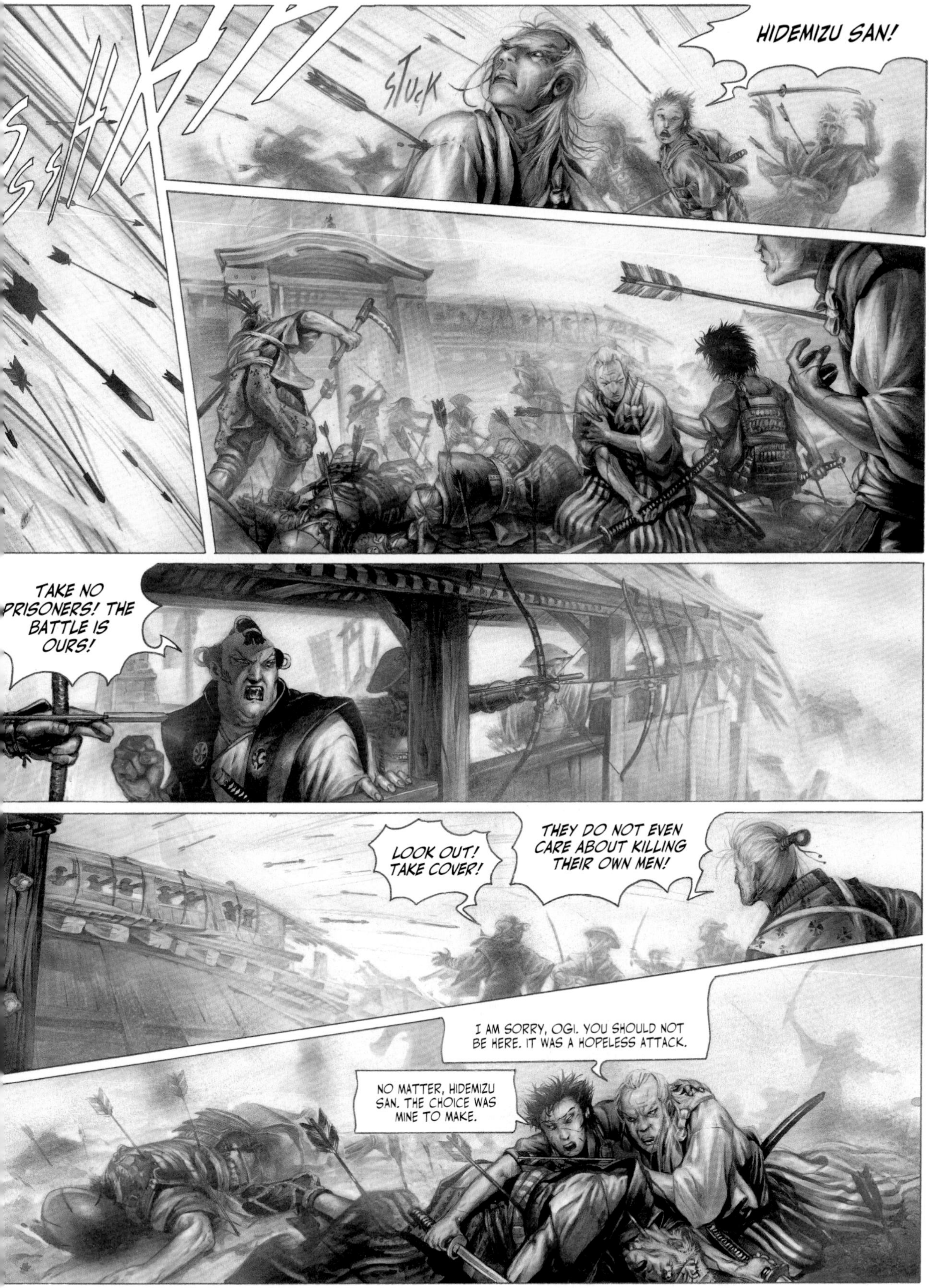
SSSHK
STUCK
HIDEMIZU SAN!
TAKE NO PRISONERS! THE BATTLE IS OURS!
LOOK OUT! TAKE COVER!
THEY DO NOT EVEN CARE ABOUT KILLING THEIR OWN MEN!
I AM SORRY, OGI. YOU SHOULD NOT BE HERE. IT WAS A HOPELESS ATTACK.
NO MATTER, HIDEMIZU SAN. THE CHOICE WAS MINE TO MAKE.

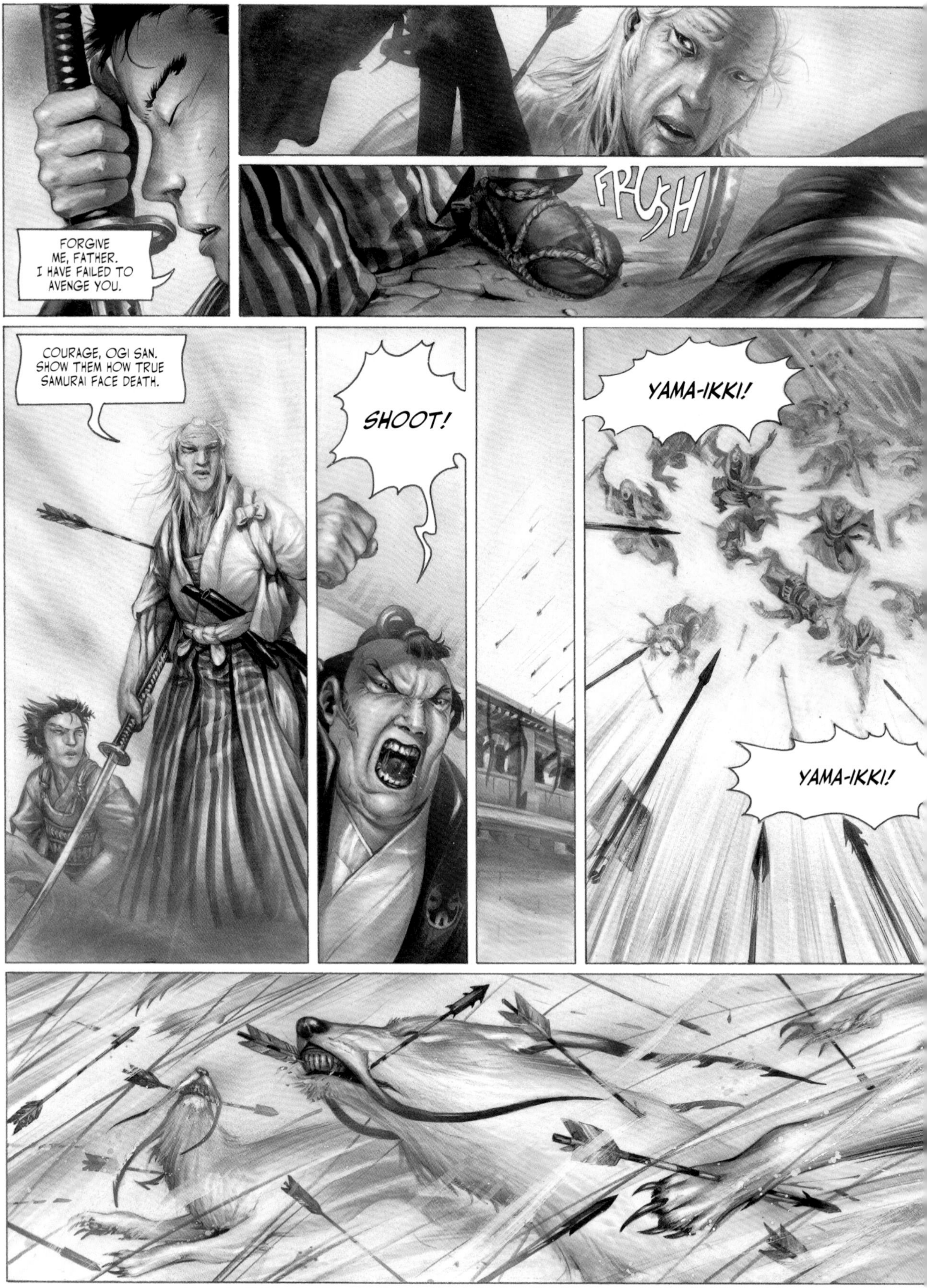

FORGIVE ME, FATHER. I HAVE FAILED TO AVENGE YOU.
FRUSH
COURAGE, OGI SAN. SHOW THEM HOW TRUE SAMURAI FACE DEATH.
SHOOT!
YAMA-IKKI!
YAMA-IKKI!

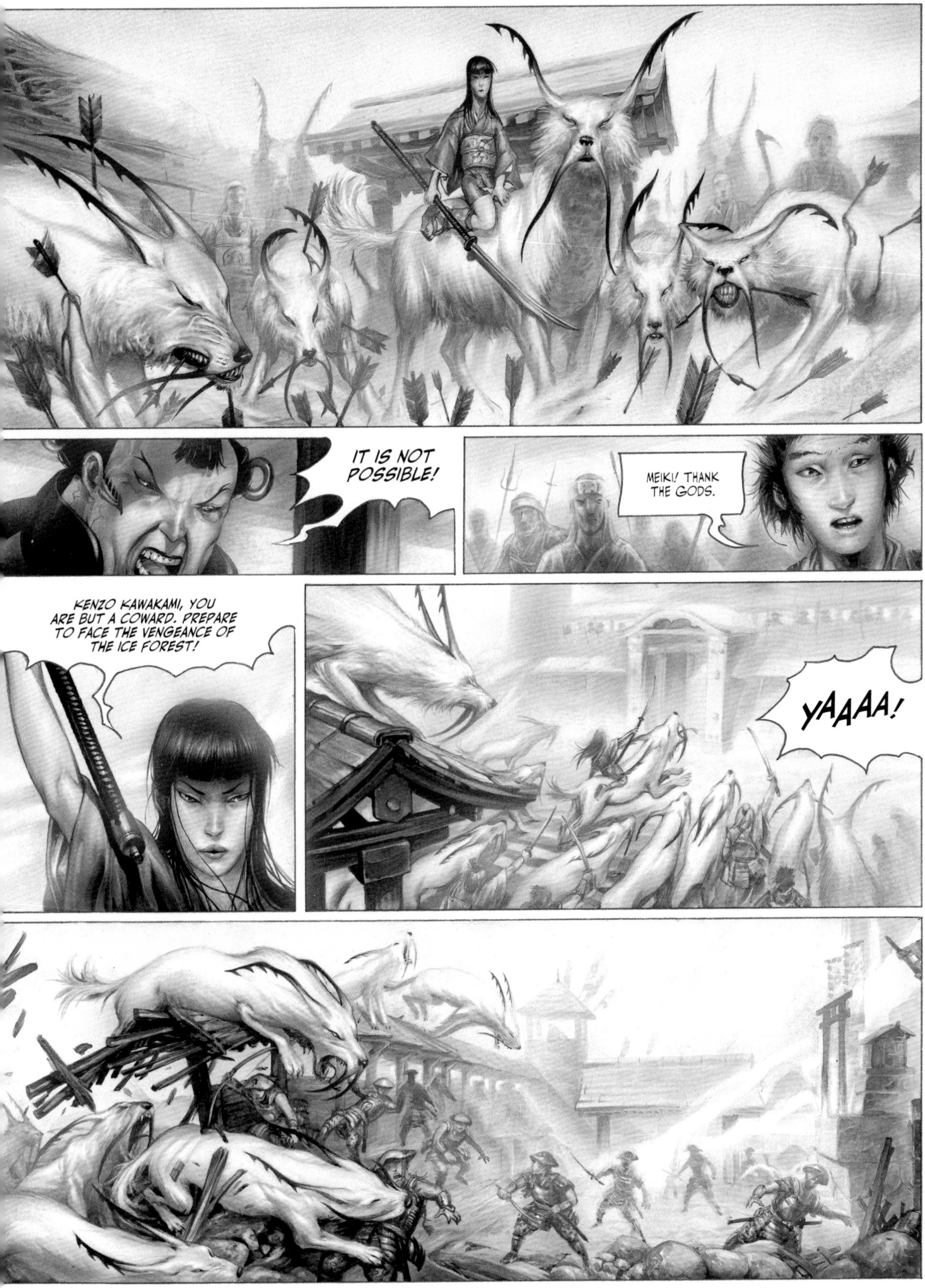
IT IS NOT POSSIBLE!
MEIKI! THANK THE GODS.
KENZO KAWAKAMI, YOU ARE BUT A COWARD. PREPARE TO FACE THE VENGEANCE OF THE ICE FOREST!
YAAAA!

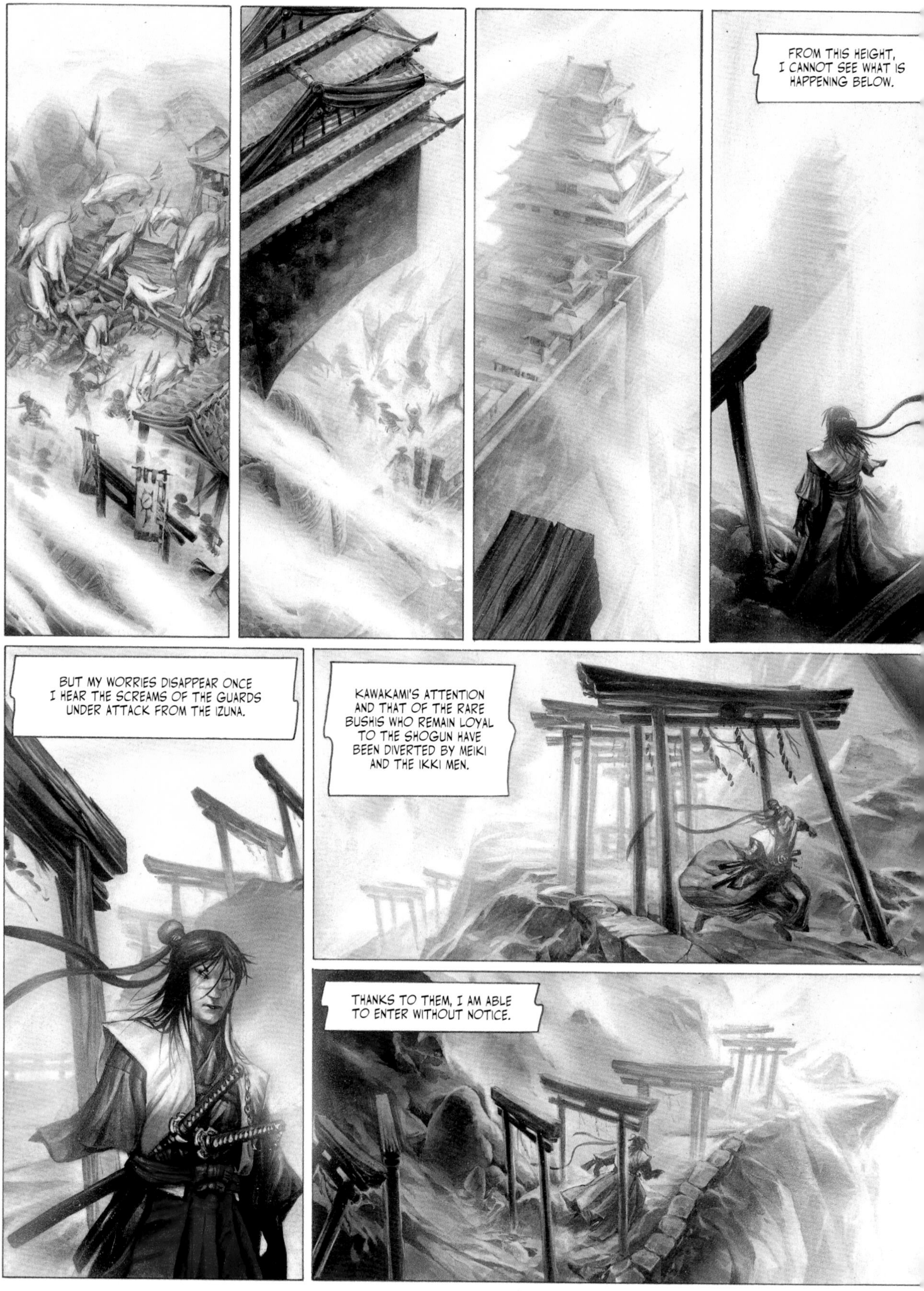
FROM THIS HEIGHT, I CANNOT SEE WHAT IS HAPPENING BELOW.
BUT MY WORRIES DISAPPEAR ONCE I HEAR THE SCREAMS OF THE GUARDS UNDER ATTACK FROM THE IZUNA.
KAWAKAMI'S ATTENTION AND THAT OF THE RARE BUSHIS WHO REMAIN LOYAL TO THE SHOGUN HAVE BEEN DIVERTED BY MEIKI AND THE IKKI MEN.
THANKS TO THEM, I AM ABLE TO ENTER WITHOUT NOTICE.

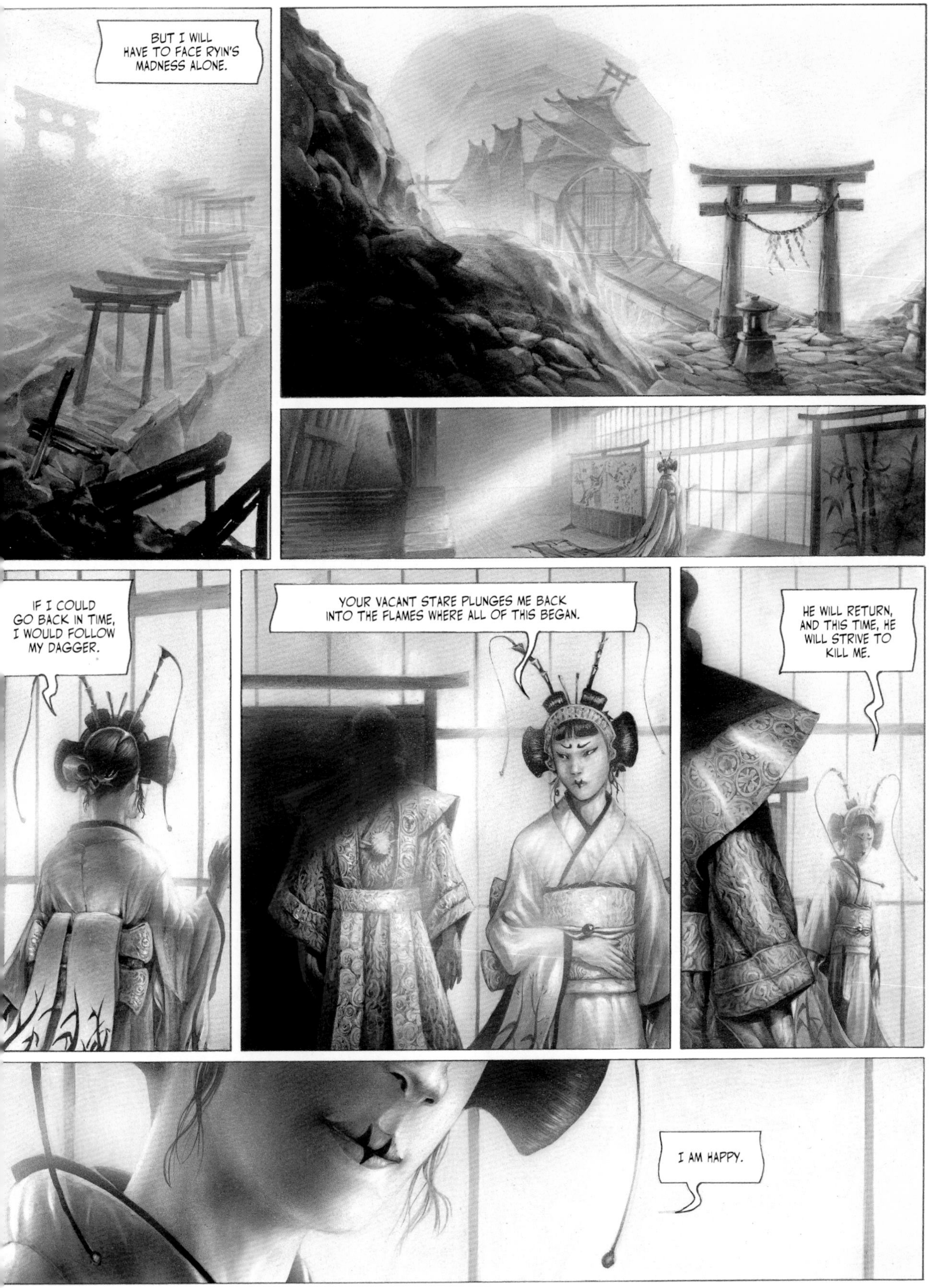
BUT I WILL HAVE TO FACE RYIN'S MADNESS ALONE.
IF I COULD GO BACK IN TIME, I WOULD FOLLOW MY DAGGER.
YOUR VACANT STARE PLUNGES ME BACK INTO THE FLAMES WHERE ALL OF THIS BEGAN.
HE WILL RETURN, AND THIS TIME, HE WILL STRIVE TO KILL ME.
I AM HAPPY.

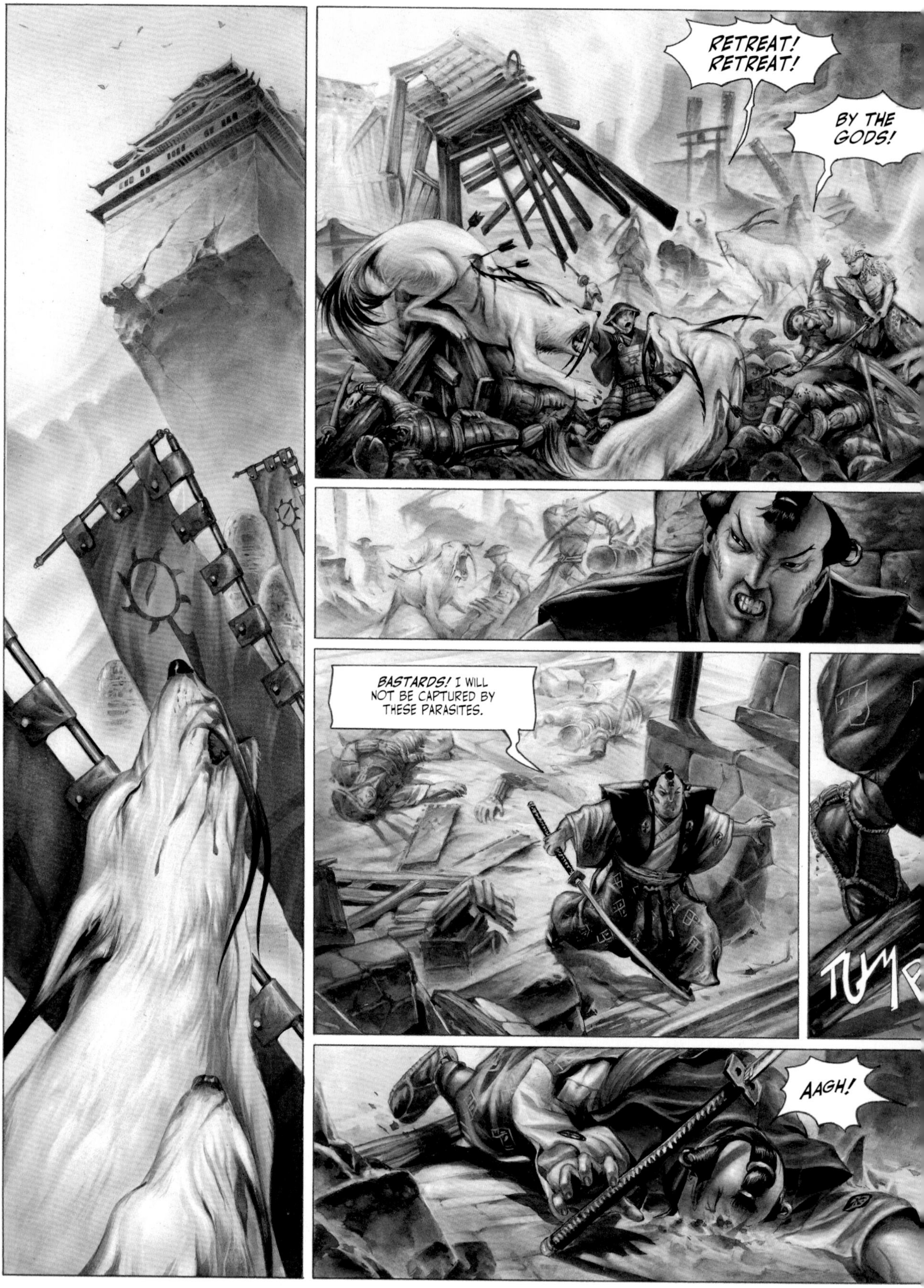
RETREAT! RETREAT!
BY THE GODS!
BASTARDS! I WILL NOT BE CAPTURED BY THESE PARASITES.
AAGH!

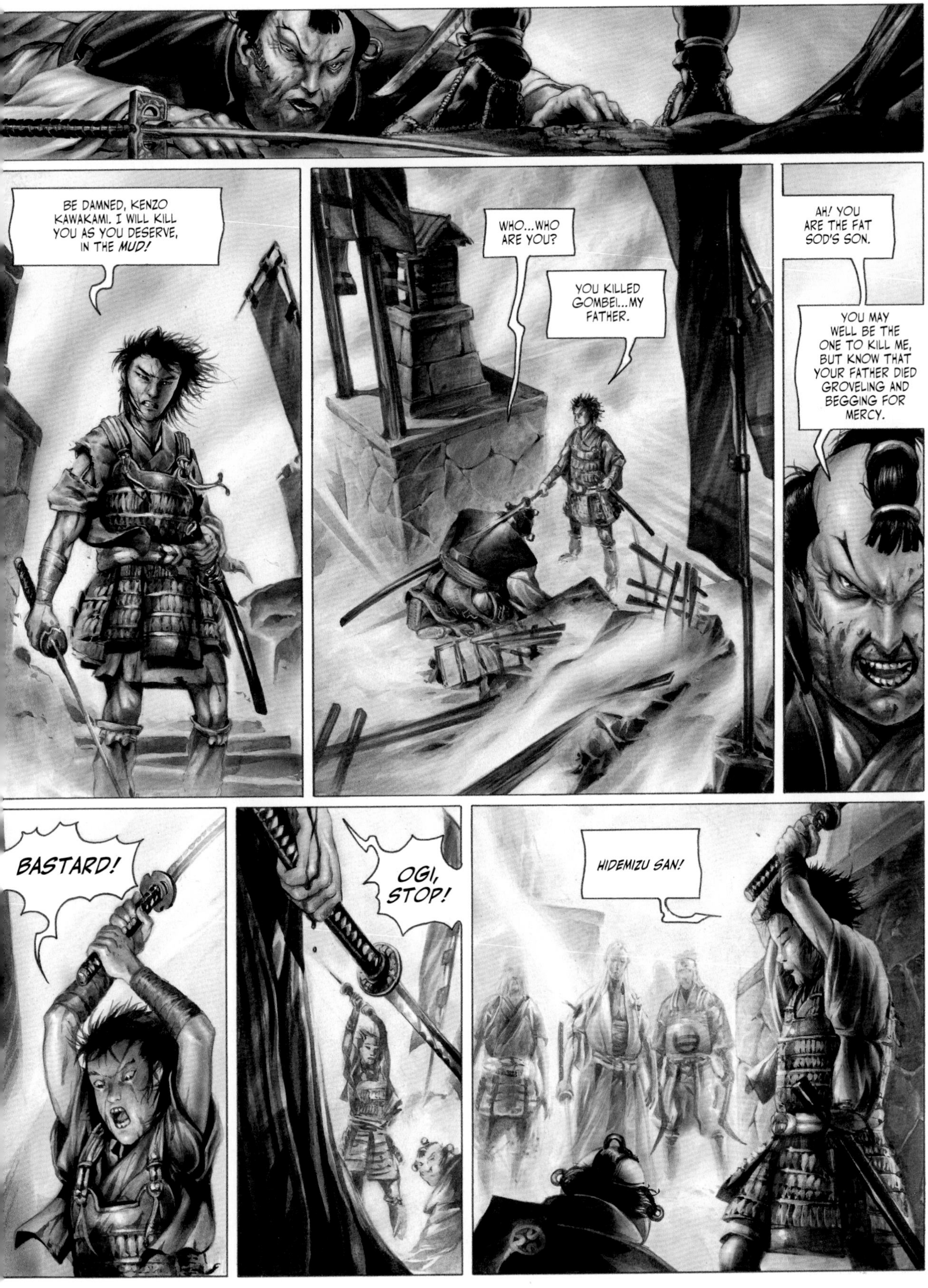
BE DAMNED, KENZO KAWAKAMI. I WILL KILL YOU AS YOU DESERVE, IN THE MUD!
WHO...WHO ARE YOU?
YOU KILLED GOMBEI...MY FATHER.
AH! YOU ARE THE FAT SOD'S SON.
YOU MAY WELL BE THE ONE TO KILL ME, BUT KNOW THAT YOUR FATHER DIED GROVELING AND BEGGING FOR MERCY.
BASTARD!
OGI, STOP!
HIDEMIZU SAN!

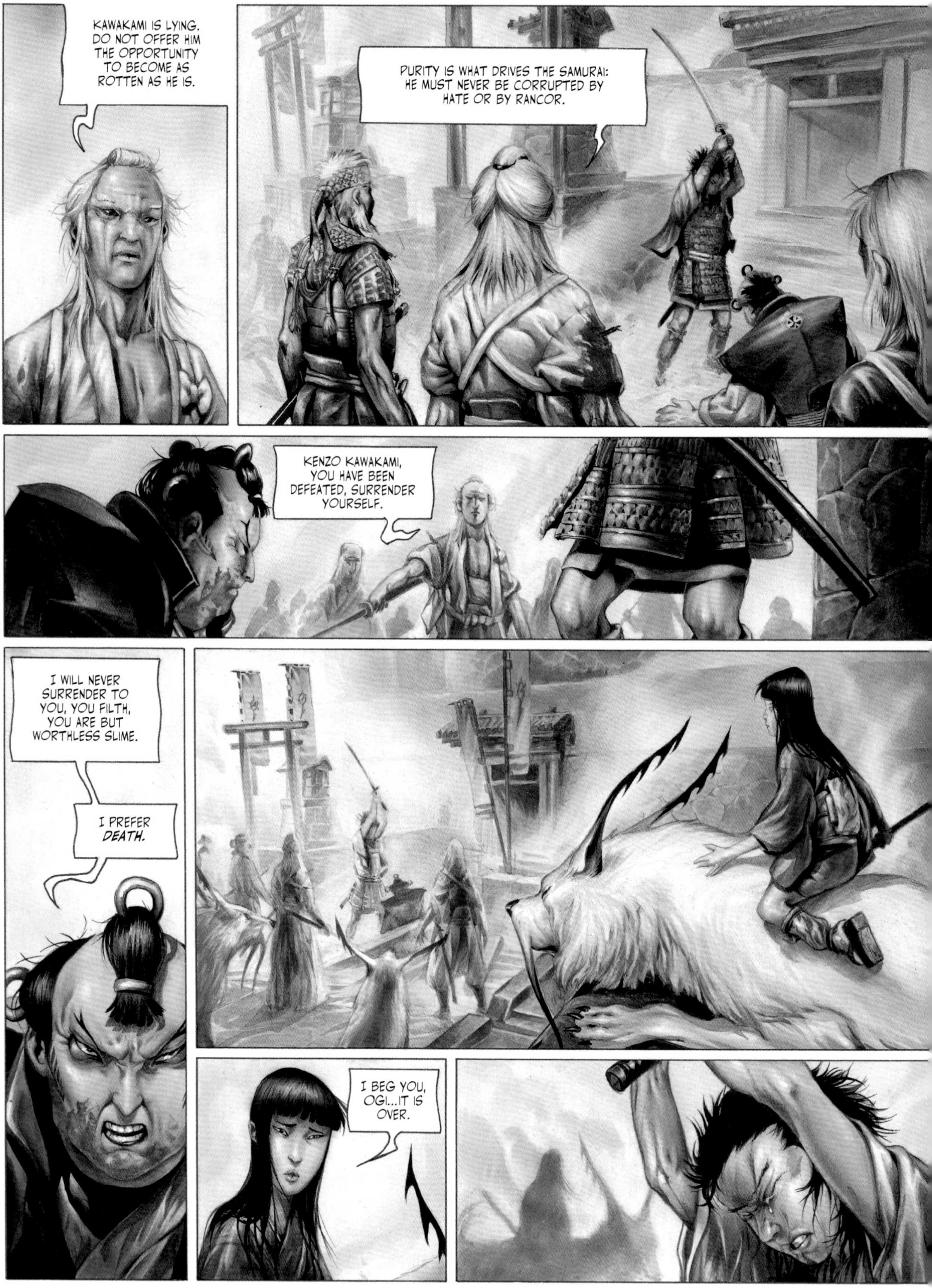
KAWAKAMI IS LYING. DO NOT OFFER HIM THE OPPORTUNITY TO BECOME AS ROTTEN AS HE IS.
PURITY IS WHAT DRIVES THE SAMURAI: HE MUST NEVER BE CORRUPTED BY HATE OR BY RANCOR.
KENZO KAWAKAMI, YOU HAVE BEEN DEFEATED, SURRENDER YOURSELF.
I WILL NEVER SURRENDER TO YOU, YOU FILTH, YOU ARE BUT WORTHLESS SLIME.
I PREFER *DEATH.*
I BEG YOU, OGI...IT IS OVER.

GOOD FOR YOU, LITTLE SAMURAI.

FOR YOU, FATHER.

EVEN SHOULD YOU OFFER YOUR BELLY TO AMATERASU, I AM CERTAIN THAT YOUR INSIDES WILL NEVER BE AS PURE AS MY FATHER'S WERE.

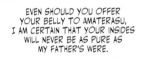

I GRANT YOU AN HONORABLE DEATH, KAWAKAMI SAN.

169

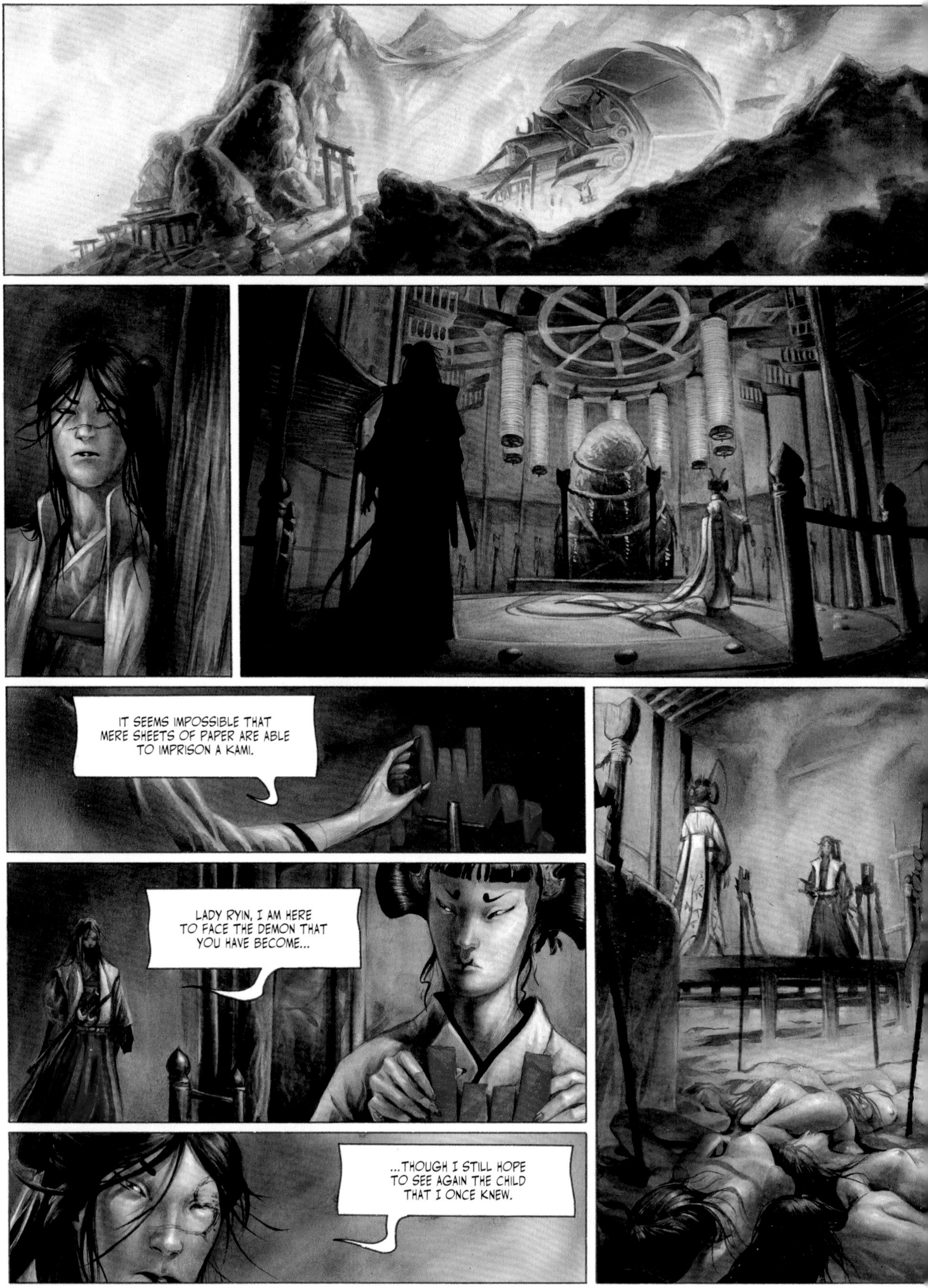
IT SEEMS IMPOSSIBLE THAT MERE SHEETS OF PAPER ARE ABLE TO IMPRISON A KAMI.
LADY RYIN, I AM HERE TO FACE THE DEMON THAT YOU HAVE BECOME...
...THOUGH I STILL HOPE TO SEE AGAIN THE CHILD THAT I ONCE KNEW.

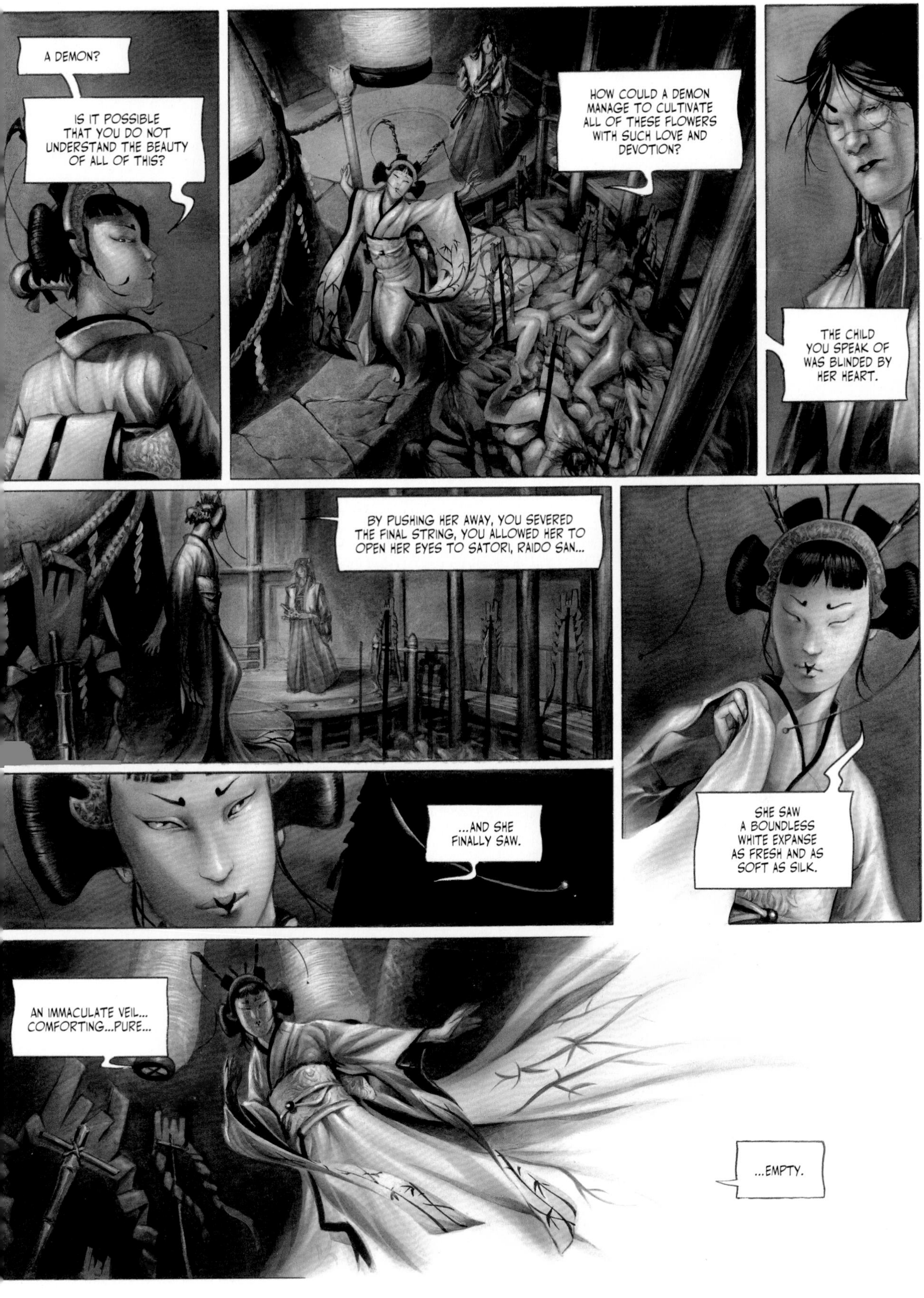
A DEMON?
IS IT POSSIBLE THAT YOU DO NOT UNDERSTAND THE BEAUTY OF ALL OF THIS?
HOW COULD A DEMON MANAGE TO CULTIVATE ALL OF THESE FLOWERS WITH SUCH LOVE AND DEVOTION?
THE CHILD YOU SPEAK OF WAS BLINDED BY HER HEART.
BY PUSHING HER AWAY, YOU SEVERED THE FINAL STRING, YOU ALLOWED HER TO OPEN HER EYES TO SATORI, RAIDO SAN...
...AND SHE FINALLY SAW.
SHE SAW A BOUNDLESS WHITE EXPANSE AS FRESH AND AS SOFT AS SILK.
AN IMMACULATE VEIL... COMFORTING...PURE...
...EMPTY.

AT THAT MOMENT, BEYOND THE LIMITS OF HER BODY, SHE ALSO TRANSCENDED HER PERCEPTION.

THAT CHILD NO LONGER EXISTS, RAIDO SAN. IT IS YOU WHO KILLED HER.

BUT TODAY, SHE HAS FINALLY TRACED THE PATH OF HER NEW EXISTENCE.

A REBIRTH.

THANKS TO A FATHER, AN OBJECT OF DESIRE...AND, FINALLY, A HUSBAND.

NO...YOU CANNOT HAVE DONE THAT!

THE WORLD HAS CHANGED, RAIDO SAN...

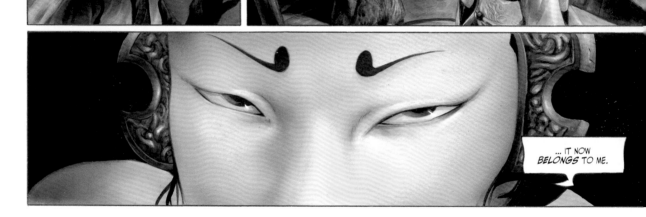

... IT NOW *BELONGS* TO ME.

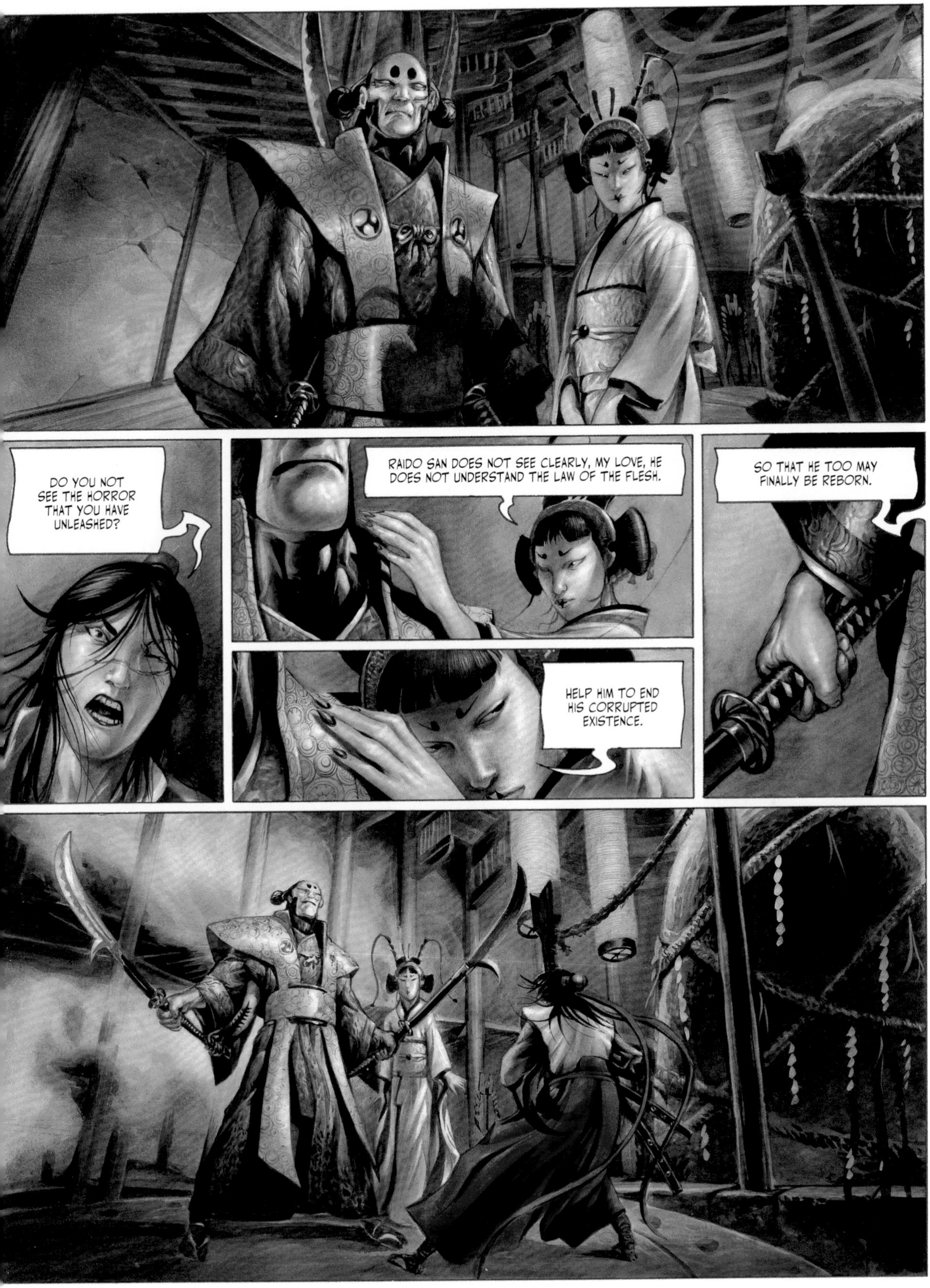
DO YOU NOT SEE THE HORROR THAT YOU HAVE UNLEASHED?
RAIDO SAN DOES NOT SEE CLEARLY, MY LOVE, HE DOES NOT UNDERSTAND THE LAW OF THE FLESH.
HELP HIM TO END HIS CORRUPTED EXISTENCE.
SO THAT HE TOO MAY FINALLY BE REBORN.

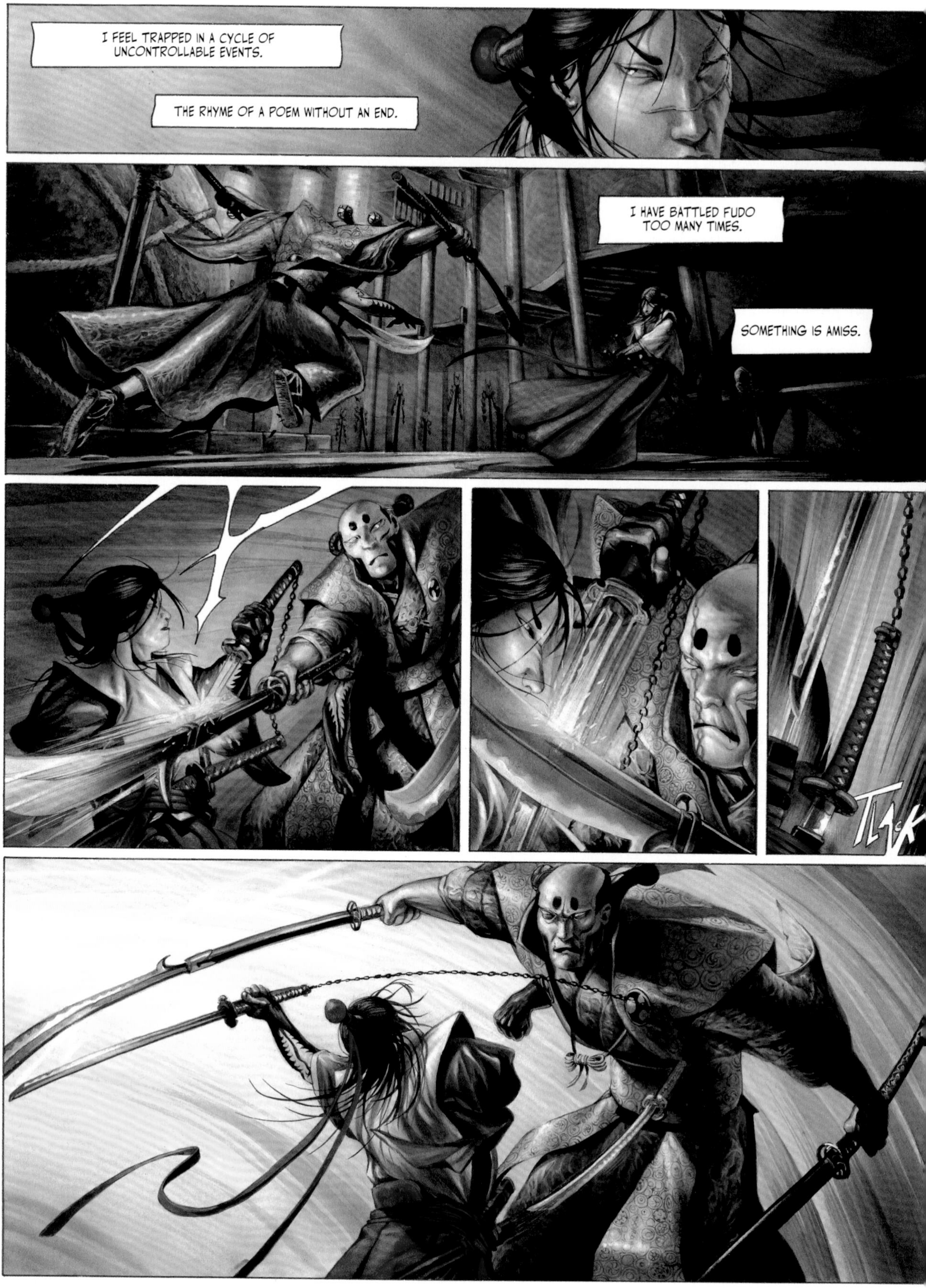
I FEEL TRAPPED IN A CYCLE OF UNCONTROLLABLE EVENTS.
THE RHYME OF A POEM WITHOUT AN END.
I HAVE BATTLED FUDO TOO MANY TIMES.
SOMETHING IS AMISS.
TLACK

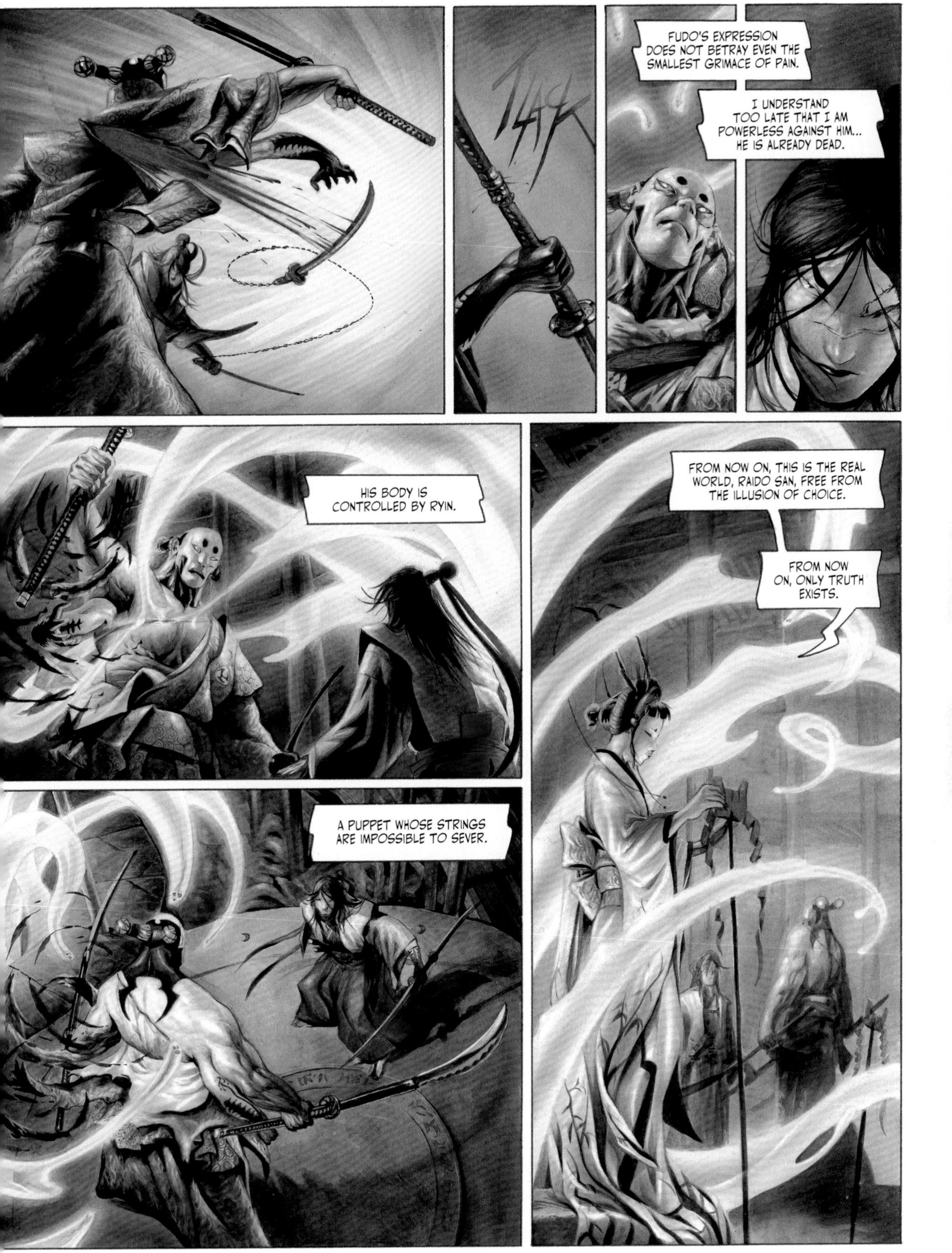
FUDO'S EXPRESSION DOES NOT BETRAY EVEN THE SMALLEST GRIMACE OF PAIN.
I UNDERSTAND TOO LATE THAT I AM POWERLESS AGAINST HIM... HE IS ALREADY DEAD.
HIS BODY IS CONTROLLED BY RYIN.
A PUPPET WHOSE STRINGS ARE IMPOSSIBLE TO SEVER.
FROM NOW ON, THIS IS THE REAL WORLD, RAIDO SAN, FREE FROM THE ILLUSION OF CHOICE.
FROM NOW ON, ONLY TRUTH EXISTS.

AND THE TRUTH IS THAT WE ARE FLESH. EVERYTHING ELSE IS A LIE.

I DID NOT WANT TO ACCEPT IT. IT IS NOT UNTIL THIS MOMENT THAT I REALIZE THAT RYIN NO LONGER EXISTS.

I MUST REACH THE BONDS OR ALL WILL BE LOST.

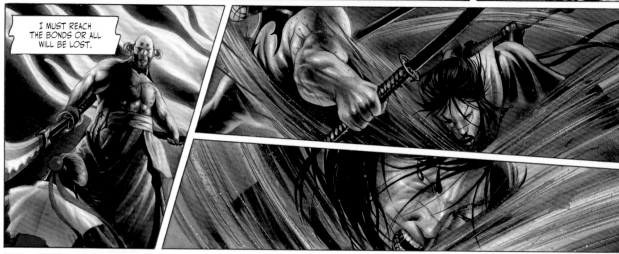

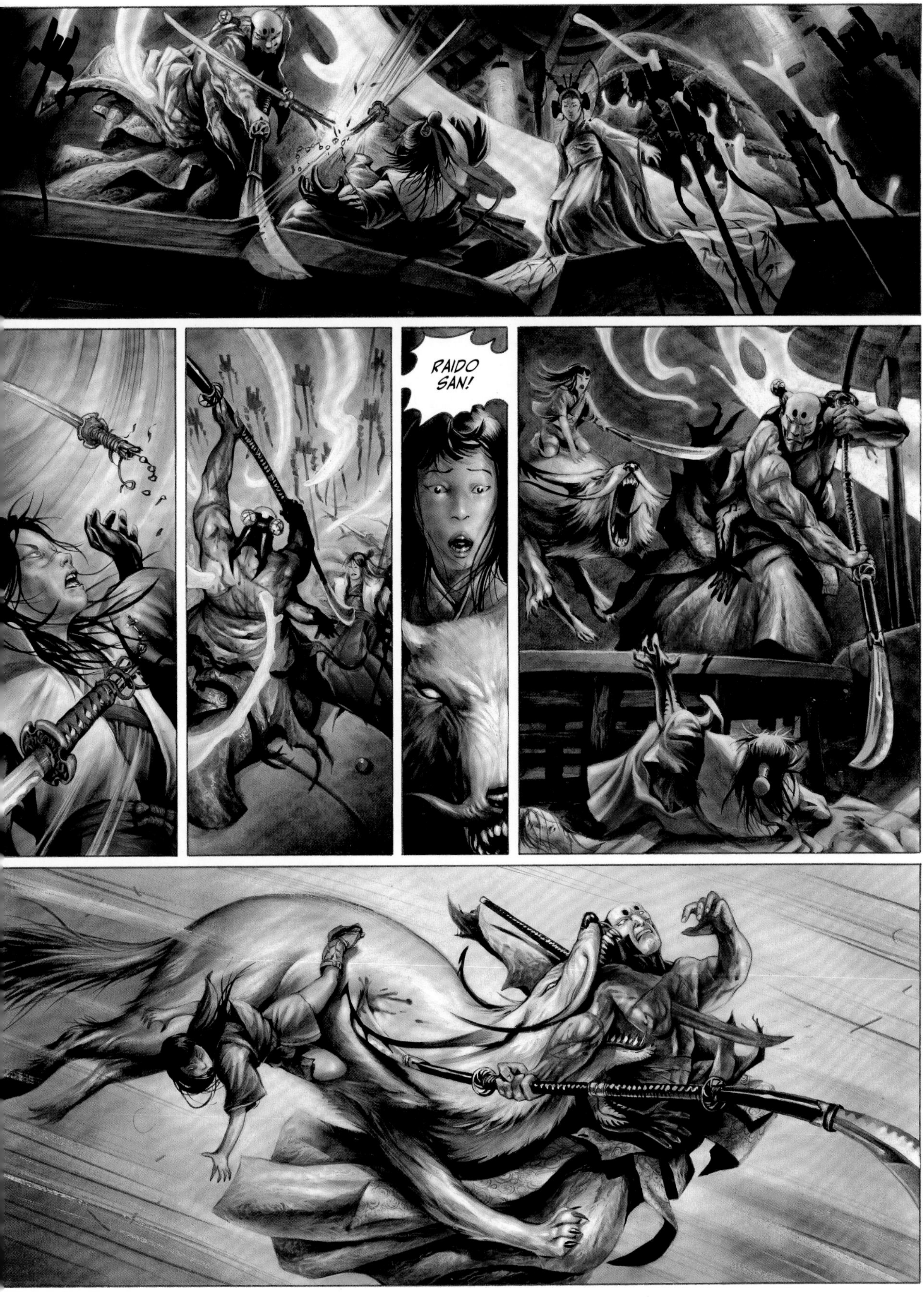
RAIDO SAN!

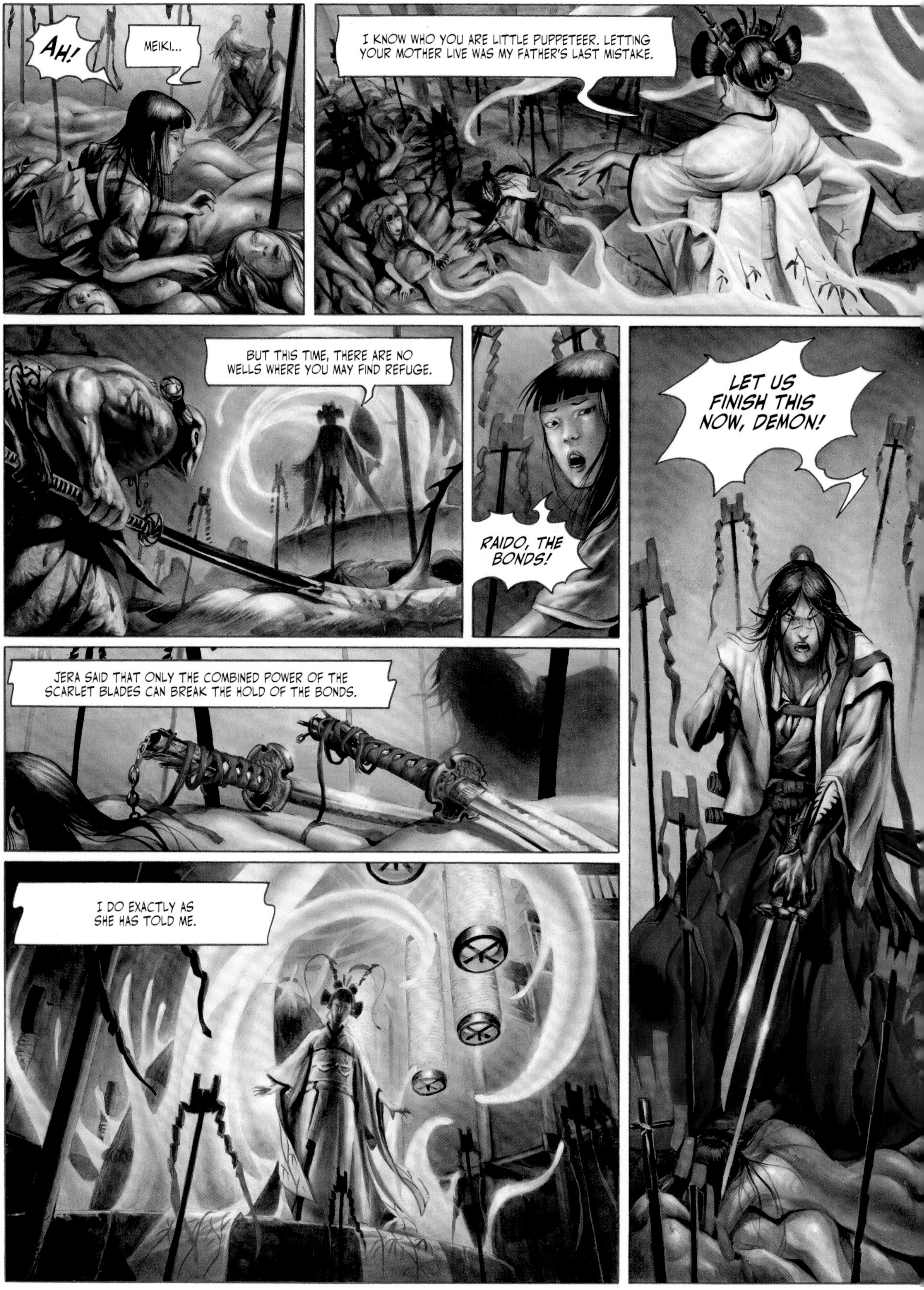
AH!
MEIKI...
I KNOW WHO YOU ARE LITTLE PUPPETEER. LETTING YOUR MOTHER LIVE WAS MY FATHER'S LAST MISTAKE.
BUT THIS TIME, THERE ARE NO WELLS WHERE YOU MAY FIND REFUGE.
RAIDO, THE BONDS!
LET US FINISH THIS NOW, DEMON!
JERA SAID THAT ONLY THE COMBINED POWER OF THE SCARLET BLADES CAN BREAK THE HOLD OF THE BONDS.
I DO EXACTLY AS SHE HAS TOLD ME.

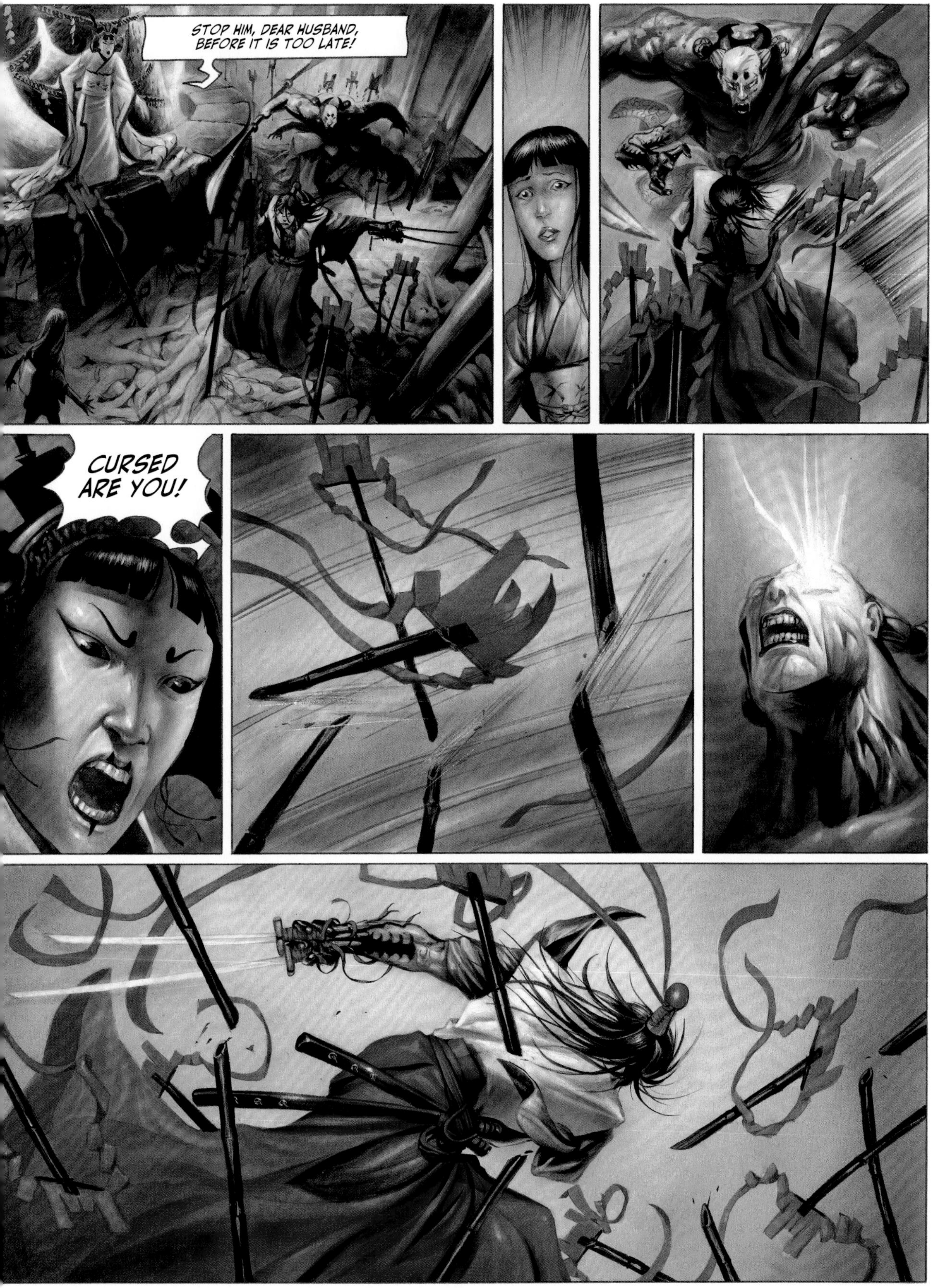
STOP HIM, DEAR HUSBAND, BEFORE IT IS TOO LATE!
CURSED ARE YOU!

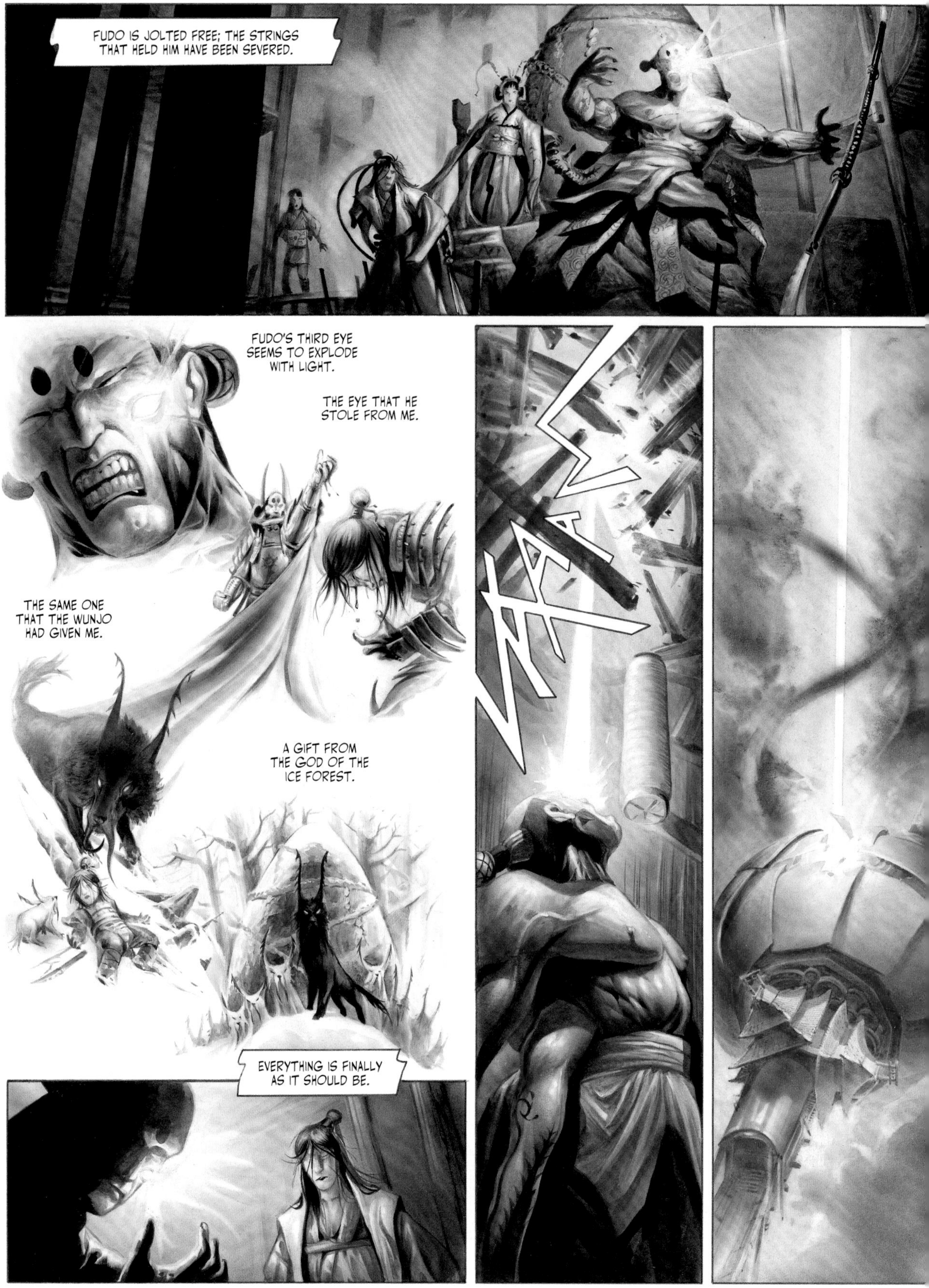
FUDO IS JOLTED FREE; THE STRINGS THAT HELD HIM HAVE BEEN SEVERED.
FUDO'S THIRD EYE SEEMS TO EXPLODE WITH LIGHT.
THE EYE THAT HE STOLE FROM ME.
THE SAME ONE THAT THE WUNJO HAD GIVEN ME.
A GIFT FROM THE GOD OF THE ICE FOREST.
EVERYTHING IS FINALLY AS IT SHOULD BE.

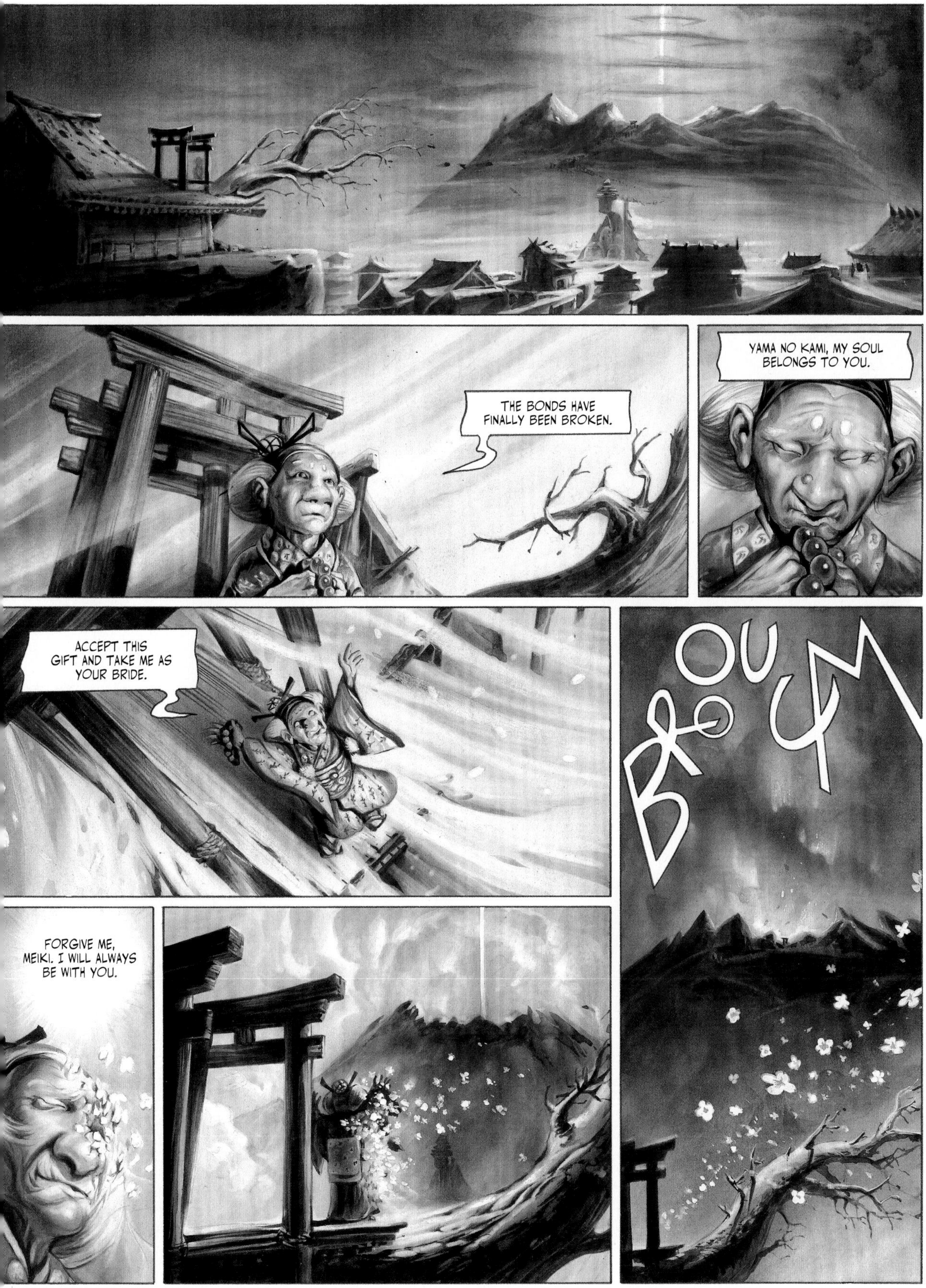

THE BONDS HAVE FINALLY BEEN BROKEN.
YAMA NO KAMI, MY SOUL BELONGS TO YOU.
ACCEPT THIS GIFT AND TAKE ME AS YOUR BRIDE.
BROOUM
FORGIVE ME, MEIKI. I WILL ALWAYS BE WITH YOU.

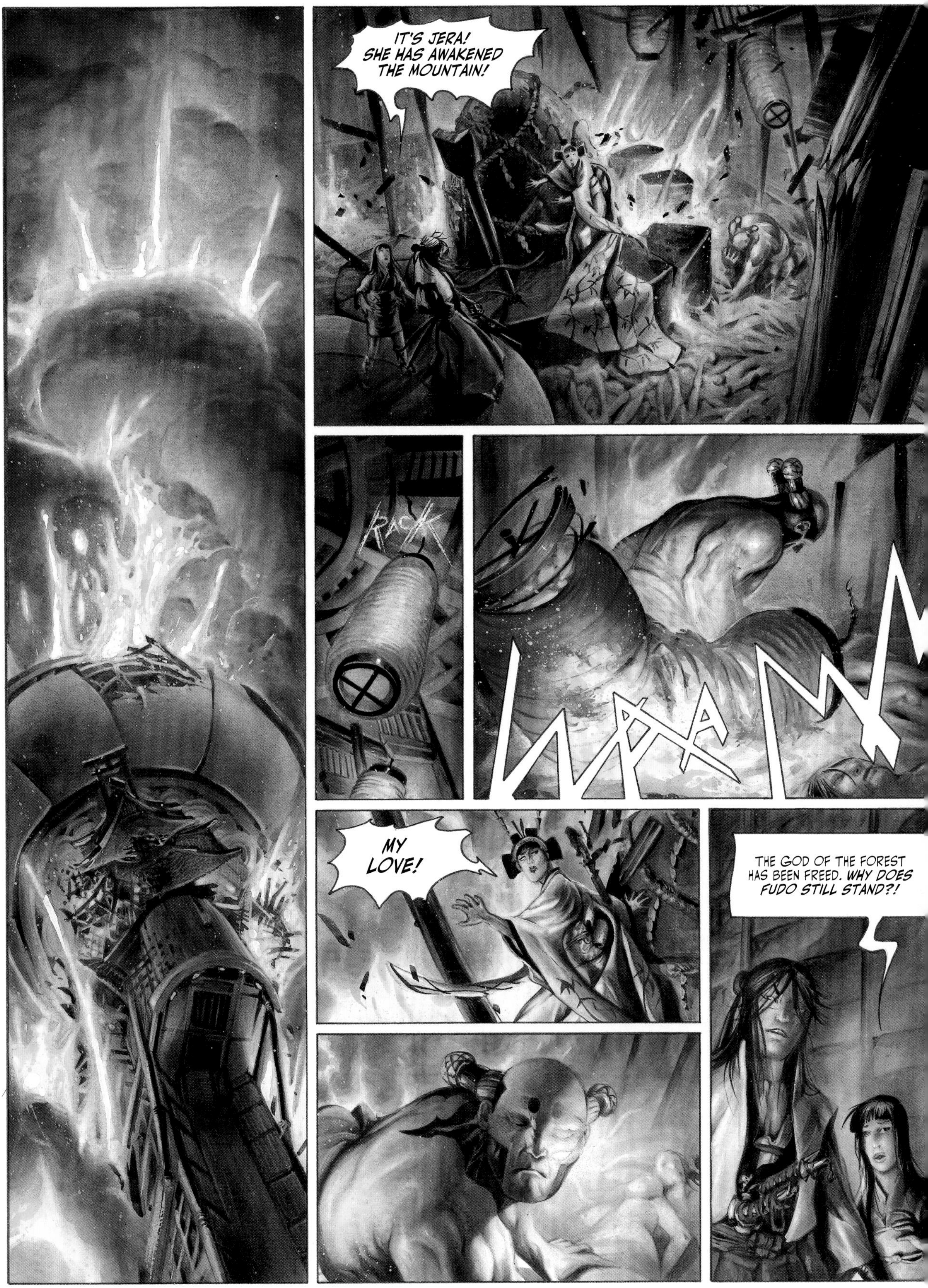
IT'S JERA! SHE HAS AWAKENED THE MOUNTAIN!
RACK
MY LOVE!
THE GOD OF THE FOREST HAS BEEN FREED. WHY DOES FUDO STILL STAND?!

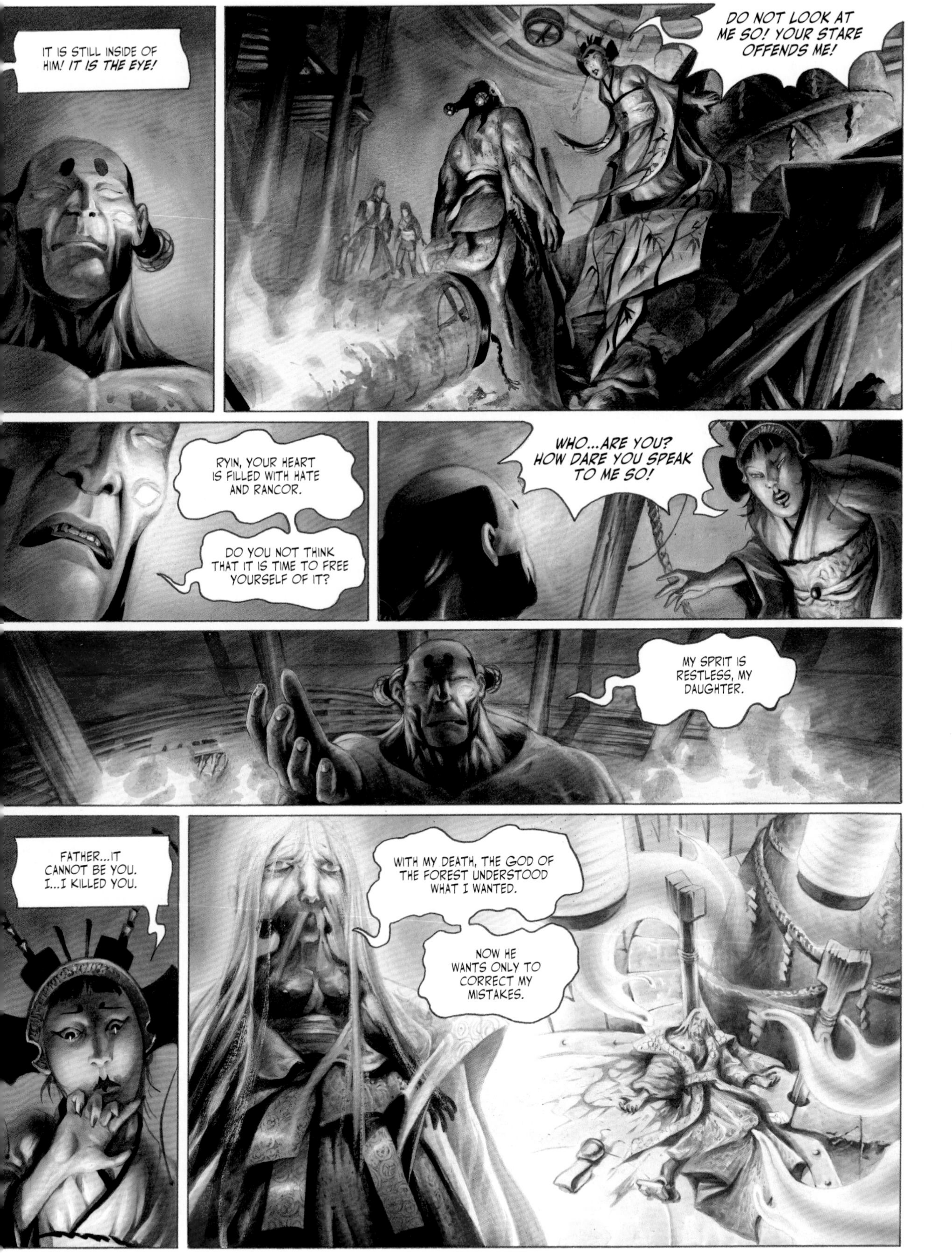

IT IS STILL INSIDE OF HIM! *IT IS THE EYE!*
DO NOT LOOK AT ME SO! YOUR STARE OFFENDS ME!
RYIN, YOUR HEART IS FILLED WITH HATE AND RANCOR.
DO YOU NOT THINK THAT IT IS TIME TO FREE YOURSELF OF IT?
WHO...ARE YOU? HOW DARE YOU SPEAK TO ME SO!
MY SPRIT IS RESTLESS, MY DAUGHTER.
FATHER...IT CANNOT BE YOU. I...I KILLED YOU.
WITH MY DEATH, THE GOD OF THE FOREST UNDERSTOOD WHAT I WANTED.
NOW HE WANTS ONLY TO CORRECT MY MISTAKES.

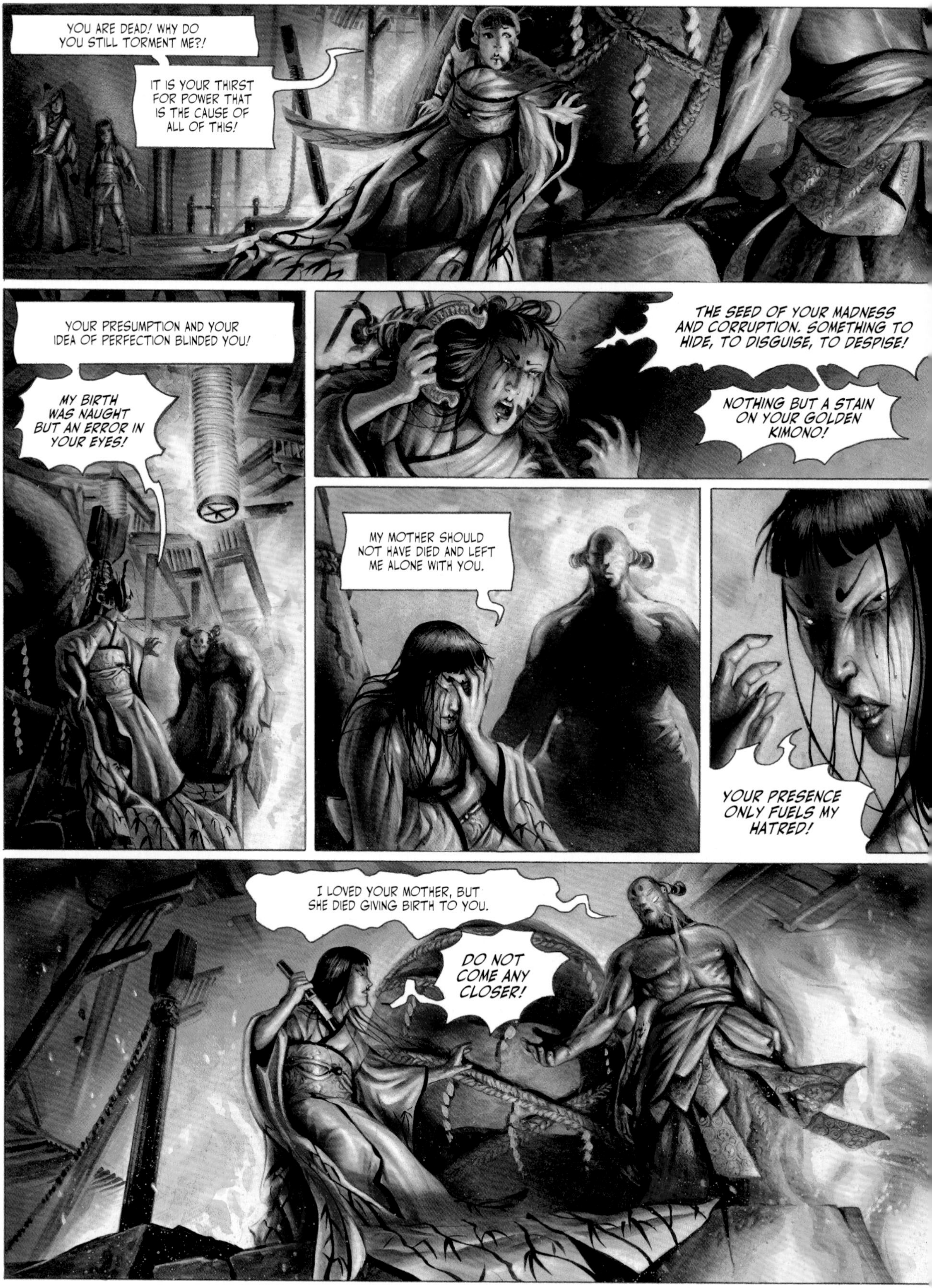
YOU ARE DEAD! WHY DO YOU STILL TORMENT ME?!
IT IS YOUR THIRST FOR POWER THAT IS THE CAUSE OF ALL OF THIS!
YOUR PRESUMPTION AND YOUR IDEA OF PERFECTION BLINDED YOU!
MY BIRTH WAS NAUGHT BUT AN ERROR IN YOUR EYES!
THE SEED OF YOUR MADNESS AND CORRUPTION. SOMETHING TO HIDE, TO DISGUISE, TO DESPISE!
NOTHING BUT A STAIN ON YOUR GOLDEN KIMONO!
MY MOTHER SHOULD NOT HAVE DIED AND LEFT ME ALONE WITH YOU.
YOUR PRESENCE ONLY FUELS MY HATRED!
I LOVED YOUR MOTHER, BUT SHE DIED GIVING BIRTH TO YOU.
DO NOT COME ANY CLOSER!

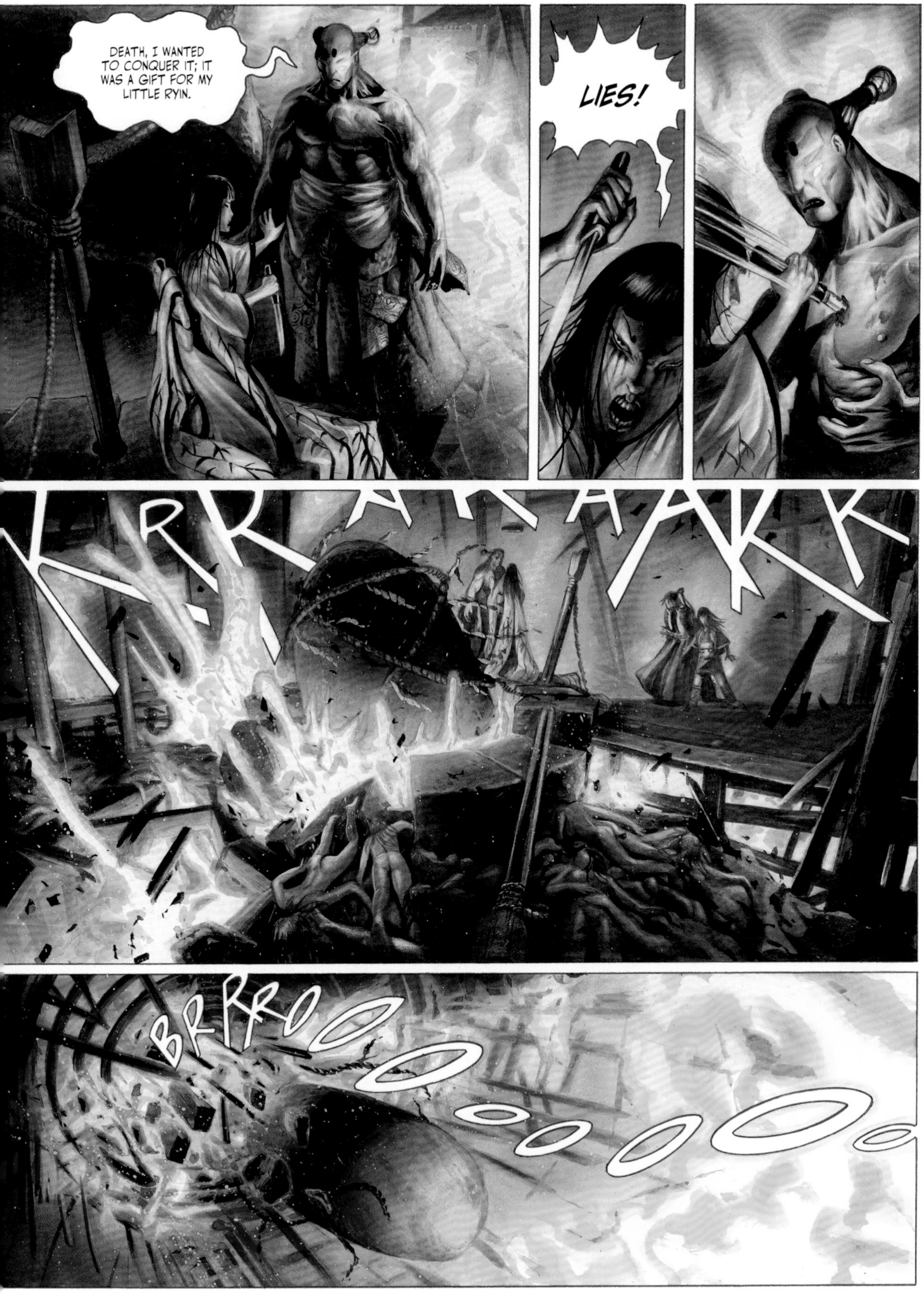
DEATH, I WANTED TO CONQUER IT; IT WAS A GIFT FOR MY LITTLE RYIN.
LIES!
KRRAAAKK
BRRROOOOOOOOO

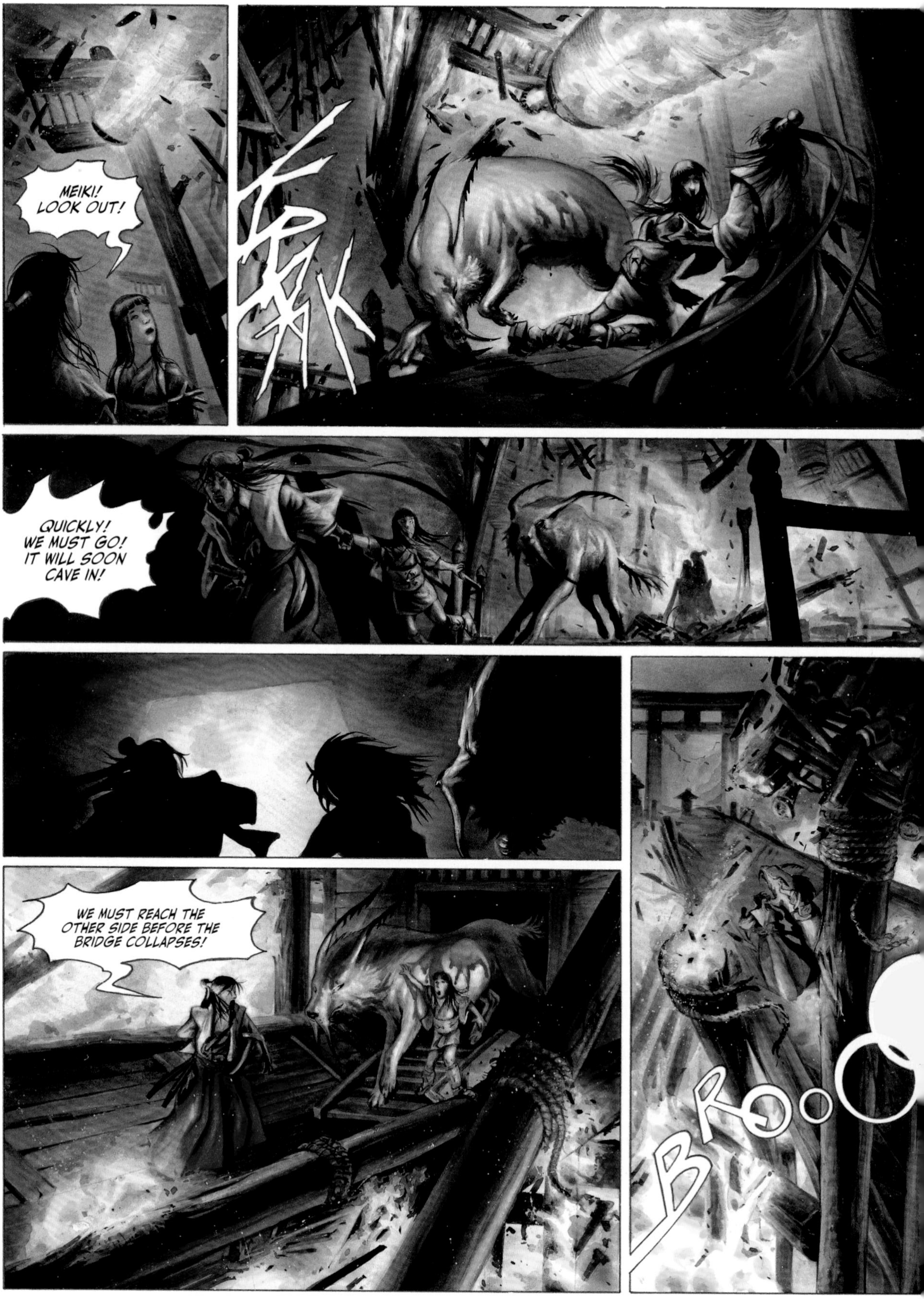
MEIKI! LOOK OUT!
QUICKLY! WE MUST GO! IT WILL SOON CAVE IN!
WE MUST REACH THE OTHER SIDE BEFORE THE BRIDGE COLLAPSES!
BROOO

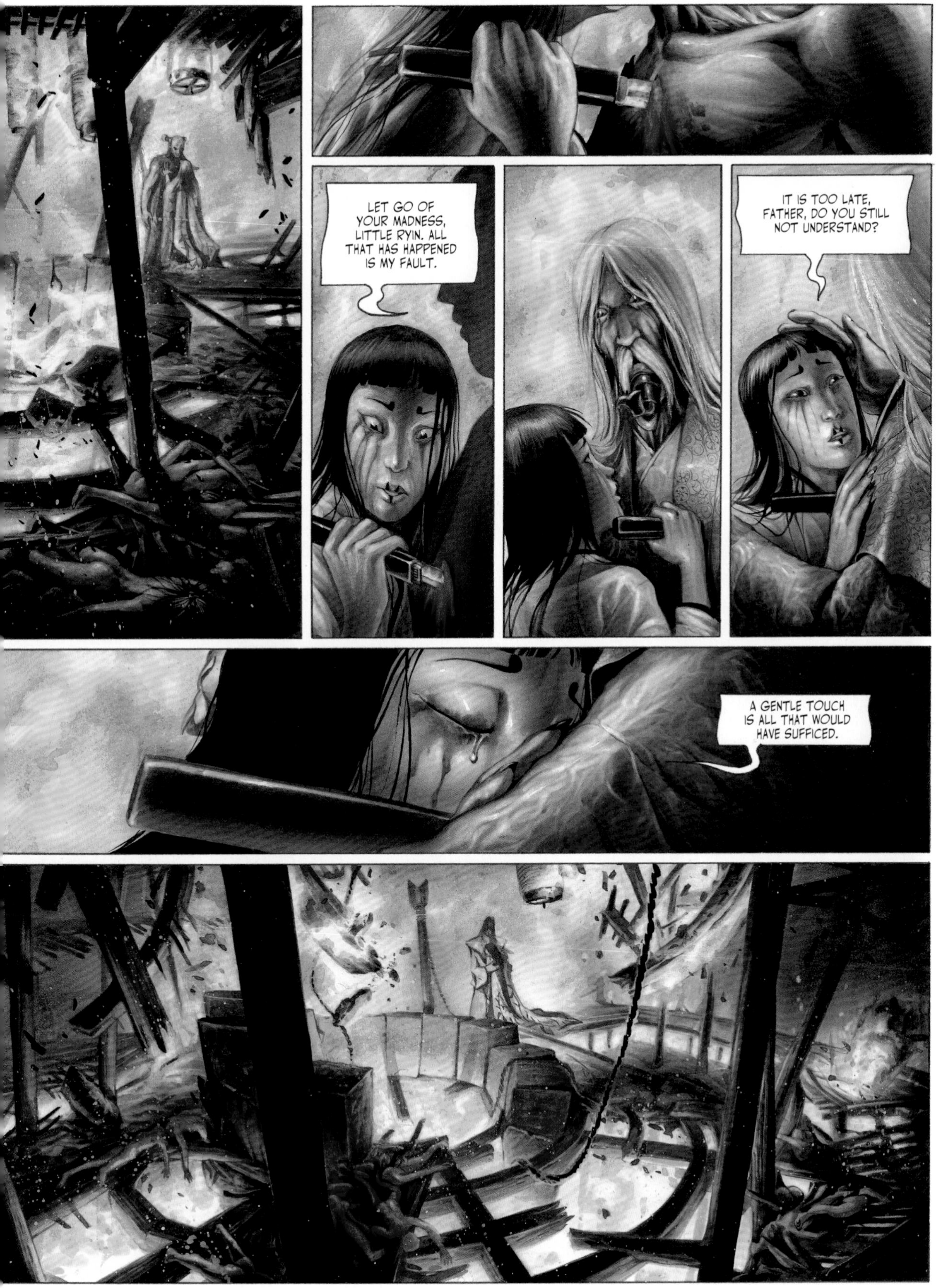
LET GO OF YOUR MADNESS, LITTLE RYIN. ALL THAT HAS HAPPENED IS MY FAULT.
IT IS TOO LATE, FATHER, DO YOU STILL NOT UNDERSTAND?
A GENTLE TOUCH IS ALL THAT WOULD HAVE SUFFICED.

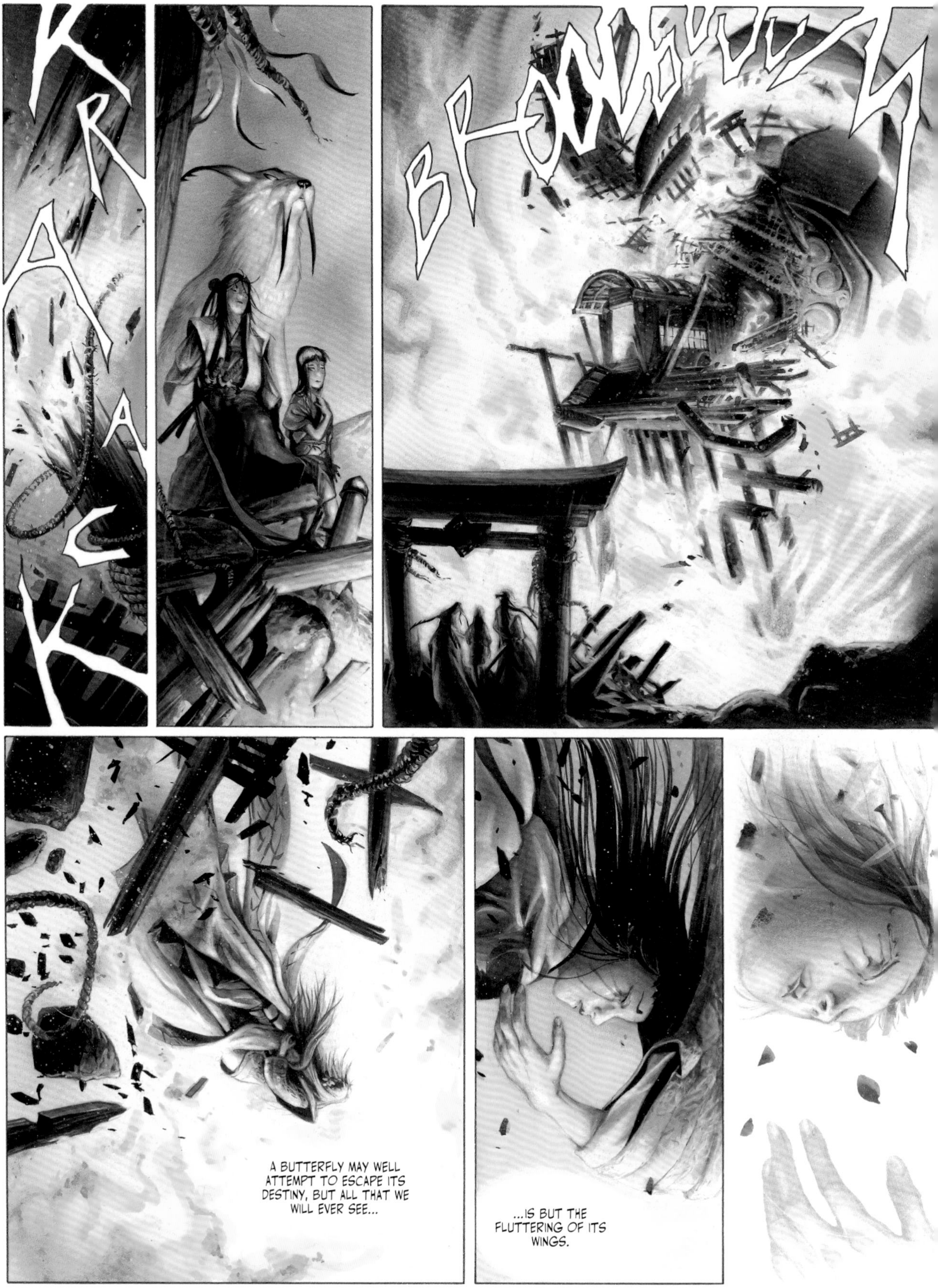
KRAKK
BROOOOOOOM
A BUTTERFLY MAY WELL ATTEMPT TO ESCAPE ITS DESTINY, BUT ALL THAT WE WILL EVER SEE...
...IS BUT THE FLUTTERING OF ITS WINGS.

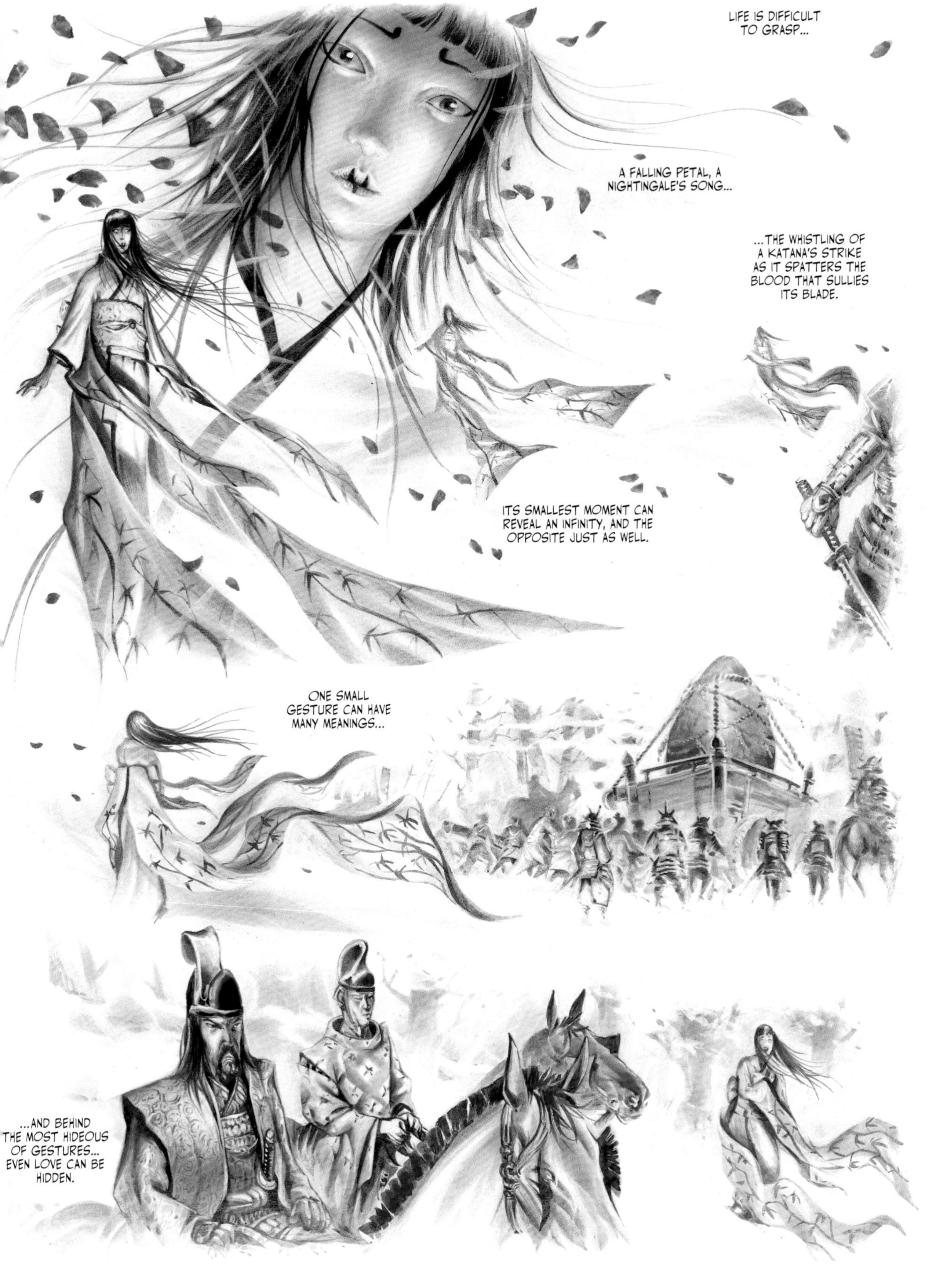
LIFE IS DIFFICULT TO GRASP...
A FALLING PETAL, A NIGHTINGALE'S SONG...
...THE WHISTLING OF A KATANA'S STRIKE AS IT SPATTERS THE BLOOD THAT SULLIES ITS BLADE.
ITS SMALLEST MOMENT CAN REVEAL AN INFINITY, AND THE OPPOSITE JUST AS WELL.
ONE SMALL GESTURE CAN HAVE MANY MEANINGS...
...AND BEHIND THE MOST HIDEOUS OF GESTURES... EVEN LOVE CAN BE HIDDEN.

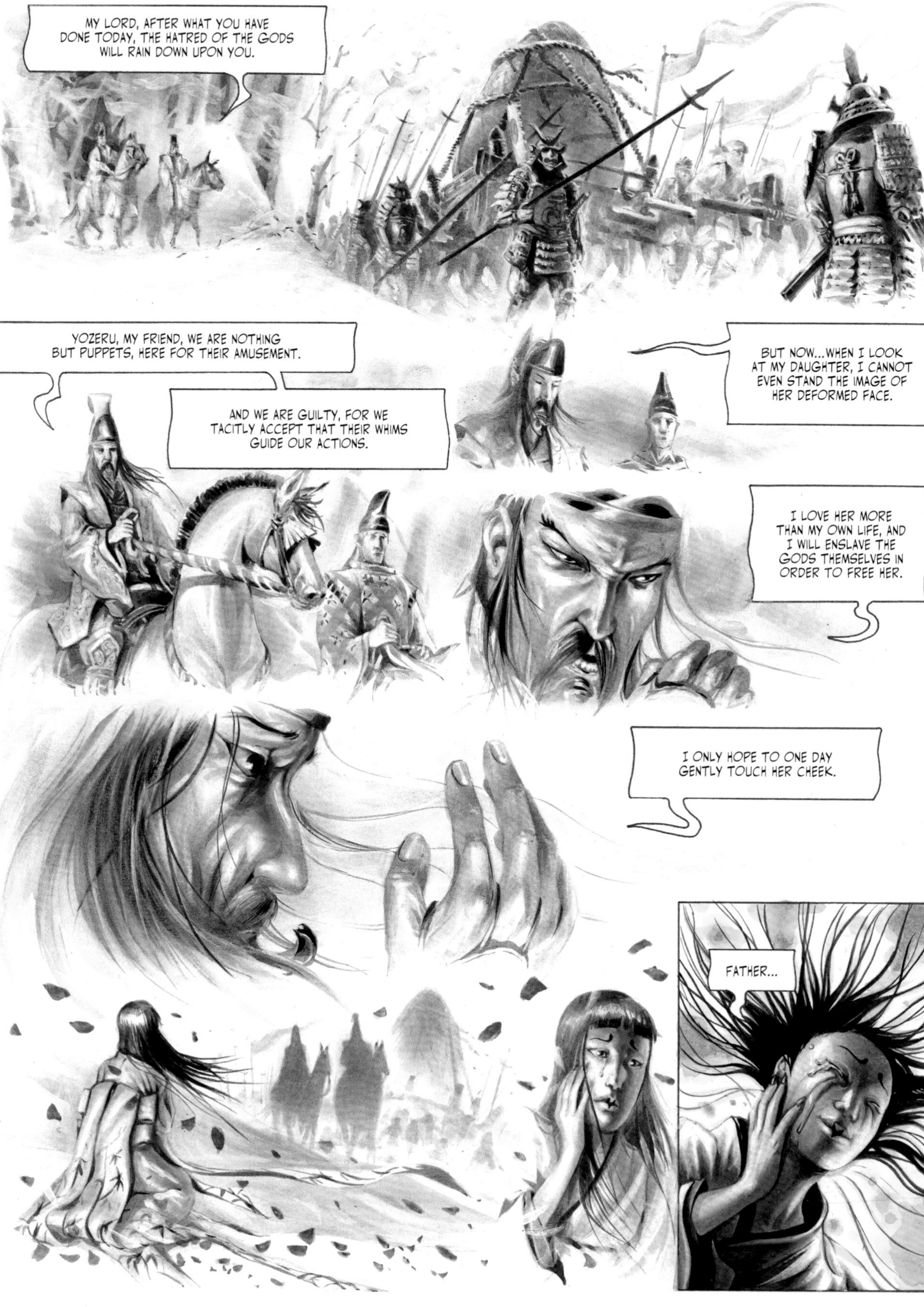
MY LORD, AFTER WHAT YOU HAVE DONE TODAY, THE HATRED OF THE GODS WILL RAIN DOWN UPON YOU.
YOZERU, MY FRIEND, WE ARE NOTHING BUT PUPPETS, HERE FOR THEIR AMUSEMENT.
AND WE ARE GUILTY, FOR WE TACITLY ACCEPT THAT THEIR WHIMS GUIDE OUR ACTIONS.
BUT NOW...WHEN I LOOK AT MY DAUGHTER, I CANNOT EVEN STAND THE IMAGE OF HER DEFORMED FACE.
I LOVE HER MORE THAN MY OWN LIFE, AND I WILL ENSLAVE THE GODS THEMSELVES IN ORDER TO FREE HER.
I ONLY HOPE TO ONE DAY GENTLY TOUCH HER CHEEK.
FATHER...

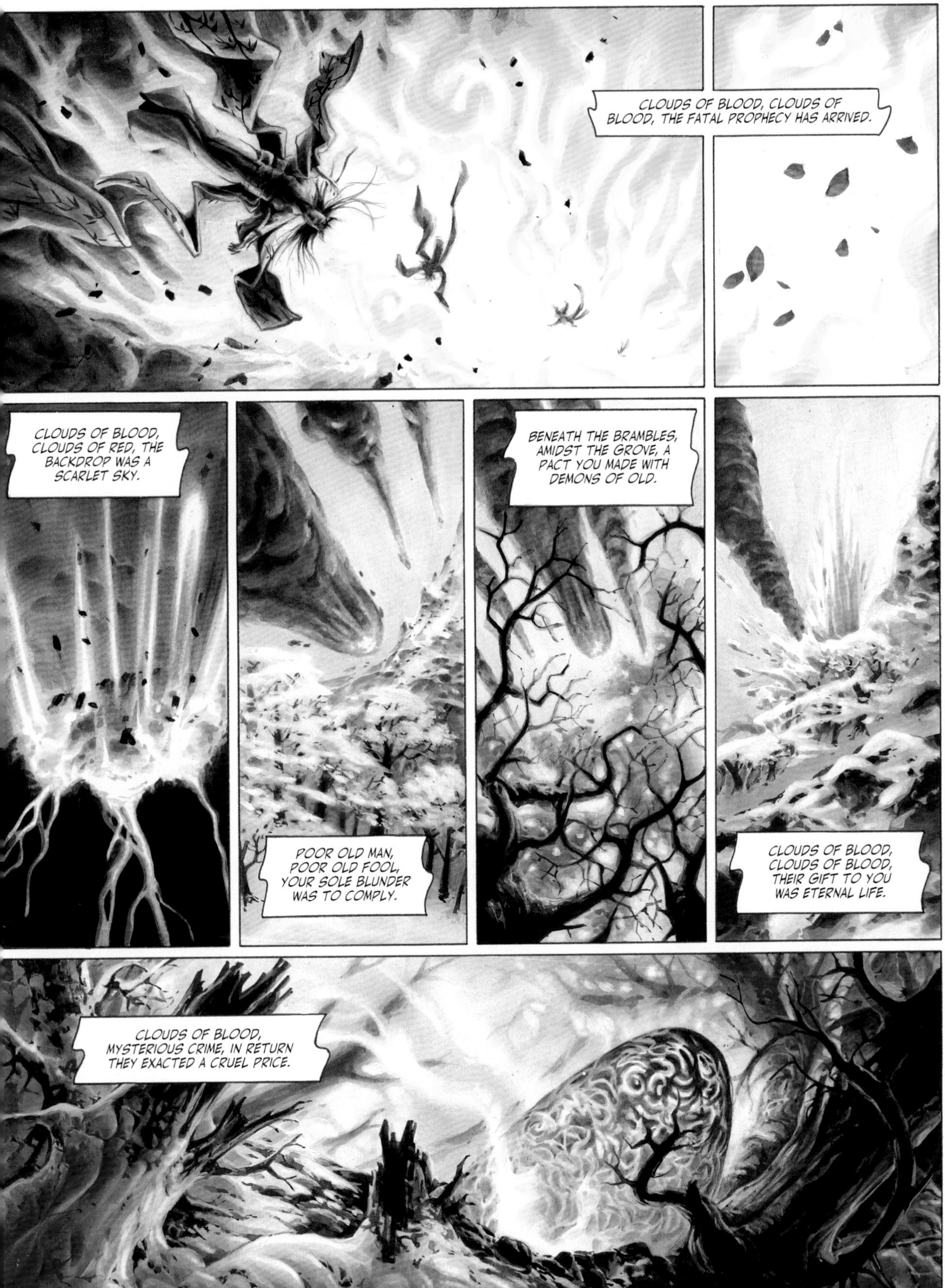
CLOUDS OF BLOOD, CLOUDS OF BLOOD, THE FATAL PROPHECY HAS ARRIVED.
CLOUDS OF BLOOD, CLOUDS OF RED, THE BACKDROP WAS A SCARLET SKY.
POOR OLD MAN, POOR OLD FOOL, YOUR SOLE BLUNDER WAS TO COMPLY.
BENEATH THE BRAMBLES, AMIDST THE GROVE, A PACT YOU MADE WITH DEMONS OF OLD.
CLOUDS OF BLOOD, CLOUDS OF BLOOD, THEIR GIFT TO YOU WAS ETERNAL LIFE.
CLOUDS OF BLOOD, MYSTERIOUS CRIME, IN RETURN THEY EXACTED A CRUEL PRICE.

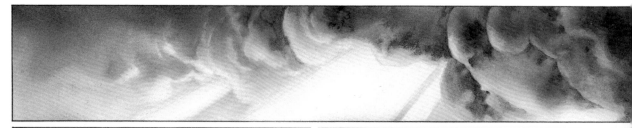

OGI, LEAVE IT WHERE IT IS. NATURE NEEDS TO REBUILD HERSELF AFTER SO MUCH DESTRUCTION.

HIDEMIZU SAN, I PRAY THAT RAIDO AND MEIKI ARE...

LOOK, OGI. I BELIEVE THAT THE KAMIS HAVE JUST ANSWERED YOUR PRAYER.

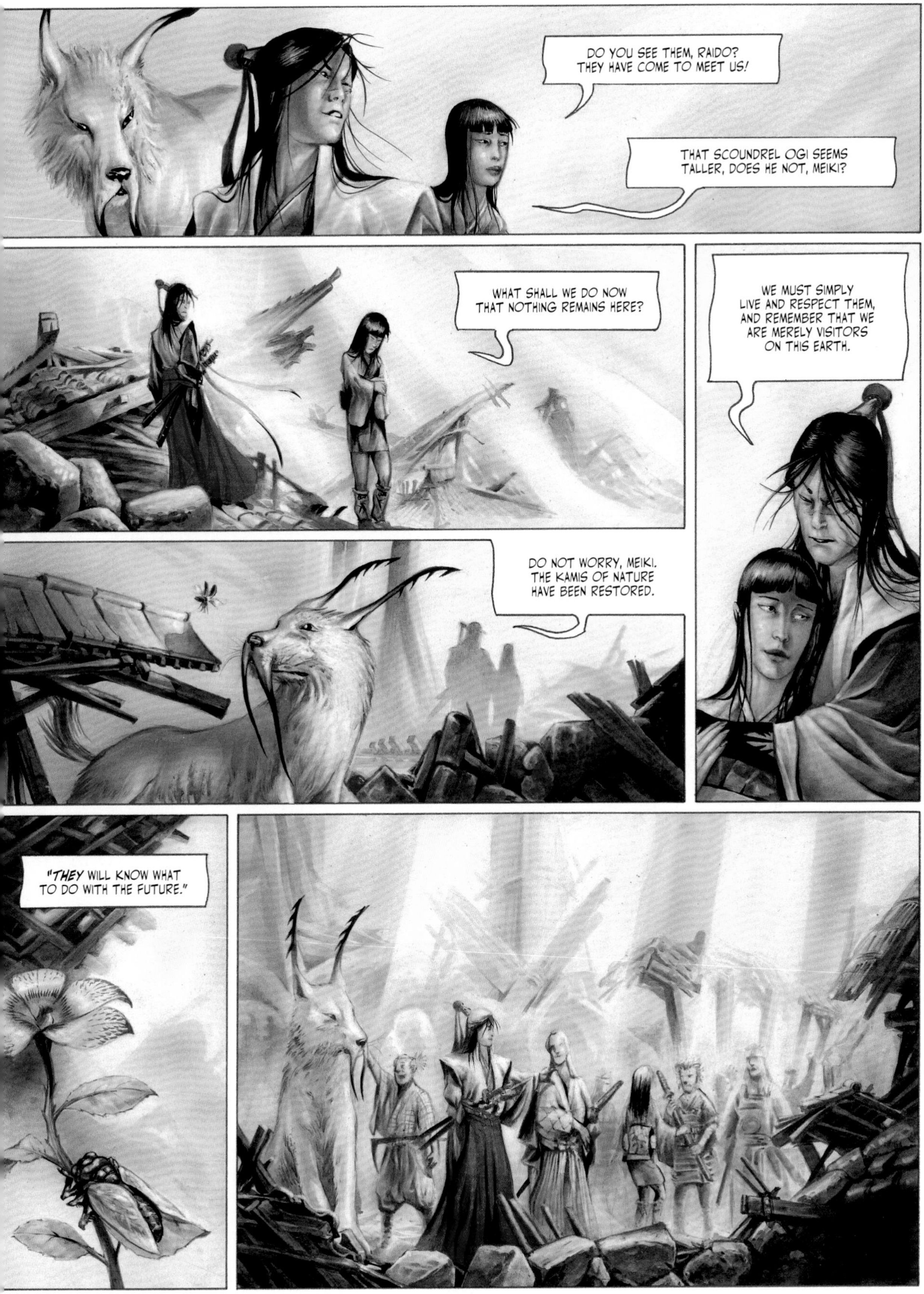
DO YOU SEE THEM, RAIDO? THEY HAVE COME TO MEET US!
THAT SCOUNDREL OGI SEEMS TALLER, DOES HE NOT, MEIKI?
WHAT SHALL WE DO NOW THAT NOTHING REMAINS HERE?
DO NOT WORRY, MEIKI. THE KAMIS OF NATURE HAVE BEEN RESTORED.
WE MUST SIMPLY LIVE AND RESPECT THEM, AND REMEMBER THAT WE ARE MERELY VISITORS ON THIS EARTH.
"THEY WILL KNOW WHAT TO DO WITH THE FUTURE."

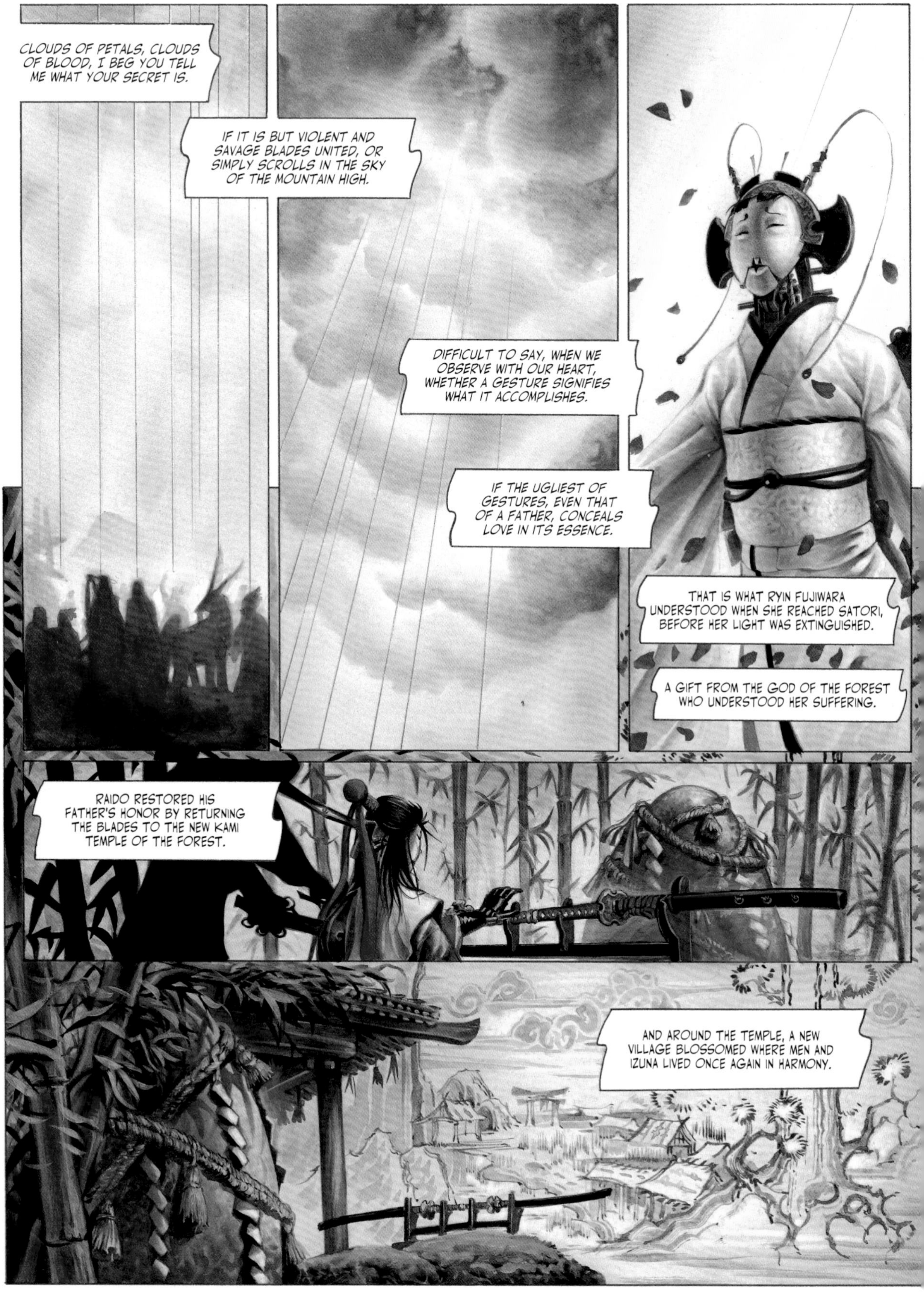
CLOUDS OF PETALS, CLOUDS OF BLOOD, I BEG YOU TELL ME WHAT YOUR SECRET IS.
IF IT IS BUT VIOLENT AND SAVAGE BLADES UNITED, OR SIMPLY SCROLLS IN THE SKY OF THE MOUNTAIN HIGH.
DIFFICULT TO SAY, WHEN WE OBSERVE WITH OUR HEART, WHETHER A GESTURE SIGNIFIES WHAT IT ACCOMPLISHES.
IF THE UGLIEST OF GESTURES, EVEN THAT OF A FATHER, CONCEALS LOVE IN ITS ESSENCE.
THAT IS WHAT RYIN FUJIWARA UNDERSTOOD WHEN SHE REACHED SATORI, BEFORE HER LIGHT WAS EXTINGUISHED.
A GIFT FROM THE GOD OF THE FOREST WHO UNDERSTOOD HER SUFFERING.
RAIDO RESTORED HIS FATHER'S HONOR BY RETURNING THE BLADES TO THE NEW KAMI TEMPLE OF THE FOREST.
AND AROUND THE TEMPLE, A NEW VILLAGE BLOSSOMED WHERE MEN AND IZUNA LIVED ONCE AGAIN IN HARMONY.

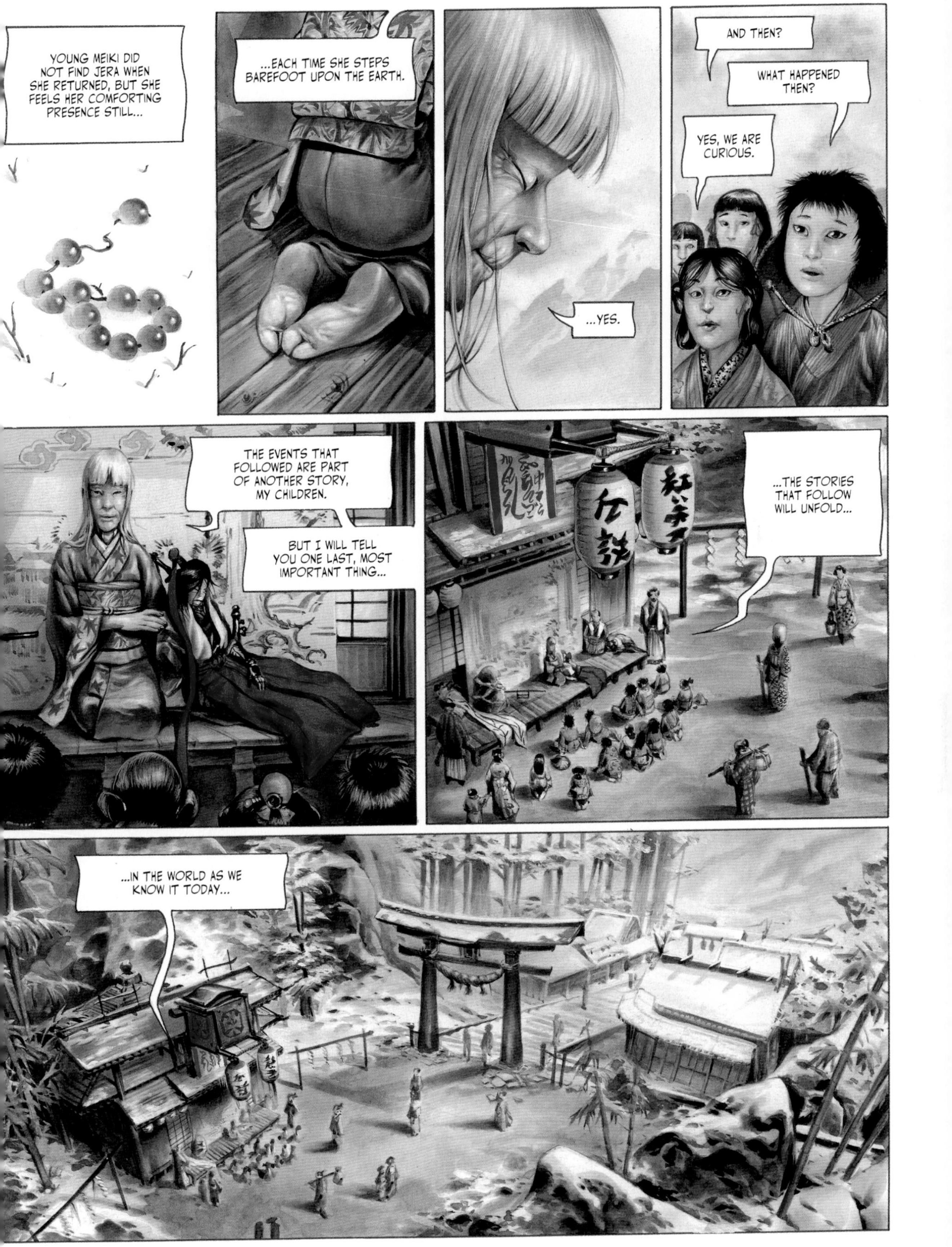
YOUNG MEIKI DID NOT FIND JERA WHEN SHE RETURNED, BUT SHE FEELS HER COMFORTING PRESENCE STILL...
...EACH TIME SHE STEPS BAREFOOT UPON THE EARTH.
...YES.
AND THEN?
WHAT HAPPENED THEN?
YES, WE ARE CURIOUS.
THE EVENTS THAT FOLLOWED ARE PART OF ANOTHER STORY, MY CHILDREN.
BUT I WILL TELL YOU ONE LAST, MOST IMPORTANT THING...
...THE STORIES THAT FOLLOW WILL UNFOLD...
...IN THE WORLD AS WE KNOW IT TODAY...

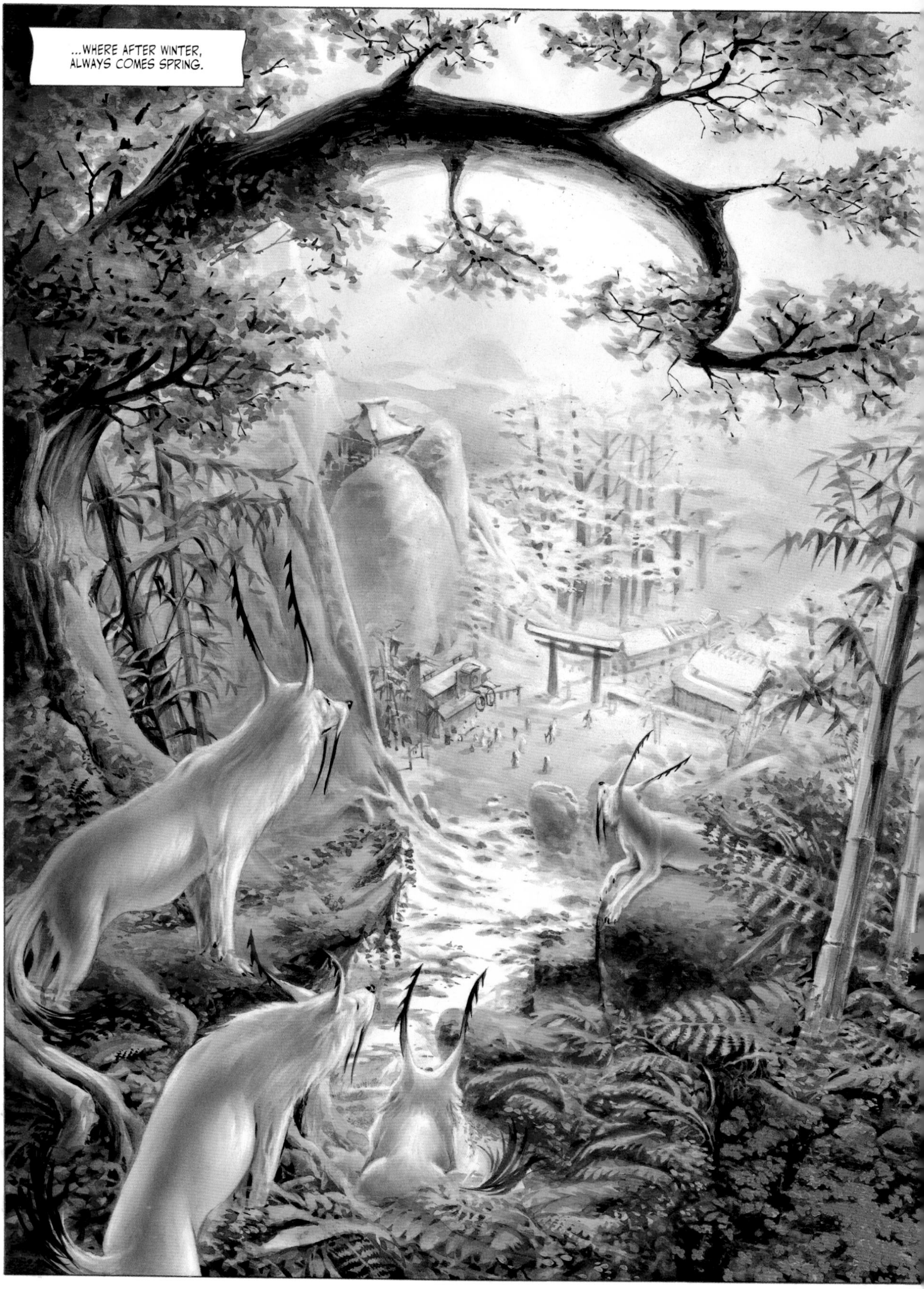
...WHERE AFTER WINTER,
ALWAYS COMES SPRING.

EN

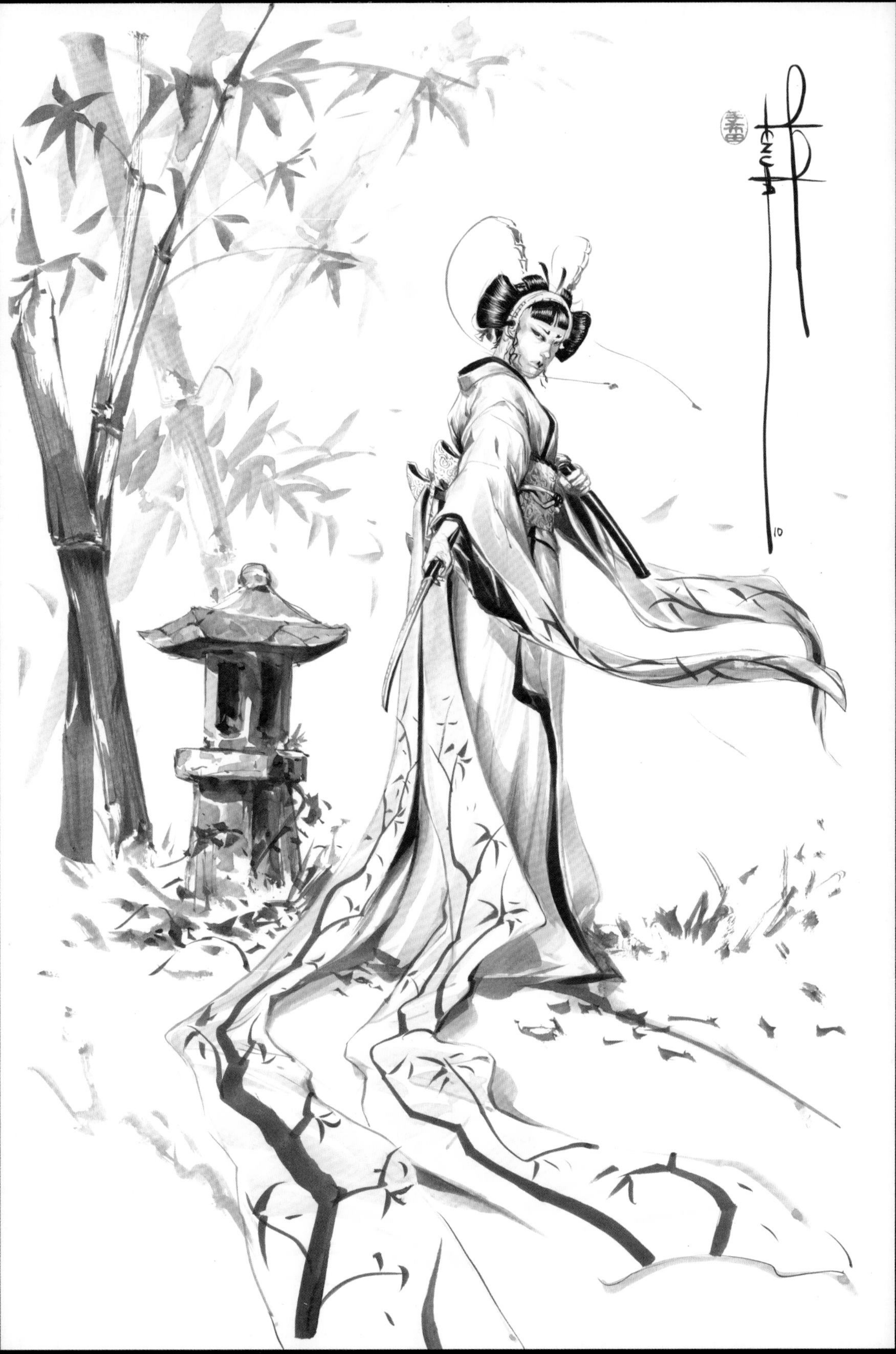

Character sketch of Lady Ryin.

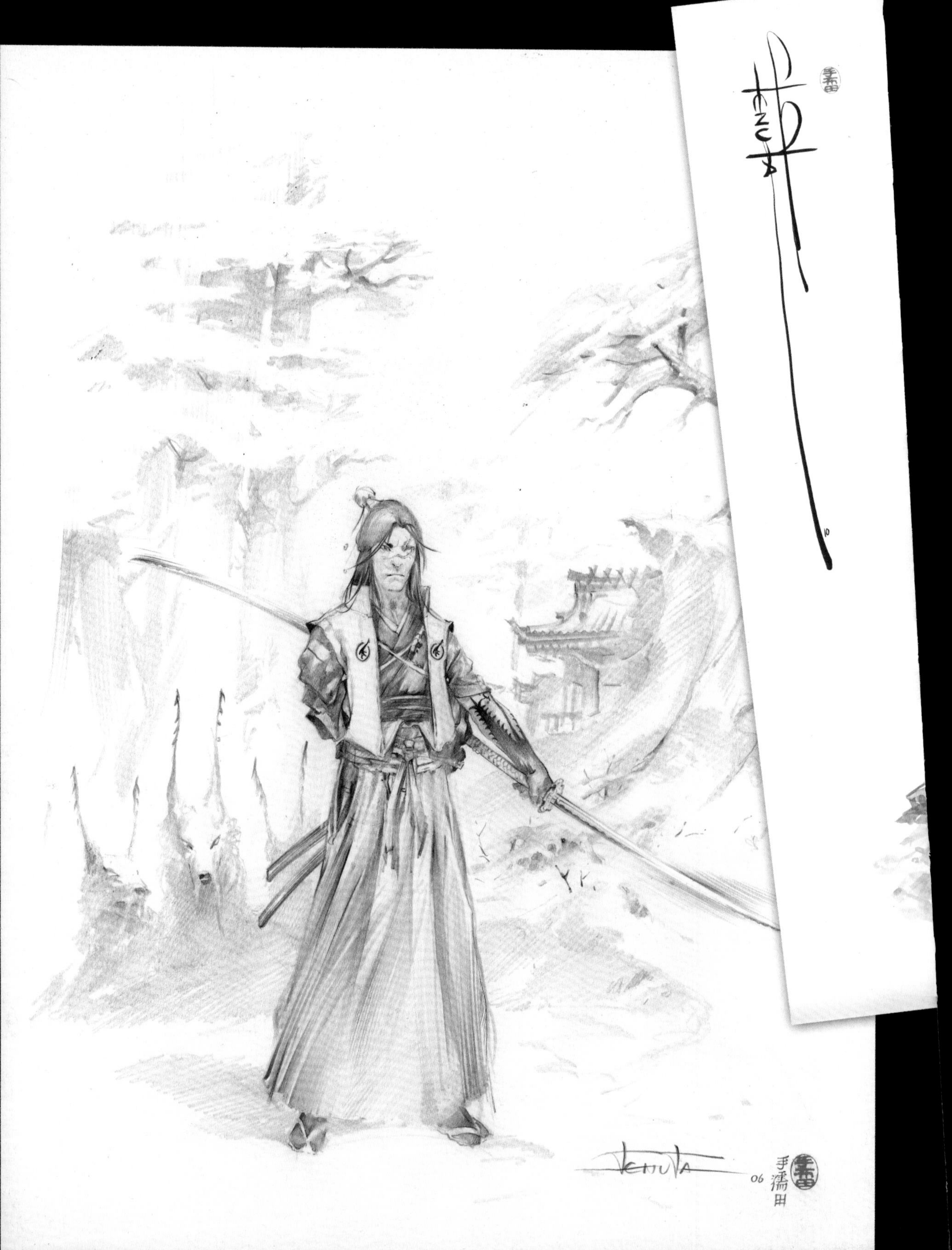

Character sketch of Raido.

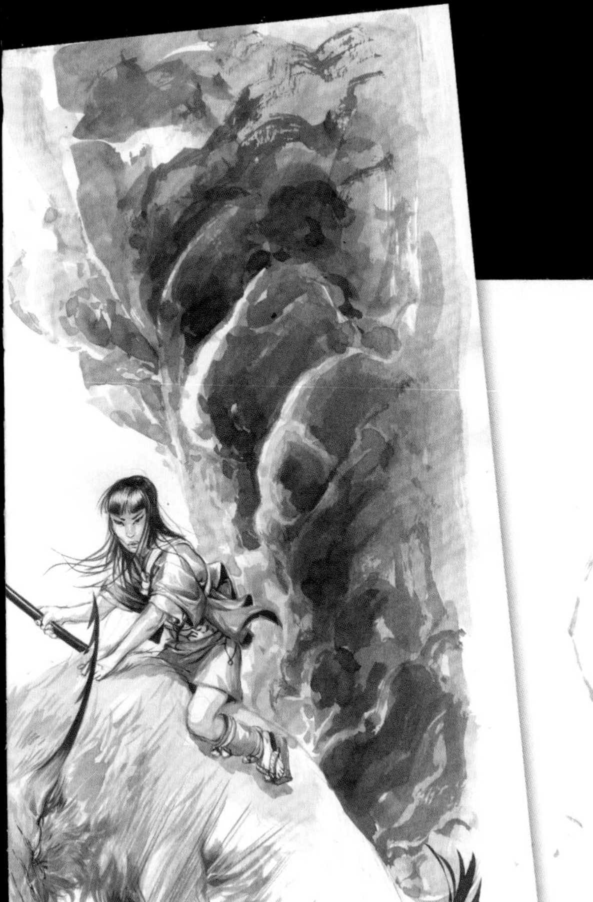

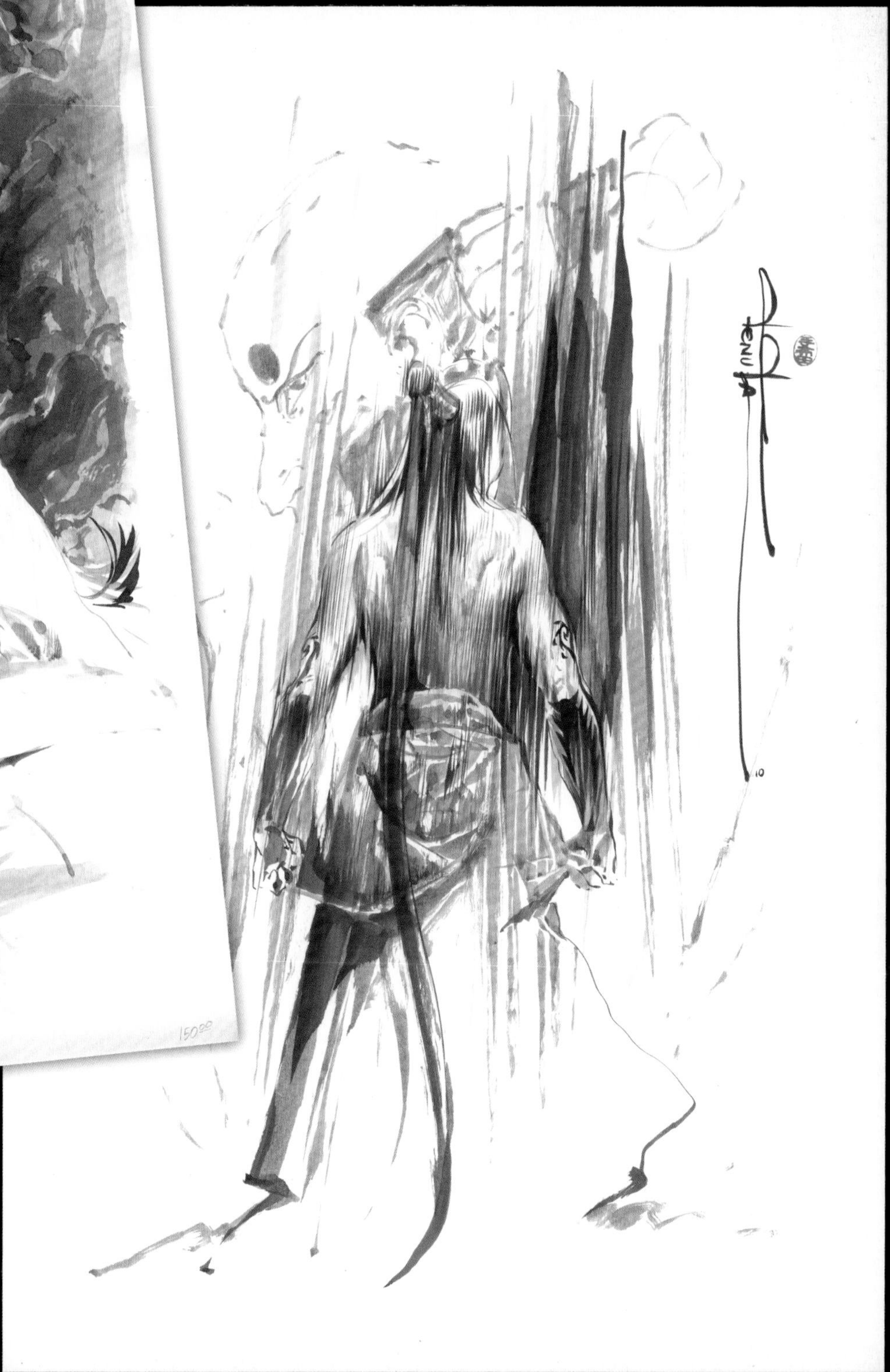

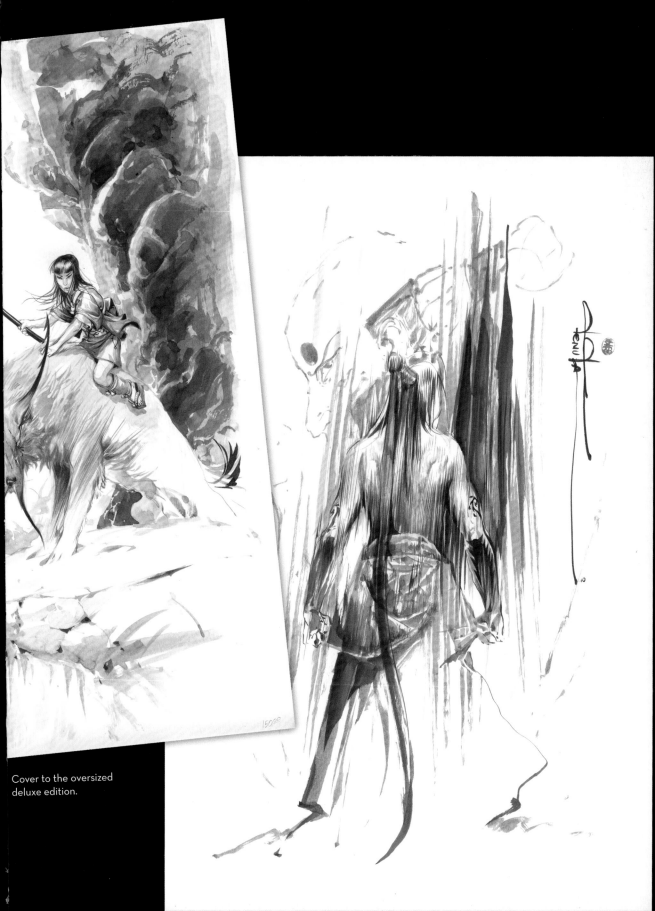

Cover to the oversized deluxe edition.

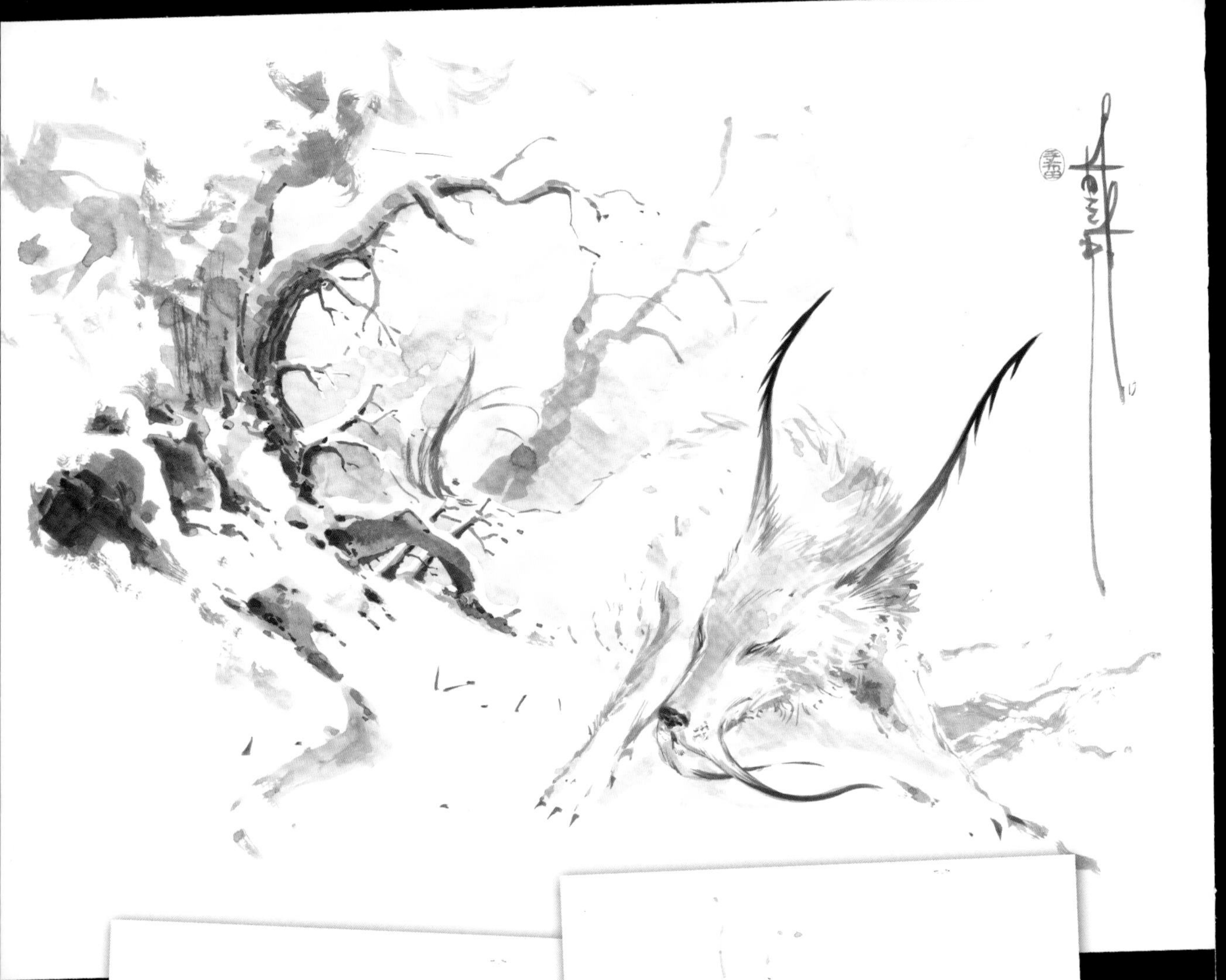

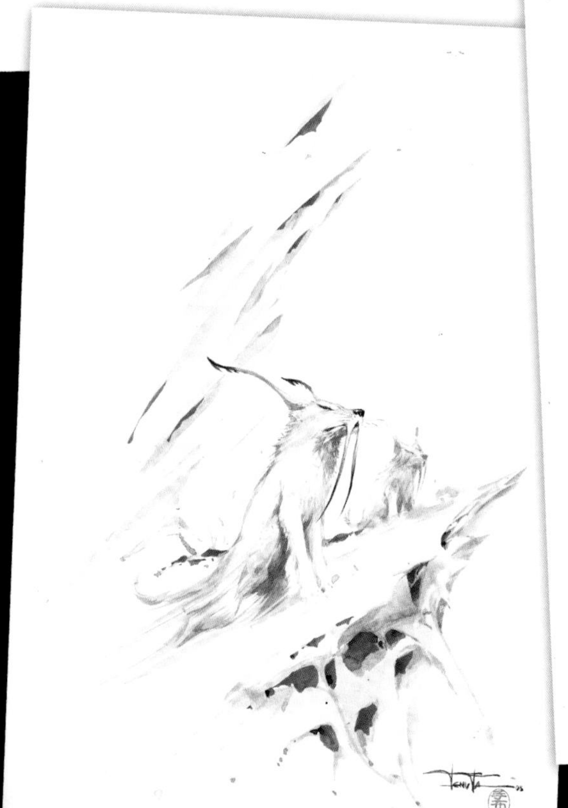

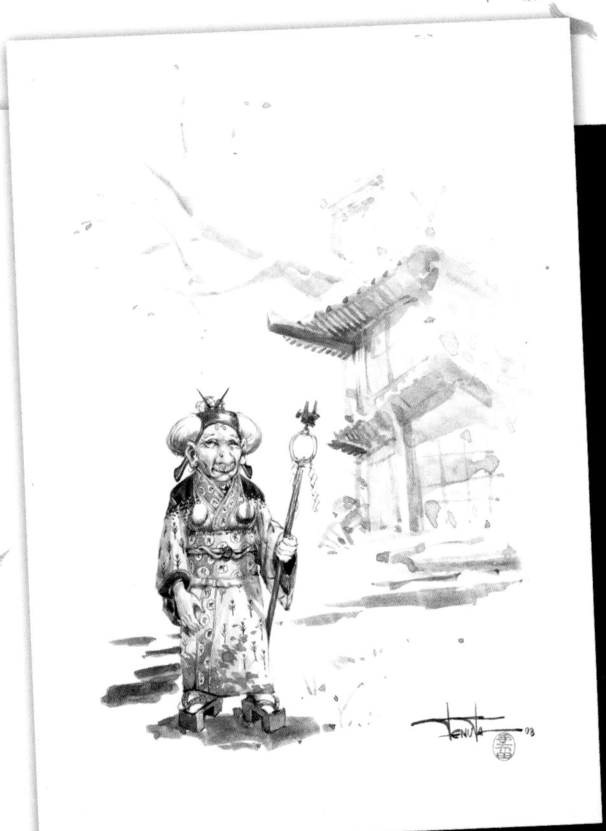

Character sketches of the Izuna wolves and Jera Isegawa.